P9-CQQ-176

Creative Organization Theory

A RESOURCEBOOK

Gareth Morgan

SAGE Publications
The Publishers of Professional Social Science
Newbury Park   London   New Delhi

Copyright © 1989 by Gareth Morgan

All rights reserved. No part of this book may be reproduced or utilized in any form or by any means, electronic or mechanical, including photocopying, recording, or by any information storage and retrieval system, without permission in writing from the publisher.

For information address:

 SAGE Publications, Inc.
2111 West Hillcrest Drive
Newbury Park, California 91320

SAGE Publications Ltd.
28 Banner Street
London EC1Y 8QE
England

SAGE Publications India Pvt. Ltd.
M-32 Market
Greater Kailash I
New Delhi 110 048 India

Printed in the United States of America

Library of Congress Cataloging-in-Publication Data

Morgan, Gareth.
    Creative organization theory : a resourcebook / Gareth Morgan.
        p.   cm.
    Bibliography: p.
    ISBN 0-8039-3444-0.   ISBN 0-8039-3438-6 (pbk.)
    1. Organization.   2. Organizational behavior.   3. Management.
    I. Title.
    HD31.M6278 1989
    658.4--dc 19

                                                          88-28288
                                                          CIP

THIRD PRINTING 1989

Julia Christensen-Hughes

_____

Creative
Organization
Theory

_____

Contents

Preface   8
Acknowledgments   10

I. Mindstretchers   11

1. Flexibility and Intelligence   12
2. What Is This?   13
3. The Need for a Tool Chest   14
4. Framing and Reframing: Seeing the Same Situation in Different Ways   15
5. What Is a Paintbrush?   16
6. What Is This?   17
7. Using Your "Right Brain"   19
8. We Learn How to See   21
9. What Is Truth?   22
10. Different Assumptions and Organizing Principles Generate Different Meanings   23
11. Developing Multiple Interpretations   24
12. Understanding Different Viewpoints   26
13. Escaping from Dominant Ideas   28
14. Interpreting Patterns, Boundaries, and Constraints   29
15. What Is an Organization?   30
16. Where's the Customer?   31
17. Viewing Your Organization as if You Were a Visitor from a Foreign Land   32
18. Some Thought Patterns   34
19. Today's Solutions Shape Tomorrow's Problems   35
20. Mindstretchers—Ideas and Solutions   36

II. Readings, Stories, and Other Resources   39

21. The Evolution of Organization Theory   41
22. Max Weber's Concept of Bureaucracy   49
23. Taylor, Schmidt, and Scientific Management   51
24. How to Kill Creativity   54
25. Working Under Mechanized Systems of Production   55
26. Computers and the Mechanization of Intellectual Work   59
27. From Bureaucracies to Networks: The Emergence of New Organizational Forms   64

28. Organization Design: An Information-Processing Perspective   68

29. Organizational Technologies   70

30. Organizational Environments   72

31. The Emergence of Turbulent Environments   74

32. The Contingency Approach: Analyzing Relations Between Organization and Environment   76

33. Differentiation and Integration: One of the Paradoxes of Management   80

34. Collective Strategy: The Management of Interorganizational Relations   82

35. Tit for Tat: A Strategy for Cooperation and Survival?   84

36. Organization and Environment: Adaptation or Selection?   87

37. Do Organizations "Enact" Their Environments?   91

38. Organizational Growth and Development   97

39. "Just in Time" Systems of Management   102

40. Japanese Management: The Art of Self-Regulation   105

41. The Challenger Disaster: A Case of Discouraged Feedback?   112

42. Information and Misinformation: Some Unintended Consequences of Performance Controls   116

43. Collaboration and Control   121

44. Peopleless Factories   124

45. Peopleless Offices   127

46. Team-Based Manufacturing: Digital Trying the Bossless System   129

47. Growing Large While Staying Small   132

48. Organizational Learning   139

49. Innovating Organizations: The Case of 3M   143

50. Culture: A Complex and Subtle Language   150

51. Corporate Culture and Core Values   157

52. Corporate Culture: The Role of Stories   159

53. Transformational Leadership   163

54. The Tandem Corporation: A Successful Corporate Culture?   166

55. ServiceMaster: Combining Vision and Control   169

56. Life on the Fast Lane at Datsun   174

57. Apple Computer and the Politics of Change   181

58. Politics at Work   188

59. Some Sources of Organizational Conflict   196

60. A Perspective on Conflict Management   198

61. Decision Making in Conflict Situations   200

62. Managing Intergroup Conflict   202

63. Rational for Whom?   207

64. Powerless Power?   209

65. Gender and Corporate Politics   213

66. Game-Playing and the Psychodynamics of Organizational Life   218

67. Groupthink: The Problems of Conformity   224

68. Some Unconscious Aspects of Organization   229

69. Hooked on Work   241

70. The Destructive Side of Technological Development   245

71. Unfolding Contradictions?   252

72. The Bhopal Disaster   255

73. The Not-Enough World of Work   260

III. Cases and Exercises   265

74. American Football: A Case of Mechanistic Organization?   267

75. Charlie Chaplin's *Modern Times*   267

76. Eagle Smelting   268

77. A Visit to McDonald's   271

78. Judging the Degree of Fit Between Organization and Environment   274

79. The Paradoxical Twins: Acme and Omega Electronics   278

80. Scholar Educational Products Inc.   283

81. The Changing Structure of Financial Services   286

82. Organizations Often Obstruct Learning   291

83. Product X   294

84. Arnold: The Paradox of Creativity   296

85. Understanding the Culture of Your Organization   297

86. Perfection or Bust   299

87. The Creation and Destruction of the Order of Maria Theresa   301

88. Sink or Swim: Reflections on a Corporate Training Program   305

89. The Nomizu Sake Company   311

90. The Fortress Insurance Company   315

91. Rainbow Financial Services   318

92. The University as a Political System   323

93. Global Inc.: A Role-Play   327

94. How Politicized Is Your Organization?   328

95. Pluralist Management   329

96. Meetings, Meetings, Meetings   330

97. The Sunnyvale Youth Center   331

98. Conflict at Riverside   335

99. The Hand Grenade   338

100. Jersey Packers   342

101. The Department of Information Services   345

102. Quality Co-Op   349

103. Who Builds the Dillworth Extension?   351

104. The Lakeside Literary Magazine   354

105. A New Direction for the Upstage Theater   357

106. Tipdale Engineering   360

107. Problems in the Machine Shop   363

108. Visibility, Autonomy, Relevance, and Relationships: Four Factors Shaping Power and Influence   364

109. Profit and Organizations: A Story of Exploitation?   367

110. Final Offer   368

About the Author   369

Preface

This *Resourcebook* marshals ideas, stories, cases, exercises, and snippets of information that will help the reader to gain a broad-based understanding of the nature and functioning of modern organizations. It has been designed to complement my book *Images of Organization*, which developed the idea that effective managers and professionals have to become skilled in the art of "reading" the situations that they are attempting to organize or manage— to understand the many and often paradoxical aspects of situations, and to forge appropriate actions.

The materials here provide springboards for gaining this kind of insight.

The *Mindstretchers* in Part I are designed to provide entertaining ways of broadening perspective and of developing creative approaches to how we interpret the world around us.

The *Readings, Stories, and Other Resources* presented in Part II are designed to present different angles on organization. Each invites us to see and appreciate a different aspect of organizational functioning, and to unravel their connections and significance.

The *Cases and Exercises* in Part III provide opportunities to develop this skill even further. Each presents a situation that is open to multiple interpretations. The invitation is to "read" and judge the circumstances presented to gain a full understanding and, if there are problems, to determine what actions will be most appropriate.

The *Resourcebook* is designed for use on courses addressing the management of organizations where an instructor coordinates and facilitates the selection and use of materials, guided by the advice of an *Instructor's Manual*. Individuals can also benefit by browsing through the contents, exploring the links with the ideas explored in *Images of Organization*. Table P.1, which identifies the detailed cross-links between *Images* and the resources presented in this volume, will be helpful to readers trying to navigate the territory on their own, although the maximum benefit from the materials usually stems from use in a group setting, where the exchange of ideas and opinions can help to sharpen one's personal insights.

Table P.1   Cross-Links with *Images of Organization*

Images of Organization

Relevant Exercises and Resources:
Resource Number

Chapter 1 (Introduction)
   1, 2, 3, 4, 5, 6, 7, 8, 9, 10, 11, 12, 13, 14, 15, 16, 17, 18, 19, 20, 21, 76

Chapter 2 (Organizations as Machines)
   22, 23, 24, 25, 26, 74, 75, 77

Chapter 3 (Organizations as Organisms)
   27, 29, 30, 31, 32, 33, 34, 35, 36, 37, 38, 78, 79, 80, 81

Chapter 4 (Organizations as Brains)
   28, 39, 40, 41, 42, 43, 44, 45, 46, 47, 48, 49, 82, 83, 84

Chapter 5 (Organizations as Cultures)
   16, 40, 50, 51, 52, 53, 54, 55, 56, 85, 86, 87, 88, 89, 90, 91

Chapter 6 (Organizations as Political Systems)
   57, 58, 59, 60, 61, 62, 63, 64, 65, 90, 91, 92, 93, 94, 95, 96, 97, 98, 99, 100, 101, 102, 103, 104, 105, 106, 107, 108, 109, 110

Chapter 7 (Organizations as Psychic Prisons)
   66, 67, 68, 69, 88

Chapter 8 (Organization as Flux and Transformation)
   19, 35, 70, 71

Chapter 9 (Organizations as Instruments of Domination)
   23, 25, 26, 56, 69, 71, 72, 73, 75, 88, 98, 107, 109, 110

Chapters 10 and 11 (The Art of Organizational Analysis)/(Imaginization)
   1, 2, 3, 4, 5, 6, 7, 8, 9, 10, 11, 12, 13, 14, 15, 16, 17, 18, 19, 20

The *Resourcebook* is the product of a number of years of teaching organization and management through the perspective of *Images of Organization*. In essence, it marshals the materials and cases that I have found helpful in developing concrete skills in organizational analysis, and I hope that it will prove helpful to others.

Some of the items have been contributed by colleagues and students, and I am grateful for their help in creating the volume. Particular thanks are due to Chris Atack, Pat Bradshaw-Campball, Robert Burns, David Dimick, Betty Hagopian, Clement Hammah, Graham Morgan, Vic Murray, Linda Smircich, Lin Ward, Sacha Warunkiw, and numerous people at Sage Publications.

—Gareth Morgan
Toronto

Acknowledgments

This *Resourcebook* draws on materials from various published and unpublished sources. Special thanks are due to the following authors whose work is featured or quoted at length in the readings and exercises that follow:

Chris Argyris
Stanley Aronowitz
Graham Astley
Chris Atack
Robert Axelrod
Edward de Bono
Mary Yoko Brannen
Dave Brown
Grant Buckler
Gibson Burrell
Gene Bylinsky
David Calabria
John Case
Harlan Cleveland
Mike Cooley
Nick Davis/
   The Observer
Terrence Deal
Brian Duke
Betty Edwards
Fred Emery
Diane Fassell
Munro Ferguson
F. Scott Fitzgerald
Wendy Fox/
   The Boston Globe
John Freeman
Jay Galbraith

Jeff Gandz
Alvin Gouldner
Larry E. Greiner
Edward T. Hall
Michael T. Hannon
Larry Hirschhorn
Irving Janis
John Junkerman
Rosabeth Moss
   Kanter
Allan Kennedy
Manfred Kets
   de Vries
Judith Knelman
Arthur Koestler
Isabelle Landry
Paul R. Lawrence
Roy Lewicki
Jay W. Lorsch
John L. McKnight
Adrian Mclean
Marshall McLuhan
Danny Miller
Victor Murray
Eric Neilsen
Newsweek reporters
Friedrich Nietzsche
Kenichi Ohmae

William Ouchi
Charles Perrow
Tom Peters
Jeffrey Pfeffer
Anatol Rapoport
Roger Rosenblatt
David Sanger
Anne Wilson
   Schaeff
Donald Schön
Gail Sheehy
Linda Smircich
Charles Stubbart
Frederick Taylor
Glen Taylor
Studs Terkel
Noel Tichy
Eric Trist
David Ulrich
John F. Veiga
Robert Waterman
Jack Weber
Max Weber
Kenneth W.
   Wessner
Allan Wilkins
John N. Yanouzas
Abraham Zaleznik

PART I

Mindstretchers

Many ideas about organization are like concrete. Once fluid, they have become firmly set; as solid as stone.

The purpose of the exercises and snippets of information in this section of the *Resourcebook* is to break up the concrete a little: by encouraging us to see how favored mindsets, assumptions, stereotypes, and everyday ways of thinking shape our views of organization in practice.

Play with the exercises and ideas as you will. There is no logical order or sequence. They are simply designed to encourage reflection on how we see and structure the world around us. Some suggested angles on the solutions to some of the mindstretchers are presented in Resource 20.

1

Flexibility and Intelligence

The test of a first-rate intelligence is the ability to hold two opposed ideas in mind at the same time and still retain the ability to function.

—F. Scott Fitzgerald

Of all forms of mental activity, the most difficult to induce even in the minds of the young, who may be presumed not to have lost their flexibility, is the art of handling the same bundle of data as before, but placing them in a new system of relations with one another by giving them a different framework, all of which virtually means putting on a different kind of thinking-cap for the moment. It is easy to teach anybody a new fact . . . but it needs light from heaven to enable a teacher to break the old framework in which the student has been accustomed to seeing.

—Arthur Koestler

2

What Is This?

Make a list of interpretations in the space below:

3

The Need for a Tool Chest

If you only have a hammer,

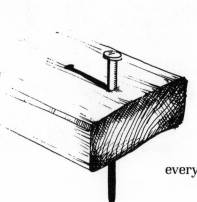

every problem tends to become a nail.

4

Framing and Reframing

Seeing the Same Situation in Different Ways

An embrace,
or a man
washing his face?

A penguin,
or an
oriental lady?

A mouse,
or a
sleeping cat?

5

What Is a Paintbrush?

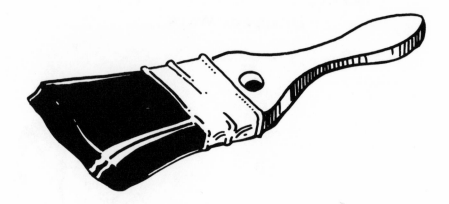

Yes, it's a picture of a paintbrush!

But what is a paintbrush?

A clue: . . . Ask yourself,

How does it work?

6

What Is This?

Can you see the cowboy hat and the man at the barber's?

Did you also see the man wearing a turban?

7

Using Your "Right Brain"

Try drawing the following picture in the space below:

Now, try drawing the picture upside down.

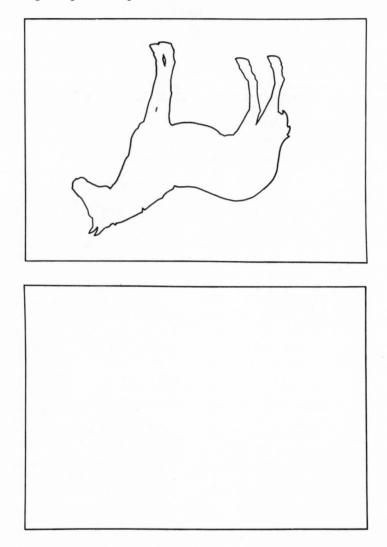

How did you do?

This exercise illustrates how we can develop new ways of seeing and new skills by approaching tasks in new ways—especially in ways that help us to break our usual stereotypes and beliefs!

See Betty Edwards, *Drawing on the Right Side of Your Brain* (Tarcher, 1979), for more on this upside-down approach to art.

8

We Learn How to See†

Eskimos are able to identify many different types of snow.

Asian peoples often know many varieties of rice.

We understand many aspects of our world through the *tools* provided by language and the other learned ways of seeing that form our culture.

The process is nicely illustrated in a story related by Marshall McLuhan about the problems that nonliterate people experience in seeing and understanding in three dimensions or perspective. The story focuses on the research of Professor John Wilson of London University, who had been involved in using film to teach African natives.

The film in question was about five minutes long and addressed problems of health and sanitation, featuring a sanitation inspector moving very slowly through an African village, removing all tins, pails, and pools of standing water. The inspector moved very deliberately, showing how the water should be poured away and rubbed into the ground to remove all potential mosquito breeding grounds, and showing how all rubbish should be placed in appropriate containers.

After the film had been shown to an audience of about 30 people, viewers were asked what they had seen. The response: They had seen a chicken.

The educators were flummoxed. As far as they were concerned, there was no chicken in the movie. But on careful examination of the individual movie frames, they found that a chicken had in fact appeared for about a second, running across the bottom right-hand segment of the screen.

Why had the Africans seen the chicken, but not the deliberate actions of the sanitation inspector? Why did they fail to grasp the story or message that the film was trying to convey?

The answer, it seems, is that they were unable to see the contents of the screen as a whole. Untrained in the art of perspective, they scanned the screen for details. As a result, they failed to see the sequence of events revealed by the consecutive frames. But their attention had been attracted to the scuttling chicken—the most active and thus visible detail in the whole film.

As McLuhan comments, literacy gives people the power to focus a little way in front of an image so that they can take in the whole image at a glance. In preliterate societies, people have not developed this skill, and do not look at objects in the way that is now commonplace. More often than not, they are wholly with the object; they go into it—empathically; the eye is used tactually, not in perspective.

The point: We *learn* to see!

Our ways of seeing are shaped by numerous hidden forces that make reality real in a culturally specific way.

†Source: Based on Marshall H. McLuhan, *The Guttenberg Galaxy, The Making of Typographic Man*. Toronto: University of Toronto Press, 1965, pp. 36-37.

9

What Is Truth?

"Do you swear to tell the truth, the whole truth, and nothing but the truth, and not in some sneaky relativistic way?"+

What is truth? A moving army of metaphors, metonymies and anthropomorphisms, in short a summa of human relationships that are being poetically and rhetorically sublimated, transposed, and beautified until after long and repeated use, a people considers them as solid, canonical, and unavoidable. Truths are illusions whose illusionary nature has been forgotten, metaphors that have been used up and have lost their imprint and that now operate as mere metal, no longer as coins.

—Nietzsche

+SOURCE: Gahan Wilson, published with permission of the *New Yorker* magazine (contributed by Linda Smircich, University of Massachusetts, Amherst, MA).

10

Different Assumptions and Organizing Principles Generate Different Designs

Examples of architecture based on the principle of compression:

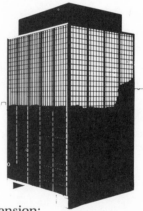

Examples of architecture based on the principle of tension:

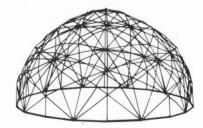

11

Developing Multiple Interpretations

Any complex situation is usually open to many interpretations.

See if you can interpret each of the following episodes from at least three different angles.

1. The Grave-Diggers' Strike

A week ago, the grave-diggers at Green Mountain cemetery laid down their tools and declared an indefinite strike. Their spokesman, Norman Babitt, said that they were "fed up with the city council's stonewalling." Their demands for a pay increase and improved fringe benefits had been rejected. The effects of the strike were immediate. A number of funerals had to be canceled and replaced with cremations. In two instances, bodies were placed in storage pending a resolution of the strike. No immediate return to work is expected.

Interpretation 1:

Interpretation 2:

Interpretation 3:

Others:

2. The Gold Banana Award†

"At Foxboro, a technical advance was desperately needed for survival in the company's early days. Late one evening, a scientist rushed into the president's office with a working prototype. Dumbfounded at the elegance of the solution and bemused about how to reward it, the president bent forward in his chair, rummaged through most of the drawers in his desk, found something, leaned over the desk to the scientist, and said, "Here!" In his hand was a banana, the only reward he could immediately put his hands on. From that point on, the small 'gold banana' pin has been the highest accolade for scientific achievement at Foxboro."

Interpretation 1:

Interpretation 2:

Interpretation 3:

Others:

†SOURCE: T. Peters and R. Waterman, *In Search of Excellence: Lessons from America's Best Run Corporations.* New York: Warner Books, 1982, pp. 70-71.

12

Understanding Different Viewpoints

The reality of organizational life usually comprises numerous different realities! To illustrate, consider the following picture:

Now describe the situation represented here as you see it, and then as you think it may be seen from the viewpoints of the different people involved:

My viewpoint:

Other viewpoints:
1.

2.

3.

How would you represent the situation in the following picture:

My viewpoint:

Other viewpoints:

1.

2.

3.

NOTE: The purpose of the exercise is not to guess exactly what the various people are thinking, but to understand how the same situation can be understood in different ways.

13

Escaping from Dominant Ideas

In his discussions of the creative process, Edward de Bono, author of *Lateral Thinking*, makes much of the need to be able to recognize and escape from the dominant ideas that structure a situation, or one's interpretation of a situation.

The trouble is, these ideas may be so ingrained that they are very hard to see. It is often difficult to identify the truly fundamental assumptions and beliefs that are shaping one's thoughts and actions. But it is important to be able to do so, to avoid being dominated by them. It is usually far easier to escape from something that is definite and explicit, rather than vague and poorly understood. It is much easier to become aware of alternatives in the former case, than in the latter.

What are the dominant assumptions and beliefs that shape how *you* think about your organization? Try and document them below:

Now try and document patterns of alternative assumptions—for example, by reversing the ideas you've identified above. In what ways can they help you to grasp new insights about how to organize. Document some of these alternatives in the space below:

14

Interpreting Patterns, Boundaries, and Constraints

Link all six dots shown below using five straight lines, without raising your pencil from the paper.

Link the following points to form a star:

15

What Is an Organization?

Conventional texts on management often define organizations as groups of people united by a common goal.

This kind of definition eliminates almost all the interesting features of organizations in practice. They are rarely so rational and so united as the definition suggests.

How would *you* define an organization?

16

Where's the Customer?

Ken Bird is the newly appointed president of a large bank. He's thinking about organization, and has just sketched the following chart:

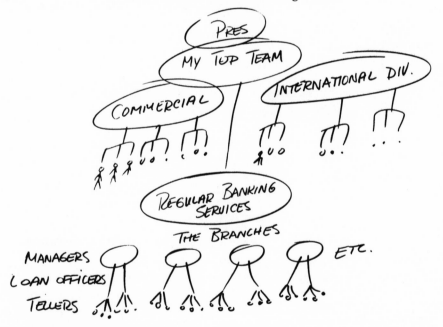

Ken wants to make his employees more conscious of the importance of the bank's customers.

He thinks: "How can I change the organization chart to symbolize the importance of the customer?

Can you help him?

17

Viewing Your Organization as if You Were a Visitor from a Foreign Land[†]

Everyday life always looks different when viewed from the outside.

To gain a fresh perspective on *your* organization (e.g., your place of work, your university, a social group), think about the following questions:

On first joining . . .

What struck you as being novel, strange, or different about the way things happened compared to your expectations or what you had become used to elsewhere?

_____

_____

Think of another organization with which you are familiar . . .

What do you consider to be odd, novel, or interesting about the way in which they do things that would be inconceivable in your present organization? What does this say about "normal" practice in your organization?

_____

_____

That's absolutely typical of us! . . .

If you wanted to convey the essence of how things are done in your organization, capturing both the good and the bad, can you think of a recent event or happening that seems to sum things up? What would it illustrate to an outsider who wanted to learn about your organization?

†SOURCE: Contributed by Adrian McLean, a partner with Bath Associates, 6, Vane St., Bath, England BA2 9DZ.

_____

_____

Heroes, villains and fools! . . .

Think about some of the stories circulating in your organization. What behaviors or character traits lead people to be considered heroes, villains, or fool? What messages do they communicate?

_____

_____

On returning to your organization from a new management course . . .

Imagine that you find a new assignment waiting for you that is tailor-made for the new ideas and skills that you've learned. You're the only member of your organization possessing these skills. What would you expect to happen as you try to implement your new ideas and approaches? What would you need to attend to in order to sustain your initiative, and what people or events would be key in determining it's fate? What does this tell you about the character of your organization?

_____

_____

How others see you . . .

What do people from other organizations say about your organization? What do they remark on when they come to visit, and what overheard or reported comments have you picked up?

_____

_____

18

Some Thought Patterns†

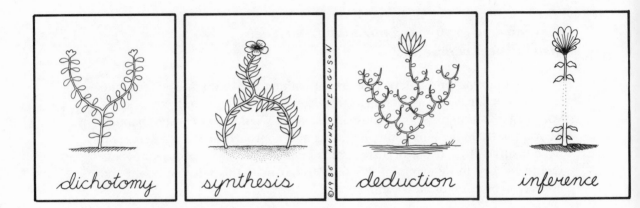

†SOURCE: Munro Ferguson.

19

Today's Solutions Shape Tomorrow's Problems!

There Was an Old Lady Who Swallowed a Fly

There was an old lady who swallowed a fly
I don't know why she swallowed the fly
Perhaps she'll die!

There was an old lady who swallowed a spider who wiggled and jiggled and
*   tickled inside her*
She swallowed the spider to catch the fly
I don't know why she swallowed the fly
Perhaps she'll die!

There was an old lady who swallowed a bird
Now how absurd to swallow a bird
She swallowed the bird to swallow the spider who wiggled and jiggled and
*   tickled inside her*
She swallowed the spider to swallow the fly
I don't know why she swallowed the fly
Perhaps she'll die!

The factory system centralized production to take full advantage of the efficiency of mechanized production systems.

Mechanized production systems dehumanized work, united the work force, and contributed to the growth and power of trade unions.

Strong unions helped to increase the level of wages and employee benefits, encouraging managers to search for alternatives to unionized labor—such as robots and low-wage labor in the Third World.

But robots don't get paid wages and subsistence wage earners can't afford to consume the products they make! . . .

20

Mindstretchers: Ideas and Solutions

Exercise 2: For example, a photo of a garbage dump; the destruction of a rural landscape; a statement on the domineering relationship between "man" and nature; a comment on the disposable society—on how humans are destroying their heritage and lack systemic balance with the planet; one person's trash is another's gold (note the prospector in the bottom right corner); a future archaeological site.

Exercise 5: A spreader; a pump; a hydraulic system, and so on. The image of what a paintbrush really is has major implications for how it is to be designed, and thus how it will function in practice.

Exercise 7: Try turning the page upside down.

Exercise 11: *The Grave-Diggers' Strike*
An illustration of the use and abuse of labor power; a statement on the callous nature of some human behavior; an expression of human alienation; a question of ethics and morality.

The Gold Banana Award
A creative means of rewarding excellence; a silly American gimmick; an example of how managers try to manipulate people; a statement on the gullibility of ambitious executives—who'd want a gold banana pin anyway; an example of how an organization fosters a corporate culture encouraging success.

Exercise 12: Who do you identify with most? Use the differences in viewpoint to gain a richer understanding of the dynamics that underpin these everyday organizational realities. Really try to get into the minds and "eyes" of the people involved.

Exercise 13: The answers here are entirely up to you. Are your assumptions mechanistic, emphasizing structure and clearly defined form? Are they more free flowing, encouraging ad hoc or evolving process? Do they emphasize values or ends over means?

Your reversal of assumptions may lead you to creative ways of thinking about organization.

Exercise 14:

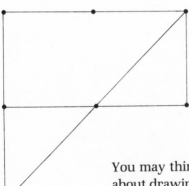
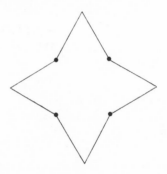

You may think this is cheating, but who said anything about drawing straight lines or not adding extra points? Why build in constraints if you don't have to?

Exercise 15: Numerous metaphors can be used, according to the organization you have in mind. For example: a machine; an anarchy; creative chaos; a living organism; an error amplifying device; a culture; an elephant, a giraffe; an octopus; an amoeba; a political system; a prison, an exploitative enterprise.

Exercise 16: Add the customers by drawing appropriate lines of interaction with bank tellers, loan officers, and so on;

or turn the organization chart upside down, place the customers at the top and make the whole organization subservient to this focus;

or depict the organization by using a picture of a tree

with roots, branches, leaves, and a wider environment. Depict the customers as birds—some are flying around inspecting the branches, others are flying away, some are nesting and roosting. Many organizations would like their customers to nest and roost;

or use computer graphics to create new symbols representing the importance of different patterns of interaction.

Organization charts are symbolic. It's significant that, for the longest time, many organizations have never included customers in the charts through which they think about themselves.

PART II

Readings, Stories, and Other Resources

The materials presented in this section of the *Resourcebook* invite you, the reader, to discern and understand different aspects of organization. Their sequence parallels the structure of *Images of Organization* focusing sequentially on the mechanical, organic, brainlike, cultural, political, deep psychological, and exploitative aspects of organization. (See Table P.1 for an overview of cross-links.) In reading the various pieces, you should gain valuable insights about the aspect of organization under consideration. These insights will help to build and refine the mosaic of ideas and knowledge necessary to understand organizations in practice.

21

The Evolution of Organization Theory

It is often difficult to capture the twists and turns in the development of a discipline in a short and evocative paper. Charles Perrow, however, has managed to pull this off in this essay "The Short and Glorious History of Organization Theory." The following extract provides the reader with a succinct overview of how organization theory developed in the period up to 1970:

THE SHORT AND GLORIOUS HISTORY OF ORGANIZATION THEORY[†]

From the beginning, the forces of light and the forces of darkness have polarized the field of organizational analysis, and the struggle has been protracted and inconclusive. The forces of darkness have been represented by the mechanical school of organizational theory—those who treat the organization as a machine. This school characterizes organizations in terms of such things as: centralized authority, clear lines of authority, specialization and expertise, marked division of labor, rules and regulations, and clear separation of staff and line.

The forces of light, which by mid-20th century came to be characterized as the human relations school, emphasizes people rather than machines, accommodations rather than machine-like precision, and draws its inspiration from biological systems rather than engineering systems. It has emphasized such things as: delegation of authority, employee autonomy, trust and openness, concerns with the "whole person," and interpersonal dynamics.

The Rise and Fall of Scientific Management

The forces of darkness formulated their position first, starting in the early part of this cen-

[†]SOURCE: Perrow, Charles, "The Short and Glorious History of Organization Theory." Reprinted by permission of the publisher from ORGANIZATION DYNAMICS, Summer 1973, © 1973 American Management Association, New York. All rights reserved.

tury. They have been characterized as the scientific management or classical management school. This school started by parading simple-minded injunctions to plan ahead, keep records, write down policies, specialize, be decisive, and keep your span of control to about six people. These injunctions were needed as firms grew in size and complexity, since there were few models around beyond the railroads, the military and the Catholic Church to guide organizations. And their injunctions worked. Executives began to delegate, reduce their span of control, keep records, and specialize. Planning ahead still is difficult, it seems, and the modern equivalent is Management by Objectives.

But many things intruded to make these simple-minded injunctions less relevant:

1. Labor became a more critical factor in the firm. As the technology increased in sophistication it took longer to train people, and more varied and specialized skills were needed. Thus, labor turnover cost more and recruitment became more selective. As a consequence, labor's power increased. Unions and strikes appeared. Management adjusted by beginning to speak of a cooperative system of capital, management, and labor. The machine model began to lose its relevancy.

2. The increasing complexity of markets, variability of products, increasing number of branch plants, and changes in technology all required more adaptive organization. The scientific management school was ill-equipped to deal with rapid change. It had presumed that once the proper structure was achieved the firm could run forever without much tampering. By the late 1930s, people began writing about adaptation and change in industry from an organizational point of view and had to abandon some of the principles of scientific management.

3. Political, social, and cultural changes meant new expectations regarding the proper way to treat people. The dark, satanic mills needed at the least a whitewashing. Child labor and the brutality of supervision in many enterprises became no longer permissible. Even managers could not be expected to accept the authoritarian patterns of leadership that prevailed in the small firm run by the founding father.

4. As mergers and growth proceeded apace and the firm could no longer be viewed as the shadow of one man (the founding entrepreneur), a search for methods of selecting good leadership became a preoccupation. A good, clear, mechanical structure would no longer suffice. Instead, firms had to search for the qualities of leadership that could fill the large footsteps of the entrepreneur. They tacitly had to admit that something other than either "sound principles" or "dynamic leadership" was needed. The search for leadership traits implied that leaders were made, not just born, that the matter was complex, and that several skills were involved.

Enter Human Relations

From the beginning, individual voices were raised against the implications of the scientific management school. "Bureaucracy" had always been a dirty word, and the job design efforts of Frederick Taylor were even the subject of a congressional investigation. But no effective counter-force developed until 1938, when a business executive with academic talents named Chester Barnard proposed the first new theory of organizations: Organizations are cooperative systems, not the products of mechanical engineering. He stressed natural groups within the organization, upward communication, authority from below rather than from above, and leaders who functioned as a cohesive force. With the spectre of labor unrest and the Great Depression upon him, Bernard's emphasis on the cooperative nature of organizations was well-timed. The year following the publication of his *Functions of the Executive* (1938) saw the publication of F. J. Roethlisberger and William Dickson's *Management and the Worker*, reporting on the first large-scale empirical investigation of productivity and social relations. The research, most of it conducted in the Hawthorne plant of the Western Electric Company during a period in which the workforce was reduced, highlighted the role of informal groups, work restriction norms, the value of decent, humane leadership, and the role of psychological manipulation of employees through the counseling system. World War II intervened, but after the war the human relations movement, building on the insights of Barnard and the Hawthorne studies came into its own.

The first step was a search for the traits of good leadership. It went on furiously at university centers but at first failed to produce more than a list of Boy Scout maxims: A good leader was kind, courteous, loyal, courageous, etc. We suspected as much. However, the studies did turn up a distinction between "consideration," or employee-centered aspects of leadership, and job-centered, technical aspects labeled "initiating structure." Both were important, but the former received most of the attention and the latter went undeveloped. The former led directly to an examination of group processes, an investigation that has culminated in T-group programs and is moving forward still with encounter groups. Meanwhile, in England, the Tavistock Institute sensed the importance of the influence of the kind of task a group has to perform on the social relations within the group. The first important study, conducted among coal miners, showed that job simplification and specialization did not work under conditions of uncertainty and nonroutine tasks.

As this work flourished and spread, more adventurous theorists began to extend it beyond work groups to organizations as a whole. We now knew that there were a number of things that were bad for the morale and loyalty of groups—routine tasks, submission to authority, specialization of task, segregation of task sequence, ignorance of the goals of the firm, centralized decision making, and so on. If these were bad for groups, they were likely to be bad for groups of groups—i.e., for organizations. So people like Warren Bennis began talking about innovative, rapidly changing organizations that

were made up of temporary leadership and role assignment, and democratic access to the goals of the firm. If rapidly changing technologies and unstable, turbulent environments were to characterize industry, then the structure of firms should be temporary and decentralized. The forces of light, of freedom, autonomy, change, humanity, creativity, and democracy were winning. Scientific management survived only in out-dated text books. If the evangelizing of some of the human relations school theorists were excessive, and, if Likert's System 4, or MacGregor's Theory Y, or Blake's 9 x 9 evaded us, at least there was a rationale for the confusion, disorganization, scrambling and stress: Systems should be temporary.

Bureaucracy's Comeback

Meanwhile, in another part of the management forest, the mechanistic school was gathering its forces and preparing to outflank the forces of light. First came the numbers men—the linear programmers, the budget experts, and the financial analysts—with their PERT systems and cost-benefit analyses. From another world, unburdened by most of the scientific management ideology and untouched by the human relations school, they began to parcel things out and give some meaning to those truisms, "plan ahead" and "keep records." Armed with emerging systems concepts, they carried the "mechanistic" analogy to its fullest—and it was very productive. Their work still goes on, largely untroubled by organizational theory; the theory, it seems clear, will have to adjust to them, rather than the other way around.

Then the words of Max Weber, first translated from the German in the 1940s—he wrote around 1910, incredibly—began to find their way into social science thought. At first, with his celebration of the efficiency of bureaucracy, he was received with only reluctant respect, and even with hostility. All writers were against bureaucracy. But it turned out, surprisingly, that managers were not. When asked, they acknowledge that they preferred clear lines of communication, clear specifications of authority and responsibility, and clear knowledge of whom they were responsible to. They were as wont to say "there ought to be a rule about this," as to say "there are too many rules around here," as wont to say "next week we've got to get organized," as to say "there is too much red tape." Gradually, studies began to show that bureaucratic organizations could change faster than nonbureaucratic ones, and that morale could be higher where there was clear evidence of bureaucracy.

What was this thing, then? Weber had showed us, for example, that bureaucracy was the most effective way of ridding organizations of favoritism, arbitrary authority, discrimination, payola, and kickbacks, and, yes, even incompetence. His model stressed expertise, and the favorite or the boss's nephew or the guy who burned up resources to make his performance look good was *not* the one with expertise. Rules could be changed; they could be dropped in exceptional circumstances; job security promoted more innovation. The sins of bureaucracy began to look like the sins of failing to follow its principles.

Enter Power, Conflict, and Decisions

But another discipline began to intrude upon the confident work and increasingly elaborate models of the human relations theorists (largely social psychologists) and the uneasy toying with bureaucracy of the "structionalists" (largely sociologists). Both tended to study economic organizations. A few, like Philip Selznick, were noting conflict and differences in goals (perhaps because he was studying a public agency, the Tennessee Valley Authority), but most ignored conflict or treated it as a pathological manifestation of breakdowns in communication or the ego trips of unreconstructed managers.

But in the world of political parties, pressure groups, and legislative bodies, conflict was not only rampant, but to be expected—it was even functional. This was the domain of the political scientists. They kept talking about power, making it a legitimate concern for analysis. There was an open acknowledgment of "manipulation." These were political scientists who were "behaviorally" inclined—studying and recording behavior rather than constitutions and formal systems of government—and they came to a much more complex view of organized activity. It spilled over into the area of economic organizations, with the help of some economists like R. A. Gordon and some sociologists who were studying conflicting goals of treatment and custody in prisons and mental hospitals.

The presence of legitimately conflicting goals and techniques of preserving and using power did not, of course, sit well with a cooperative systems view of organizations. But it also puzzled the bureaucratic school (and what was left of the old scientific management school), for the impressive Weberian principles were designed to settle questions of power through organizational design and to keep conflict out through reliance on rational-legal authority and systems of careers, expertise, and hierarchy. But power was being covertly contested and exercised in covert ways, and conflict was bursting out all over, and even being creative.

Gradually, in the second half of the 1950s and in the next decade, the political-science view infiltrated both schools. Conflict could be healthy, even in a cooperative system, said the human relationists; it was the mode of resolution that counted rather than prevention. Power became reconceptualized as "influence," and the distribution was less important, said Arnold Tannenbaum, than the total amount. For the bureaucratic school—never a clearly defined group of people, and largely without any clear ideology—it was easier to just absorb the new data and theories as something else to be thrown into the pot. That is to say, they floundered, writing books that went from topic to topic, without a clear view of organizations, or better yet, producing "readers" and leaving students to sort it all out.

Buried in the political-science viewpoint was a sleeper that only gradually began to undermine the dominant views. This was the idea, largely found in the work of Herbert Simon and James March, that because man was so limited —in intelligence, reasoning powers, information at his disposal, time available, and means of ordering his preferences clearly—he generally seized on the first acceptable alternative when deciding, rather than looking for the best; that he rarely changed things unless they really got bad, and even then he continued to try what had worked before; that he limited his search for solutions to well-worn paths and traditional sources of information and established ideas; that he was wont to remain preoccupied with routine, thus preventing innovation. They called these characteristics "cognitive limits on rationality" and spoke of "satisficing" rather than maximizing or optimizing. It is now called the "decision making" school, and is concerned with the basic question of how people make decisions.

This view had some rather unusual implications. It suggested that if managers were so limited, then they could be easily controlled. What was necessary was not to give direct orders (on the assumption that subordinates were idiots without expertise) or to leave them to their own devices (on the assumption that they were supermen who would somehow know what was best for the organization, how to coordinate with all the other supermen, how to anticipate market changes, etc.). It was necessary to control only the *premises* of their decisions. Left to themselves, with those premises set, they could be predicted to rely on precedent, keep things stable and smooth, and respond to signals that reinforce the behavior desired of them.

To control the premises of decision making, March and Simon outline a variety of devices, all of which are familiar to you, but some of which you may not have seen before in quite this light. For example, organizations develop vocabularies, and this means that certain kinds of information are highlighted, and others are screened out—just as Eskimos (and skiers) distinguish many varieties of snow, while Londoners see only one. This is a form of attention-directing. Another is the reward system. Change the bonus for salesmen and you can shift them from volume selling to steady-account selling, or to selling quality products or new products. If you want to channel good people into a different function (because, for example, sales should no longer be the critical functions as the market changes, but engineering applications should), you may have to promote mediocre people in the unrewarded function in order to signal to the good people in the rewarded one that the game has changed. You cannot expect most people to make such decisions on their own because of the cognitive limits on their rationality, nor will you succeed by giving direct orders, because you yourself probably do not know whom to order where. You presume that once the signals are clear and the new sets of alternatives are manifest, they have enough ability to make the decision but you have had to change the premises for their decisions about their career lines.

It would take too long to go through the dozen or so devices, covering a range of decisions areas (March and Simon are not that clear or systematic about them, themselves, so I have summarized them in my own book), but I think the message is clear.

It was becoming clear to the human relations school, and to the bureaucratic school. The human relationists had begun to speak of changing stimuli rather than changing personality. They had begun to see that the rewards that can change behavior can well be prestige, money, comfort, etc., rather than trust, openness, self-insight, and so on. The alternative to supportive relations need not be punishment, since behavior can best be changed by rewarding approved behavior rather than by punishing disapproved behavior. They were finding that although leadership may be centralized, it can function best through indirect and unobtrusive means such as changing the premises on which decisions are made, thus giving the impression that the subordinate is actually making a decision when he has only been switched to a different set of alternatives. The implications of this work were also beginning to filter into the human relations school, through an emphasis on behavioral psychology (the modern version of the much maligned stimulus-response school) that was supplanting personality theory (Freudian in its roots, and drawing heavily, in the human relations school, on Maslow).

For the bureaucratic school, this new line of thought reduced the heavy weight placed upon the bony structure of bureaucracy by highlighting the muscle and flesh that make these bones move. A single chain of command, precise division of labor, and clear lines of communication are simply not enough in themselves. Control can be achieved by using alternative communication channels, depending on the situation; by increasing or decreasing the static or "noise" in the system; by creating organizational myths and organizational vocabularies that allow only selective bits of information to enter the system; and through monitoring performance through indirect means rather than direct surveillance. Weber was all right for a starter, but organizations had changed vastly, and the leaders needed many more means of control and more subtle means of manipulation than they did at the turn of the century.

The Technological Qualification

By now the forces of darkness and forces of light had moved respectively from midnight to noon to about 4 A.M. and 8 P.M. But any convergence or resolution would have to be on yet new terms, for soon after the political-science tradition had begun to infiltrate the established schools, another blow struck both of the major positions. Working quite independently of the Tavistock Group, with its emphasis on sociotechnical systems, and before the work of Burns and Stalker on mechanistic and organic firms, Joan Woodward was trying to see whether the classical scientific principles of organization made any sense in her survey of

a hundred firms in South Essex. She tripped and stumbled over a piece of gold in the process. She picked up the gold, labeled it "technology," and made sense out of her otherwise hopeless data. Job-shop firms, mass-production firms, and continuous-process firms all had quite different structures because the type of tasks, or the "technology," was different. Somewhat later, researchers in America were coming to very similar conclusions based on studies of hospitals, juvenile correctional institutions, and industrial firms. Bureaucracy appeared to be the best form of organization for routine operations; temporary work groups, decentralization, and emphasis on interpersonal processes appeared to work best for nonroutine operations. A raft of studies appeared and are still appearing, all trying to show how the nature of the task affects the structure of the organization.

This severely complicated things for the human relations school, since it suggested that openness and trust, while good things in themselves, did not have much impact, or perhaps were not even possible in some kinds of work situations. The prescriptions that were being handed out would have to be drastically qualified. What might work for nonroutine, high-status, interesting, and challenging jobs performed by highly educated people might not be relevant or even beneficial for the vast majority of jobs and people.

It also forced the upholders of the revised bureaucratic theory to qualify their recommendations, since research and development units should obviously be run differently from mass-production units, and the difference between both of these and highly programmed and highly sophisticated continuous-process firms was obscure in terms of bureaucratic theory. But the bureaucratic school perhaps came out on top, because the forces of evil—authority, structure, division of labor, etc.—no longer looked evil, even if they were not applicable to a minority of industrial units.

The emphasis on technology raised other questions, however. A can company might be quite routine, and a plastics division nonroutine, but there were both routine and non-routine units within each. How should they be integrated if the prescription were followed that, say, productions should be bureaucratized and R&D not? James Thompson began spelling out different forms of interdependence among units in organizations, and Paul Lawrence and Jay Lorsch looked closely at the nature of integrating mechanisms. Lawrence and Lorsch found that firms performed best when the differences between units were *maximized* (in contrast to both the human relations and the bureaucratic school), as long as the integrating mechanisms stood half-way between the two—being neither strongly bureaucratic nor nonroutine. They also noted that attempts at participative management in routine situations were counterproductive, that the environments of some kinds of organizations were far from turbulent and customers did not want innovations and changes, that cost reduction, price and efficiency were trivial considerations in some firms, and so on. The technical insight was demolishing our comfortable truths right and left. They were also being questioned from another quarter.

Enter Goals, Environments, and Systems

The final seam was being mined by the sociologists while all this went on. This was the concern with organizational goals and the environment. Borrowing from the political scientists to some extent, but pushing ahead on their own, this "institutional school" came to see that goals were not fixed; conflicting goals could be pursued simultaneously, if there were enough slack resources, or sequentially (growth for the next four years, then cost-cutting and profit-taking for the next four); that goals were up for grabs in organizations, and units fought over them. Goals were, of course, not what they seemed to be, the important ones were quite unofficial; history played a big role; and assuming profit as the preeminent goal explained almost nothing about a firm's behavior.

They also did case studies that linked the organization to the web of influence of the environment; that showed how unique organizations were in many respects (so that, once again, there was no one best way to do things for all organizations); how organizations were embedded in their own history, making change difficult. Most striking of all, perhaps, the case studies revealed that the stated goals usually were not the real ones; the official leaders usually were not the real ones; the official leaders usually were not the powerful ones; claims of effectiveness and efficiency were deceptive or even untrue; the public interest was not being served; political influences were pervasive; favoritism, discrimination, and sheer corruption commonplace. The accumulation of these studies presented quite a pill for either the forces of light or darkness to swallow, since it was hard to see how training sessions or interpersonal skills were relevant to these problems, and it was also clear that the vaunted efficiency of bureaucracy was hardly in evidence. What could they make of this wad of case studies?

We are still sorting it out. In one sense, the Weberian model is upheld because organizations are not, *by nature*, cooperative systems; top managers must exercise a great deal of effort to control them. But if organizations are tools in the hands of leaders, they may be very recalcitrant ones. Like the broom in the story of the sorcerer's apprentice, they occasionally get out of hand. If conflicting goals, bargaining, and unofficial leadership exists, where is the structure of Weberian bones and Simonian muscle? To what extent are organizations tools, and to what extent are they products of the varied interests and group strivings of their members? Does it vary by organization, in terms of some typological alchemy we have not discovered? We don't know. But at any rate, the bureaucratic model suffers again; it simply has not reckoned on the role of the environment. There are enormous sources of variations that the neat, though by now quite complex, neo-Weberian model could not account for.

The human relations model has also been badly-shaken by the findings of the institutional school, for it was wont to assume that goals were given and unproblematical, and that anything that promoted harmony and efficiency for an organization also was good for society. Human relationists assumed that the problems created by organizations were largely limited to the psychological consequences of poor interpersonal relations within them, rather than their impact on the environment. Could the organization really promote the psychological health in terms of the goals of the organization itself? The neo-Weberian model at least called manipulation "manipulation" and was skeptical of claims about autonomy and self-realization.

But on one thing all the varied schools of organizational analysis now seemed to be agreed: organizations are systems—indeed, they are open systems. As the growth of the field has forced ever more variables into our consciousness, flat claims of predictive power are beginning to decrease and research has become bewilderingly complex. Even consulting groups need more than one or two tools in their kit-bag as the software multiplies.

The systems view is intuitively simple. Everything is related to everything else, though in uneven degrees of tension and reciprocity. Every unit, organization, department, or work group takes in resources, transforms them, and sends them out, and thus interacts with the larger system. The psychological, sociological, and cultural aspects of units interact. The systems view was explicit in the institutional work, since they tried to study whole organizations; it became explicit in the human relations school, because they were so concerned with the interactions of people. The political science and technology viewpoints also had to come to this realization, since they deal with parts affecting each other (sales affecting production; technology affecting structure).

But as intuitively simple as it is, the systems view has been difficult to put into practical use. We still find ourselves ignoring the tenets of the open-system view, possibly because of the cognitive limits on our rationality. General systems theory itself had not lived up to its heady predictions; it remains rather nebulous. But at least there is a model for calling us to account and for stretching our minds, our research tools, and our troubled nostrums.

REFERENCES

Barnard, C. *The Functions of the Executive.* Cambridge, MA: Harvard University Press, 1938.

Roethlisberger, F. J., and W. Dickson. *Management and the Worker.* Cambridge, MA: Harvard University Press, 1939.

22

Max Weber's
Concept of Bureaucracy

The term "bureaucracy" was coined in the eighteenth century by the French economist Vincent de Gourney. But it was most explicitly defined in the early twentieth century by German sociologist Max Weber.

Weber was a very perceptive observer of history, and noted that the story of society and the rise of civilization was a story of power and domination. He noted that different social epochs were characterized by different forms of political rule, and that for a ruler or group of rulers to sustain power, it was essential for them (a) to gain legitimacy and (b) to develop some kind of administrative apparatus to sustain their power.

He saw the bureaucratic form of organization as the tool of a centralized administration, where the legitimacy of those in power was underpinned by a respect for the rule of law. In a bureaucracy, laws, rules, procedures, and predefined routines are dominant. They give form to a clearly defined system of administration where the exercise of "due process" is all important. As we all know, bureaucracies are supposed to operate "by the rules." They are places where individual initiative, enterprise, judgment, and creativity are supposed to take second place—if they are permitted at all!—to the policies and procedures that have been defined or authorized by those in charge of the organization as a whole.

Weber observed that the bureaucratic approach to organization mechanized the process of administration, exactly as machines had routinized production in industry. And his writings make frequent reference to how this process of mechanization squeezes out the human dimension. For example:

The decisive reason for the advance of bureaucratic organization has always been its purely technical superiority over any other form of organization. The fully developed bureaucratic mechanism compares with other organizations exactly as does the machine with the non-mechanical modes of production.

Precision, speed, unambiguity, knowledge of the files, continuity, discretion, unity, strict subordination, reduction of friction and of material and personal costs—these are raised to the optimum point in the strictly bureaucratic administration. . . .

Its specific nature . . . develops the more perfectly the more the bureaucracy is "dehumanized", the more completely it succeeds in eliminating from official business, love, hatred, and purely personal, irrational, and emotional elements which escape calculation. (Weber 1946, 214-17)

For Weber, the bureaucracy was a rational-legal form of organization that carried mechanistic principles into all areas of social life. His writings illustrate how a respect for legal order ultimately serves to create rigid, rule-bound institutions.

The following characteristics, which capture the main elements of Weber's concept of bureaucracy, illustrate how a legalistic approach to administration shapes organizations into mechanistic structures:

1. "The regular activities required for the purposes of the bureaucratically governed structure are distributed in a fixed way as official duties."

2. "A specified sphere of competence . . . is marked off as part of a systematic division of labour. . . ."

3. The official "is subject to strict and systematic discipline and control in the conduct of his office."

4. All operations are governed by "a consistent system of abstract rules . . . [and] consist in the application of these rules to particular cases."

5. "The organization of offices follows the principle of hierarchy; that is, each lower office is under the control and supervision of a higher one."

6. Officials are "subject to authority only with respect to their impersonal official obligations."

7. "Candidates [for bureaucratic positions] are selected on the basis of technical qualifications. In the most rational case, this is tested by examinations, or guaranteed by diplomas certifying technical training, or both. They are appointed, not elected."

8. Being a bureaucratic official "constitutes a career. There is a system of 'promotion' according to seniority or to achievement, or both" (Blau 1955, 1).

REFERENCES

Blau, P. M. *The Dynamics of Bureaucracy*. Chicago: University of Chicago Press, 1955.

Mouzelis, N. *Organization and Bureaucracy*. London: Routledge & Kegan Paul, 1976.

Weber, M. *Max Weber: Essays in Sociology*, translated and edited by H. H. Gerth and C. Wright Mills. New York: Oxford University Press, 1946.

Weber, M. *The Theory of Social and Economic Organization*, translated by A. M. Henderson and T. Parsons. New York: Oxford University Press, 1947.

23

Taylor, Schmidt, and Scientific Management†

Frederick Taylor was by all accounts a very colorful personality. The following paragraphs present a slightly edited version of his own story of the early days of Scientific Management. It is instructive in revealing Taylor's attitude to the workmen of his day, and how his system of management served to mechanize the worker, in effect by splitting the functions of hand and brain. Taylor's Scientific Management engineered giant leaps in efficiency. But it also dehumanized the workplace. Under its influence, more and more people became employed to provide "hands," with their managers providing all the brains.

One of the first pieces of work undertaken by us, when we started to introduce scientific management into the Bethlehem Steel Company, was to handle pig iron on task work. The opening of the Spanish War found some 80,000 tons of pig iron placed in small piles in an open field adjoining the works. Prices for pig iron had been so low that it could not be sold at profit, and therefore had been stored. With the opening of the Spanish War the price of pig iron rose, and this large accumulation of iron was sold. This gave us a good opportunity to show the workmen, as well as the owners and managers of the works, on a fairly large scale the advantages of task work over the old-fashioned day work and piece work, in doing a very elementary class of work.

The Bethlehem Steel Company had five blast furnaces, the product of which had been handled by a pig iron gang for many years. This gang, at this time, consisted of about 75 men. They were good, average pig-iron handlers, were under an excellent foreman who himself had been a pig-iron handler, and the work was done, on the whole, about as fast and as cheaply as it was anywhere else at that time.

A railroad switch was run out into the field, right along the edge of the piles of pig iron. An inclined plank was placed against the side of a car, and each man picked up from his pile a pig of iron weighing about 92 pounds, walked up the inclined plank and dropped it on the end of the car.

We found that this gang were loading on the

SOURCE: Pages 41-47 from SCIENTIFIC MANAGEMENT by Frederick Taylor. Copyright 1947 by Harper & Row, Publishers, Inc. Reprinted by permission of Harper & Row, Publishers, Inc.

average about 12½ long tons per man per day. We were surprised to find, after studying the matter, that a first-class pig-iron handler ought to handle between 47 and 48 long tons per day, instead of 12½ tons. This task seemed to us so very large that we were obliged to go over our work several times before we were absolutely sure that we were right. Once we were sure, however, that 47 tons was a proper day's work for a first-class pig-iron handler, the task which faced us as managers under the modern scientific plan was clearly before us. It was our duty to see that the 80,000 tons of pig iron was loaded onto the cars at the rate of 47 tons per man per day. And it was further our duty to see that this work was done without bringing on a strike among the men, without any quarrel with the men, and to see that the men were happier and better contented when loading at the new rate of 47 tons than they were when loading at the old rate of 12½ tons.

Our first step was the scientific selection of the workman. In dealing with workmen under this type of management, it is an inflexible rule to talk to and deal with only one man at a time, since each workman has his own special abilities and limitations, and since we are not dealing with men in masses, but are trying to develop each individual man to his highest state or rate or efficiency and prosperity. Our first step was to find the proper workman to begin with. We therefore carefully watched and studied these 75 men for three or four days, at the end of which time we had picked out four men who appeared to be physically able to handle pig iron at the rate of 47 tons per day. A careful study was then made of each of these men. We looked upon their history as far back as practicable and thorough inquiries were made as to the character, habits, and the ambition of each of them. Finally we selected one from among the four as the most likely man to start with. He was a *little* Pennsylvania Dutchman who had been observed to trot back home for a mile or so after his work in the evening, about as fresh as he was when he came trotting down to work in the morning. We found that upon wages of $1.15 a day he

had succeeded in buying a small plot of ground, and that he was engaged in putting up the walls of a little house for himself in the morning before starting to work and at night after leaving. He also had the reputation of being exceedingly "close," that is, of placing a very high value on a dollar. As one man whom we talked to about him said, "A penny looks about the size of a cart-wheel to him." This man we will call Schmidt.

The task before us, then, narrowed itself down to getting Schmidt to handle 47 tons of pig iron per day and making him glad to do it. This was done as follows. Schmidt was called out from among the gang of pig-iron handlers and talked to somewhat in this way:

"Schmidt, are you a high-priced man?"

"Well, I don't know vat you mean."

"Oh yes, you do. What I want to know is whether you are a high-priced man or not."

"Well, I don't know vat you mean."

"Oh, come now, you answer my questions. What I want to find out is whether you are a high-priced man or one of these cheap fellows here. What I want to find out is whether you want to earn $1.85 a day or whether you are satisfied with $1.15, just the same as all those cheap fellows are getting."

"Did I vant $1.85 a day? Vas dot a high-priced man? Vell, yes I vas a high-priced man."

"Oh, you're aggravating me. Of course you want $1.85 a day—every one wants it! You know perfectly well that has very little to do with your being a high-priced man. For goodness' sake answer my questions, and don't waste any more of my time. Now come over here. You see that pile of pig iron?"

"Yes."

"You see that car?"

"Yes."

"Well, if you are a high-priced man, you will load that pig iron on that car tomorrow for $1.85. Now do wake up and answer my question. Tell me whether you are a high-priced man or not."

"Vell—did I got $1.85 for loading dot pig iron on dot car tomorrow?"

"Yes, of course you do, and you get $1.85 for loading a pile like that every day right through the year. That is what a high-priced man does, and you know it just as well as I do."

"Vell, dot's all right. I could load dot pig iron on the

car tomorrow for $1.85, and I get it every day, don't I?"

"Certainly you do—certainly you do."

"Vell, den, I vas a high-priced man."

"Now, hold on, hold on. You know just as well as I do that a high-priced man has to do exactly as he's told from the morning till night. You have seen this man here (the supervisor) before, haven't you?"

"No, I never saw him."

"Well, if your are a high-priced man, you will do exactly as this man tells you tomorrow, from morning till night. When he tells you to pick up a pig and walk, you pick it up and you walk, and when he tells you to sit down and rest, you sit down. You do that right straight through the day. And what's more, no back talk. Now a high-priced man does just what he's told to do, and no back talk. Do you understand that? When this man tells you to walk, you walk; when he tells you to sit down, you sit down, and you don't talk back at him. Now you come on to work here tomorrow morning and I'll know before night whether you are really a high-priced man or not."

This seems to be rather rough talk. And indeed it would be if applied to an educated mechanic, or even an intelligent laborer. With a man of the mentally sluggish type of Schmidt it is appropriate and not unkind, since it is ef-fective in fixing his attention on the high wages which he wants and away from what, if it were called to his attention, he probably would consider impossibly hard work. . . .

Schmidt started to work, and all day long, and at regular intervals, was told by the man who stood over him with a watch, "Now pick up a pig and walk. Now sit down and rest. Now walk—now rest," etc. He worked when he was told to work, and rested when he was told to rest, and at half-past five in the afternoon had his 47½ tons loaded on the car. And he practically never failed to work at this pace and do the task that was set him during the three years that the writer was at Bethlehem. And throughout this time he averaged a little more than $1.85 per day, whereas before he had never received over $1.15 per day, which was the ruling rate of wages at that time in Bethlehem. That is, he received 60 per cent higher wages than were paid to other men who were not working on task work. One man after another was picked out and trained to handle pig iron at the rate of 47½ tons per day until all of the pig iron was handled at this rate, and the men were receiving 60 per cent more wages than other workmen around them.

24

How to Kill Creativity

In 1982, Machine Design *carried this provocative checklist on the relationship between management and creativity.*

How to Kill Creativity

- Always pretend to know more than anybody around you.
- Police your employees by every procedural means that you can devise.
- Run daily checks on the progress of everyone's work.
- Be sure that your professionally-trained staff members do technicians' work for long periods of time.
- Erect the highest possible barrier between commercial decision-makers and your technical staff.

- Be certain not to speak to employees on a personal level, except when announcing raises.
- Try to be the exclusive spokesman for everything for which you are responsible.
- Say yes to new ideas, but do nothing about them.
- Call many meetings.
- Put every new idea through channels.
- Stick to protocol.
- Worry about the budget.
- Cultivate the not-invented-here syndrome.

Note the relationship between these managerial attitudes and practices, and the everyday functioning of many bureaucratic organizations!

25

Working Under Mechanized Systems of Production

The following two accounts of work under mechanized systems of production capture a range of experience: on an assembly line and in an airline reservations office. Each illustrates the tension created between people and their work in situations where people are no more than tools. They speak to the forces that have given such a boost to the unionization and radicalization of the work force, and to the search for new work designs that can provide a better balance between the human and technical aspects of work.

LORDSTOWN:
Disruption on the Assembly Line†

Every day I come out of there I feel ripped off. I'm gettin' the shit kicked out of me and I'm helpless to stop it. A good day's work is being tired but not exhausted. Out there all I feel is glad when it's over.

I don't even feel useful now. They could replace me; I don't even feel necessary. . . . They could always find somebody stupider than me to do the job.

> —*Lordstown assembly line worker, twenty years old.*

The Lordstown complex of the General Motors Company sprawls along a huge, flat cornfield alongside Route 45 near Warren, Ohio. The facility is called a "complex" because it includes several plants doing different things. The older plants—the Fisher Body shop making subassemblies such as fenders for Chevrolet cars, and the smaller truck plant—are no different from the many similar factories oper-

†SOURCE: Aronowitz, Stanley, *False Promises: The Shaping of American Working Class Consciousness*, New York: McGraw-Hill, pp. 21-27, copyright 1974; used by permission.

ated by the company in other complexes throughout the United States. The big news is the new Chevrolet assembly plant which rolls out 800 Vega passenger cars a day. . . .

The new plant began to hire workers in 1966, but there was no sign that there was to be anything unusual about the work until the model changeover in the late summer and autumn of 1971. Until then, the 700 assembly line workers turned out slightly more than 60 cars an hour. In the late summer GM introduced its new production methods and, at the same time, brought in a new management, the GM Assembly Division (GMAD). A few automatic robot machines were brought into the body shop to replace human labor in welding operations, the number of moving parts in the car was reduced to permit one car to be assembled every 36 seconds, and the parts were made smaller for easier handling. . . .

At Lordstown, efficiency became the watchword. At 60 cars an hour, the pace of work had not been exactly leisurely, but after GMAD came in the number of cars produced almost doubled. Making one car a minute had been no picnic, especially on a constantly moving line. Assembly work fits the worker to the pace of the machine. Each work station is no more than 6 to 8 feet long. For example, within a minute on the line, a worker in the trim department had to walk about 20 feet to a conveyor belt transporting parts to the line, pick up a front seat weighing 30 pounds, carry it back to his work station, place the seat on the chassis, and put in four bolts to fasten it down by first hand-starting the bolts and then using an air gun to tighten them according to standard. It was steady work when the line moved at 60 cars an hour. When it increased to more than 100 cars an hour, the number of operations in this job were not reduced and the pace became almost maddening. In 36 seconds the worker had to perform at least eight different operations, including walking, lifting, hauling, lifting the carpet, bending to fasten the bolts by hand, fastening them by air gun, replacing the carpet, and putting a sticker on the hood. Sometimes the bolts fail to fit into the holes; the gun

refuses to function at the required torque; the seats are defective or the threads are bare on the bolt. But the line does not stop. Under these circumstances the workers often find themselves "in the hole," which means that they have fallen behind the line.

"You really have to run like hell to catch up, if you're gonna do the whole job right," one operator named Jerry told me when I interviewed him in the summer of 1972. "They had the wrong-sized bolts on the job for a whole year. A lot of times we just miss a bolt to keep up with the line."

In all plants workers try to make the work a little easier for themselves. At Lordstown, as in other automobile plants, there are many methods for making the work tolerable. Despite the already accelerated pace, workers still attempt to use the traditional relief mechanism of "doubling up." This method consists of two workers deciding that they will learn each other's operation. One worker performs both jobs while the other worker is spelled. At Lordstown, a half-hour "on" and a half-hour "off" is a fairly normal pattern. The worker who is on is obliged to do both jobs by superhuman effort. But workers would rather race to keep up with the line than work steadily—in anticipation of a half-hour off to read, lie down, go to the toilet, or roam the plant to talk to a buddy. Not all jobs lend themselves to this arrangement, especially those where a specific part like a front seat must be placed on all models; here the work is time consuming, and full of hassles. But there are many operations where doubling up is feasible, particularly light jobs which have few different movements. Fastening seat belts and putting on windshield wipers are examples.

"The only chance to keep from going nuts," said one worker, "is to double up on the job. It's the only way to survive in the plant. . . . "

The company claims that doubling up reduces quality. The method engenders a tendency for workers to miss operations, especially when they fall behind, according to one general foreman. Some workers believe that the company blames workers for doubling up as an excuse to explain its own quality control failures. There is a widespread feeling among the line workers that the doubling-up "issue" has more to do with the company's program of harassment than the problem of quality control.

The tenure of the previous management at the Chevrolet division of GM was characterized by a plethora of shop floor agreements between foremen and line workers on work rules. These agreements were not written down, but were passed from worker to worker as part of the lore of the job. As in many workplaces, a new line supervisor meant that these deals had to be "renegotiated."

When GMAD took over at Lordstown, management imposed new, universally applicable rules, which in fact, were applied selectively. On Mondays, "when there are not many people on the line," the company tolerates lateness. On Tuesdays, when young workers come back from their long weekends, "they throw you out the door" for the rest of the shift for coming in fifteen minutes or a half-hour late. "When the company gets a bug up its ass to improve quality, they come down on you for every little mistake. But then things start going good on the cars, so they start to work on other areas. Then you are not allowed to lay down—not allowed to read on the job; no talkin' (you can't talk anyway the noise is so terrific); no doubling up."

Efficiency meant imposing on workers the absolute power of management to control production. GMAD instituted a policy of compulsory overtime at the time of the model changeover. The "normal" shift became ten hours a day and there were no exceptions to the rule. Absenteeism and lateness became the objects of veritable holy crusades for the new management. Nurses refused to grant permission for workers to go home sick. The company began to consider a worker a voluntary quit if he stayed off for three days and failed to bring a doctor's note certifying his illness. Doctors were actually sent to workers' homes to check up on "phony" illnesses in an effort to curb absenteeism.

The average hourly rate for production line workers was $4.56 an hour in mid-1972. In addition, annual cost of living increases geared to the consumer price index had been incorporated into the contract. Gross base weekly earnings for ten hours a day were more than $195. With overtime, some workers had made more than $13,000 a year. Besides, GM workers have among the best pension, health insurance, and unemployment benefits programs in American industry. Certainly, there is no job in the Warren area whose terms compare with the high wages and benefits enjoyed by the GM workers. Equally significant, GM is among the few places in the area still hiring a large number of employees. The steel mills, electrical plants, and retail trades offer lower wages to unskilled workers and less steady employment to low-seniority people. For some, General Motors is "big mother." Many workers echo the sentiment of Joe, a forty-five-year-old assembly line worker who said that GM offered better wages and working conditions than he had ever enjoyed in his life—"I don't know how anybody who works for a living can do better than GM." Compared to the steel mill where he did heavy and dirty jobs, GM was "not near as hard."

Of course Joe has had differences with company policies. The job was "too confining." He didn't like to do the same thing every day. He objected to the company harassment of the men and had actually voted for a strike to correct some of the injustices in the plant. But, like many others, Joe had "married the job" because he didn't know where else he could get a retirement plan which would give him substantial benefits after thirty years of service, full hospital benefits, and real job security.

GMAD likes workers like Joe too. They know Joe isn't going anywhere. They believe him when he says he is sick and, if he misses installing parts on a car he can "chalk it up." In such cases, he simply tells the foreman about the missing operations and the "repairmen will take care of it."

Yet high wages and substantial fringe benefits have not been sufficient to allay discontent among the young people working on the line. If other area employers paid wages competitive with GM wages, GM would have serious difficulty attracting a labor force. The wages are a tremendous initial attraction for workers and explain why many are reluctant to leave the ship. . . .

The drama of Lordstown is the conflict between the old goals of decent income and job security, which have lost their force but are by no means dead, and the new needs voiced by young people for more than mindless labor.

BERYL SIMPSON[††]

[Prior to her present job as an employment counselor, she had been an airline reservationist for twelve years.]

My job as a reservationist was very routine, computerized. I hated it with a passion. Getting sick in the morning, going to work feeling, Oh, my God! I've got to go to work.

I was on the astrojet desk. It has an unlisted number for people who travel all the time. This is a special desk for people who spend umpteen millions of dollars traveling with the airlines. They may spend ten thousand dollars a month, a hundred thousand a month, depending on the company. I was dealing with the same people every day. This is so-and-so from such-and-such a company and I want a reservation to New York and return, first class. That was the end of the conversation. They brought in a computer called Sabre. It's like an electric typewriter. It has a memory drum and you can retrieve that information forever. Sabre was so expensive, everything was geared to it. Sabre's down, Sabre's up, Sabre's this and that. Everything was Sabre.

With Sabre being so valuable, you were allowed no more than three minutes on the telephone. You had twenty seconds, busy-out time it was called, to put the information into Sabre. Then you had to be available for another phone call. It was almost like a production line. We adjusted to the machine. The casualness, the informality that had been there previously was no longer there. The last three or four years on the job were horrible.

They monitored you and listened to your conversations. If you were a minute late for work, it went into your file. I had a horrible attendance record—ten letters in my file for lateness, a total of ten minutes. You took thirty minutes for lunch, not thirty-one. If you got a break, you took ten minutes, not eleven.

When I was with the airlines, I was taking eight tranquilizers a day. I came into this business, which is supposed to be one of the most hectic, and I'm down to three a day. Even my doctor remarked, "Your ulcer is healed, it's going away." With the airline I had no free will. I was just a part of the stupid computer. . . .

[††]SOURCE: Terkel, Studs, "Working: People Talk About What They Do All Day and How They Feel About What They Do," pp. 82-83, New York: Pantheon Books, a Division of Random House, Inc., copyright 1974; used by permission.

26

Computers and the Mechanization of Intellectual Work[†]

Computers are two-edged swords. They bring the promise of liberation from toil and routine, yet often end up just intensifying systems of control. In the following pages, Mike Cooley—an engineer and trade unionist who has been involved in a search for alternative modes of cooperative work design as a member of the Lucas Aerospace Combine Shop Stewards Committee in England—argues that many of the current trends in computer usage are heading to a deskilling of intellectual work, and reproducing the same kinds of problems that occurred following the introduction of machine technology in industry in the first half of this century. More often than not, computers are being used to create alienating work and to replace rather than augment human intelligence.

There is still a widespread belief that automation, computerisation and the use of robotic devices will free human beings from soul destroying, routine, backbreaking tasks and leave them free to engage in more creative work. It is further suggested that this is automatically going to lead to a shorter working week, longer holidays and more leisure time—that in an all round way it is going to result in 'an improvement in the quality of life.' It is usually added, as a sort of occupational bonus, that the masses of data we will have available to us from computers will make our decisions so much more creative, scientific and logical, and that as a result we will have a more rational form of society.

I want to question some of these assumptions, and attempt to show that we are beginning to repeat in the field of intellectual work, most of the mistakes already made in the field of skilled manual work at an earlier historical stage when it was subjected to the use of high capital equipment. I move from manual to intellectual work quite deliberately because I resent the division between the two and I therefore draw parallels throughout.

In my view it would be a mistake to regard the computer as an isolated phenomenon. It is necessary to see it as part of a technological continuum discernible over the last 400 years or so. I see it as another means of production and as such it has to be viewed in the context

[†]SOURCE: Excerpted from M. Cooley, *Architect or Bee? The Human-Technology Relationship*, Langley Technical Services, 95 Sussex Place, Slough SLI INN, England; used by permission. A new edition, updated and greatly extended, has been published by Chatto and Windus (1987), Bedford Square, London WC1B3RP.

of the society that has given rise to it. Consequently, I look critically at technological change as a whole in order to provide the framework for questioning the way computers are used today. . . . The equipment and processes described are not necessarily the most advanced or the latest in their field. They are chosen because they are typical of the kind of changes that are taking place in design. The problems I see arising within the design activity in the areas described will be universally applicable whether one is talking about computers in insurance, bank, newsprint industry or any other field.

The Equipment

The first piece of equipment considered is one which is being used to replace the function that was traditionally known as draughting. Up to the 1940's the draughtsman was the centre of the design activity. He could design a component, draw it, stress it out, specify the material for it and the lubrication required. Nowadays, each of these is fragmented down to isolated functions. The designer designs, the draughtsman draws, the metallurgist specifies the material, the stress analyst analyses the structure and the tribologist specifies the lubrication. Each of these fragmented parts can be taken over by equipment such as this automatic draughting equipment.

With this equipment, the draughtsman no longer needs to produce a drawing and so the subtle interplay of interpretation and modification as the commodity was being designed and related to the skilled manual workers on the shop floor, is being ruptured. What the draughtsman now does is work on the digitiser and input the material through a graticule or teletype. An exact reading is set of the length of each line, the tolerance and other details. The design comes out as a tape which is expanded in the computer after which it operates some item of equipment such as a jig borer or a continuous path milling machine. After that, the equipment itself will do the inspecting. If

perchance you want a drawing in order to show the customer exactly what they are purchasing—and that's the only reason you would bother to do it—then you can produce one on a master plotter very accurately. You can get a less accurate one on the microplatter which also produces an aperture card.

What is important in all this is not only that the fragmented functions of the designer have been inbuilt into the computer, but the highly skilled and satisfying work on the shop floor has also been destroyed. It is no longer a question of supply and demand, of a slump or a boom; these jobs have been technologically eliminated and yet they were some of the most satisfying and fulfilling jobs on the shop floor.

Quite apart from the suffering of those involved and the destruction of the creativity the worker used in doing the job, what must be of concern to all of us is where the next generation of skills is coming from. Skills which will need to be embodied in further levels of machines. The feel for the physical world about us is being lost due to the intervention of computerised equipment, and work is becoming an abstraction from the real world. In my view, profound problems face us in the coming years due to this process. . . .

In the past, skilled workers have had in the main, a tacit understanding of mathematics through their ability to analyse the size and shape of components by actually working on them. More and more, that knowledge has been abstracted away from the labour process and has been rarified into mathematical functions. . . . At present that knowledge has been taken away and rarified into a computer programme where only a small group of people can work on it. What would have gone on in reality is conceptualised, objectivised and fed to the computer. In its present mode of usage the computer is a tool for silencing the common sense and creativity of the skilled worker on the shop floor.

A major application of Manned Computer Graphics is in the field of structural analysis. Equations required for the analysis of the structure are automatically set up and are solved automatically upon request of the analytical output. Displacement, loads, shear and moments are computed and conveniently displaced for perusal. Changes of input conditions are easily facilitated and the corresponding output is displayed upon request. Constraining forces may be placed by using a light pen. . . . This equipment represents a deskilling process because it becomes possible to use designers and stress analysts with much less ability and experience than was previously required. . . .

What all this represents in fact, is that the knowledge which previously existed in the consciousness of the stress analyst, which was his or her knowledge, taken home every night and which was part of that person's bargaining power, has now been extracted from them. It has been absorbed and objectivised into the machine through the intervention of the computer and is now the property of the employer, so the employer now appropriates part of the worker himself through the intervention of the computer and not just the surplus value of the product. Thus we can say that the worker has conferred 'life' on the machine and the more he gives to the machine the less there is left of himself. . . .

When one considers all the uses for computerised equipment one gets the immediate impression that it must automatically improve the creativity of the designer concerned. However, there are enormous problems involved which require discussion. The complex communications that go on between human beings during problem solving activities are being distanced by the computer and by the systems interfacing the people with the computer with attendant consequences that are very serious and far reaching. Look at the job of a building designer for example. In the past, when designing a building, he would go out to the site to see how the structure was progressing. He would discuss it with the site engineer and maybe modify the design. Now it is possible to have a display on the site so that visits are unnecessary because the designer and engineer can have an abstracted conversation via the equipment. The designer's drawings will be transmitted electronically and displayed on the screen so the physical contact between the designer and the site is cut out. Apart from the design implications, the system will tie people down to the machine more and more and the break of getting away from the drawing office and on to the site, which was always one of the perks of the job, will no longer be acceptable.

In spite of the power of this equipment to do some really good work, it brings in its wake all the problems which high capital equipment bought to manual work at an earlier stage. . . .

Rate of Change

A discernible feature about modern equipment of any kind is the rate of change that is now driving us along at an incredible tempo. Over the last century alone the speed of communication has increased by 10^7, of travel by 10^2, of data handling by 10^6. Over the same period energy resources have increased by 10^3 and weapon power by 10^6. We are being drawn along in this tremendous technological inferno and it means that the knowledge we have, and the basis upon which we judge the world about us is becoming obsolete at an ever increasing rate, just like the equipment. It is now the case in many fields of endeavour that simply to stand still, you have to spend 15% of your time updating your knowledge. The problems for older workers are really enormous. . . .

It has been said that if you could divide knowledge into quartiles of outdatedness, all those over the age of 40 would be in the same quartile as Pythagoras and Archimedes. This alone shows the incredible rate of change, and the stress it places upon design staff, particularly the older ones should not be underestimated. What is happening is that the organic composition of capital is being changed. Processes are becoming capital intensive rather than labour intensive. . . . We are confronted therefore with massive and growing structural unemployment. More and more we are moving into a position where large numbers of people are going to be denied the right to work at all.

Seething Industrial Discontent

Pronouncements on the dehumanisation of work in so called technologically advanced societies have tended to concentrate on manual tasks. This is not surprising since despotism in the factory is now so great as to be counter productive. In addition to our well known problems in Great Britain, there are those experienced in other industrial nations. At Fiat in Italy the absentee rate is 18%. In Sweden the Government has introduced protective workshops for those who need protecting from the advanced technology which we had always been given to understand would liberate all of us. Along with these examples, the sabotage of products at the General Motors plant in Lordstown, U.S.A., reveals but the tip of a great iceberg of seething industrial discontent.

In my view the computer is the Trojan Horse with which Taylorism is going to be introduced into intellectual work. When a human being interacts with a machine, the interaction is between two dialectical opposites. The human is slow, inconsistent, unreliable but highly creative, whereas the machine is fast, reliable but totally non creative.

Originally it was held that these opposite characteristics—the creative and the non-creative—were complementary and would provide for a perfect human/machine symbiosis, for example, in the field of Computer Aided Design. However, it is not true that design methodology is such that it can be separated into two disconnected elements which can then be combined at some particular point like a chemical compound. The process by which these two dialectical opposites are united by the designer to produce a new whole is a complex, and as yet an ill defined and researched area. The sequential basis on which the elements interact is of extreme importance.

The nature of that sequential interaction, and indeed the ratio of the quantitative to the qualitative depends upon the commodity under design. Even where an attempt is made to define the proportion of the work that is creative, and the proportion that is non creative, what cannot readily be stated is the stage at which the creative element has to be introduced, when a certain stage of the non creative work has been completed. The very subtle process by which the designer reviews the quantitative information assembled and then makes the qualitative judgement is extremely complex. Those who seek to introduce computerised equipment into this interaction attempt to suggest that the quantitative and the qualitative can be arbitrarily divided and that the computer can handle the quantitative.

The speed at which computers are capable of carrying out immense computations is almost impossible to grasp. For example, to calculate all the stresses in the Gyretron—the space frame centre piece of EXPO 67, a computer was employed for two hours. A mathematical graduate could have performed the same calculations but would have taken about 30,000 years! This is equivalent to about 1,000 mathematicians working for their entire lifetimes.

The Faster the Better

Where computerized systems like this are installed, the operators are subjected to work which is alienating, fragmented and of an ever increasing tempo. As the human being tries to keep pace with the rate at which the computer can handle the quantitative data in order to be able to make the qualitative value judgements, the resulting stress is enormous. Some systems we have looked at increase the decision making rate by 1800 or 1900%, and work done by Bernholz in Canada has shown that getting a designer to interact in this way will mean that the designer's creativity, or ability to deal with the new problems, is reduced by 30% in the first hour, by 80% in the second hour, and thereafter the designer is shattered! The crude introduction of computers into the design activity in keeping with the Western ethic 'the faster the better' may well result in a plummeting of the quality of design.

There are arrangements in some systems where there is a set length of time for handling the data (17 seconds is an example). If you do not comply with this you are downgraded to 'headscratching status' as they call it. The anxiety of those involved can be measured, for they display all the signs of stress such as perspiration, higher pulse rate and increased heartbeat. Suppose the image is about to disappear from the screen and you haven't finished with it. You can hold or recall it, but everyone in the office knows when you have become a headscratcher. You are being paced by the machine, and the pace at which you work is becoming more and more visible. There comes a time when your efficiency as an operative unit is inadequate. . . .

Why Diminish the Human Intellect?

. . . The more I look at human beings, the more impressed I become with the vast bands of intelligence they can use. We often say of a job "It's as easy as crossing a road", yet as a technologist I am ever impressed with people's ability to do just that. They go to the edge of the pavement and work out the velocity of the cars coming in both directions by calling up a massive memory bank which will establish whether its a mini or a bus because there is significance in actual size. They then work out the rate of change of the image and from this assess the velocity. They do this for vehicles in both directions in order to assess the closing velocity between them. At the same time they are working out the width of the road and their own acceleration and peak velocity. When they decide they can go, they will just fit in between the vehicles.

The above computation is one of the simple ones to do, but you should watch one of our skilled workers at Lucas Aerospace going through the diagnostic procedures of finding out what has gone wrong with an aircraft generator. There you see real intelligence at work. A human being using total information processing capability can bring to bear synaptic connections of 10^{14}, but the most complicated robotic device with pattern recognition capability has only about 10^3 intelligence units.

Why do we deliberately design equipment to enhance the 10^3 machine intelligence and diminish the 10^{14} intellect? Human intelligence brings with it culture, political consciousness, ideology and other aspirations. In our society these are regarded as somewhat subversive, a very good reason then to try and suppress it or eliminate it altogether, and this is the ideological assumption present all the time.

As designers we don't even realise we are suppressing intellects, we are so preconditioned to doing it. That is why we have this terrific drive in certain fields of artificial intelligence. Fred Margulies of the Austrian Trade Union Movement commenting recently on this waste of human brainpower said "The waste is a twofold one, because we not only make no use of the resources available, we also let them perish and dwindle. Medicine has been aware of the phenomenon of atrophy for a long time. It denotes the shrinking of organs not in use such as muscles in plaster. More recent research of social scientists supports the hypothesis that atrophy will also apply to mental functions and abilities."

To illustrate the capabilities of human brainpower, I quote Sir William Fairbairn's definition of a millwright of 1861.

"The millwright of former days was to a great extent the sole representative of mechanical art. He was an itinerant engineer and mechanic of high reputation. He could handle the axe, the hammer and the plane with equal skill and precision; he could turn, bore or forge with the despatch of one brought up to these trades and he could set out and cut furrows of a millstone with an accuracy equal or superior to that of the miller himself. Generally, he was a fair mathematician, knew something of geometry, levelling and mensuration, and in some cases possessed a very competent knowledge of practical mathematics. He could calculate the velocities, strength and power of machines, could draw in plan and section, and could construct buildings, conduits, or water courses in all forms and under all conditions required in his professional practice. He could build bridges, cut canals and perform a variety of tasks now done by civil engineers."

All the intellectual work has long since been withdrawn from the millwright's function.

27

From Bureaucracies to Networks:
The Emergence of New Organizational Forms

Most of us are familiar with the bureaucratic organization that is specified in almost every detail and run in a tightly controlled way by the executive at the top. Many government organizations with their rigid departmental divisions and clearly defined roles and rules, mobilized through a hierarchical chain of command, provide obvious examples.

While this kind of organization once dominated many aspects of society, most bureaucracies are in the process of being reshaped along with the changing demands and challenges of the world around them. Sometimes the changes are quite marginal. Many organizations often resist fundamental change—because people, for one reason or another, wish to cling to a hierarchical model. But in some cases, significant transformations in organization can be achieved. The following pages explore some

of these changes, and how the bureaucratic approach to management is being challenged and replaced by newer forms of organization that are much more like networks than hierarchical structures. Conceptually, the range of organizational forms to be discussed can be represented by a continuum ranging from the rigid bureaucracy on the one hand (model 1) to the loosely coupled network, or organic form of organization (model 6), on the other. The aim of the discussion is twofold:

(a) to illustrate how a bureaucracy can, in principle, begin to transform itself over time from one form of organization into another (but probably not all the way from model 1 to models 5 and 6); and

(b) to contrast the principles that underpin organizations at different ends of the continuum.

EXHIBIT 27.1

Model 1	Model 2	Model 3	Model 4	Model 5	Model 6
The rigidly organized bureaucracy	The bureaucracy run by a senior executives' group	The bureaucracy that has created cross-departmental teams and task forces	The matrix organization	The project-based organization	The loosely coupled organic network

⟵————————————————————————————⟶

MECHANISTIC/BUREAUCRATIC
Organized for Stability

ORGANIC NETWORK
Organized for
flexibility and change

The purpose of the discussion is to provide a series of images and general principles against which you can identify the organizations with which you are familiar. A visual illustration of each model is presented in Exhibit 27.2.

Model 1

This is Weber's classical bureaucracy described in the opening paragraph (and in Resource 22). It represents the traditional organizational pyramid under the strict control of the chief executive. The organization has tried to codify all important operational principles, and is run in accordance with those principles. Meetings are viewed as a waste of time, and are rarely necessary, because almost every contingency is well understood: The organization is operating in an ultrastable environment.

Model 2

This organization is finding that the environment is generating novel problems, issues, and concerns on an ongoing basis. It is impossible to codify all appropriate responses. The chief executive has thus decided to create a "management team," comprising himself and the heads of principal departments, which meets on a weekly basis. This team makes all policy decisions, and settles the problems that cannot be handled through the organization's normal routines. Each department head exercises clearly defined authority in relation to his or her area of influence. Managerial styles vary from department to department, being shaped by the personality of the department head and the kind of task being performed. Some departments are highly authoritarian; others are more participative.

Model 3

This organization has found that the senior management team cannot handle all the issues that require an interdepartmental perspective, and has created a number of project teams and task forces involving staff at lower levels of the organization. The departmental structure and sense of organizational hierarchy, however, are very strong. The members of the teams and task forces tend to see their primary loyalty as being to their department head rather than to the team to which they belong. They realize that promotion is largely a departmental affair. They sit in team meetings as representatives of their department. They tend to give the "departmental line" on issues, and report back to their departmental head on what happens. When real problems arise, they are thus usually "delegated upward" for resolution by the senior management team. Team leaders feel that they have relatively little power, and find it difficult to develop commitment and momentum in relation to the activities that they're charged with managing. The organization *looks* as if it is moving toward a "matrix" or project-team structure, but in reality it operates like a loosely structured bureaucratic organization where information is passed up the hierarchy, and decisions down.

Model 4

This organization has decided to organize itself in a matrix form. Its special character rests in the fact that it has decided to give more or less equal priority to functional departments such as finance, administration, marketing, sales, production and R&D, and to various business or product areas. Thus people working in the various product or business teams that cut across the functional areas have to work with two perspectives in mind: functional and end product. This dual focus, under ideal conditions, allows the various operating teams to combine functional skills and resources with an orientation driven by the key tasks and challenges from the organization's environment—such as those relating to the need to fine-tune products for specific market segments or the needs of specific geographic areas.

EXHIBIT 27.2   Schematic illustrations of the six models

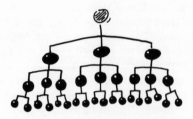

Model 1: The Rigid Bureaucracy

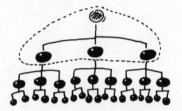

Model 2: The Bureaucracy with a senior "management" team.

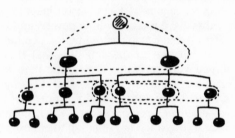

Model 3: The Bureaucracy with Project Teams and Task Forces.

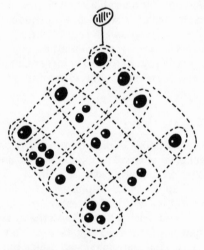

Model 4: The Matrix Organization

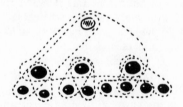

Model 5: The Project Organization

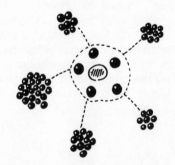

Model 6: The Loosely-coupled Organic Network

Model 5

This organization has decided to tackle most of its core activities through project teams. Notionally, there may be functional departments—but they only play a supporting role. Key specialist belong to teams, and make their main contributions through their team. The organization recognizes that its future lies in the dynamism and innovativeness of these teams, and tries to give them a free rein within the parameters and values that senior managers have used to define the strategic direction of the organization. The organization is much more like a network of interaction than a bureaucratic structure. The teams are powerful, exciting, and dynamic entities. Coordination is informal. There is frequent cross-fertilization of ideas, and a regular exchange of information, especially between team leaders and the senior management group. Much effort is devoted to creating shared appreciations and understandings of the nature and identity of the organization and its mission, but always within a context that encourages a learning-oriented approach. The organization is constantly trying to find and create the new initiatives, ideas, systems, and processes that will contribute to its success.

Model 6

This organization has decided to become, and stay, a loosely coupled network. Rather than employ large numbers of people, it has decided to operate in a subcontracting mode. It has a small core of staff who set a strategic direction and provide the operational support necessary to sustain the network, but it contracts other individuals and organizations to perform key operational activities. Its network at any given time operationalizes the "ideas" that the central group wishes to develop. For example, the organization may be in the fashion industry. It has created a name and image—"it's label"—but contracts out market surveys, product design, production, distribution, and so on. In the public eye, the firm has a clear identity. But in reality, it is a network of firms held together by the product of the day. It changes from month to month as different ideas and products come on line, and as the core organization experiments with different partners. The firm is really a system of firms—an open-ended system of ideas and activities, rather than an entity with a clear structure and definable boundary.

Models 1 through 6 are really different "species" of organizations. A firm beginning as model 1 may over time evolve into model 2, 3, perhaps even 4. And if it is prepared to engage in a major "revolution," it may develop the features of models 5 and 6. But in reality, the transformation process from one end of the continuum to the other is extremely difficult to make, and the required change is more than structural—it is cultural and political as well. The culture and politics of many organizations constrain the degree of change and transformation in which they can successfully engage, even though such change may be highly desirable for meeting the challenges and demands of the wider environment.

28

Organization Design:
An Information-Processing Perspective

Jay Galbraith (1974, 1977), building on the work of James Thompson (1967), suggests that as the amount of uncertainty facing an organization increases, coordination mechanisms (such as goal-setting, hierarchy, and rules) must usually be supplemented by design action that either reduces the need for information or increases information-processing capacities.

Creation of slack resources reduces the interdependence between subunits (by creating loose rather than tight coupling) and allows time for appropriate action to be initiated. Ex-

amples include extension of production and planning targets; padding of budgets to cope with contingencies; or use of stocks of supplies, work in progress, and finished goods to buffer discontinuities in input, throughput, and output.

Creation of self-contained tasks reduces the interdependence and degree of information exchange. Examples include the use of product or geographic groups (incorporating functional specialisms) rather than functional organization, "chunking" the organization into strategic

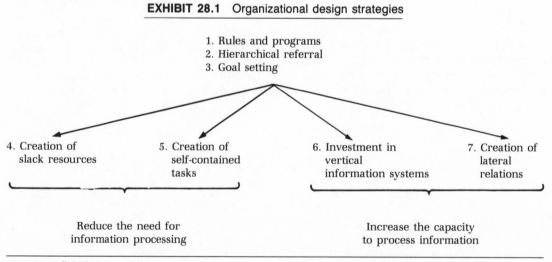

EXHIBIT 28.1 Organizational design strategies

SOURCE: Galbraith (1974, 300).

business units (SBUs), less division of labor, or the use of autonomous work groups instead of fragmented production processes.

Investment in vertical information systems allows the organization to automate control in a way that replaces hierarchical supervision. Examples include sophisticated production and cost controls that monitor activities on an ongoing basis, identifying significant departures from plans for managerial attention.

Creation of lateral relations creates selective forms of joint decision making that push the decision-making process down the organization to where information is available. Examples include direct contact between people who share a problem, use of liaison and coordinator roles, task forces, teams, and matrix organizations.

These strategies, which can be used one at a time or in combination, ease the ability of organizations to handle nonroutine problems for which they cannot plan.

Galbraith argues that when faced with environmental uncertainty, organizations must choose one of these strategies, or find means of operating on the environment to reduce the uncertainty. Otherwise performance will suffer.

REFERENCES

Galbraith, J. R. "Organization Design: An Information Processing View." *Interfaces* 4 (1974): 28-36.

Galbraith, J. R. *Organization Design*. Reading, MA: Addison-Wesley, 1977.

Thompson, J. D. *Organizations in Action*. Englewood Cliffs, NJ: Prentice-Hall, 1967.

29

Organizational Technologies

The technology used in an organization takes many forms. It is reflected

(a) in *equipment* (e.g., robots, machines, trucks, trains, computers, slide rules, hand calculators, pens, pencils);

(b) in how the equipment is linked into *some form of productive system* (e.g., as an assembly line; or decentralized system of semiautonomous production cells); and

(c) in *problem-solving and decision-making techniques* (e.g., algorithms, computer programs, decision trees, ways of routinizing judgments).

Over the years, many organization theorists have produced typologies for distinguishing between different types of technology.

For example, Joan Woodward (1965) in a famous study of English organizations produced a classification distinguishing between three different kinds of production processes:

Unit and Small-Batch Production
  Production of units to customers' requirements
  Production of prototypes
  Fabrication of large equipment in stages
  Production of small batches to customers' orders
Large-Batch and Mass Production
  Production of large batches
  Production of large batches on assembly lines
  Mass production

Process Production
  Intermittent production of chemicals in multipurpose plant
  Continuous-flow production of liquids, gases, and crystalline substances

James Thompson (1967) has also focused on differences in production systems, offering the following classification:

Long-linked technology—which involves serial interdependence in the sense that act C can be performed only after act B, which in turn can only be performed after act A, and so on; for example, assembly-line manufacturing;

Mediating technology—which requires operating in standardized ways with many diverse clients; for example, the telephone company, the post office; and

Intensive technology—which calls on a variety of techniques in order to achieve changes; selection of techniques is determined by feedback from the object itself; for example, an electronics laboratory developing and testing a new product.

As Charles Perrow (1970) has noted, the organizational significance of a particular technology is often related to the character of the raw material to which it is applied. First, there is the question of variability—the number of exceptional cases encountered. Second, there is the question of the extent to which the variations are understood, and hence the amount of discretion and nature of the "search processes" required to deal with the exceptional circumstances. These factors influence the extent to which technology and related organizational structures and processes can be routinized. Perrow uses these two dimensions of technology to distinguish between the following basic situations where there are

—few exceptions and analyzable searches (i.e., routinized manufacture);
—few exceptions and unanalyzable searches (i.e., craft manufacture);
—many exceptions and analyzable searches (i.e., an engineering approach); and
—many exceptions and unanalyzable searches (i.e., nonroutine manufacture).

This classification incorporates the basic ideas underlying the typologies of Woodward and Thompson (given that their classifications speak to the degree of underlying routineness) and also has the advantage that it applies to a wide range of organizations using "soft" as well as "hard" technology—that is, to "people-processing" organizations such as schools and hospitals, and to "information-processing" organizations, such as computer firms, marketing agencies, R&D outfits and government administrations, as well as to manufacturing firms.

To a degree, all organizations face a choice in the technology that they employ, in that they can choose to routinize their activities in different ways and to different degrees (e.g., by using assembly-line or team-based work sta-

tions in a factory or by using programmed learning or individualized development in a school). Technology is thus not a completely independent force. But research suggests that once a basic technology has been selected, successful organization depends on developing compatible organizational structures, control and coordination systems, and managerial styles. Highly routinized tasks can be organized and managed in a mechanistic way (assuming people are prepared to tolerate the mechanistic structures thus defined). But nonroutine, high-discretion tasks require more open and flexible approaches to organization. (Note the parallels with Burns and Stalker's (1961) distinction between mechanistic and organic organization.)

The technology within an organization can and will usually vary between different divisions and departments. Hence structures, controls, and managerial styles will have to match these variations to provide the basis for success.

REFERENCES

Burns, Tom, and G. M. Stalker. *The Management of Innovation*. London: Tavistock, 1961.

Perrow, C. *Organizational Analysis: A Sociological View*. Belmont, CA: Wadsworth, 1970.

Thompson, J. D. *Organizations in Action*. New York: McGraw-Hill, 1967.

Woodward, J. *Industrial Organization: Theory and Practice*. New York: Oxford University Press, 1965.

30

Organizational Environments

Everything exists in the context of a wider environment.

Consider the human being: Molecules exist within cells, which exist as part of a more complex organ, which forms part of a body, which constitutes one body within a population of similar bodies, which exists as a population alongside other populations, forming part of a wider ecology, and so on.

In a similar way, organizations comprise individuals who belong to groups, within departments or divisions forming the overall organization. In turn, the organization belongs to a wider population, for example, an industry, existing alongside other populations in a wider organizational ecology. And so on.

The concept of "an environment" is created by drawing a boundary at some level within a system of relations, thereby separating a particular element from the rest of the system. It is thus a somewhat arbitrary concept, and runs the danger of rupturing the complex network of interdependence that constitutes the system as a whole. The concept does have advantages, however, focusing attention on the detailed relations between a particular element of a system, and everything else in the context at large.

Organizational theorists and researchers have made use of this idea, using the distinction between organization and environment to highlight the key boundary transactions that sustain an organization on a day-to-day basis, and influence its long-term survival. For example, in its everyday functioning, an organiza-tion interacts with customers, competitors, suppliers, labor unions, shareholders, government agencies, and other individuals and organizations that have an immediate influence on the organization's well-being. These relations constitute what Dill (1958) has called the organization's *task environment*. But permeating and extending beyond this there are forces that constitute a broader *contextual environment*: cultural, social, political, technological, economic, demographic, and other factors that shape the organization's overall operations.

Nowadays, organizations must keep in touch with both these aspects of the environment.

They require a detailed knowledge of their task environment and potential changes in that environment. And they also need an understanding of the broader context and the implications of the changes that are occurring in that context.

Some organizations exist in relatively stable task environments. But, increasingly, change is becoming the order of the day. More than ever, organizations have to be sensitive to the possibility of dramatic changes in technologies, markets, social values and attitudes, and other factors with a capacity to transform their operations. Many of these changes often originate in the contextual environment, far removed from issues that are the focus of the organization's day-to-day concerns. Consider, for example, how changing political attitudes have gradually led to the regulation and deregulation of whole industries, or of how developments in microcomputing, which were once no more than "wild ideas" in scientific laboratories, are influencing the products and administrative processes in almost every industry (Morgan, 1988).

Intelligent organizations scan their environments and position themselves to deal with the challenges that lie ahead. Sometimes they can do this by fine-tuning existing activities to keep up with the latest production technology or market trend (as the U.S. automobile industry did in the 1960s). But sometimes they have to conduct major transformations (e.g., as happened in the U.S. auto industry in the face of new competition from Japan in the 1970s and 1980s, and as is happening in the financial services sector in the 1980s as information technology and other contextual forces transform the products and services offered by banks, insurance companies, brokerage houses, and the like). As Emery and Trist (1965) have noted, many organizations are now encountering turbulent environments where the fundamental challenges and changes are arising *in the context as a whole* as a result of the interaction of technological, social, and other forces that do not fall neatly within the domain of any single organization or industry.

During the last two decades, numerous organizational researchers have concerned themselves with understanding environmental turbulence, and its impact. Some have focused on sources of uncertainty arising from factors such as the pace of market and technological innovation (e.g., Lawrence and Lorsch 1967). Others have focused on understanding the pattern of interconnection within the environment, particularly with regard to the dependence of one organization upon another, for example, in terms of the control and flow of key resources (e.g., Pfeffer and Salancik 1978). Such factors influence the pace of change and to some degree an organization's ability to control the direction of that change.

Many of the most important challenges facing the modern organization rest in striking an appropriate balance with its environment. More and more, the task of strategic management becomes that of reading the environment, and of creating initiatives that will resonate with the changes that are occurring. In this way, organizations can develop a capacity to *adapt* to critical changes, and, through the management of key and environmental relations with government, customers, competitors, and potential collaborators actually *shape* the changes that are occurring.

REFERENCES

Burns, T., and G. M. Stalker. *The Management of Innovation.* London: Tavistock, 1961.

Dill, W. R. "Environment as an Influence on Managerial Autonomy." *Administrative Science Quarterly* 2 (1958): 409-43.

Emery, F. E., and E. L. Trist. "The Causal Texture of Organizational Environments." *Human Relations* 18 (1965): 21-32.

Lawrence, P. R., and J. W. Lorsch. *Organization and Environment.* Cambridge, MA: Harvard Graduate School of Business Administration, 1967.

Morgan, G. *Riding the Waves of Change.* San Francisco: Jossey-Bass, 1988.

Pfeffer, J., and G. R. Salancik. *The External Control of Organizations: A Resource Dependence Perspective.* New York: Harper & Row, 1978.

31

The Emergence of Turbulent Environments[†]

In their paper *The Causal Texture of Organizational Environments (1965)*, Fred Emery and Eric Trist identified four domains of interest in organizational behavior. They are illustrated here as four kinds of interdependency, where L indicates some potentially lawful connection, and the suffix 1 refers to the organization and the suffix 2 to the environment:

$$L(11), L(12)$$
$$L(21), L(22)$$

L(11) refers to processes within the organization: the area of internal interdependencies; L(12) and L(21) to exchanges between the organization and its environment: the area of transactional interdependencies from either direction; and L(22) to processes through which parts of the environment become related to each other: that is, its causal texture, the area of interdependencies that belong within the environment itself.

One of the seminal contributions of their paper was to draw attention to the causal texture of environments, and to argue that the connections within this domain may be qualitatively different from those in other domains. Another was to show how the causal texture of environments is changing in a way that reflects an increasing complexity calling for new kinds of strategic management. They identify four idealized types of environment to illustrate their point:

The *placid-randomized* environment reflects the simplest form of environmental texture in which goods and bads are relatively unchanging and randomly distributed. Interconnection between elements of the environment is weak. Under such circumstances, the best strategy for an organization is to do its best on a purely local basis (like a firm in an open and perfectly competitive market). There is no distinction between strategy and tactics, and the best tactics can be learned through trial and error. Under these conditions, organizations can survive as single and quite small units.

The *placid-clustered* environment is more complicated. The environment is still placid, but the distribution of goods and bads is not random; they hang together in clumps and clusters. Thus it may be far better for the organization to be in one part of the environment than another. Under these circumstances, it becomes worthwhile to get to know the wider environment and its threats and its opportunities and to adjust one's actions to take account of the presence of the others one meets at random. Here a distinction develops between strategy and tactics. There is a need to formulate plans that will allow one to achieve an important objective (e.g., gaining command of a resource niche or market opportunity) while recognizing and avoiding potential pitfalls along the way. A short-term gain may thus have to be forgone for more important long-run oppor-

†SOURCE: Adapted from F. E. Emery and E. L. Trist, "The Causal Texture of Organizational Environments." *Human Relations*, 1965, 21-32.

tunities. This kind of environment encourages planning, a concentration of resources, and the development of special competencies. Organizations in this environment thus tend to grow in size, become hierarchical, and tend toward centralized control and coordination.

The *disturbed-reactive* environment is similar to the placid clustered except that it has more than one organization of the same kind. Under these circumstances, each organization has to take account of the other in a serious way, considering that what it knows can be known by others, and that in the long run both may be competing for the same part of the environment. Knowing this, each will wish to improve its own chances by hindering the others, and will know that the others will wish to do likewise, and know that each knows this. Appropriate strategy and tactics thus resemble those of a military operation where one side wishes to outwit the other. This places a premium on the ability to launch initiatives that allow one to move at will, and to draw off the enemy, that is, to make and meet competitive challenge. Under these circumstances, decentralization, speed, and quality of decision making, and the ability to live off or absorb others and to compete, compromise, or negotiate become valuable capacities that can be used in appropriate situations. As Emery and Trist put it, "One has to know when not to fight to the death."

The *turbulent field* is even more complex and is distinguished by the fact that significant variances for component organizations can arise from the field itself. In other words, it is characterized by dynamic processes that are not necessarily dependent on one's own actions or those of one's competitors. The growth to meet the demands of disturbed-reactive environments, the effects of the competitive cut and thrust that characterize such environments, the effects of research-based development, and increasing interdependence between different facets of society combine to create turbulent conditions in which the very ground is in motion. Under such circumstances, the consequences of actions become increasingly unpredictable and can assume dimensions well beyond what one expects, with chance connections and events combining to create major transformations within the field. Such environments, which are emerging in all areas of life, are like nothing that we've known before, and call for new forms of strategic action. Emery and Trist suggest that individual organizations, however large, cannot cope with turbulence through traditional methods of forecasting and planning, or expect to adapt successfully on the basis of their own actions. Rather, they must search for forms of collaborative action, and for value consensus that can help reduce the number of independent lines of action contributing to turbulence, to arrive at shared norms and standards that can provide the basis for evolving patterns of relations. Collective strategies involving networks of organizations linked by shared values and ideals emerge as the ideal means for coping with turbulent times.

32

The Contingency Approach:
Analyzing Relations Between Organization and Environment

The contingency approach to organization stresses that effective organizations succeed in achieving a "good fit" *internally*—in terms of relations between organizational structure, managerial styles, technology employed, and the needs, values, and abilities of employees—and *externally*—in relation to the environment. One of the major strategic tasks facing the top management of any organization is to achieve this internal and external balance, and thus keep the organization finely tuned to meet emerging challenges.

Here are profiles of three successful types of organization identified in research by Miles and Snow (1978). Each type achieves a different configuration of organization-environment relations.

Defender organizations focus on sustaining a profitable environmental niche by being highly cost-effective and use price competition, an emphasis on quality, and other "barriers" to discourage entry from potential competitors. They build their organizations around a very clearly defined understanding of the domain in which they are operating—identifying and "sealing off" a segment of the total market to create as much stability as possible—and use a highly efficient core technology to deliver competitively priced products. The structure of organization and style of management is made subservient to the primary task of effi-

cient, effective production. The firm has a very clear conception of what it is doing, and defends, defends, defends. So long as the environment is stable, or can be stabilized, the defender firm can be very effective.

Prospector organizations focus on developing a relationship with the environment based on finding, developing, and exploiting new opportunities. This kind of organization is driven by a quest for innovation, moving from one product or activity to another, exactly as gold miners used to move from one claim to another. The successful prospector firm recognizes that it is much better at innovation and the development of prototype products than at the efficient long-term production of those products. It thus tends to see its products as relatively short-term ventures, and uses technologies, organizational structures, and managerial styles that create and support the required flexibility. It recognizes that it must have a capacity to "keep on the move" so that it can evolve along with changing opportunities. This kind of organization is ideally suited for dealing with turbulent environmental conditions.

Analyzer organizations try to combine the strengths of both the defender and the prospector by developing an ability to produce a range of high-quality products very efficiently, while remaining open to new opportunities. The analyzer is always scanning the environment for new opportunities, but only embarks on those opportunities when their viability has been clearly established. In terms of innovation and development, they tend to *follow* prospector firms, imitating and refining their products, producing them with a focus on quality and lower costs. These are the organizations that eventually make the prospector's innovations mainstream. Analyzer firms are very much "market driven," using R&D and production capacities in a supporting role. They place emphasis on responding quickly, and use technologies and organizational styles that support this. They usually have a well-understood core technology that can be easily retooled and adapted to fit the needs of new product designs. The organization often adopts the matrix form, and is usually differentiated in-

ternally according to the nature of the challenges of the specific tasks being faced. While some parts of the organization are geared to achieve a high degree of flexibility and change, others may be more traditional and stable.

The defender-analyzer-prospector typology fits the contingency approach to organization presented in *Images of Organization*, summarized in the diagram in Exhibit 32.1 (Morgan 1986, 63).

Defender organizations strive to develop congruent relations along the left-hand side of the diagram (line A); *prospector* organizations strive for a position toward the right-hand side (line B); *analyzer* firms try to occupy the middle range (line C).

This integrated model can be turned into a

EXHIBIT 32.1   Congruence and incongruence between organizational subsystems

SOURCE: From Morgan (1986, 63).

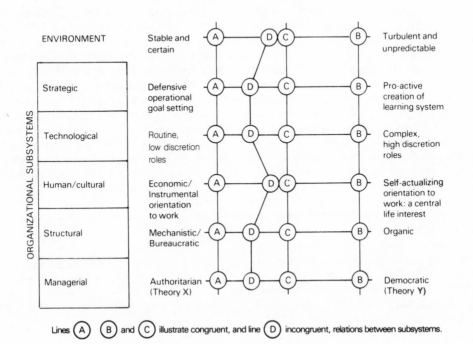

Profile of Organizational Characteristics

Lines (A) (B) and (C) illustrate congruent, and line (D) incongruent, relations between subsystems.

powerful diagnostic scheme for analyzing the relations between an organization and its environment by focusing on the following questions, and using the following chart to plot the characteristics of the organization that you wish to understand. (Note: this analysis can be performed for each of the principal departmental or other groupings within an organization. Generally, questions one and two should be answered with the total organization in view; questions three to six can be answered at the subunit level, given that different departments or groups within the organization will often be at different points on the various scales.)

How stable is the organizational environment? Is there a niche that can be defended, or is the environment in a continuous state of flux? (On a scale of 1-5, use 1 to signify a high degree of stability, and 5, conditions of rapid, unpredictable change.)

What kind of strategy is being employed? Defensive, analytical, prospecting? (Use 1 to characterize a strong defensive orientation, 5 to characterize an aggressive prospector; analyzer organizations will fall somewhere between, according to their degree of openness to environmental change).

What kind of technology is being employed? Is the emphasis on creating a highly routinized and fragmented system along the lines of an assembly line (point 1 on the scale)? Or is the emphasis on complete flexibility and dynamic teamwork (point 5)? Various degrees of nonroutineness and autonomy can be ranked at intermediate points on the scale, signifying the various degrees of job enrichment, autonomy, and self-organization found in practice.

How motivated are the firm's employees? Are they inclined to act as mindless "cogs in wheels," doing no more than they're told (point 1), or do they strive to become fully involved with their jobs, relishing autonomy and responsibility (point 5)? Again, rank intermediate degrees of involvement somewhere in between.

How is the organization structured? Is it a rigid bureaucracy (point 1), or a dynamic project-based organization/organic network (point 5)? Is it a bureaucracy that has been modified to create a measure of team activity (point 2), or a well-developed matrix organization where a real measure of autonomy and responsibility is delegated to the teams (points 3 or 4)?

What kind of managerial style is being used? Is it highly directive and authoritarian (point 1)? Or is there an emphasis on delegating a high degree of authority and responsibility to where it's needed (point 5)? Again, intermediate degrees of openness can be ranked in between.

As noted earlier, some of these questions can be answered in relation to the principal departmental and other groupings within the organization. In all probability, the plottings for each will vary, signifying the differentiation within the organization. These differences may be the source of important and difficult tensions (see Resource 33 in this *Resourcebook*).

Contingency theory hypothesizes that congruent relations between the six variables identified above provide the basis for effective operation; incongruencies are often accompanied by ineffectiveness. Where the profiles of subunits are at variance with overall challenges posed by the environment, it is important that they be brought into line, or remain differentiated, but in a way that does not subvert the organization's overall ability to deal with the challenges emerging from the environment. For example, in a turbulent environment, the bureaucratic characteristics of a particular area of the finance and administration department (though eminently suited for detailed administration within these departments) should not be allowed to dominate the organization as a whole.

REFERENCES

Miles, R. E., and C. C. Snow. *Organization Strategy, Structure and Process.* New York: McGraw-Hill, 1978.

Morgan, G. *Images of Organization.* Beverly Hills, CA: Sage, 1986.

Plot your analysis on the following chart:

1. How stable is the organization's environment?

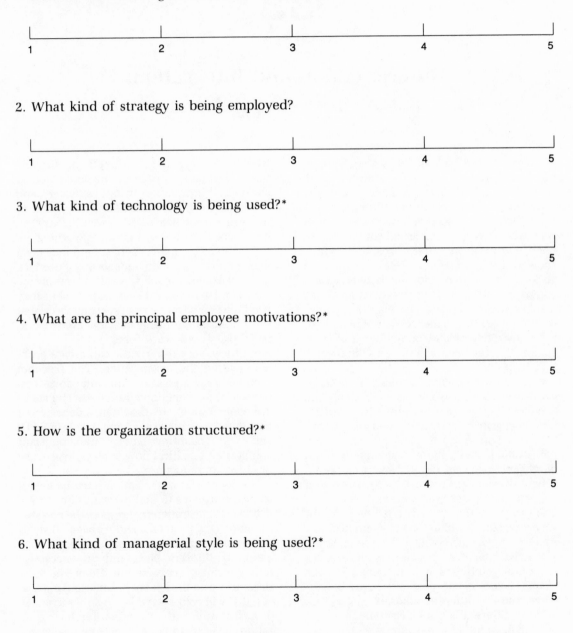

2. What kind of strategy is being employed?

3. What kind of technology is being used?*

4. What are the principal employee motivations?*

5. How is the organization structured?*

6. What kind of managerial style is being used?*

*This analysis should be applied to each of the principal departmental or other groupings within the organization.

33

Differentiation and Integration:
One of the Paradoxes of Management

All organizations have to find ways of breaking overall tasks into smaller elements and, then, of tying them together again. This is the problem of differentiation and integration!

In 1967, Paul Lawrence and Jay Lorsch of Harvard University published an important book, *Organization and Environment*, which showed that successful organizations seem to strike an optimum relationship between these competing dimensions of organization. They manage to differentiate in a way that allows them to meet the challenges and demands of their environment, and yet find ways of overcoming the fragmentation that this differentiation typically creates.

When an organization fragments itself, there are usually forces at work that will enhance the fragmentation process. For example, when different departments are established to specialize in production, sales, marketing, finance, administration, R&D, these departments often develop distinctive managerial styles, corporate subcultures, organizational structures and routines, and specialized aims and objectives. The effect is often to create many different suborganizations within the same organization. And they can be incredibly difficult to integrate and tie back together, because the differences are often reinforced and sustained by the values, beliefs, aims, and objectives of employees in the different subunits.

These differences can be very important in helping the subunits to meet the tasks that they have been assigned. For example, the production department may need to be dominated by a concern for precision, order, regularity, and routine. The R&D department may need to nurture a freewheeling "do as you please" atmosphere to preserve a creative working environment. The finance department may need to be preoccupied with budgets and a need for prudent expenditure and sound systems of control. The hard-pressed sales department may need the flamboyant corporate subculture that helps to sustain its highly individualistic, "work-hard, play-hard" work force.

But these very differences can create problems within the organization. The freedom granted R&D and sales can antagonize employees in production and finance. The rigorous control sought by the finance department may threaten to make work impossible in R&D, and so on. The differences can fuel important conflicts and political power plays, with very negative consequences.

The successful organization must be aware of this, and strive to find patterns of differentiation and integration that respect the need for diversity. Organizational and managerial styles will need to vary to accommodate the requirements of different tasks and the successful manager must recognize this. He or she must strive to create the kind of balance and integration that will hold everything together in an appropriate way, without hampering the organization's overall ability to meet the challenges of the wider environment, and the key tasks on which its survival ultimately depends.

The integration can take many forms:

structural—for example, through use of appropriate committees or task forces, the appointment of coordinators or troubleshooters, having an appropriate physical location to create tight or loose coupling, or to optimize interaction or isolation;

cultural—for example, by encouraging core values, attitudes, and corporate philosophies that will create an underlying sense of unity, or communicate a respect and rationale for differences; and

political—for example, by managing conflicts and differences effectively, and orchestrating initiatives that will help to keep the organization as whole in touch with the key issues and challenges that it must meet.

The methods and approaches that will prove successful will vary from one situation to another. To understand why, consider how the above ideas on differentiation and integration apply in the Acme and Omega case study (Resource 79) and in understanding the problems of the Fortress Insurance Company (Resource 90).

REFERENCE

Lawrence, P. R., and J. W. Lorsch. *Organization and Environment*. Cambridge, MA: Harvard Business School, 1967.

34

Collective Strategy:
The Management of Interorganizational Relations

In turbulent environments, new ways of managing change have to be developed. One extremely promising new direction has emerged from the work of Eric Trist (1983), who has argued that if one can begin to organize whole "domains" of interaction at an interorganizational level, one can do much to moderate the turbulence of the modern environment. The logic of Trist's argument is powerful yet extremely simple: The complexity and turbulence of modern environments is in large part the effect of individualized lines of action. Hence, if one can begin to reshape these patterns of behavior (a) by establishing "referent organizations" (such as trade associations, labor-management committees, or special purpose organizations that negotiate policies and develop programs that can unite a wide range of different actors), and (b) by encouraging other kinds of interorganizational collaborations (based on formal or informal networking, joint ventures, strategic alliances, and so on), one can have a major effect on the pattern of competition and cooperation in the environment at large. It is interesting that these developments are fast becoming realities as trade associations increase in power and influence, and as major sections of the economy reorganize to meet the future. The way in which the financial services sector is being reorganized as banks, trust companies, insurance companies, brokerage houses, and other organizations merge, acquire each other, and generally realign provides an obvious example.

As a growing number of organization theorists have suggested (see the references), these developments require that we rethink the whole nature of strategy-making in organizations to recognize the importance of joint action and collective strategy as a means of linking organization and environment. Traditionally, the emphasis in business policy and strategy-making in most sectors of the economy has been focused on (a) responding to external threats and opportunities, (b) negotiating resource interdependencies with critical stakeholders, and (c) strategic maneuvering in relation to competitors. In contrast, the scope for collaboration has been much neglected.

By developing and reshaping relations with potential competitors, and by thinking about organizing in a way that unites whole domains in the manner advocated by Trist, promising new developments can emerge.

As Astley (1984) points out, there are strong ecological arguments in favor of this kind of interorganizational cooperation. In nature we find numerous examples of intra- and interspecies cooperation, and organizations may do well to learn to develop the lessons in collaboration that can be drawn—to enhance what Kenneth Boulding has called the "survival of the fitting," not just the "survival of the fittest." The next resource in this *Resourcebook* offers interesting insights on how this can be done.

REFERENCES

Astley, W. G. "Toward an Appreciation of Collective Strategy." *Academy of Management Review*, 1984, 526-35.

Astley, W. G., and C. J. Fombrun. "Collective Strategy: The Social Ecology of Organizational Environments." *Academy of Management Review*, 1983, 576-86.

Astley, W. G., and A. H. Van de Ven. "Central Perspectives and Debates in Organization Theory." *Administrative Science Quarterly*, 1983, 245-73.

Boulding, K. E. *Evolutionary Economics*. Beverly Hills, CA: Sage, 1981.

Emery, F. E., and E. L. Trist. *Toward a Social Ecology*. Harmondsworth: Penguin, 1972.

Fombrun, C. J., and W. G. Astley. "Strategies of Collective Action: The Case of the Financial Services Industry." In *Advances in Strategic Management*, 125-29. Greenwich, CT: JAI Press, 1983.

Morgan, G. "Rethinking Corporate Strategy: A Cybernetic Perspective." *Human Relations*, 1983, 345-60.

Trist, E. L. "New Directions of Hope: Recent Innovations Interconnecting Organizational, Industrial, Community and Personal Development." *Regional Studies*, 1979, 439-51.

Trist, E. L. "Referent Organizations and the Development of Inter-Organizational Domains." *Human Relations*, 1983, 269-84.

35

Tit for Tat:
A Strategy for Cooperation and Survival?

In 1979, Robert Axelrod, Professor of Political Science at the University of Michigan, ran a tournament for computer programs addressing the Prisoner's Dilemma. The winning program was the shortest of all those submitted and based on the simple principle of tit for tat. Adopting the principle: Cooperate on the first move, and thereafter do exactly what the opposing player does, the program defeated all the complex strategies built into the other programs.

The results of this computer experiment have profound implications for our understanding of competition and collaboration, and the merits of collaboration in a competitive world. It shows that even in "zero-sum" situations, it is possible for everyone to win.

In the following paragraphs, Judith Knelman writes about her conversation with Anatol Rapoport, author of the winning program.

HOW CAN I WIN IF YOU DON'T LOSE?
Games Where the Winner Doesn't Take All[†]

It's commonly believed so-called zero-sum games like Monopoly, poker and bridge, in which what one player wins represents the loss to his opponents, are an imitation of life. Success means someone else's failure, a feast someone else's famine. Survival of the fittest means it's you or the other guy: to keep on top of the competition, you have to deprive others of what you all want.

Anatol Rapoport, professor emeritus at University of Toronto, director of the Institute for Advanced Studies in Vienna, . . . demonstrates,

[†]SOURCE: Knelman, Judith, "How Can I Win if You Don't Lose?" University of Toronto *Graduate*, January/February 1984, 20-21; used by permission.

among other things, the folly of this notion . . . in a statistical analysis of how people tend to resolve conflict.

By means of a program of strategy he has worked out for a simple game called the Prisoner's Dilemma, which looks something like tick-tack-toe and takes even less time to play, he is able to show that life is not a zero-sum game at all. Not only is it not necessary for the winner to take all: it is impossible. The winner does best by sharing and never attempting to put one over on the opponent. To win, you quietly follow the other person's lead, never trying to outmanoeuvre him except in immediate retaliation.

Life, says Rapoport, is a mixed motive game in which the interests of people partly coincide and partly conflict. To get what they want, they have to co-operate. They must trust each other consistently and be prepared to share the rewards available.

The game, which was discovered and circulated in the early 1950s, has aroused a tremendous amount of interest in academic circles, he says, because it demonstrates an important moral lesson: that the meek shall inherit the earth. When it is played in a situation that simulates society or evolution—a tournament environment wherein every player uses his own peculiar strategy consistently against every other player and then against himself— those who co-operate do much better than those who try to trick their opponents.

"Think of two scorpions in a bottle," he suggests. "If neither attacks, both will survive. If one attacks, the other retaliates, and both die. An even worse situation for the scorpions develops when one has to plot its strategy for survival on the assumption that the other may attack at any time."

The game worked out to represent the prisoner's dilemma mathematically gives each prisoner two alternatives. Each is told that if both keep quiet they will both get a sentence of two years, but if one rats he will get off free while the accomplice will get five years. The catch is that if they rat on one another, both

will get four years. If each is sure that the other will keep quiet as well, that is the best course for both. But can they trust each other?

The dilemma of the game is in the circumstance that it is in the best interest of each prisoner to implicate the other whether or not the other co-operates. If the other keeps quiet, he will still get a two-year sentence, while telling on the other gets him off free. As betrayal by both results in a four-year sentence, while keeping quiet could result in a five-year sentence, it's best to rat no matter what the other does. However, if neither rats, both get only two years.

Robert Axelrod decided to extend this problem to a tournament using computers to find the best consistent strategy for this sort of dilemma, which regularly confronts individuals and governments, in the form of potential rewards rather than punishments. The goal is to do as well as possible in your dealings with others over the long term. Rapoport won over all the other experts with the shortest and simplest program submitted, TIT FOR TAT, which shows that you do not have to deprive others in order to succeed yourself. His strategy is to co-operate or defect according to the lead of the other player. Even the most successful of the rival programs came to grief when they had to play against themselves, but TIT FOR TAT did nothing to hurt itself. It demonstrates the golden rule, do unto others as you would have them do unto you.

You play the game over and over again with the same partner, so that what happens in one game influences what happens in the next. You also play it over and over again with other people, just as you interact more than once with a large group of people in your everyday life. The idea is to accumulate the highest overall score. It is not necessary to vanquish individual rivals in order to do this. . . .

The research has obvious implications in many areas from domestic to international. Rapoport uses it to plead publicly for nuclear disarmament. . . . He thinks that like two scorpions in a bottle we are doomed if we do not trust our rivals. And even if our trust is not justified, he points out—if the other side does not disarm and we do—we may actually be safer than if we remained armed, since once we are no longer a threat they would have no need to attack us.

"I have no use for either superpower," says Rapoport. "I very much admire the small democratic countries that are not powerful." Canada, he says, is "sensible." It has the advantages of the U.S. without succumbing to the excesses. . . . As in the game, the secret of suc-cess lies in the correct definition of the problem. "You make your choice by asking not 'How do I do better'," says Rapoport, "but 'How do we do better?' You have to trust each other to co-operate. Then the answer is obvious."

REFERENCES

Hofstadter, D.H.R. "Metamagical Themas." *Scientific American*, May 1983, 16-26.

Rapoport, Anatol. *Fights, Games and Debates*. Ann Arbor: University of Michigan Press, 1960.

36

Organization and Environment:
Adaptation or Selection?†

Do successful organizations adapt to the changes occurring in their external environment?

Or, does the environment select the organizations that are to survive?

These questions lie at the heart of a debate in organization theory between "adaptation theorists" and "population ecologists."

While the "adaptationists" focus on the relations between individual organizations and their environment, arguing that organizations can and do adapt to environmental changes, the "population ecologists" focus on the dynamics of change at the level of whole populations of organizations. They argue that adaptation is easier said than done, and that the pattern of environmental change is such that "selection pressures" may favor or eliminate entire groups of organizations, such as industries, and that the changing structure and distribution of organizations in a society reflects the operation of such selection processes (Aldrich, 1979, 28).

The essential argument against the viability of the adaptation view is captured by Michael Hannan and John Freeman (1977), two key proponents of the population ecology perspective, in the following terms:

According to the adaptation perspective, subunits of the organization, usually managers or dominant coalitions, scan the relevant environment for opportunities and threats, formulate strategic responses, and adjust organizational structure appropriately.

The adaptation perspective is seen most clearly in the literature on management. Contributors to it usually assume a hierarchy of authority and control that locates decisions concerning the organization as a whole at the top. It follows, then, that organizations are affected

†SOURCE: Excerpted from M. T. Hannan and J. H. Freeman, "The Population Ecology of Organizations," *American Journal of Sociology*, 1977, 929-64, University of Chicago Press; used by permission.

by their environments according to the ways in which managers or leaders formulate strategies, make decisions, and implement them. Particularly successful managers are able either to buffer their organizations from environmental disturbances or to arrange smooth adjustments that require minimal disruption of organizational structure. . . . Clearly leaders of organizations do formulate strategies and organizations do adapt to environmental contingencies. As a result, at least some of the relationship between structure and environment must reflect adaptive behaviour or learning. But there is no reason to presume that the great structural variability among organizations reflects only or even primarily adaptation.

There are a number of obvious limitations on the ability of organizations to adapt. That is, there are a number of processes that generate structural inertia. The stronger the pressures, the lower the organizations' adaptive flexibility and the more likely that the logic of environmental selection is appropriate. As a consequence, the issue of structural inertia is central to the choice between adaptation and selection models. . . .

Inertial pressures arise from both internal structural arrangements and environmental constraints. A minimal list of the constraints arising from internal considerations follows.

1. An organization's investment in plant, equipment, and specialized personnel constitutes assets that are not easily transferable to other tasks or functions. The ways in which such sunk costs constrain adaptation options are so obvious that they need not be discussed further.

2. Organizational decision makers also face constraints on the information they receive. Much of what we know about the flow of information through organizational structures tells us that leaders do not obtain anything close to full information on activities within the organization and environmental contingencies facing the subunits.

3. Internal political constraints are even more important. When organizations alter structure, political equilibria are disturbed. As long as the pool of resources is fixed, structural change almost always involves redistribution of resources across subunits. Such redistribution upsets the prevailing system of exchange among subunits (or subunit leaders). So at least some subunits are likely to resist any proposed reorganization. Moreover, the benefits of structural reorganization are likely to be both generalized (designed to benefit the organization as a whole) and long-run. Any negative political response will tend to generate short-run costs that are high enough that organizational leaders will forego the planned reorganization. (For a more extensive discussion of the ways in which the internal political economy of organizations impedes change or adaptation, see Downs, 1967; and Zald, 1970.)

4. Finally, organizations face constraints generated by their own history. Once standards of procedure and the allocation of tasks and authority have become the subject of normative agreement, the costs of change are greatly increased. Normative agreements constrain adaptation in at least two ways. First, they provide a justification and organizing principle for those elements that wish to resist reorganization (that is, they can resist in terms of a shared principle). Second, normative agreements preclude the serious consideration of many alternative responses. For example, few research-oriented universities seriously consider adapting to declining enrollments by eliminating the teaching function. To entertain this option would be to challenge central organization norms.

The external pressures toward inertia seem to be at least as strong. They include at least the following factors:

1. Legal and fiscal barriers to entry and exit from markets (broadly defined) are numerous. Discussion of organizational behaviour typically emphasizes barriers to entry (state licensed monopoly positions, and so on). Barriers to exit are equally interesting. There are an increasing number of instances in which political deci-

sions prevent firms from abandoning certain activities. All such constraints on entry and exit limit the breadth of adaptation possibilities.

2. Internal constraints on the availability of information are paralleled by external constraints. The acquisition of information about relevant environments is costly particularly in turbulent situations where the information is most essential. In addition, the type of specialists employed by the organization constrains both the nature of the information it is likely to obtain (see Granovetter, 1973) and the kind of specialized information it can process and utilize.

3. Legitimacy constraints also emanate from the environment. Any legitimacy an organization has been able to generate constitutes an asset in manipulating the environment. To the extent that adaptation (for example, eliminating undergraduate instruction in public universities) violates the legitimacy claims, it incurs considerable costs. So external legitimacy considerations also tend to limit adaptation.

4. Finally, there is the collective rationality problem. One of the most difficult issues in contemporary economics concerns general equilibria. If one can find an optimal strategy for some individual buyer or seller in a competitive market, it does not necessarily follow that there is a general equilibrium once all players start trading. More generally, it is difficult to establish that a strategy that is rational for a single decision maker will be rational if adopted by a large number of decision makers. A number of solutions to this problem have been proposed in competitive market theory, but we know of no treatment of the problem for organizations generally. Until such a treatment is established, we should not presume that a course of action that is adaptive for a single organization facing some changing environment will be adaptive for many competing organizations adopting a similar strategy.

A number of these inertial pressures can be accommodated within the adaptation framework. That is, one can modify and limit the perspective in order to consider choices within the constrained set of alternatives. But to do so greatly limits the scope of one's investigation. We argue that in order to deal with the various inertial pressures the adaptation perspective must be supplemented with a selection orientation. . . .

This "selection" orientation tends to emphasize the importance of environmental competition, on the one hand, and of resource scarcity (as a factor influencing the number of organizations that an environment can sustain), on the other, as two forces that "select" or eliminate specific types of organizations. As a consequence, populations of organizations can survive or fail as a result of natural evolutionary processes, regardless of the actions taken by individual organizations.

Needless to say, this implication of the selection view has generated a sharp reaction from the adaptationists—for it leaves little room for good management and effective strategic decision making to have a significant influence on the long-term success of an organization.

In marshalling their view, the adaptationists point to the fact that strategic decision making can be critical in sealing the fate of an organization and that organiza-

tions can do much to organize their environment. For example, by engaging in collaborative actions with other major actors in the environment—potential competitors, firms in other industries, governments, unions, and the like—organizations can reshape and even eliminate many potential threats. They can be proactive in relating to the environment, and not just reactive. They also point to the fact that it is all too easy to emphasize the competitive and threatening aspects of environmental forces, underplaying the importance of synergistic, mutually sustaining patterns of interaction. Evolution, from this viewpoint, is not a deterministic force, but a process of "coevolution" through which individuals and organizations cocreate the futures they eventually face.

REFERENCES

Aldrich, H. *Organizations and Environments.* Englewood Cliffs, NJ: Prentice-Hall, 1979.

Astley, W. G. "Toward an Appreciation of Collective Strategy." *Academy of Management Review,* 1984, 526-35.

Astley, W. G., and A. H. Van de Ven. "Central Perspectives and Debates in Organization Theory." *Administrative Science Quarterly,* 1983, 245-73.

Downs, Anthony. *Inside Bureaucracy.* Boston: Little, Brown, 1967.

Granovetter, Mark S. "The Strength of Weak Ties." *American Journal of Sociology* 78 (May 1973): 1360-80.

Hannan, M. T., and J. H. Freeman. "The Population Ecology of Organizations." *American Journal of Sociology,* 1977, 929-64.

Van de Ven, A. H., and W. F. Joyce, eds. *Perspectives on Organizational Design and Behavior.* New York: John Wiley, 1981.

Zald, Mayer. "Political Economy: A Framework for Analysis." In *Power in Organizations,* edited by M. N. Zald, 221-61. Nashville, TN: Vanderbilt University Press, 1970.

37

Do Organizations "Enact" Their Environments?

How concrete is the environment facing an organization?

The distinction drawn between organization and environment creates a sharp division between the world inside and outside the organization. But how "real" is that distinction? Is the environment something that is independent of an organization, or is it in some measure a product of its own decisions, actions, and subjective constructions? For example, to what extent does an organization make and shape its environment through the processes that it uses to read, interpret, and judge the significance of what it sees in the world "out there," by selecting the domain in which it acts and determining the direction in which it develops?

This issue is the subject of a fascinating paper by Linda Smircich and Charles Stubbart (1985): "Strategic Management in an Enacted World."

They argue that there are three ways of thinking about one's environment.

(a) as an *objective* and unambiguous "reality" that has an existence of its own, and affects an organization directly and unambiguously;

(b) as an independent, real domain, that is at best a *perceived* phenomenon that is understood in incomplete and, at times, distorted ways; and

(c) as an *enacted* or socially constructed domain that is as much the consequence of the language, ideas, and concepts through which people attempt to make sense of the wider world as it is of the "reality" to which these social constructions relate.

The differences between these three views of the environment are illustrated in Exhibit 37.1

Each of these three ways of thinking about "the environment" has enormous implications for the way an organization is managed. For example, if one sees the environment as an objective reality (as in much of conventional organization theory), an organization and its managers have little option but to deal with the environment as a given: a deterministic force. If one sees the environment as a domain that, at best, is imperfectly perceived, it leads people to focus on the problems of "flawed understanding," and of trying to improve one's understanding as a means of dealing with the reality with which one is faced. If one sees the environment as an enacted domain, on the other hand, people are encouraged to recognize that the process of understanding and relating to the environment can be creative and flexible— one is not facing a domain of "hard reality," so much as interacting with a domain that can be understood, shaped, and, to a degree, managed in novel ways.

Smircich and Stubbart belong to a growing group of "interpretive organization theorists" who recognize that people in every walk of life play a large part in enacting their realities, and have a much greater influence on the world than they usually recognize (see, for example, Burrell and Morgan, 1979; Morgan, 1984). As they put it, the world is, essentially, an ambiguous realm of experience that is made concrete by the people who interpret it, and who

EXHIBIT 37.1 A Visual Representation of the Three Models of Environment

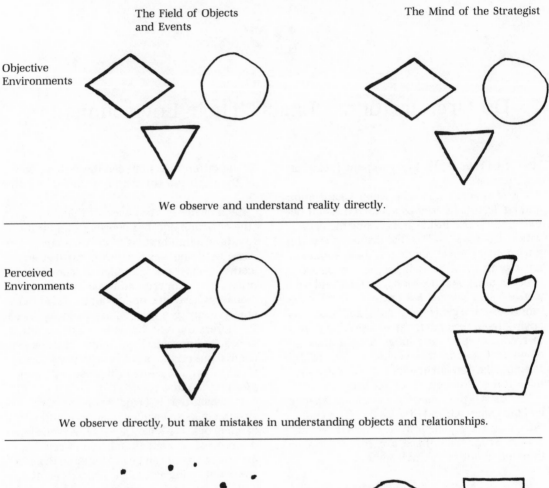

The Field of Objects
and Events

The Mind of the Strategist

Objective
Environments

We observe and understand reality directly.

Perceived
Environments

We observe directly, but make mistakes in understanding objects and relationships.

Enacted
Environments

We organize and interpret ambiguous events and experiences.

(Adapted from an unpublished segment of Smircich & Stubbart's original paper)

act on the basis of these interpretations. People's interpretations construct reality and, through subsequent actions based on those interpretations, actually shape future realities. Realities are not given; they are *made*! Smircich and Stubbart provide two examples that serve to illustrate the point:

(a) *For centuries people have scanned the heavens in search of constellations. In the process, they have learned to "see" "the Big Dipper" by drawing imaginary lines, a construction that proves very useful for orienting oneself in relation to the night sky. But there is no "Big Dipper" as such. Organizational managers and strategists make sense of the world in a similar way. Just as there are stars in the heavens, there are real things out there in the organization's environment—people, automobiles, oilwells, competitor firms, governments, etc. But these only become meaningful when imaginary lines are drawn to shape the universe with which one is concerned. The imaginary lines and the interpretations to which they give form then became "the realities" with which managers and decisions makers deal.*

(b) *The music industry essentially comprises people that provide music and people that listen to music. Firms in this industry shape themselves and their interests through all kinds of socially constructed concepts, values, assumptions and conventions that segment "the market" and "the industry" into different categories, focusing on different "tastes" and listening styles. The industry evolves as a result of the interpretations that shape understanding of a very amorphous phenomenon.*

The "enactment" or "interpretive view" thus has very important theoretical and practical implications for how we understand organizations and their ability to deal with the challenges that they face. Smircich and Stubbart highlight three issues that are of particular importance, suggesting that organizations and their managers should:

(1) abandon the prescription that organizations should adapt to their environment;
(2) rethink constraints, threats, and opportunities; and

(3) think differently about the role of strategic management and strategic managers.

Their argument is as follows:

* * *

1. Abandoning the Prescription That Organizations Should Adapt to Their Environments[†]

The conventional wisdom of strategic management urges organizations to adapt to their environments. This taken-for-granted maxim is more problematic than it appears. It obscures a good deal of the complexity, ambiguity, and abstractness in the strategic management process.

A brief example drawn from the American steel industry illustrates this point:

In 1950 America's steel industry was the most powerful in the world. Accounting for nearly one half of global steel output, it produced more steel than all of Europe combined, nearly three times as much as the Communist Bloc, and almost twenty times as much as Japan. Moreover, the large American steel firms enjoyed an undisputed position that had gone virtually unchallenged by foreign competitors during the preceding five decades (Adams & Mueller, 1982, p. 73).

By 1980, American steel producers lagged behind the Soviet Union, Japan, and Europe. The United States had become the world's largest importer of steel. American integrated steel producers increasingly suffered from outdated technology, inefficient plants, declining productivity, labor unrest, and inadequate cash flow for facility investment needs. The integrated companies vigorously called for import quotas or trigger-pricing levels that would choke off the flood of imports, imports said to be dumped at unfair prices by companies subsidized by foreign governments.

To the casual observer, the integrated steel companies seem to be having difficulties in adjusting to a hostile environment. The managers of the Big Eight steel companies feel that their problems have been caused by foreign competitors and government intervention. . . . Big

†SOURCE: Linda Smircich and Charles Stubbart, "Strategic Management in an Enacted World," *Academy of Management Review*, 1985, 724-36; used by permission.

Steel claims helplessness in the face of forces beyond their control and invites sympathy for their plight. Industry analysts, on the other hand, reproach steel executives for their conservatism and resistance to creative thinking (Ignatius, 1979; Lawrence & Dyer, 1983).

Regardless of which explanations one accepts, important questions remain: What should the managers of Big Steel do now? Should the steel companies build new facilities? Should they diversify? Merge? Should they sell plants to workers? Should they import semi-finished steel? Which actions are the adaptive ones?

When one theorizes from the present into the past as strategic analysts often do, one finds what seems to be a powerful argument about adaptation to an objective "environment." But the power of this explanation ends in the present. Although the argument about environmental adaptation may initially seem appealing, it does not provide much help for strategists in the here and now. The advice from much strategic management literature that stresses fit, congruence, and alignment is not sufficient for dealing with issues in day-to-day management. The executives in an industry cannot simply stand outside the action and adjust themselves to trends; their actions make the trends. Thus, if every firm rushes to take advantage of an opportunity, the opportunity vanishes. Trends are complex functions of multilateral behavior, making future outcomes problematic. The nature of what constitutes adaptation can be stated only *retrospectively*, never prospectively. Accordingly, the admonition to adapt to trends and forces is not very helpful.

An interpretive perspective argues that strategic managers can manage their organizations only on the basis of their knowledge of events and situations. But events and situations are *always* open to multiple interpretations. The facts *never* speak for themselves. If facts seem to "go without saying," it is only because observers happen to be saying very similar things.

For example, many commentators and par-ticipants in steel convey the impression that the industry is a scene of unrelieved devastation, using imagery reminiscent of the Alamo, Custer's last stand, or The Apocalypse, but other views can be brought to bear. To foreign steel producers the U.S. domestic market is a fragile opportunity. U.S. minimills are doing fine. The President of the United States views the situation as a painful, but necessary, evolutionary step into the golden age of techno-information, an era when former steelworkers will repair home computers, when kindly foreign governments will subsidize the cost of U.S. domestic steel. None of these views is dictated by the "environment." Each view flows from applying certain preconceived, limited frameworks to available contexts. Many other guiding images or views are possible. It is in terms of these multiple views that expectations and strategic action will congeal and shape the future. Old visions of what the industry is, how it works, who the participants are, and which strategic avenues are open, are becoming unglued. Out of this turmoil, new visions may emerge. Will the future bring a rapprochement with labor? Does the turmoil foreshadow the *reawakening* of a sleeping giant? Can one hear the *death knell* of steel? Whatever is possible *depends* on which visions people believe and act on—not on environmental fiat.

Analysis of a firm's environment cannot aspire to the status of a science, because there are no independent, authoritative observers. Instead, the choice of frameworks and interpretations becomes a creative and political art. Strategists need to concentrate on their choices vis-à-vis frameworks and interpretations. Novel and interesting frameworks may stimulate novel and interesting environments that could in turn preface novel and interesting strategic initiatives.

2. Rethinking Constraints, Threats, Opportunities

Managers face a tidal wave of situations, events, pressures, and uncertainties, and they naturally resort to collective discussion (in the broadest sense) to negotiate an acceptable set of relationships that provides satisfactory explanations of their social worlds. The scope and meaning of events are funneled down to manageable dimensions by formal and informal processes leading to industry wisdom. Huff (1982) points out that industry groups and other industry forums provide organized sense-making mechanisms.

A corresponding problem occurs, however, when strategic managers, by holding untested assumptions, unwittingly collude to restrict their knowledge. They may suffer from "collective ignorance" (Weick, 1979).

Evidence of the fragile nature of industry wisdom often draws attention (Cooper & Schendel, 1983). What everyone knows about an industry translates into an opportunity for those who do not know. Many, if not most, really novel and exciting new strategies that invade an industry, are perpetrated by outsiders who do not know the rules. Consider the introduction of Lite beer by the Miller Brewing unit of Philip Morris. Traditional companies knew that a diet beer could not be sold, but a foolish interloper tested the assumption and thereby enacted the most significant product innovation in beer industry history.

These observations about the way social reality is formed in organizational settings suggest a powerful prescription for strategic managers. They must look first to themselves and their actions and inactions, and not to "the environment" for explanations of their situations. Indeed, recent research on organizational crises (Nystrom & Starbuck, 1984; Starbuck, 1983) reveals that in many cases top managers' thinking patterns, not external environments, cause crises. As Karl Weick advises:

If people want to change their environment, they need to change themselves and their actions—not someone else. . . . Problems that never get solved, never get solved because managers keep tinkering with everything but what they do (Weick, 1979, p. 152).

Because of the temptation to assign convenient blame, the contributions of strategic management research should help managers reflect on the way in which managers' actions create and sustain their particular organizational realities. With the development of a greater capacity for self-reflection, corporate officials, governmental policy makers, and all organization members can examine and critique their own enactment processes. By maintaining a dual focus of attention—an ability to transcend the momentary situation in which they are entangled and to see and understand their actions within a system of meaning that is continually open to reflection and reassessment—strategic managers can challenge the apparent limits and test the possibilities for organizational existence.

3. Thinking Differently About the Role of Strategic Managers

The enactment model places strategy makers in an entirely different role from that envisaged by the objective or perceived models. Environmental scanning in those models sends managers "out" to collect facts and to amass an inventory of information (King & Cleland, 1978). A strategic manager is portrayed as a decision-formulator, an implementer of structure, and a controller of events who derives ideas from information.

The interpretive perspective, on the other hand, defines a strategist's task as an imaginative one, a creative one, an art. In the chaotic world, a continuous stream of ecological changes and discontinuities must be sifted through and interpreted. Relevant and irrelevant categories of experience must be defined. People make sense of their situation by engaging in an interpretive process that forms the basis for their *organized* behavior. This interpretive process spans both intellectual and emotional realms. Managers can strategically influence this process. They can provide a vision to account for the streams of events and actions that occur—a universe within which organizational events and experiences take on meaning. The best work of strategic managers inspires splendid meanings (Davis, 1982; Peters, 1978; Pfeffer, 1981; Pondy, 1976; Smircich & Morgan, 1982).

REFERENCES

Adams, W., and H. Mueller. "The Steel Industry." In *The Structure of American Industry*, edited by W. Adams, 73-135. New York: Macmillan, 1982.

Burrell, G., and G. Morgan. *Sociological Paradigms and Organizational Analysis*. London: Heinemann, 1979.

Cooper, A. C., and D. Schendel. "Strategic Responses to Technological Threats." In *Business Policy and Strategy: Concepts and Readings*, edited by D. J. McCarthy, 207-19. Homewood, IL: Irwin, 1983.

Davis, S. M. "Transforming Organizations: The Key to Strategy Is Context." *Organizational Dynamics* 3, no. 10 (1982): 64-80.

Huff, A. S. "Industry Influences on Strategy Reformulation." *Strategic Management Journal* 3 (1982): 119-31.

Ignatius, D. "Who Killed the Steel Industry?" *The Washington Monthly*, 11 March 1979, 9-19.

King, W. R., and D. I. Cleland. *Strategic Planning and Policy*. New York: Van Nostrand Reinhold, 1978.

Lawrence. P., and D. Dyer. *Renewing American Industry*. New York: Free Press, 1983.

Morgan, G. "Opportunities Arising from Paradigm Diversity." *Administration and Society*, 1984, 306-27.

Nystrom, P. C., and W. H. Starbuck. "To Avoid Organizational Crises, Unlearn." *Organizational Dynamics* 4, no. 12 (1984): 53-65.

Peters, T. J. "Symbols, Patterns and Settings: An Optimistic Case for Getting Things Done." *Organizational Dynamics* 2, no. 7 (1978): 3-23.

Pfeffer, J. "Management as Symbolic Action: The Creation and Maintenance of Organizational Paradigms." In *Research in Organizational Behavior*, edited by L. L. Cummings and Barry M. Staw, vol. 3, 1-52. Greenwich, CT: JAI Press, 1981.

Pondy, L. R. "Leadership Is a Language Game." In *Leadership: Where Else Can We Go?* edited by M. McCall and M. Lombardo, 87-88. Durham, NC: Duke University Press, 1976.

Pondy, L. R., P. Frost, G. Morgan, and T. Dandridge. *Organizational Symbolism*. Greenwich, CT: JAI Press, 1983.

Smircich, L. "Organizations as Shared Meanings." In *Organizational Symbolism*, edited by L. R. Pondy, P. Frost, G. Morgan, and T. Dandridge, 56-65. Greenwich, CT: JAI Press, 1983.

Smircich, L., and G. Morgan. "Leadership: The Management of Meaning." *Journal of Applied Behavioral Science* 18, no. 3 (1982): 257-73.

Starbuck, W. H. "Organizations as Action Generators." *American Sociological Review* 48 (1983): 91-102.

Weick, K. E. *The Social Psychology of Organizing*. Reading, MA: Addison-Wesley, 1979.

38

Organizational Growth and Development

Many organization theorists have concerned themselves with understanding the life cycle of organizations: how they are born, grow, and die.

In an early contribution in the field, Larry Greiner argued that growing organizations move through five phases of development, each of which ends with a management crisis. The following excerpt from his article "Evolution and Revolution as Organizations Grow" illustrates how periods of evolution, characterized by prolonged periods of growth with no major upheaval in organizational practice, give way to periods of revolution. If managers can anticipate where their organization is in the overall cycle, they may be able to anticipate and deal with upcoming crises:

Phases of Growth†

. . . let us now examine in depth the five specific phases of evolution and revolution. As shown in the *Exhibit*, each evolutionary period is characterized by the dominant *management style* used to achieve growth, while each revolutionary period is characterized by the dominant *management problem* that must be solved before growth can continue. The patterns presented seem to be typical for companies in industries with moderate growth over a long time period; companies in faster growing industries tend to experience all five phases more rapidly, while those in slower growing industries encounter only two or three phases over many years.

It is important to note that *each phase is both an effect of the previous phase and a cause for the next phase.* For example, the evolutionary management style in Phase 3 of the Exhibit is "delegation," which grows out of, and becomes the solution to, demands for greater "autonomy" in the preceding Phase 2 revolution. The style of delegation used in Phase 3, however, eventually provokes a major revolutionary crisis that is characterized by attempts to regain control over the diversity created through increased delegation.

The principal implication of each phase is that management actions are narrowly prescribed if growth is to occur. For example, a

†SOURCE: Reprinted by permission of the *Harvard Business Review*. An excerpt from "Evolution and Revolution as Organizations Grow" by Larry E. Greiner (July-August, 1972). Copyright © 1972 by the President and Fellows of Harvard College; all rights reserved.

company experiencing an autonomy crisis in Phase 2 cannot return to directive management for a solution—it must adopt a new style of delegation in order to move ahead.

Phase 1: Creativity . . .

In the birth stage of an organization, the emphasis is on creating both a product and a market. Here are the characteristics of the period of creative evolution:

• The company's founders are usually technically or entrepreneurially oriented, and they disdain the management activities; their physical and mental energies are absorbed entirely in making and selling a new product.

• Communication among employees is frequent and informal.

• Long hours of work are rewarded by modest salaries and the promise of ownership benefits.

• Control of activities comes from immediate marketplace feedback; the management acts as the customers react.

. . . *The leadership crisis*: All of the foregoing individualistic and creative activities are essential for the company to get off the ground. But therein lies the problem. As the company grows larger production runs require knowledge about the efficiencies of manufacturing. Increased numbers of employees cannot be managed exclusively through informal communication; new employees are not motivated by an intense dedication to the product or organization. Additional capital must be secured, and new accounting procedures are needed for financial control.

Thus the founders find themselves burdened with unwanted management responsibilities. So they long for the "good old days," still trying to act as they did in the past. And conflicts between the harried leaders grow more intense.

At this point a crisis of leadership occurs, which is the onset of the first revolution. Who is to lead the company out of confusion and solve the managerial problems confronting it?

Quite obviously, a strong manager is needed who has the necessary knowledge and skill to introduce new business techniques. But this is easier said than done. The founders often hate to step aside even though they are probably temperamentally unsuited to be managers. So here is the first critical development choice—to locate and install a strong business manager who is acceptable to the founders and who can pull the organization together.

Phase 2: Direction . . .

Those companies that survive the first phase by installing a capable business manager usually embark on a period of sustained growth under able and directive leadership. Here are the characteristics of this evolutionary period:

• A functional organization structure is introduced to separate manufacturing from marketing activities, and job assignments become more specialized.

• Accounting systems for inventory and purchasing are introduced.

• Incentives, budgets, and work standards are adopted.

• Communication becomes more formal and impersonal as a hierarchy of titles and positions builds.

• The new manager and his key supervisors take most of the responsibility for instituting direction, while lower-level supervisors are treated more as functional specialists than as autonomous decision-making managers.

. . . *The autonomy crisis:* Although the new directive techniques channel employee energy more efficiently into growth, they eventually become inappropriate for controlling a larger, more diverse and complex organization. Lower-level employees find themselves restricted by a cumbersome and centralized hierarchy. They have come to possess more direct knowledge about markets and machinery than do the leaders at the top; consequently, they feel torn between following procedures and taking initiative on their own.

Exhibit 38.1   The five phases of growth

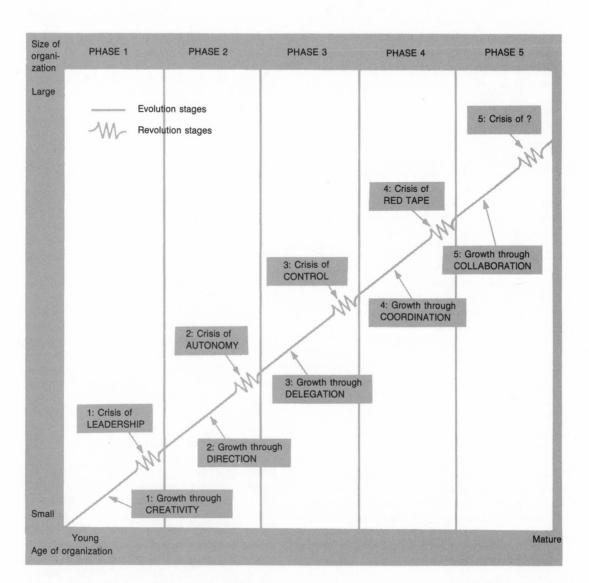

Thus the second revolution is imminent as a crisis develops from demands for greater autonomy on the part of lower-level managers. The solution adopted by most companies is to move toward greater delegation. Yet it is difficult for top managers who were previously successful at being directive to give up respon- sibility. Moreover, lower-level managers are not accustomed to making decisions for themselves. As a result, numerous companies flounder during this revolutionary period, adhering to centralized methods while lower-level employees grow more disenchanted and leave the organization.

Phase 3: Delegation . . .

The next era of growth evolves from the successful application of a decentralized organization structure. It exhibits these characteristics:

- Much greater responsibility is given to the managers of plants and market territories.
- Profit centers and bonuses are used to stimulate motivation.
- The top executives at headquarters restrain themselves to managing by exception, based on periodic reports from the field.
- Management often concentrates on making new acquisitions which can be lined up beside other decentralized units.
- Communication from the top is infrequent, usually by correspondence, telephone, or brief visits to field locations.

The delegation stage proves useful for gaining expansion through heightened motivation at lower levels. Decentralized managers with greater authority and incentive are able to penetrate larger markets, respond faster to customers, and develop new products.

. . . *The control crisis*: A serious problem eventually evolves, however, as top executives sense that they are losing control over a highly diversified field operation. Autonomous field managers prefer to run their own shows without coordinating plans, money, technology, and manpower with the rest of the organization. Freedom breeds a parochial attitude.

Hence, the Phase 3 revolution is under way when top management seeks to regain control over the total company. Some top managements attempt a return to centralized management, which usually fails because of the vast scope of operations. Those companies that move ahead find a new solution in the use of special coordination techniques.

Phase 4: Coordination . . .

During this phase, the evolutionary period is characterized by the use of formal systems for achieving greater coordination and by top executives taking responsibility for the initiation and administration of these new systems. For example:

- Decentralized units are merged into product groups.
- Formal planning procedures are established and intensively reviewed.
- Numerous staff personnel are hired and located at headquarters to initiate company-wide programs of control and review for line managers.
- Capital expenditures are very carefully weighted and parcelled out across the organization.
- Each product group is treated as an investment centre where return on invested capital is an important criterion used in allocating funds.
- Certain technical functions, such as data processing, are centralized at headquarters, while daily operating decisions remain decentralized.
- Stock options and company wide profit sharing are used to encourage identity with the firm as a whole.

All of these new coordination systems prove useful for achieving growth through more efficient allocation of a company's limited resources. They prompt field managers to look beyond the needs of their local units. While these managers still have much decision-making responsibility, they learn to justify their actions more carefully to a "watchdog" audience at headquarters.

. . . *The red-tape crisis*: But a lack of confidence gradually builds between line and staff, and between headquarters and the field. The proliferation of systems and programs begins to exceed its utility; a red-tape crisis is created. Line managers, for example, increasingly resent heavy staff direction from those who are not familiar with local conditions. Staff people, on the other hand, complain about uncooperative and uninformed line managers. Together both groups criticise the bureaucratic paper system that has evolved. Procedures take precedence over problem solving, and innovation is dampened. In short, the organization has become too large and complex to be managed through formal programs and rigid systems. The Phase 4 revolution is under way.

Phase 5: Collaboration . . .

The last observable phase in previous studies emphasizes strong interpersonal collaboration in an attempt to overcome the red-tape crisis. Where Phase 4 was managed more through formal systems and procedures, Phase 5 emphasizes greater spontaneity in management action through teams and the skillful confrontation of interpersonal differences. Social control and self-discipline take over from formal control. This transition is especially difficult for those experts who created the old systems as well as for those line managers who relied on formal methods for answers.

The Phase 5 evolution, then, builds around a more flexible and behavioral approach to management. Here are its characteristics:

- The focus is on solving problems quickly through team action.
- Teams are combined across functions for task-group activity.
- Headquarters staff experts are reduced in number, reassigned, and combined in interdisciplinary teams to consult with, not to direct, field units.
- A matrix-type structure is frequently used to assemble the right teams for the appropriate problems.
- Previous formal systems are simplified and combined into single multipurpose systems.
- Conferences of key managers are held frequently to focus on major problem issues.
- Educational programs are utilized to train managers in behavioral skills for achieving better teamwork and conflict resolution.
- Real-time information systems are integrated into daily decision making.
- Economic rewards are geared more to team performance than to individual achievement.
- Experiments in new practices are encouraged throughout the organization.

. . . *The ? crises*: What will be the revolution in response to this stage of evolution? Many large U.S. companies are now in the Phase 5 evolutionary stage, so the answers are critical. While there is little clear evidence, I imagine the revolution will centre around the "psychological saturation" of employees who grow emotionally and physically exhausted by the intensity of teamwork and the heavy pressure for innovative solutions.

My hunch is that the Phase 5 revolution will be solved through new structures and programs that allow employees to periodically rest, reflect, and revitalize themselves. We may even see companies with dual organization structures: a "habit" structure for getting the daily work done, and a "reflective" structure for stimulating perspective and personal enrichment. Employees could then move back and forth between the two structures as their energies are dissipated and refueled.

One European organization has implemented such a structure. Five reflective groups have been established outside their regular structure for the purpose of continuously evaluating five task activities basic to the organization. They report directly to the managing director, although their reports are made public throughout the organization. Membership in each group includes all levels and functions, and employees are rotated through these groups on a six-month basis.

Other concrete examples now in practice include providing sabbaticals for employees, moving managers in and out of "hot spot" jobs, establishing a four-day workweek, assuring job security, building physical facilities for relaxation *during* the working day, making jobs more interchangeable, creating an extra team on the assembly line so that one team is always off for reeducation, and switching to longer vacations and more flexible working hours.

The Chinese practice of requiring executives to spend time periodically on lower-level jobs may also be worth a nonideological evaluation. For too long U.S. management has assumed that career progress should be equated with an upward path toward title, salary, and power. Could it be that some vice presidents of marketing might just long for, and even benefit from, temporary duty in the field sales organization?

39

"Just in Time" Systems of Management

"Protect the core technology"
"Buffer and buffer to minimize external influence"
"Build for stability rather than change"

Many approaches to organization have been dominated by a concern to stabilize in the face of changing circumstances, rather than to organize in a way that flows with change. A dramatic exception is found in the introduction of Just in Time (JIT) systems of management, first introduced in Japan, that build production processes around variable inputs. The results can be dramatic, allowing assembly lines to be redesigned to produce variations of the same products, that often incorporate customer-specified modifications. For example, on a Toyota production-line, the molds for producing a particular model of car can be changed in a matter of minutes.

The key to JIT management rests in new systems of inventory control that eliminate large stocks of parts and other raw materials in favor of JIT delivery (e.g., four hours rather than four days). But, as the following discussion suggests, the system requires many changes in organization and management as well.

The Transformative Impact of "Just-in-Time" Systems of Management[†]

Many branches of manufacturing, retailing, distribution, and other service industries are being transformed by the introduction of "Just-in-Time" (JIT) principles of management. JIT systems are an offshoot of systems designed to cut inventory and work in progress. Facilitated by the use of computers in manufacturing and stock control and by automated information systems that create on-line relations with suppliers, this approach has generated manufacturing systems in which inventory is kept to a minimum (for example, four-hour supply instead of four-day supply) and relations among suppliers, manufacturers, and retailers are

[†]SOURCE: Gareth Morgan, *Riding The Waves of Change*, pp. 21-23. San Francisco, Jossey Bass Inc. 1988. Reproduced with permission of the publishers.

closely coordinated to ensure that everything arrives immediately before it is needed. Though often seen as a technology for reducing overhead, JIT systems actually transform the management process and will probably have a major impact on the location and structure of manufacturing and related service industries.

Some of these latent consequences of JIT systems are illustrated in [Exhibit 39.1]. The coordination necessary for just-in-time delivery transforms relations among suppliers, manufacturers, and retailers. Formerly, a manufacturing firm may have seen itself as a separate organization. Under a JIT system, it must see itself as part of a broad interorganizational network and realize that it is this wider network of relations that must be managed. It is thus not uncommon to find manufacturers taking some responsibility for the management of their suppliers and engaging in novel methods of collaboration. Suppliers, manufacturers, and retailers increasingly have to develop new mindsets consistent with this network view of their identities.

Similarly, JIT systems transform the patterns of management and control required in an organization. Four-hour margins allow little room for error or prolonged decision making, and spread responsibility and control through-

EXHIBIT 39.1 The "fracture" surrounding 'just-in-time" (JIT) management

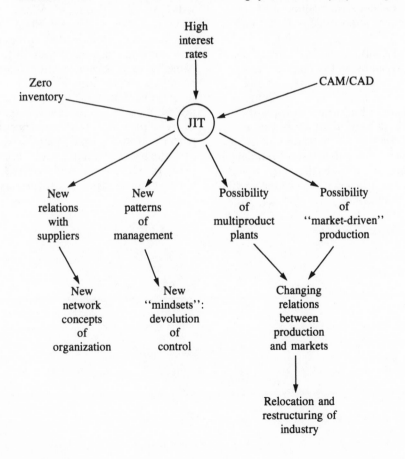

out the system. JIT systems can work effectively only if those involved are primed to spot potential problems and take corrective action. These systems thus call for a new type of involvement in the work process and dissolve traditional relations between workers and managers. Every person in the system becomes a kind of manager and quality controller. Introduction of JIT systems transforms managerial hierarchies, reduces the need for middle managers, and depends for its success on the evolution of philosophies, attitudes, and mindsets that facilitate the diffusion and evolution of control. Though often introduced as a technology, it must be supported by a corporate culture that is open to these other developments. The company that uses or tries to use JIT thus invariably finds itself examining the values, beliefs, assumptions, and principles that underlie almost every aspect of its operations.

JIT systems also lend great flexibility to production systems, allowing the manufacture of different products on the same production line in almost any sequence. This flexibility is creating a potential for production plants to become "market driven" in the sense that production schedules can, in principle, be made directly responsive to the demands of retailers: customer orders can activate the system, and the product can be adapted in accordance with customers' requirements. JIT systems thus have important implications for product design and customer service and unleash possibilities for customized mass manufacture that have not previously existed. These systems also have important impacts on the economics of location and distribution. The flexibility created by JIT systems allows for the emergence of small-scale multiproduct plants located close to relevant markets, instead of the traditional large-scale single-product plants located in industrial centers. The new technology may thus end up transforming the nature of manufacturing and the location of entire industries. Extending this scenario, it does not take much to imagine how future manufacturing systems may be based on localized networks of firms held together by various subcontracting arrangements and shared management systems, geared to providing multiple products to local markets.

JIT symbolizes the unfolding effects of a "fracture line." Independent forces combine to create new management systems that have the capacity to generate further changes in the structure and identity of organizations and interorganizational relations, in patterns and philosophies of management, in corporate culture and the relations between people and their work, and in the scale, pattern, and location of industry. By tracing these consequences, many of which have yet to unfold, it is possible to glimpse what the future may have in store.

40

Japanese Management:
The Art of Self-Regulation

Ever since the Japanese started taking American industry apart, the role and influence of culture on organization has become a hot topic. But if you look carefully beneath the surface of Japanese culture, you will find incredibly powerful processes of cybernetic self-regulation. In the following reading, William Ouchi, author of Theory Z, *explores critical aspects of the Japanese system of management. Try understanding these principles in terms of the ideas of cybernetics, as explored in* Images of Organization *(1986, especially pages 84-85), as well as those of culture.*

Decision Making[†]

Probably the best known feature of Japanese organizations is their participative approach to decision making. In the typical American organization the department head, division manager, and president typically each feel that "the buck stops here"—that they alone should take the responsibility for making decisions. Recently, some organizations have adopted explicitly participative modes of decision making in which all of the members of a department reach consensus on what decision to adopt. Decision making by consensus has been the subject of a great deal of research in Europe and the United States over the past twenty years, and the evidence strongly suggest that a consensus approach yields more creative decisions and more effective implementation than does individual decision making.

Western style participative decision making is by now a fairly standardized process. Typically, a small group of not more than eight or ten people will gather around a table, discuss the problem and suggest alternative solutions. During this process, the group should have one or more leaders skilled at managing relationships between people so that underlying disagreements can be dealt with constructively. The group can be said to have achieved a consensus when it finally agrees upon a single alternative and each member of the group can honestly say to each other member three things:

1. I believe that you understand my point of view.

†SOURCE: William Ouchi, *Theory Z*, © 1981, Addison Wesley Publishing Co., Inc., Reading, Massachusetts. Pages 39-55. Reprinted with permission.

2. I believe that I understand your point of view.

3. Whether or not I prefer this decision, I will support it, because it was arrived at in an open and fair manner.

At least a few managers instinctively follow this approach in every company, government office, and church meeting, but the vast majority do not. Some companies have officially instituted this consensual approach throughout, because of its superiority in many cases to individual decision making. However, what occurs in a Japanese organization is a great deal more far reaching and subtle than even this participative approach.

When an important decision needs to be made in a Japanese organization, everyone who will feel its impact is involved in making it. In the case of a decision where to put a new plant, whether to change a production process, or some other major event, that will often mean sixty to eighty people directly involved in making the decision. A team of three will be assigned the duty of talking to all sixty to eighty people and, each time a significant modification arises, contacting all the people involved again. The team will repeat this process until a true consensus has been achieved. Making a decision this way takes a very long time, but once a decision is reached, everyone affected by it will be likely to support it. Understanding and support may supersede the actual content of the decision, since the five or six competing alternatives may be equally good or bad. What is important is not the decision itself but rather how committed and informed people are. The "best" decision can be bungled just as "worst" decisions can work just fine.

A friend in one of the major Japanese banks described their process. "When a major decision is to be made, a written proposal lays out one 'best' alternative for consideration. The task of writing the proposal goes to the youngest and newest member of the department involved. Of course, the president or vice-president knows the acceptable alternatives, and the young person tries like heck to figure out what those are. He talks to everyone, soliciting their opinions, paying special attention to those who know the top man best. In so doing he is seeking a common ground. Fortunately, the young person cannot completely figure out from others what the boss wants, and must add his own thoughts. This is how variety enters the decision process in a Japanese company. The company relies so heavily on socializing employees with a common set of values and beliefs that all experienced employees would be likely to come up with similar ideas. Too much homogeneity would lead to a loss of vitality and change, so the youngest person gets the assignment."

Frequently, according to my informant, this young person will in the process make a number of errors. He will suggest things that are technically impossible or politically unacceptable, and will leave things out. Experienced managers never over-direct the young man, never sit him down and tell him what the proposal should say. Even though errors consume time, effort, and expense, many will turn out to be good ideas. Letting a young person make one error of his own is believed to be worth more than one hundred lectures in his education as a manager and worker.

Ultimately, a formal proposal is written and then circulated from the bottom of the organization to the top. At each stage, the manager in question signifies his agreement by affixing his seal to the document. At the end of this *ringi* process, the proposal is literally covered with the stamps of approval of sixty to eighty people.

American managers are fond of chiding the Japanese by observing that, "If you're going to Japan to make a sale or close a deal and you think it will take two days, allow two weeks and if you're lucky you'll get a 'maybe.' It takes the Japanese forever to make a decision." True enough, but Japanese business people who have experience dealing in the United States will often say, "Americans are quick to sign a contract or make a decision. But try to get them to implement it—it takes them forever!"

Remember that this apparently cumbersome decision process takes place within the framework of an underlying agreement on philosophy, values, and beliefs. These form the basis for common decision premises that make it possible to include a very large number of people in each decision. If, as in some Western organizations, each of the sixty people has a fundamentally different view of goals and procedure, then the participative process would fail. Because the Japanese only debate the suitability of a particular alternative to reach the agreed-upon values, the process can be broadly participatory yet efficient. In Western-style consensual processes, by comparison, often underlying values and beliefs need to be worked out, and for that reason decision making teams are deliberately kept small.

Another key feature of decision making in Japan is the intentional ambiguity of who is responsible for what decisions. In the United States we have job descriptions and negotiations between employees for the purpose of setting crystal clear boundaries on where my decision authority ends and yours begins. Americans expect others to behave just as we do. Many are the unhappy and frustrated American businessmen or lawyers returning from Japan with the complaint that, "If only they would tell me who is really in charge, we could make some progress." The complaint displays a lack of understanding that, in Japan, no one individual carries responsibility for a particular turf. Rather, a group or team of employees assumes joint responsibility for a set of tasks. While we wonder at their comfortableness in not knowing who is responsible for what, they know quite clearly that each of them is completely responsible for all tasks, and they share that responsibility jointly. Obviously this approach sometimes lets things "fall through the cracks" because everyone may think that someone else has a task under control. When working well, however, this approach leads to a naturally participative decision making and problem solving process. But

there is another important reason for the collective assignment of decision responsibility.

Many Americans object to the idea of lifetime employment because they fear the consequences of keeping on an ineffective worker. Won't that create bottlenecks and inefficiency? Clearly the Japanese have somehow solved that problem or they couldn't have achieved their great economic success. A partial answer comes from the collective assignment of decision responsibility. In a typical American firm, Jim is assigned sole responsibility for purchasing decisions for office supplies, Mary has sole responsibility for purchasing maintenance services and Fred is solely responsible for purchasing office machines. If Fred develops serious problems of a personal nature, or if he becomes ill or has some other problem that seriously impedes his ability to function at work, a bottleneck will develop. Office machine orders will not be properly processed or perhaps will not be processed at all. The whole company will suffer, and Fred will have to be let go.

In a Japanese company, by comparison, Mitsuo, Yoshito, and Nori will comprise a team collectively responsible for purchasing office supplies, maintenance services, and office machines. Each of them participates in all significant decisions in purchasing any of those goods or services. If Nori is unable to work, it is perfectly natural and efficient for Mitsuo and Yoshito to take up his share of the load. When Nori returns to work again, he can step right back in and do his share. This does mean that Mitsuo and Yoshito probably will have to work harder than usual for perhaps six months or a year, and they may also have to draw on Masao, who used to work in purchasing but has now been transferred to the computer section. This flow of people can be accomplished only if Mitsuo and Yoshito are confident that the organization has a memory and know that their extra efforts now will be repaid later. Fairness and equity will be achieved over the long run. It also depends upon the practice of job rotation, so that short-run labor needs can be filled internally without having to hire and fire people as such needs come and go. As with all other characteristics of the Japanese management system, decision making is embedded in a complex of parts that hang together and rely upon trust and subtlety developed through intimacy.

Collective Values

Perhaps that most difficult aspect of the Japanese for Westerners to comprehend is the strong orientation to collective values, particularly a collective sense of responsibility. Let me illustrate with an anecdote about a visit to a new factory in Japan owned and operated by an American electronics company. The American company, a particularly creative firm, frequently attracts attention within the business community for its novel approaches to planning, organizational design, and management systems. As a consequence of this corporate style, the parent company determined to make a thorough study of Japanese workers and to design a plant that would combine the best of East and West. In their study they discovered that Japanese firms almost never make use of individual work incentives, such as piecework or even individual performance appraisal tied to salary increases. They concluded that rewarding individual achievement and individual ability is always a good thing.

In the final assembly area of their new plant long lines of young Japanese women wired together electronic products on a piece-rate system: the more you wired, the more you got paid. About two months after opening, the head foreladies approached the plant manager. "Honorable plant manager," they said humbly as they bowed, "we are embarrassed to be so forward, but we must speak to you because all of the girls have threatened to quit work this Friday." (To have this happen, of course, would be a great disaster for all concerned.) "Why," they wanted to know, "can't our plant have the same compensation system as other Japanese companies? When you hire a new girl, her starting wage should be fixed by her age. An eighteen-year-old should be paid more than a sixteen-year-old. Every year on her birthday, she should receive an automatic increase in pay. The idea that only one of us can be more productive than another must be wrong, because none of us in final assembly could make a thing unless all of the other people in the plant had done their jobs right first. To single one person out as being more productive is wrong and is also personally humiliating to us." The company changed its compensation system to the Japanese model.

Another American company in Japan had installed a suggestion system much as we have in the United States. Individual workers were encouraged to place suggestions to improve productivity into special boxes. For an accepted idea the individual received a bonus amounting to some fraction of the productivity savings realized from his or her suggestion. After a period of six months, not a single suggestion had been submitted. The American managers were puzzled. They had heard many stories of the inventiveness, the commitment, and the loyalty of Japanese workers, yet not one suggestion to improve productivity had appeared.

The managers approached some of the workers and asked why the suggestion system had not been used. The answer: "No one can come up with a work improvement idea alone. We work together, and any ideas that one of us may have are actually developed by watching others and talking to others. If one of us was singled out for being responsible for such an idea, it would embarrass all of us." The company changed to a group suggestion system, in which workers collectively submitted suggestions. Bonuses were paid to groups which would save bonus money until the end of the year for a party at a restaurant or, if there was enough money, for family vacations together. The suggestions and productivity improvements rained down on the plant.

One can interpret these examples in two quite different ways. Perhaps the Japanese commitment to collective values is an anachronism that does not fit with modern industrialism but brings economic success despite that collectivism. Collectivism seems to be inimical to the kind of maverick creativity exemplified in Benjamin Franklin, Thomas Edison, and John D. Rockefeller. Collectivism does not seem to provide the individual incentive to excel which has made a great success of American enterprise. Entirely apart from its economic effects, collectivism implies a loss of individuality, a loss of the freedom to be different, to hold fundamentally different values from others.

The second interpretation of the examples is that the Japanese collectivism is economically efficient. It causes people to work well together and to encourage one another to better efforts. Industrial life requires interdependence of one person on another. But a less obvious but far-reaching implication of the Japanese collectivism for economic performance has to do with accountability.

In the Japanese mind, collectivism is neither a corporate nor individual goal to strive for nor a slogan to pursue. Rather, the nature of things operates so that nothing of consequence occurs as a result of individual effort. Everything important in life happens as a result of teamwork or collective effort. Therefore, to attempt to assign individual credit or blame to results is unfounded. A Japanese professor of accounting, a brilliant scholar trained at Carnegie-Mellon University who teaches now in Tokyo, remarked that the status of accounting systems in Japanese industry is primitive compared to those in the United States. Profit centers, transfer prices, and computerized information systems are barely known even in the largest Japanese companies, whereas they are a commonplace in even small United States organizations. Though not at all surprised at the difference in accounting systems, I was not at all sure that the Japanese were primitive. In fact, I thought their system a good deal more efficient than ours.

Most American companies have basically two accounting systems. One system summarizes the overall financial state to inform stockholders, bankers, and other outsiders. That system is not of interest here. The other system, called the managerial or cost accounting system, exists for an entirely different reason. It measures in detail all of the particulars of transactions between departments, divisions, and key individuals in the organization, for the purpose of untangling the interdependencies between people. When, for example, two departments share one truck for deliveries, the cost accounting system charges each department for part of the cost of maintaining the truck and driver, so that at the end of the year, the performance of each department can be individually assessed, and the better department's manager can receive a larger raise. Of course, all of this information processing costs money, and furthermore may lead to arguments between the departments over whether the costs charged to each are fair.

In a Japanese company a short-run assessment of individual performance is not wanted, so the company can save the considerable expense of collecting and processing all of that information. Companies still keep track of which department uses a truck how often and for what purposes, but like-minded people can interpret some simple numbers for themselves and adjust their behavior accordingly. Those insisting upon clear and precise measurement for the purpose of advancing individual interests must have an elaborate information system. Industrial life, however, is essentially integrated and interdependent. No one builds an automobile alone, no one carries through a banking transaction alone. In a sense the Japanese value of collectivism fits naturally into an industrial setting, whereas the Western individualism provides constant conflicts. The image that comes to mind is of Chaplin's silent film "Modern Times" in which the apparently insignificant hero played by Chaplin successfully fights against the unfeeling machinery of industry. Modern industrial life can be aggravating, even hostile, or natural: it all depends on the fit between our culture and our technology.

Holistic Concern for People

Anthropologist Thomas Rohlen has described in detail the process of inducting young trainees into a Japanese bank. Training culminates in a formal ceremony held in the company auditorium. The bank president stands at the podium, the training director at his side. The young trainees sit on the front rows with their mothers, fathers, and siblings behind them. The president welcomes the new members into the bank family, challenging them to live up to the expectations of their trainers and leaders. He speaks also to the parents, accepting from them the challenge of providing for their children not only honest work, but also accepting the obligation to see to their complete physical, intellectual, and moral development. A representative of the parents next takes the podium, thanking the bank for offering this opportunity to their offspring and reaffirming the charge to the trainees to be as loyal to their new family as they are to their blood family. Finally, a representative of the trainees rises to speak, thanking both parents and bank for their support and pledging to work hard to meet their expectations.

Most Western organizations practice an attitude of "partial inclusion," an understanding between employees and employer that the connection between them involves only those activities directly connected with the completion of a specific job. Many Western social scientists have argued that partial inclusion maintains the emotional health in individuals. Being partially included in a number of organizations makes moving from one social domain to another easy, and tensions that have built up in one setting can be released in another. The Japanese organization, by contrast, forms inclusive relationships. A set of mechanisms provides for the social support and emotional release necessary for emotional equilibrium. One such mechanism is the capacity of group members to

"change hats" and later the nature of their relationships to one another for a short time in order to provide this social release and balance. Consider one example: At one American-owned plant in Japan, a golfing day with the manager became a twice yearly tradition. A train ride of four hours each way, plus golf, consumed an entire day for this important event. The American plant manager, to prepare for the outing, made a list of critical issues of strategy and management that he felt were on the minds of his subordinates. As the group approached the first "tee", he produced his list and set the agenda for the next eighteen holes. His subordinates were discouraged and disappointed by this, and the day proceeded in a desultory fashion.

A Japanese manager interpreted this story for me. A Japanese company, he points out, is a quite formal and at times even an authoritarian setting. Rarely will an employee disagree openly with a superior or voice complaints. When people anticipate a lifetime of working together, they cannot afford to let deep rifts develop. Thus a stylized pattern of interaction develops. Conflict and refusal would disturb the harmony that must underlie the work relationship. On the other hand, no company can remain healthy with suppressed disagreement, conflict, and complaint. A symbolic change of roles in which different patterns of behavior are acceptable provides one outlet. In the golf outing, for example, the implication was that boss and subordinates were competing as equals. With the physical setting away from the place of work, the acceptable patterns of behavior are also meant to be far removed from the daily norm. At these times subordinates can feel free to ask questions and to raise objections suppressed in the office and expect the boss to respond sympathetically. In a similar manner, office parties with drinks and dinner permit the subordinates to adopt the guise of mild inebriation to tell the boss off and give opinions unspeakable under ordinary conditions. Thus the organization provides the group with a change of venue necessary to healthy social relations.

The [holistic] orientation of Japanese organizations stems from both historical accident and underlying social and cultural forces. According to one commonly held view, the historical accident is that industrialism rushed into Japan after having been held out for decades by a feudal political system. Companies were forced to build plants near to the villages where they could recruit workers. With no long and gradual urbanization as Europe had, Japan found itself with a sparsely-distributed rural population faced with the onrush of industrialization. Each plant sent recruiters to village homes asking mothers and fathers to send their offspring to work in the plant twenty or thirty miles away. Village parents who loved their children would simply not release them to go to live and work in a strange place. The companies had to build dormitories, to provide a healthy diet, and to assure parents that their children would receive the moral, intellectual, physical, and domestic training that would prepare them for life. In the case of young women, the company arranged for training in domestic skills needed by a young wife. No partial inclusion, no tentative, tenuous link between company and employee was possible in this setting. Rather, it was a complete and whole relationship which formed between employee and employer.

Some Japan experts argue that the underlying social patterns developed under feudalism prepared the Japanese for dependent relationship on a paternalistic force to meet their needs and to give their loyalty in return. If such an attitude had existed, it surely would have supported the [holistic] work relationship.

When economic and social life are integrated into a single whole, then relationships between individuals become intimate. Rather than a connection through a single work relationship, individuals interconnect through multiple bonds. This one closely-knit relationship makes it impossible to escape the frustrations and tensions by spending time with another, completely unrelated group. Intimacy of this sort discourages selfish or dishonest action in the group, since abused relationships cannot be left behind. People who live in a company dormitory, play on a company baseball team, work together in five different committees, and know the situation will continue for the rest of their lives will develop a unique relationship. Values and beliefs become mutually compatible over a wide range of work and non-work related issues. Each person's true level of effort and of performance stands out, and the close relationship brings about a high level of subtlety in understanding of each other's needs and plans. This mixture of supports and restraints promotes mutual trust, since compatible goals and complete openness remove the fears of or desires for deception. Thus intimacy, trust, and understanding grow where individuals are linked to one another through multiple bonds in a [holistic] relationship.

Social scientists have long noted that [holistic] relationships develop in "total institutions," but have regarded these as anomalies limited to prisons, mental hospitals, religious orders, and military units. Amitai Etzioni (1965) of Columbia University asserts that a [holistic] network comprises an effective means of social control, one in which individuals can be free but also capable of a peaceful co-existence. But Etzioni, like others, has also contended that this form of social control is fundamentally incompatible with modern industrial society, because industrialism inevitably leads to a high degree of specialization of labor, frequent moving between employers, and consequently only a partial inclusion in the group. The Japanese show clear evidence that [holism] in industrial life is possible. The final question must address whether [holism] and intimacy in industrial life are desirable. In grasping just how we Americans really differ from the Japanese lies the key to what we can learn from them.

REFERENCES

Etzioni, A. "Organizational Control Structure." *Handbook of Organizations*, edited by J. G. March. Chicago: Rand McNally, 1965.

Morgan, Gareth. *Images of Organization*. Beverly Hills, CA: Sage, 1986.

41

The Challenger Disaster:
A Case of Discouraged Feedback?

*Many organizations discourage feedback and learning, especially when power-
ful members become committed to the achievement of predetermined goals at
almost any cost. One of the most famous recent examples is found in the case
of the ill-fated space shuttle, Challenger. In the following article, David Sanger
of the* New York Times *gives us a glimpse of aspects of the corporate culture,
power politics, and misinformation systems that lay behind the disaster on 28
January 1986.*

ENGINEERS SAY THEY WERE PUNISHED[†]

The rocket engineers who told a Presidential panel three months ago that they had argued strenuously against launching the space shuttle Challenger in cold weather on Jan. 28 have now informed the panel they have been severely punished for their testimony by their employer, Morton Thiokol Inc.

In wide-ranging testimony given at a closed session of the commission on May 2 and made public in documents today, the engineers, whose warnings the night before the launching were overruled by Morton Thiokol's management, said that in recent months they had been stripped of their authority, deprived of their staffs and prevented from seeing critical data about the investigation of the Challenger disaster. It occurred 74 seconds after the launching and took the lives of the seven crew members.

William P. Rogers, chairman of the commission, today called the engineers' most recent testimony "shocking," adding that they were being "punished for being right." His rebuke of the company that built the rockets that caused the disaster was included in more than 300 pages of testimony taken by the commission May 2 at what was apparently to be their last executive session.

[†]SOURCE: "Engineers Tell of Punishment for Shuttle Testimony," by David E. Sanger, of May 11, 1986. Copyright © 1986/87 by The New York Times Company. Reprinted by permission.

Company Denies Demotions

A Morton Thiokol executive present at the May 2 hearing denied the engineers had been demoted but conceded that they had been reassigned in what he said was a broader company reorganization.

The report of punishments, as well as other testimony disclosed today, strongly suggests that in the aftermath of the disaster, Morton Thiokol and at least one key official of the National Aeronautics and Space Administration attempted to sharply control what kind of information was given to the commission investigating the disaster.

In the most striking instance, Allan J. McDonald, the Thiokol engineer whose testimony in February was the first to assert that the Challenger had been launched over the objections of many of its designers, said, according to the documents released today, that soon after his testimony he was confronted in private by Lawrence B. Mulloy, at the time the head of space agency's booster rocket program for the shuttle.

Mr. Mulloy, he said, warned him, "You're giving information to the commission without going through your own management, without going through NASA," and questioned his motivations.

"I Told Him to Calm Down"

Another Thiokol engineer, Roger M. Boisjoly, who had written an apparently ignored memorandum last summer warning that there "could be a catastrophe of the highest order" if the company failed to fix the rocket's safety seals, which quickly became suspect in the investigation, said he, too, had been "put on the sideline."

"Do you feel that may be in retaliation for your testimony?" Mr. Rogers asked at the May 2 hearing.

"I think that is a possibility, a distinct possibility." Mr. Boisjoly responded.

In both public and private sessions, commission members have urged employees of the space agency and its contractors to approach members directly if there was any evidence about the accident that had not yet come to light.

Pressure Is Suspected

Sources close to the commission suggested recently that the May 2 testimony released today was the first solid evidence that some workers, in fact, were under pressure not to come forward. "The only thing you can conclude," said one source, who insisted on anonymity, "is that someone, somewhere, decided to make an example of Boisjoly and McDonald."

In the course of hundreds of hours of hearings, it was the testimony of Mr. Boisjoly and Mr. McDonald that proved the most damaging, both to the space agency and to Morton Thiokol, which has manufactured the solid-fuel booster rockets since the inception of the shuttle program.

Until the two engineers first testified, several weeks after the Challenger disintegrated, the space shuttle disaster appeared to the commission and the public as an inexplicable accident, caused by a freak hardware failure that no one could have been reasonably expected to foresee. However, the testimony showed that the joints connecting segments of the rocket together had been a critical source of trouble for several years, and that NASA had kept flying the shuttle despite mounting evidence that the critical safety seals eroded in flight. Later evidence has virtually proven that a burn-through of the joint caused the disaster.

Mr. McDonald's initial testimony was particularly embarrassing to Morton Thiokol because he described, in painstaking detail, how, on the night before the disaster, the company's engineers had been unanimously opposed to launching. He said they became concerned as soon as they heard the temperature at Cape Canaveral would be in the low 30's, or nearly 20 degrees lower than for any previous launching. The engineers were overruled by their managers.

"I felt management was under a lot of pressure to launch," Mr. Boisjoly told the commission on Feb. 25.

Until shortly after the accident, Mr. McDonald had been head of Thiokol's solid-rocket-motor project, managing a large staff at a plant outside Brigham City, Utah.

Engineer's Function Curtailed

Asked what he is doing now, Mr. McDonald told the commission: "I have a title called director of special projects." He added, "The people that all work for me work for somebody else." He said he was "set aside" because of the testimony he gave the commission, and later described how he had to borrow copies of test results related to the accident investigation that were apparently widely available to other employees.

"So, you were in effect punished for being right?" Mr. Rogers asked.

"I felt I was," said Mr. McDonald.

But Mr. McDonald was contradicted by Joseph Kilminster, his superior at Thiokol who signed a document the night before launching giving NASA the go-ahead to launch the Challenger. "There was certainly no demotion involved that I know of," he said.

Mr. McDonald shot back: "I was not demoted. They just took my people away and gave me a more menial job."

Later in the hearing, Mr. Rogers said he was "very upset" by the testimony, saying "the whole idea of the program is to have an openness and to have an honest exchange of views."

"To have something happen to him," Mr. Rogers said of Mr. Mcdonald, "is shocking, and I just hope that you convey that to management," he said to Mr. Kilminster.

Since his testimony, Mr. McDonald has apparently communicated regularly with commission members, commenting on test results he suspected were biased or inaccurate, and providing additional detail. It was this back-channel communication that apparently angered Mr. Mulloy, who until Friday headed the solid-rocket motor project at the Marshall Space Flight Center in Huntsville, Ala. He responded, moving to another post at Marshall, NASA said on Friday.

Mr. McDonald, recounting his confrontation with the NASA official, said, "Mr. Mulloy came into my office and slammed the door and, as far as I was concerned, was very intimidating to me."

"He was obviously very disturbed and wanted to know what my motivation was, and I won't use his exact words, for doing what I was doing," Mr. McDonald testified.

Mr. Mulloy, however, recalled a different version of events, testifying: "I came to Mr. McDonald's door and asked him if he had a moment, and he said he did, and I then closed the door. I didn't realize I slammed it. I was not upset."

Mr. Mulloy said the topic was his contention that Mr. McDonald had not objected to the launching the night before the Challenger disintegrated, as he had testified.

Other parts of the May 2 testimony by Morton Thiokol officials appear to raise new questions in the investigation, never addressed in public sessions. One engineer, Robert Ebeling, said he had repeatedly expressed the opinion, "We shouldn't ship any more rocket motors until we got it fixed," but that opinion had never been passed on to higher management at Thiokol for some reason.

Another apparent mystery to emerge from the testimony is why Morton Thiokol, the month before the Challenger disaster, wrote a letter to NASA requesting that the agency remove concern about the O ring erosion from its list of critical flight problems.

Brian Russell, a Thiokol engineer, testified that because the O-ring was getting so much attention within the company, including from a special task force, it only created more paperwork to keep the topic on the list of concerns reviewed on a monthly basis. One apparent reason for the Thiokol request, which NASA apparently never acted on, was concern by Marshall Space Flight officials that there were too many unresolved issues on a list of technical problems associated with the rocket. The officials asked Thiokol to reduce the number, though it is not clear whether they were to actually fix the problems, or merely scratch them off the list.

"Why would you write a letter saying let's close it out now?" asked Mr. Rogers.

"Because I was asked to do it," Mr. Russell responded.

"I see," said Mr. Rogers, with apparent irony. "well, that explains it."

"It explains it," interjected Robert Rummel, another commission member, "but it really doesn't make any sense."

42

Information and Misinformation: *Some Unintended Consequences of Performance Controls*

An organization's information and control systems can have a dramatic impact on how it operates: often producing many undesirable results. The following report of how some members of the police force in Britain have responded to the statistical control through which their overall performance is measured provides frightening insights on the distortions that can occur.

CRIME: THE GREAT COP-OUT[†]

Police boasts about clearing up unsolved crimes are often deceitful. As serving policeman Ron Walker discovered, crimes are routinely passed off as 'solved' by extracting phoney confessions from tame criminals. NICK DAVIES, Home Affairs Correspondent, reports:

The detective inspector was beside himself with rage. He had just been passed the latest official figures showing the clear-up rates for each of the police stations in Kent.

"They're crooked," he barked.

"They're ridiculous. Anybody can see they are crooked."

Then he turned to the junior detectives in the CID room. "And there'll be none of that here," he told them. "There'll be no dodgy write-offs here. No way." The new detective constable, Ron Walker, watching the scene seven years ago, was impressed.

But the "dodgy write-offs" did not stop. As Walker moved from one station to another in the Kent Police, in and out of the CID, he kept stumbling across the same dishonest fiddle—scores of unsolved crimes being "written off" in fraudulent confessions.

The idea of write-offs had been promoted in

[†]SOURCE: "Crime: The Great Cop Out," *The Observer*, Sunday 13 July 1986, p. 11. Reproduced by permission of The Observer Ltd., London.

the mid-1970s as a legitimate way of clearing up crime. The Home Office encouraged police to visit criminals in prison to take statements. The Attorney-General agreed that such criminals would not be prosecuted for their confessions if it served no useful purpose.

But there were no safeguards, no need to check that the statements were true. For detectives, under pressure for results, and for the criminals, looking for a risk-free way of earning favours from the police, the system was wide open to abuse. In Kent's police stations, Walker found detectives quite unashamed of their activities.

"On one occasion, I was in the office with another detective constable—a very experienced man who I had always thought was an excellent policeman. He was on the phone to someone in the statistics office at the force HQ.

"He was making a list of unsolved burglaries, checking that they were still outstanding. I wandered over to his desk and it was covered in blank statement forms.

"When he came off the phone, he just sat there and started writing out this statement—a completely phoney confession writing off all these burglaries.

"There was another occasion when one of the senior detectives came into the office waving this little bundle of write-offs, laughing about it and complaining that he had had so many crimes written off that he could clear up every offence in his patch for the rest of the year. He was saying he would have to feed them into the system slowly over the months so that the figures didn't go over the top.

"It was a bad joke the way things were being run. There was this change of direction coming about: junior officers just wanted promotion; the senior officers just wanted good clear-up rates; helping the public became less and less important."

Walker's disaffection spilled over into open conflict when a cynical senior officer torpedoed a major inquiry he had been running. By cultivating an informer and mounting a round-the-clock surveillance, Walker had identified two particularly active local burglars. He was poised to arrest them red-handed when the senior officer intervened.

He was worried that if they were arrested and charged, the two burglars would refuse to admit all the offences they had committed, which would make the crime figures look bad. He proposed instead to have a quiet word with them, to tell them that if they left his patch and committed crime elsewhere, he would not give them any trouble. "I exploded," said Walker, "but I never got to arrest the two burglars."

About this time, Walker also stumbled on another abuse—phantom crimes, which were being invented by detectives and then "admitted" by willing criminals, so that the crime figures were artificially improved.

"A detective had nicked this gullible young lad who was prepared to play ball with him. I saw him get on to a PC from this lad's area and tell him to go out and get some vehicle numbers, so that he could get the names and addresses off the computer and put them down as stolen cars. The next thing you know, the lad is confessing to stealing them."

The abuses split Kent's detectives. "Some of them were right into this, visiting prisons and turning out write-offs like a machine. There were some who turned a blind eye and just hid. And some of us wanted to fight it, but we didn't know how."

Seething with indignation, Walker decided to leave the CID and return to uniform. Then he was breathalysed and charged with driving over the (drinking) limit; when a senior officer told him not to worry, that his CID job was still open to him, Walker told him he had had enough of the corruption. Back in uniform, Walker made decisions and secretly set out to turn his detective skills on his former colleagues. He became a one-man anti-corruption squad.

He gathered statistics for every sub-division in Kent. They told their own story: in 1978, before the abuses took off, a typical Kent division was solving 24.4 percent of its burglaries. A year later, the figure had shot up to 69.5 per cent, an astonishing leap.

Clear-up rates differed wildly across the county: while some stations were clearing up less than 10 per cent, others were scoring over 90 per cent. Yet this was happening without any apparent questions or criticisms from leaders of the force.

Unknown to Walker, however, alarm bells had also begun to ring in the (British government) Home Office. The Inspector of Constabulary began to monitor the use of write-offs; a Home Office research paper noted tactfully that with the sudden expansion of the write-off system "there could be said to be weight behind the criticism that justice is not seen to be done."

But it was Walker who followed through and gathered hard evidence. Checking through the station officer's log, he noted two particular offenders whose names had been entered unusually often for having cleared-up crimes. From central records, he obtained a list of all the offences recently cleared by the two men and then began a minute examination.

One of them, Robert H, had written-off 87 offences, including 73 burglaries, when he was visited in Borstal by two Kent detectives. It was an eloquent confession, the sort detectives love to hear, full and frank with just enough detail of each offence to show first-hand knowledge.

He began by explaining himself. "When I was arrested, I admitted a lot of offences to the police. However, I only admitted a few of the offences I had actually committed." He then apologised that he was unable to name anybody who had helped commit the offences, nor the people to whom he had sold the stolen goods. Nor could he return any of the goods because he had not kept anything. Then he reeled off the offences.

"About the beginning of October," he recalled at one point, "I did a place in Letchworth Avenue. I climbed on to the porch and got in through an upstairs window that was open. I had a look around and took some jewellery.

"The same day as that one, I did one in Robin Hood Lane. I got in through a skylight in the conservatory and forced a window in the back. I had a look around and took some jewellery and some money. A few days later, I did a place in Marston Walk . . . [and so on]."

It was pure baloney. The details of the break-ins were correct, just as they had been recorded when the victims had reported the crimes. But Robert H had not committed them, for Walker discovered that "about the beginning of October," when a burglar climbed on that porch in Letchworth Avenue, Robert H had been locked up inside Canterbury Prison.

The detectives had slipped up because Robert H's record sheet was not up to date. Robert H had been in prison from 10 September to 8 October—a discovery that wiped out nine of the offences which he claimed to have committed. But there was more.

Digging deeper into Robert H's background, Walker established that he had spent two periods under close supervision in a day centre run by the probation service. Walker called the man who runs the centre and took a detailed record of the days and times when it could be proved that Robert H was there; then he checked back through the confession: seven of his admissions were undoubtedly false and a further 18 were highly suspect.

But the falseness of the confession was not the most important point. "The question that had to be answered was that if this man had not been at the scenes of these burglaries, how could he know in such detail what had happened there? It must have been fed to him."

Walker then began investigating the second write-off, in which Ernie C, a veteran with 24 years of criminal activity, admitted committing 54 burglaries in a six-month period. It was another long, detailed confession—and its very length gave Walker an idea.

He phoned the prison where Ernie C had been visited by two Kent detectives and asked how long they had been in the prison. The times had been logged at the prison gate: they had arrived at 3:20 p.m. and left at half-past-four. Just one hour 10 minutes in the prison.

Walker calculated that it would have taken them at least 10 minutes to get from the main gate to Ernie C and back. Which left one hour. It would take a full hour to write out a statement as long as his, yet the Kent detectives claimed that inside one hour they had persuaded him to confess, got him to recall crimes committed two years previously, elicited the detail and then written it all down.

And, once again, they had slipped up because of a fault in the records. Combing back through the records, Walker found that Ernie C had confessed to burglary which had also been admitted by someone else. He probed further.

He established that a Kent man had reported a burglary in which thieves had stolen money from his electricity meter. Ernie C was now admitting this break-in. Meanwhile, the Kent man had admitted that he stole the money from the meter himself and had invented the story of the break-in to cover himself. But the station records had not been straightened out.

There was one further slip-up. The detectives had been sloppy in checking Ernie C's record and had allowed him to "confess" to a burglary which, Walker established, had been committed when he had already been in police custody for an hour.

As an exercise, Walker then took the two write-offs he had proved were fraudulent, and examined the effect they had on the clear-up rate for the police sub-division which recorded them.

The sub-division had declared a clear-up rate of 49.3 per cent for the period when the write-offs were produced: 375 burglaries committed and 185 "detected." Subtracting the 127 burglaries written off fraudulently, the number of detected offences dropped to 58, and the clear-up rate fell to only 15.5 per cent. And Walker knew there was at least one other suspect write-off for the same station in the same period.

"It meant the detectives could afford to spend plenty of time taking it easy. In just a couple of days work they could get enough crimes written off to keep the crime figures looking right for the next six months."

Walker continued to look for evidence of abuse and had no trouble finding it. Late last summer, one of the area's most active juvenile criminals—"a one-man crime wave"—was arrested for burglary. To Walker's amazement,

he was given bail without any objection from the arresting officer.

It then transpired that, after his arrest, the criminal had agreed to plead guilty and to ask for some 30 other offences to be taken into consideration. A few weeks later, he was arrested again, having continued his one-man crime wave while on bail.

"They knew that if they didn't oppose bail, he would go out and commit more offences, but they didn't mind as long as he agreed to ask for a lot of offences to be taken into consideration. It didn't matter that the people of Kent were burgled, as long as the books 'looked good.' About one-third of the offences to which he admitted could not have been committed by him."

He found evidence, too, of phantom crimes. Looking through a sheet of offences prepared for a suspect to "take into consideration," he noticed half a dozen odd ones. All were for the theft of 5 rear fog lamps; none of them had a crime report number, which is normally given to each crime as soon as it is reported by its victim.

Either there had been an unusual series of administrative errors or these were phantoms. The names and addresses of the supposed victims were recorded on the sheet. Those contacted by The Observer last week confirmed Walker's suspicions that they had never lost a rear fog lamp, let alone reported one stolen.

Having got his evidence, Walker's problem was to decide what to do with it. "I was worried about it from the survival point of view. I didn't see how I could use the evidence without putting paid to my career and jeopardising my family and their welfare." After months of agonising, he decided to approach Scotland Yard on a confidential basis to ask them to investigate without disclosing his role. Things went badly from the start.

On 6 January this year, he phoned the Yard's anti-corruption squad, CIB 2, and outlined his story. They told him that to comply with the procedures we would have to lodge the complaint with his own force. Nervous that this would disclose his role, he approached a Kent superintendent he trusted, who advised him that he would have to go through the formal channels whatever the risk.

It was two weeks before the inquiry was launched and he was interviewed by a superintendent from the Yard's Serious Crimes Squad. Within four days, Walker's wife was being cut dead by other police wives and Walker, who was by then on sick leave, was told that the force was buzzing with gossip about what he had done.

A week later—with his cover already blown—the whole inquiry was compromised by a leak, apparently from the Yard, to the Daily Mail, who ran a small story outlining the inquiry and effectively putting every detective in Kent on notice to cover his tracks. There was worse to come.

Walker had repeatedly stressed that the evidence he had presented amounted only to a few random examples of widespread and routine abuse. But the Director of Public Prosecutions asked the Yard Superintendent to concentrate only on the incidents for which Walker had produced evidence: His allegations about systematic abuse in Kent and in other forces were put on one side.

The superintendent from the Yard then diligently set about investigating the two phoney write-offs that Walker had described. He criss-crossed the country, a sergeant helping him with the paperwork, interviewing everyone involved. Two weeks ago, he submitted a 450-page report to the director of Public Prosecutions and the Police Complaints Authority. The report confirms that the write-offs are phoney.

His inquiry was severely hampered because key documents have gone missing. The original hand-written versions of the two write-offs have mysteriously vanished, making it impossible to assess whether they were really signed by the criminals involved and whether they even knew of their contents. Records of offences "taken into consideration" have been destroyed within the past month.

The detectives have tried to discredit Walker, claiming that he has a vendetta against one of them because he failed to prosecute two men who assaulted Walker in a night-club. They have suggested that if there are errors in the confessions, it reflects pressure of work or genuine mistakes.

The Director of Public Prosecutions may now decide that there is insufficient evidence to prosecute the officers. It may then be said that there is no other evidence to justify further inquiries into the allegations. The Police Complaints Authority is known to be deeply concerned about the case and keen to broaden its scope, but it does not have the resources to do so. Walker fears he has jeopardised his career and his family without achieving justice, which is why he has now taken the ultimate risk of speaking out in public.

43

Collaboration and Control

Complex systems cannot be controlled externally, for the system inevitably has an inner logic and dynamic of its own. In complex systems, control resides in the pattern of relations that comprise the system itself.

This has major implications for the management of complex organizations, suggesting that command and attempts at unilateral control need to be replaced by a more collaborative process. In the following excerpt, "Control: The Twilight of Hierarchy," Harlan Cleveland provides a clear and persuasive explanation of why more openness and participation is more than just an ideological choice.

CONTROL:
The Twilight of Hierarchy†

Some people collect coins or stamps or snuffboxes or forgeries of Salvador Dali paintings. I have taken to collecting Canutes—instances of behavior reminiscent of the legendary Danish monarch who stood on an English beach and commanded the tides to stand still as proof of his power. According to the Viking historians, he intended the waters to give him a wetting, as an object lesson in humility for his courtiers who believed him to be all-powerful. But Canute's name has gone down in myth as a metaphor for attempts to avoid the unavoidable, and it is in this sense that we evoke his memory here.

The information environment created by the fusion of computers and telecommunications is full of examples of contemporary Canutish behavior. The trouble seems to be that we have adopted uncritically for the management of *information* concepts that have proven useful during the centuries when *things* were the dominant resources and the prime objects of commerce, politics, power and prestige. When we do this, our inherited wisdom is somehow

†SOURCE: Excerpted from "Control: The Twilight of Hierarchy," Haran Cleveland, *New Management* (vol. 3, no. 2, pp. 14-18), Copyright © 1985. Reprinted by permission of John Wiley & Sons, Inc.

transmuted into folly. Nowhere is this truer than in the exercise of power in management, administration, and politics.

Knowledge is power, as Francis Bacon wrote in 1597. So the wider the spread of knowledge, the more power gets diffuse. For the most part, individuals and corporations and governments don't have a choice about this; it is the ineluctable consequence of creating, through education, societies with millions of knowledgeable people.

We see the results all around us, and around the world. More and more work gets done by horizontal process, or it doesn't get done. More and more decisions are made with wider and wider consultations, or they don't "stick." The Japanese call it consensus. The Indonesians call it mushyawara. The communists call it collective leadership. We call it teamwork, or committee work. If the Census Bureau counted each year the number of committees per thousand population, we would have a rough quantitative measure of the bundle of changes called the information society.

In the new knowledge environment we have to rethink the very nature of rule, power, and authority. A revolution in the technology of organization—the twilight of hierarchy—is already well under way.

Information has always been the basis of human organization, of course. Those with better or more recent information (Moses with his tablets, generals with their fast couriers, kings with their spies and ambassadors, speculators with their quick access to markets for gold, diamonds, or ownership shares, security forces with their sources of rumor and gossip) held sway over the rest of humankind.

But once information could be spread fast and wide—rapidly collected and analyzed, instantly communicated, readily understood by millions—the power monopolies that closely held knowledge made possible were subject to accelerating erosion. Strangely, both the monopolies and their victims have often been slow to perceive the trend.

Modern King Canutes

In the old days when only a few people were well educated and "in the know," leadership of the uninformed was likely to be organized in vertical structures of command and control. Leadership of the informed is different: It results in the necessary action only if exercised mainly by persuasion, bringing into consultation those who are going to have to do something to make the decision work. Where people are educated and are not treated this way, they either balk at the decisions made or have to be dragooned by organized misinformation backed by brute force. Recent examples of both results have been on display in Poland.

This is the origin of Chester Barnard's seminal theory of the executive function: Authority is delegated upward. As director of an organization, you have no power that is not granted to you by your subordinates. Eliciting their continual (and if possible cheerful) cooperation is your main job as director; without it, you cannot get the most routine tasks (for which others are holding you, not your staff, responsible) accomplished. Indeed, nowadays in many offices orders that used to be routinely accepted are now resisted or refused. In the modern American office, if you want a cup of coffee you don't take that coworker, the secretary, off her or his own work to get it for you.

In this environment the King Canute prize for 1981 was easily won by Secretary of State Alexander Haig. Shortly after the attempted assassination of President Reagan, Haig announced on television from the White House that "I am in control here. . . ." That produced neither reassurance nor anger from the American people but nervous laughter, as in watching theater of the absurd. We the people know by instinct that in our pluralistic democracy no one is, can be, or is even supposed to be "in control." By constitutional design reinforced by the information-rich conditions of work, we live in a nobody-in-charge society.

We all know other Canutes and courtiers whose absurdities don't get on national television: executives who give orders when they should be asking questions, managers who think of their coworkers as superiors or subordinates, impatient doers who don't have time for lateral consultation—in sum, the builders of bureaucratic pyramids who haven't learned how to work by consultation and consensus.

In an information-rich polity, the very definition of control changes. Very large numbers of people empowered by knowledge—coming together in parties, unions, factions, lobbies, interest groups, neighborhoods, families, and hundreds of other structures—assert the right or feel the obligation to "make policy."

Decision making proceeds not by "recommendations up, orders down," but by development of a shared sense of direction among those who must form the parade if there is going to be a parade. Collegial not command structures become the more natural basis for organization. Not "command and control" but "conferring and networking" become the mandatory modes for getting things done.

"Planning" cannot be done by a few leaders, or even by the brightest whiz-kids immured in a systems analysis unit or a planning staff. Real-life planning is the dynamic improvisation by the many on a general sense of direction. The sense of direction is announced by only a few of the many, but only after genuine consultation with those who will have to improvise on it.

More participatory decision making implies a need for much information, widely spread, and much feedback, seriously attended, as in biological processes. Participation and public feedback become conditions precedent to decisions that stick.

Secrecy goes out of fashion, because secrets are so hard to keep. That means more openness, not as ideological preference but as a technological imperative. . . .

44

Peopleless Factories

We are rapidly approaching the age of complete automation. In the following Fortune *story, Gene Bylinsky shows how Allen-Bradley, a Milwaukee manufacturer of industrial controls, can operate a computerized factory full tilt while turning out different versions of a product, even in lots of a single unit. The story allows us to glimpse an important trend in manufacturing that is almost sure to transform the workplace, and the ability of manufacturers to serve their markets.*

A BREAKTHROUGH IN AUTOMATING THE ASSEMBLY LINE[†]

IT IS 7:30 A.M. on the eighth floor of an 80-year-old Allen-Bradley Inc. building on Milwaukee's South Side. Two-and-a-half hours ago, an IBM mainframe computer at the company's nearby headquarters relayed yesterday's orders to a master scheduling computer. Now, at the scheduling computer's command, what may be the world's most advanced assembly line comes to life with pneumatic sighs and birdlike whistles. Lights flash. Without human intervention, plastic casings the size of pocket transistor radios start marching through 26 complex automated assembly stations.

Bar code labels, computer-printed on the spot and pasted on each plastic casing by a mechanical arm, tell each station which of nearly 200 different parts to install in what combination. As the casings move along a conveyor belt, tiny mechanical fingers insert springs, another mechanical arm places covers over the casings, and automatic screwdrivers tighten the screws. At the end of the line a laser printer zaps detailed product information onto the side of each finished plastic box. The boxes are then packaged, sorted into customer orders, and shunted into chutes ready for shipment—all automatically. The four technicians who stand by to unclog jams are rarely needed. Elapsed time per box from start to finish: 45 minutes.

Allen-Bradley's speciality is industrial controls. The 600 units produced each hour on the automated assembly line are contactors and

†SOURCE: Excerpted from Gene Bylinsky, "A Breakthrough in Automating the Assembly Line," *Fortune* (May 26), © 1986 Time Inc. All rights reserved.

relays that serve as electromechanical starters and controllers for industrial electric motors. With this futuristic assembly line, which started up in April 1985, Allen-Bradley achieved a milestone in the development of computer-integrated manufacturing, CIM for short: the ability to make different versions of a product at mass-production speeds in lots as small as a single unit.

Other companies can suit a customer's specialized needs on their assembly lines—Deere & Co. can tailor-make tractors, and General Motors can turn out automobiles with different engines and stereo equipment. But they cannot do it automatically without slowing down or stopping. No one else has achieved what John C. Rothwell, manager of the Allen-Bradley line, calls, "the dream of the Japanese"—which is "to make goods flow like water through the line." To be sure, contactors and relays are not as complex as cars and farm machinery, but Allen-Bradley's remarkable assembly line points the way toward making more complicated products rapidly in lots of one.

Allen-Bradley is using its contactor line as a showcase for other products, particularly its so-called blue-collar computers that run machines on factory floors. Visitors, more than 2,000 so far, have streamed in to see the line and come away impressed. Allied Automotive, a Southfield, Michigan, division of Allied Signal, held four seminars for executives in Milwaukee last winter so they could see the Allen-Bradley line. "Our products are very different, but their concepts can be applied to almost any assembly operation," says George R. Seeger, director of technology planning at Allied Automotive. Says Charles Montpas, engineering supervisor of GM's AC Spark Plug division, "What they have is what we'd like to have in place."

Thanks to its automated line, Allen-Bradley has been able to come late to a highly competitive world market and establish itself as a leader. The company, which Rockwell International acquired last year for $1.6 billion in cash, had historically concentrated on the big U.S. market for industrial controls. Contactors and

relays account for about 10% of Allen-Bradley's annual sales of $1.2 billion. But they are a crucial part of the other electrical equipment that Allen-Bradley sells. . . .

A team of nearly 30 engineers, technicians, accountants, and other specialists tackled the factory-of-the-future project. Even as the contactor and relay housings were being redesigned for ease of automated manufacture, engineers and technicians raced against a self-imposed deadline to develop the entire manufacturing process, including the assembly machines. Allen-Bradley wound up building 60% of the machinery itself. The rest came from outside suppliers.

The decision to make contactors and relays in lots of one if a customer so desired presented the biggest engineering challenge. "It was a mind blower," says Yost. "Nobody had ever done it before." The key was finding a way to identify the products being assembled so the line would not have to be stopped to make a different version. The Japanese *kanban* (just in time) technique uses serial numbers and special dummy objects to identify the start of a new batch. But that approach does not permit making lots of one at mass-production speeds.

The breakthrough came when engineers hit on using different bar codes to identify the various contactors and relays. Bar codes had been used in manufacturing to track parts in inventory, the way goods are monitored in supermarkets. In the Allen-Bradley arrangement, a bar code stands for the catalogue number of the device to be made and also serves as the label that tells all the machines on the assembly line exactly what operations to perform. Developing the bar code system meant finding a new way to formulate bar codes on the spot and print them as the contactor and relay shells moved by. Once the company engineers solved that problem with a specially adapted high-speed printer, "a lot of things fell into place," says Yost. The use of bar codes enables Allen-Bradley to make products in two sizes with 999 possible combinations of parts.

So contactors and relays of different sizes

and types freely intermingle on Allen-Bradley's assembly line. Flexible assembly machines responding to specific bar codes make nearly instantaneous changes without slowing production. For example, when a bar code tells a screwdriver assembly that a larger contactor frame is approaching, the screwdriver moves upward and puts a larger screw higher on the frame. Occasionally, a bar code cannot be read properly because of poor printing or a defective label; when that happens, an alarm summons an attendant. That happens much less frequently than in supermarkets, where bar codes on packages are harder for a laser reader to track because they are often passed over at an angle.

Scrutiny by scores of computer-controlled sensors helps ensure quality control. As a grinding machine processes the faces of tiny magnets for the controllers, for instance, a laser gauge measures the surfaces to keep them within tolerances as small as one-sixth the diameter of a human hair. In conventional manufacturing, magnets would have been first ground and then put into an inspection machine that culls the bad ones. Here there are no defective magnets. At Allen-Bradley, 3,500 automatic inspection steps have boosted product quality far beyond what less automated production can achieve.

Tracy O'Rourke, Allen-Bradley's president and chief executive, claims that no competitor anywhere can beat him on price or quality for IEC contactors and relays. One big user, impressed by the company's ability to deliver a finished product the next day, switched his business to Allen-Bradley from a European supplier. Depending on the competitiveness of the market, the going rate for one of the controllers produced on the innovative Allen-Bradley line is anywhere from $8 in Australia to $20 in the U.S. Allen-Bradley's cost is $6.42. Concedes an official of Square D Corp., Allen-Bradley's hometown rival, "Sure, they've scooped us with this line." Square D is not saying how much it spends to make a contactor; Allen-Bradley assumes it is more than $6.42.

Turning out variegated products at will and with unheard-of speed also allows Allen-Bradley to do away with most of its parts inventory. The company manufactures everything it needs for the contactors and relays except springs, electrical coils, and screws. A local supplier delivers springs on a just-in-time basis. Screws and coils, ordered in economically large quantities, are stored until needed. The four technicians load assembly machines overnight with just enough raw materials and parts to take care of the next day's run.

Since Allen-Bradley did not make IEC contactors and relays before building the model assembly line, the company's major union, the United Electrical Workers, has raised no objections. "The process of automatic manufacturing creates more and more work for Allen-Bradley," says William Mollenhauer, chief steward of Milwaukee Local 1111. "Our job security will be stable because we will make the devices for that automation."

Allen-Bradley is now developing additional automated lines to make larger IEC contactors and relays. Some will be assembled by programmable robots. Says James J. Kinsella, division vice president and general manager of power products at Allen-Bradley, "We're No. 1 in all the markets we serve, and we intend to stay there." For U.S. companies, the Allen-Bradley lesson is that computer-integrated manufacturing provides an alternative to going offshore or going out of business.

45

Peopleless Offices

Computerized data systems are transforming office work in numerous sectors of society. In the following Canadian Business *report, we see how electronic data exchange is revolutionizing distribution and retailing. Just as automated manufacturing is creating peopleless factories, modern information systems are making offices and office workers unnecessary. More and more, organization is becoming synonymous with electronic information exchange.*

PLUGGED-IN PURCHASING[†]

With $900 million in canned and dry goods crossing the loading docks of Provigo Distribution Inc. every year, the Montreal-based company faced a huge amount of paperwork. Even though it computerized its inventory and purchase order system in 1984, the grocery chain still had to place orders with most of its 400 suppliers by telephone and match up purchase orders, shipping documents and invoices manually. Incompatibility between Provigo's computer and those of its suppliers prevented buyers from exchanging the necessary forms electronically. In addition to the higher administrative costs of doing business this way, there were also inventory expenses. Because it often takes several days for Canada Post to deliver purchase orders, costly additional stock

had to be kept in storage to service the needs of Provigo's 842 stores.

But Provigo's old way of doing things is changing thanks to electronic data interchange (EDI). A sophisticated version of Telexing or sending magnetic disks through the mail, EDI is a means of transmitting common business documents between otherwise incompatible computer systems. Twenty-two of Provigo's largest suppliers are now sent their orders electronically via General Electric, Crowntek and Telecom Canada communications networks. The suppliers, in turn, use the network to bill the grocery chain. Maurice Dignard, corporate manager of Provigo's user and affiliated stores, hopes that by the end of the year 85% of the chain's orders and invoices will be handled this

†SOURCE: Grant Buckler, "Plugged-In Purchasing," *Canadian Business*, August 1987, pp. 23-23; used by permission.

way. "EDI has reduced errors—in one case by 60%—and speeded up the ordering process," he says.

Provigo is just one of many large organizations that have seen the reduced inventories, improved cash flow and increased customer satisfaction that result from the implementation of EDI. After a relatively slow start in Canada (EDI has been used by the US transportation industry since the mid-1970s), there is now significant electronic exchange of data in the food, transportation, warehousing and automotive industries, as well as in the electrical and office products fields. Currently, 200 to 300 companies across the country use EDI.

At present, EDI can handle a wide variety of business documents. Some common ones include purchase orders, invoices, debit and credit notes, bills of lading, and shipping and receiving notices. "EDI touches every facet of business," says Alain Charbonneau, section manager for Telecom Canada's Envoy 100 electronic mail service. Eventually, even electronic funds transfer will be on-line in Canada as it already is in the US. Letting customers input their order electronically will give salespeople more time to talk to their customers about new products and customer needs and to provide other kinds of support. As a result of EDI, the role of frontline sales staff will change. "A lot of the conventional sales people as we know them today will be playing a stronger marketing role," says EDI user Bob Farrell, manager of business services at Westinghouse Sales and Distributions Inc., in Toronto.

The key to EDI is software that acts as a middleman, translating each element of a business document—item, quantity, unit price and total owing, for example—from the format used by the local computer to an EDI standard. Transmission from one computer to another via telephone line hook-ups is then very simple. You just dial the number of the intended recipient and the translated message is sent via a communications network to an electronic "mailbox" (like those used by electronic mail services). Only the intended recipient has access to this mailbox, which is protected by a user identification code and a password. EDI software on the receiving computer then converts the message from the standard format to one it understands. The entire process takes only a few seconds for each transaction.

46

Team-Based Manufacturing:
Digital Trying the Bossless System†

In many industries, assembly lines and scientific management are rapidly becoming things of the past. The following article illustrates how Digital Equipment has been experimenting with a team-based form of organization that places primary emphasis on the ingenuity, learning, and self-organizing capacities of employees.

ENFIELD, Conn.—The inside of the Digital Equipment Corp. plant here looks much less like a factory than a warehouse full of machines and office desks deposited haphazardly. Equipment, people and the odd potted plant seem randomly scattered about the cavernous, 10,000-square-foot building. No neat aisles divide the space, no obvious paths cut through the maze.

In one particular touch of incongruity, a volleyball net stands ready at one end of the room.

This, it turns out, is new management. It's an experiment—or, as one Digital official calls it, "an investment"—in the team management approach.

And according to Digital officials, it works.

The plant's 180 employees produce printed circuit board modules for computer storage systems. At other Digital plants, similar modules are made in assembly lines, where one

person does the same job, or operates the same machine, all day.

At Enfield, by contrast, each board is put together from start to finish by one of several teams. The 18 people on each team divide the work among themselves and assemble the modules from the moment the raw materials are delivered to the plant to the time the finished product is shipped out the door. Each person is expected to be able to do all the roughly 20 jobs involved in making a module.

Workers set their own hours, plan their own schedules, check their own work and take team responsibility for each board. There are no time clocks, no security guards, no quality control officers and every employee has a key to the building.

The system is not new—several thousand similar operations have emerged at other companies and plants across the country during the last 10 years. But it's new for Digital, and

†SOURCE: Wendy Fox, "Digital Trying the Bossless System," *The Boston Globe*, October 14, 1984, pp. 89-92; used by permission (courtesy of *The Boston Globe*).

although it affects a very small portion of the company's 73,000 employees worldwide (including about 28,000 in Massachusetts), company officials are supportive and say they are willing to extend it to other parts of the company.

"We do a lot of experimenting as a company," says Greg Plakias, Digital's group manufacturing manager of storage systems. "We encourage it, we reward it. We believe that if the investment and the concept is successful, then other parts of the company will reach in and take segments that are most applicable to their organization."

Enfield plant manager Bruce Dillingham says the new system has decreased by 40 percent the time needed to produce one printed circuit board, reduced by half the amount of scrap that is common in the industry and has produced twice as many perfectly working modules than other production systems.

The theory behind such new forms of participatory management, says Homer Hagedorn, a management consultant at Arthur D. Little in Cambridge, is basically that, "People will be more interested in what they're doing and do a faster and higher quality job."

Employees at the Digital plant say that's exactly how they feel.

"This gives me a little more experience how to put the whole board together and how to check it," says Betty Stebbins, a grandmother from Springfield who's worked for Digital for five years and at the Enfield plant for one. "You're sort of proud because you see the end product."

Plakias won't give specific numbers on productivity and savings, but says the year-old experiment "is going very well."

"We have always felt that traditional hardware manufacturers invest enormously in robotics and automation and pay little attention to ways to improve the product through innovative work systems and people," Plakias says. Digital is trying to increase its productivity with fewer people, he says, while at the same time emphasizing individual involvement in the process and personal pride in the product.

As Plakias says, the company is trying to achieve a balance "between the social part of one's life and the work part of one's life."

The Enfield system was Dillingham's idea, and he, in turn, got the idea by talking with other plant managers across the country.

"It's just the stuff I believe in," he says now.

As the concept for the plant evolved and the Enfield building was built, employees were involved from the beginning. In addition to the usual architects, engineers and accountants, Digital also employed an anthropologist.

The simplicity and efficiency of the building alone, Dillingham says, saved Digital about $500,000 over the normal set-up costs of a new plant.

Digital elected to avoid tying up money in long-term supplies, and the plant was designed with very little stockroom space.

A four-walled modular conference room can be moved to any part of the vast plant floor for meetings. Some of the desks are arranged in clusters of four, radiating out from a floor-to-ceiling pillar that holds telephone and electrical lines. Others are in pairs, facing each other, to increase eye contact and conjunction between workers.

The volleyball net and exercise equipment at one end of the floor are for employees as well as their families. ("We're trying to balance work and family," Dillingham says.)

Team members interview and train new workers and give each other certification tests as they learn new parts of the manufacturing process. Pay increases are based on improved levels of skill, as opposed to seniority or authority.

There are only three managers in addition to Dillingham.

"Everybody is a teacher here and everybody is a learner," Dillingham says. "People are responsible for themselves, that's the trick."

Hagedorn says that sometimes causes problems: "You have to get built into the system a willingness on the part of the peer group to reject very unsuitable people. Sometimes that's hard to do."

Dillingham says his goal is to have an atmosphere that is informal, relaxed and trusting, where people are self-motivated, creative, open and flexible.

"We don't want a lot of clones here," he says. "We want a lot of individuals. Everybody here knows everything I do. We're not paying you for a job here: we're trying to use the total person."

Plakias says Digital wants to produce at the Enfield plant in one day what is produced at other plants in 10. But the real goal, he says, is to emphasize each worker's achievement and involvement.

"Productivity is good, but it comes in many ways," he says. "Primarily, this is an investment in our most valued asset and that's people.

The concept we have designed here is one of very few layers of supervision and management . . . We have an environment here that has no functional structure. It's a team concept."

The system is not without snags.

Because there are no large stocks of supplies, vendors who are late with their deliveries or deliver faulty raw materials for the modules "can shut us down immediately," says David LaBrecque, a team member. "But we've identified a small number of vendors with excellent track records," he says, and so far, small inventories haven't been a problem.

Although Dillingham believes his system "will work anywhere," he also acknowledges that "It's not for everyone.

"It's a threatening system. We don't need as many people. The role of professional people has changed to one of learning."

Many workers don't want to work in a place where all workers are equal in terms of authority and there is no opportunity to become a supervisor.

Plakias counters by saying, "Instead of getting better at what you're good at, you get better by adding to what you have. As you gain more knowledge about how to build a product and manage the administrative aspects of the product, you become more valuable."

And, in fact, some people, like Joseph Talbot who was a supervisor for nine years with Digital in Springfield before coming to Enfield, prefer being part of a team than wielding their authority over others.

"I had 17 people under me," he said recently at the plant, bending over a table, making miniscule adjustments to a circuit board. "After a while, it gets to be a drag. I have to learn the manufacturing end of it. This gives you the overall picture."

Hagedorn at Arthur D. Little says he expects to see management systems like the one here spread to other companies because, "Many people are a little more comfortable doing this kind of work."

But unions are not always comfortable when traditional job classifications are erased and positions are not defined. And, Hagedorn says, the Enfield system won't necessarily work everywhere for many reasons:

"The whole notion of job enrichment and job enlightenment has probably been somewhat oversold. As somebody said recently, it really isn't much of an enrichment of the job if what you do is wash the spoons on Monday and wash the glassware on Tuesday."

47

Growing Large While Staying Small[†]

As companies become large, they often become inflexible. Many organizations now recognize this and are striving to find ways of building around small units that can be run in a flexible, entrepreneurial fashion. Some companies talk about "cloning" as a basis for growth. Others talk of "spawning," or "chunking." Whatever the vocabulary, the principle is the same: Organize around small units that are differentiated in terms of product or focus, yet clearly linked to the larger corporation through shared values that give coherence to the whole. The approach reflects a holographic principle whereby essential characteristics of the whole are built into all the constituent parts, creating a whole comprising smaller wholes. As a case in point, consider Magna International.

"WHO DO YOU TELL PEOPLE YOU work for?"

Margaret Barry, 23, an assembler at an auto-parts plant near Toronto, Ontario, shrugs as if the question were every bit as stupid as it sounds. She is, after all, sitting in her boss's office in the middle of a working day. "Cam-Slide," she says. "Or Magna. It doesn't matter."

In other circumstances, it might. Cam-Slide Manufacturing employs about 150 people and expects sales of maybe $15 million (Canadian) this year. Magna International Inc. has 10,300 employees and about $1 billion (Canadian, or close to $750 million U.S.) in annual sales. There's usually a difference, in the minds of factory workers as in the minds of managers, between working for a small, single-plant enterprise and working for a multinational giant.

The difference between Cam-Slide and Magna, however, is like the difference between a neighborhood and the city it's a part of. Magna—the city—is a large, diversified auto-parts manufacturer, complete with brick-and-smoked-glass headquarters, a well-regarded stock (traded over the counter in the United States), and a hefty growth rate, sustained since the days when gasoline cost 30¢ a gallon. Within its corporate borders is a collection of, at last count, 100 enterprises much like Cam-Slide. All but 10 are wholly owned by Magna, all operate under their own names, and all have exactly one factory apiece. Most Magna plants

[†]SOURCE: Excerpted from John Case, "How to Grow without Getting Big," pp. 108-14. Reprinted with permission, *Inc.* magazine, December, 1986. Copyright © 1986 by *Inc.* Publishing Company, 38 Commercial Wharf, Boston, MA 02110.

employ fewer than 200 people. If a plant gets more work than it can handle, Magna won't add to it; instead, it "clones" the facility and starts a new operation.

"In essence," says Magna chairman and chief executive officer Frank Stronach, "we are made up of many, many small businesses."

Magna is hardly the only big company to rest on a foundation of small ones. W. L. Gore & Associates Inc., Dana Corp., and a few others set limits on the size of their facilities. Giants like Johnson & Johnson and 3M Co. spin off autonomous divisions whenever a unit gets too big. At Magna, though, the number of small plants reflects not only a management philosophy, but also a powerful strategy for growth.

Over the past decade, Magna's sales grew at a compound annual rate of 34%. Its work force expanded from 913 to 10,300. In the last fiscal year alone, Magna opened 11 new plants— nearly one every month—and added about 2,700 new employees. Despite the fact that it is utterly dependent on the highly cyclical auto industry, the company has expanded in every year but one. In the past two years, its sales more than doubled.

In the glamourless business of making parts for new cars, such growth is news enough. The fact that Magna has grown not by building bigger and bigger divisions, but by creating more and more small ones, makes the company an oddity even to the experts. "This is an industry where size has always been the name of the game," one muses. "But Stronach has proven that this small-plant concept can work pretty well."

Exactly how well the concept could work in practice didn't become plain until the early 1980s. Until then, Stronach's company had been on a kind of shakedown cruise, its CEO slowly evolving some rather unorthodox ideas about management and growth.

Stronach, born in 1932, moved to Toronto from his native Austria in 1954. Trained as a tool-and-die-maker, he eventually set up a small manufacturing shop, Multimatic Investments Ltd., in—sure enough—a garage. He soon landed a contract producing sun-visor brackets

for General Motors of Canada and after a couple of years was employing 20 people. "Then my foreman," he recalls now, "began acting a little strange." Herman Koob, it turned out, wanted to go out on his own. Stronach remonstrated—"We get along fine; there's got to be a better way"—but Koob was adamant.

"Next day," Stronach says, "I said to the foreman, 'Why don't we open up a new factory together?' " Stronach would put up the money, Koob would run the plant, and they would share in the ownership. Koob agreed to the plan. The plant the two set up—Dieomatic Inc. —prospered, too. In the years that followed, Stronach repeated the process several times and bought a few other companies, including taking control, through merger, of a publicly held aerospace-and-defense-oriented manufacturer called Magna Electronics Ltd. By 1978, he was head of a fair-size company, now named Magna International Inc., with about 18 plants, most of them producing metal trim for new cars.

Philosophically, Stronach had always been predisposed to keeping his plants small. "If you have a thousand people in a factory," he says, repeating one of his favorite homilies, "each one becomes a number. It's basically incompatible with the human spirit." The late Bill Gore, who built a new W. L. Gore & Associates plant every time an old one reached about 200 employees, once observed that his employees started smiling more when the size of their group was reduced (see "The Un-Manager," INC., August 1982). It's an observation Stronach would find congenial.

As managers, though, Gore and Stronach were looking for different things. Gore felt that the intimacy of a small plant helped people work together and share responsibility—"lattice management," he called his system. Stronach chooses to focus on accountability and entrepreneurship instead. Responsibility for a factory's operation, he believes, always lies squarely with the plant manager, the "number-one guy." Keep the plant small, and its manager will know every employee, every machine, every job. Let it grow too big, and suddenly that knowledge—and the account-ability that goes with it—gets lost in the spread-ing bureaucracy. Stronach has also evolved a system of incentives to encourage growth. If there's enough work not only for the existing plant but for a new one as well, a manager can develop a plan for a new factory. Though he can continue to manage only one—the new or the old—he's entitled to a share of the profits from both enterprises.

To an outsider, the chances for growth of any sort in the auto-parts business would have looked bleak in the early '80s. After the second oil shock, touched off by the 1979 revolution in Iran, came the most serious recession since the '30s; U.S. and Canadian vehicle production dropped 42% in three years. Surprisingly, though, the downturn spurred the suppliers' business. "Auto companies saw the handwriting on the wall," explains Michael R. Hottinger, a 13-year GM veteran who is now an executive vice-president at Magna, "and began to enter-tain proposals for new ways of building cars." Chief among these new ways was outsourcing —farming out the production of parts and com-ponents that the Big Three had previously built themselves.

Between 1980 and '85, estimates Gregory Macosko, an auto-industry consultant, each of the Big Three increased its outsourcing by 5 to 10 percentage points. In the auto business, that's a fast-growing market—and Magna, with dozens of managers scrambling to win the new contracts, was positioned smartly to take ad-vantage of it. "The way that guy [Stronach] set it up," Macosko adds, "a lot of young guys had a great deal of entrepreneurial freedom." As the new work poured in, he offered them the opportunity not to expand, but to clone.

Cam-Slide's family tree illustrates the process; it's Magna's history in microcosm. In 1978, a young tool-and-die maker named Manfred Gingl, who had spent the previous two years managing a division called Speedex manufac-turing, opened a plant called Maple Stamping Inc., which produced metal trim. Moving on to yet another start-up, Gingl put George Schacht in charge of Maple. Schacht promptly bid on

a job producing seat tracks for Chrysler Corp. His bid was successful, and he followed it up with more seat-track bids.

In 1981, after two more start-ups and a stint as corporate vice-president, Gingl became president and chief operating officer of Magna. When Schacht went off to another plant in 1983, Gingl asked a recent hire, Stefan Boekamp, to take over as Maple's acting general manager. Boekamp, too, began quoting, and before long he had enough work to convince Gingl to let him open a new plant.

That plant was Cam-Slide, Margaret Barry's employer. It opened in early 1984. But in a mat-ter of months, Boekamp had landed yet another big job, an $8-million contract to produce seat adjusters for Ford Motor Co.'s 1986 Taurus/ Sable models, and so he began laying plans for yet another plant. Last May, he opened up Slide-Master Inc. A modern, 80,000-square-foot factor, it is next door to Cam-Slide. . . .

As prime recruiter, Gingl may have the most critical job at Magna. "That's 70% of my work; 90% of all the managers are people I brought in to Magna," he says. "I go on shopping trips." His secret is the fact that he, like Stronach, was born in Austria and speaks fluent German. Like a major-league baseball scout scouring Latin America for overlooked prospects, he cruises Western Europe, mainly West Germany and Austria. The results of his expeditions are reflected in the ubiquitous German accents around Magna and in the number of managers with names like Wolfgang and Gunther. About 70% of Magna's managers, Gingl estimates, are immigrants.

Why Europe? It costs Magna about $15,000, Gingl says, to move a manager to Canada, and many of them need instruction in English as well as training in the ways of the company. Like Reinlaender, most recruits are likely to spend a couple of weeks in the corporate of-fice and several months in a division, learning plant management. But, adds Gingl, his alter-natives are sparse. Finding entrepreneurial managers with tool-and-die backgrounds in the United States or Canada is hard, and if you do find them, they are likely to have their own businesses. In West Germany, by contrast, technical training in tool-and-die making is well developed, but there is little tradition of entrepreneurship.

From the recruits' point of view, Magna's attraction is the opportunity to play on a larger diamond. "We can offer them a much bigger realm of decision making," Gingl says. "That's what makes the difference."

"In Germany," confirms Reinlaender, "I had to get five signatures to spend 50,000 marks [U.S. $25,000]. Here, I'm fully responsible for Cam-Slide."

In many respects, Magna's managers do run their shops, as Stefan Boekamp says, like private businesses. Each general manager decides what contracts to bid on, which ones to accept, and how to get the product out the door. "*Nobody* comes in here to tell me how to do my job," says Peter Voss, manager of Dortec, another division. "I would throw them out." Managers even compete for contracts. Boekamp and Reinlaender, who run similarly equipped factories with similar product lines, find themselves bidding against each other frequently. (Though plants can submit competitive bids on a job, only one bid from Magna goes out to a customer.)

The fact remains, however, that Magna is not 100 individual businesses; it's a single company with some clearly defined strategic priorities and a distinct corporate identity. Fred Gingl enforces the one, Frank Stronach the other. Though both men prefer to manage by what Stronach calls "persuasion, ingenuity, and incentives" rather than by command, neither the strategy nor the corporate philosophy is up for grabs. The company is structured accordingly.

The first layer of oversight is what Magna calls "group" offices—eight in all, each with between 10 and 20 plants. Part of the groups' function is coordination: they maintain sales offices in Detroit and act as clearinghouses for quotes. But they also have the formidable task of arbitrating plant managers' claims on company capital. If a manager wants to replace a machine, he borrows money from the group. If he wants to build a new plant, he approaches

the group with his proposal.

Where the basic product decisions are concerned, though, the groups are still very much accountable to the man who creates them and who appoints their top managers: Fred Gingl. "For the last six or eight years," says Gingl, "every decision about where a factory goes, how big it is, who the manager is, and what products they will make came through my office somehow." In effect, the groups are conduits for Gingl's priorities. For example, he wants Magna to start developing modular seating systems, which it would then sell to the auto manufacturers as fully assembled units. Integram Group, formed last August to coordinate all seat-related divisions, is charged with dispensing the company's capital in this area. Plant managers whose proposals fit in with the overall strategy will benefit accordingly.

Magna's corporate philosophy, developed and propagated mainly by Stronach, imposes an entirely different set of constraints on the company's managers. Magna sets a minimum wage —currently $8 (Canadian) an hour—for unskilled production workers and provides all of its employees with an extensive list of benefits, from fully paid health and dental care to the free use of a 95-acre park situated in woodlands north of Toronto. A Corporate Constitution, published in the annual report (and incorporated in Magna's organizational laws), binds management to distribute 10% of each year's pretax profits to employee accounts, mostly in the form of company stock, thus ensuring that each worker has at least a small equity interest. Posters on the walls of every plant explain the connection between the plant and Magna; announce Magna's commitment to fair treatment, safety, and job security; and encourage any workers with grievances to contact human-relations officers (anonymously, if they wish) at the group or corporate level.

All these measures reflect an atmosphere in which the worker's interests are taken seriously. Fred Gingl, called one day by a factory worker who feared he was about to be let go, met with the man at five that afternoon. "No complaint that reaches this office will be left longer than a day," he says. Jim Gray's job as a human-relations officer for the CMT Group is, in effect, to make sure complaints don't get to Stronach's or Gingl's level. He reports spending 60% of his time handling individual problems and disputes. He has no power other than persuasion, but the company's culture lends him a good deal of authority. In one case, a manger was preparing to fire an employee for repeated fighting and sexual harassment—an open-and-shut case, Gray acknowledges. The manager nevertheless felt compelled to check with Gray before dismissing the man.

Inevitably, Stronach and his plant managers don't always see eye-to-eye. Last year, he decided that Magna's factories should abolish time clocks—a decision, he admits, that the company had a "hell of a time" convincing its more traditional managers to carry out. But there's no question who's in charge. In July, for example, Magna opened the first of what Stronach says will be a series of state-of-the-art day-care centers for its workers' children. This one, housed in a new building within walking distance of Cam-Slide, was established by headquarters and given to the CMT Group. Suppose CMT didn't want it? "Mr. Stronach would step in," says center director Wendy Campbell, no uncertainty in her voice.

Sometime in 1987, Stronach promises, Magna will promulgate an employee charter of rights which will be enforced by an advisory board of prominent citizens and a hired staff of ombudsmenlike human-relations workers. The board's officers will be located outside Magna and its activities financed by an independent trust fund.

To Stronach, every such move is one more step toward his vision of a "fair-enterprise" society. But the culture has implications for the company as well. The National Automobile, Aerospace & Agricultural Implementation Workers' Union of Canada, for example, has never succeeded in its attempts to organize Magna, despite wages that are, Stronach acknowledges, below those of many unionized companies in the industry. That's partly because of Magna's small plants, each of

which has to be organized separately. But it's also because of the benefits, the profit sharing, and the atmosphere of respect for labor that Magna's culture creates. "The last thing Frank Stronach wants is to get the operation unionized," says John Miller, a securities analyst with a division of Dean Witter Reynolds Canada Inc., in Toronto. "His philosophy makes sure that workers in the plant aren't being abused, and if they have grievances, they'll be heard."

Stronach's philosophy also imbues Magna's divisions with a sense of common purpose. If you subscribe, as Stronach does, to the notion that good management means a contented labor force, the culture is a form of quality control. It ensures that Magna's companies are well managed for the long term as well as for the short term—and that things never reach the point here that workers want, or need, a union.

For the moment, Magna's growth is continuing apace. The company has already secured so many contracts for the 1987 and 1988 model years that its sales will rise almost regardless of how many vehicles Detroit produces. According to a recent report on Magna by Goldman, Sachs, revenues in fiscal 1988 are likely to rise nearly 50% to $1.5 billion (Canadian). Every car produced in North America would then contain an average of $117 (Can.) worth of Magna parts, up from about $73 in 1986.

The company structure is also evolving. Late in September, Magna announced the creation of a supergroup, dubbed Atoma, to include four existing groups and 31 divisions. The long-range plan envisioned by Stronach is to spin off separate public companies, with roughly half of their stock controlled by Magna and half distributed to existing Magna shareholders. As long as the new companies make money and stick to Stronach's principles—the latter, he says, "is nonnegotiable"—they will be allowed to run themselves. Atoma is likely to be the first such spin-off.

No amount of decentralization, however, will get Magna around its never-ending problem: finding enough people to run its plants. Even Gingl's overseas sources may be drying up. "We just can't find people," says Leonard Johnson.

Constitutional Monarch a "Magna Charta"
for both management and labor

According to Frank Stronach, Magna's unusual corporate structure is a model of a "fair-enterprise system," his own personal amalgam of capitalism and socialism. Its heart is Magna's legally binding Corporate Constitution—which mandates, among other things, that every employee own equity in the company. "The working class," says Stronach, "has the moral right to participate in capital building."

Magna's performance over the years lends Stronach's liberal-minded philosophy a certain credibility even with traditionally minded business executives. But what's most interesting about the philosophy is that it's as much promanagement as it is prolabor.

Take that constitution, for example, which local wags have been quick to dub the Magna Charta. It mandates that 10% of Magna's pretax profits be distributed to the company's 10,000 employees, mostly in the form of stock. But it also allows up to 6% of the profits to be distributed to Stronach's handful of top managers. Last year, Stronach took home $1.8 million (Canadian), his first lieutenants an average of $650,000 apiece.

Magna's employees, who among them now own about 6% of the company, might be a significant voting bloc in many corporations. Not Magna. Workers, like most other outside stockholders, own Class A shares—one share, one vote. Class B shares, mostly in the hands of Stronach and other top managers, carry 500 votes. Conventional shareholder democracy cuts in only in extreme circumstances—if management fails to earn 4% on share capital in a given year, say, or fails to distribute profits as the constitution specifies. But even then, all the Class A shareholders can do is elect two delegates to the company's 4-person board.

Since the company has right of first refusal on a manager's Class B shares, the system erects a stone-wall defense against an unfriendly takeover. That's no small matter in this age of acquisitions, particularly since Magna's familial culture would be unlikely to thrive under absentee management. But the price of protection against would-be raiders is insulation from existing shareholders, including the employees. That's a system, all right, but there's no doubt about who runs it.

Gingl agrees: "I have dozens of new ideas for products, but I don't have the people to take on the challenge." For the future, the company hopes to cultivate its own managers: it has already established a tool-and-die training center and is sending some of its brightest prospects for a business-and-manufacturing education at General Motors Institute. But it's not yet clear whether such moves will be sufficient to support the company's rate of growth.

Nor can decentralization alone solve the fundamental issue of Magna's position in the marketplace. "Magna is entering what I call never-never land," says Dennis DesRosiers, who heads an automotive research firm in Toronto. "They're competing in a league now with the Rockwells, the Danas, the Eatons. Vehicle companies expect Magna to have the resources of the giants, and it doesn't yet." The number of competitors, moreover, is growing, as major Japanese parts companies begin to set up shop in the United States and Canada.

As People Express Airlines discovered, a fast-growing young company can be inordinately vulnerable once well-heeled competitors begin to take it seriously. Like People's employees,

Magna's have accepted relatively low wages in return for an unusual corporate culture and an ownership stake in the company. Increased competition could easily slow the company's growth and cause the stock to fall. Workers, their savings tied up mainly in the stock, might then be more receptive to union overtures. A unionized Magna would probably lose both the cost advantages and the managerial flexibility that have made it so formidable a competitor.

For now, though, Magna has defied all such cautions. It has kept its employees happy, and it has made all the right moves in the market-place. It has grown big enough to compete in a giant industrial market while maintaining the accountability and entrepreneurship of the small, individually managed plant. Margaret Barry works for Cam-Slide; she works for Magna. Which one, as she says, doesn't really matter.

It's the combination that counts.

48

Organizational Learning

In an era of turbulence and change, it is vital that organizations learn to learn. Over the last decade, a number of people writing in diverse fields have generated many important insights about learning, and how it can be developed in organizational contexts. (See, for example, Argyris and Schön, 1978; Bateson, 1972; Botkin et al., 1979.) In the following paragraphs, Chris Argyris and Donald Schön explore the distinction between single-loop learning (what Botkin calls "maintenance learning") and double-loop learning (Botkin's innovative learning) and the need for organizations to learn to learn on a continuous basis (deutero-learning).

Single-Loop Learning[†]

Quality control inspectors detect a defect in product; they feed that information back to production engineers, who then change production specifications to correct that defect. Marketing managers observe that monthly sales have fallen below expectations; they inquire into the shortfall, seeking an interpretation which they can use to devise new marketing strategies which will bring the sales curve back on target. When organizational turnover of personnel increases to the point where it threatens the steady performance of the task system, managers may respond by investigating the sources of worker dissatisfaction; they look for factors they can influence—salary levels, fringe benefits, job design—so as to reestablish the stability of their work force.

In these examples, members of the organization respond to changes in the internal and external environments of the organization by detecting errors which they then correct so as to maintain the central features of organizational theory-in-use. These are learning episodes which function to preserve a certain kind of constancy. As Gregory Bateson has pointed out (Bateson, 1972), the organization's ability to remain stable in a changing context denotes a kind of learning. Following his usage, we call this learning single-loop. There is a single feedback loop which connects detected outcomes of actions to organizational strategies and assumptions which are modified so as to keep organizational performance within the ranges set by organizational norms. The norms themselves—for product quality, sales or task performance—remain unchanged. . . .

[†]SOURCE: Excerpted from C. Argyris and D. Schön, *Organizational Learning: A Theory of Action Perspective.* Argyris/Schön, *Organizational Learning,* © 1978, Addison-Wesley Publishing Co., Inc., Reading, Massachusetts. Pages 18-28. Reprinted with permission.

Double-Loop Learning

Organizations are continually engaged in transactions with their internal and external environments. Industrial corporations, for example, continually respond to the changing pattern of external competition, regulation and demand, and to the changing internal environment of worker's attitudes and aspirations. These responses take the form of error detection and error correction. Single-loop learning is sufficient where error correction can proceed by changing organizational strategies and assumptions within a constant framework of norms for performance. It is concerned primarily with effectiveness—that is, with how best to achieve existing goals and objectives and how best to keep organizational performance within the range specified by existing norms. In some cases, however, error correction requires an organizational learning cycle in which organizational norms themselves are modified.

Consider an industrial firm which has set up a research and development division charged with the discovery and development of new technologies. This has been a response to the perceived imperative for growth in sales and earnings and the belief that these are to be generated through internally managed technological innovation. But the new division generates technologies which do not fit the corporation's familiar pattern of operations. In order to exploit some of these technologies, for example, the corporation may have to turn from the production of intermediate materials with which it is familiar to the manufacture and distribution of consumer products with which it is unfamiliar. But this, in turn, requires that members of the corporation adopt new approaches to marketing, managing, and advertising; that they become accustomed to a much shorter product life cycle and to a more rapid cycle of changes in their pattern of activities; that they, in fact, change the very image of the business they are in. And these requirements for change come into conflict with another sort of corporate norm, one that requires predictability in the management of corporate affairs.

Hence, the corporate managers find themselves confronted with conflicting requirements. If they conform to the imperative for growth, they must give up on the imperative for predictability. If they decide to keep their patterns of operations constant, they must give up on the imperative for growth, at least insofar as that imperative is to be realized through internally generated technology. A process of change initiated with an eye to effectiveness under existing norms turns out to yield a conflict in the norms themselves.

If corporate managers are to engage this conflict, they must undertake a process of inquiry which is significantly different from the inquiry characteristic of single-loop learning. They must, to begin with, recognize the conflict itself. They have set up a new division which has yielded unexpected outcomes; this is an error, in the sense earlier described. They must reflect upon this error to the point where they become aware that they cannot correct it by doing better what they already know how to do. They must become aware, for example, that they cannot correct the error by getting the new division to perform more effectively under existing norms; indeed, the more effective the new division is, the more its results will plunge the managers into conflict. The managers must discover that it is the norm for predictable management which they hold, perhaps tacitly, that conflicts with their wish to achieve corporate growth through technological innovation.

Then the managers must undertake an inquiry which resolves the conflicting requirements. The results of their inquiry will take the form of a restructuring of organizational norms, and very likely a restructuring of strategies and assumptions associated with those norms, which must then be embedded in the images which encode organizational theory-in-use.

We call this sort of learning double-loop. There is in this sort of episode a double feedback loop which connects the detection of error not only to strategies and assumptions for effective performance but to the very norms which define effective performance. . . .

We give the name "double-loop learning" to those sorts of organizational inquiry which resolve incompatible organizational norms by setting new priorities and weightings of norms, or by restructuring the norms themselves together with associated strategies and assumptions.

In these cases, individual members resolve the interpersonal and intergroup conflict which express incompatible requirements by creating new understandings of the conflicting requirements, their sources, conditions, and consequences—understandings which then become embedded in the images and maps of organization. By doing so, they make the new, more nearly compatible requirements susceptible to effective realization . . .

Deutero-Learning

Since World War II, it has gradually become apparent not only to business firms but to all sorts of organizations that the requirements of organizational learning, especially for double-loop learning, are not one-shot but continuing. There has been a sequence of ideas in good currency—such as "creativity," "innovation," "the management of change"—which reflect this awareness.

In our earlier example, to take one instance, managers of the industrial firm might conclude that their organization needs to learn how to restructure itself, at regular intervals, so as to exploit the new technologies generated by research and development. That is, the organization needs to learn how to carry out single- and double-loop learning.

This sort of learning to learn Gregory Bateson has called deutero-learning (that is second-order learning). Bateson illustrates the idea through the following story:

A female porpoise . . . is trained to accept the sound of the trainer's whistle as a "secondary reinforcement." The whistle is expectably followed by food, and if she later repeats what she was doing when the whistle blew, she will expect again to hear the whistle and receive food.

The porpoise is now used by the trainers to demonstrate "operant conditioning" to the public. When she enters the exhibition tank, she raises her head above the surface, hears the whistle and is fed. . . .

But this pattern is (suitable) only for a single episode in the exhibition tank. She must break that pattern to deal with the class of such episodes. There is a larger context of contexts which will put her in the wrong. . . .

When the porpoise comes on stage, she again raises her head. But she gets no whistle. The trainer waits for the next piece of conspicuous behavior, likely a tail flip, which is a common expression of annoyance. This behavior is then reinforced and repeated (by giving her food).

But the tail flip was, of course, not regarded in the third performance.

Finally the porpoise learned to deal with the context of contexts—by offering a different or new piece of conspicuous behavior whenever she came on stage.

Each time the porpoise learns to deal with a larger class of episodes, she learns about the previous contexts for learning. Her creativity reflects deutero-learning.

When an organization engages in deutero-learning, its members learn, too, about previous contexts for learning. They reflect on and inquire into previous episodes of organizational learning, or failure to learn. They discover what they did that facilitated or inhibited learning, they invent new strategies for learning, they produce these strategies, and they evaluate and generalize what they have produced. The results become encoded in individual images and maps and are reflected in organizational learning practice.

The deutero-learning cycle is relatively familiar in the context of organizational learning curves. Aircraft manufacturers, for example, project the rate at which their organizations will learn to manufacture a new aircraft and base cost estimates on their projections of the rate of organizational learning. In the late 1950s, the Systems Development Corporation undertook the "Cogwheel" experiment, in which members of an aircraft-spotting team were invited to inquire into their own organizational learning and then to produce conditions which would enable them more effectively to learn to improve their performance (Chapman and Kennedy, 1956). In these examples, however, deutero-learning concentrates on single-loop learning; emphasis is on learning for effectiveness rather than on learning to resolve conflicting norms for performance. But the concept of deutero-learning is also relevant to double-loop learning. How, indeed, can organizations learn to become better at double-loop learning? How can members of an organization learn to carry out the kinds of inquiry essential to double-loop learning? What are the conditions which enable members to meet the test of organizational learning? And how can they learn to produce those conditions? . . .

REFERENCES

Argyris, C., and D. Schön. *Organizational Learning: A Theory of Action Perspective.* Reading, MA: Addison Wesley, 1978.

Bateson, G. *Steps to an Ecology of Mind.* New York: Ballantine, 1972.

Botkin, J. W., M. Elnadsra, and M. Malitza. *No Limits to Learning.* Oxford: Pergamon, 1979.

Chapman, R. L., and John L. Kennedy. *The Background and Implications of the Systems Research Laboratory Studies.* Systems Development Corporation, 1956.

49

Innovating Organizations:
The Case of 3M

Innovation in a large organization rarely happens by chance. It has to be organized!

Jay Galbraith (1982) has studied what it takes to keep innovation alive in large corporations, and has argued that it must be built into the very core of the way an organization does business. In particular, he suggests that managers must

• *be aware of the distinction between innovation on the one hand, and day-to-day operations on the other;*

• *develop two organizations to handle each of these functions, or at least differentiate the functions to a sufficient degree; and*

• *develop transition processes that transfer the ideas from the innovative organization to the operating organization.*

He also argues that innovation must be encouraged by

• *developing appropriate roles that recognize the need for idea generation, the sponsorship or championing of promising ideas, and the kind of orchestration that is necessary to steer promising ideas through the political and other aspects of corporate functioning that might otherwise quash them;*

• *separating idea generation from the normal controls on day-to-day functioning, especially bureaucratic ones;*

• *preparing the ground for the reintegration of good ideas into the mainstream organization;*

• *providing special risk funds, available from multiple sources, to generate adequate levels of financial support without draining operating budgets;*

• *building the processes of idea generation into the very fabric of the organization and its core values; and*

• *providing adequate rewards for successful innovations and sponsors.*

Many features of this approach to innovation are evident in the following account of how innovation is encouraged and managed in 3M as reported by Tom Peters and Robert Waterman in the book In Search of Excellence:

3M: *A Major Case in Point*†

Our study was primarily of giants—the huge corporations, which seldom seem as innovative as they "ought" to be. 3M qualifies as a giant: fifty-first on the Fortune 500 list, sales of $6.1 billion in 1980. But 3M has innovated: more than 40,000 products in total, well over 100 major new-product offerings each year, 40 plus divisions, with new ones being formed every year. And it has been successful. A tidy after-tax profit of $678 million on that just over $6 billion in sales, which puts it fifth in return on sales among the majors (the Fortune 100) behind only Sohio, Kodak, IBM, and American Home Products.

3M is in a lot of businesses. The largest, about 17 percent of sales, is tape and allied products, including Scotch Tape. Others are graphic systems, abrasives, adhesives, building materials, chemicals, protective products, photographic products, printing products, static control, recording materials, electrical products, and health care products. But despite the diversity, a common theme prevails at 3M. The company is dominated by chemical engineers who do most of their wizardry with coating and bonding technology. Sticking to that central discipline doesn't mean just mundane product-line extensions. Among the new products within the last two years, Fortune notes, are a "suntan lotion that won't wash off when the wearer goes for a swim; a stapler that a surgeon can use to close incisions quickly with metal staples; a film for offset printing that requires no costly silver; and a potion that makes the grass grow slower."

Peter Drucker observes, "Whenever anything is being accomplished, it is being done, I have learned, by a monomaniac with a mission," and 3M fosters the notion that commitment is the sine qua non of good product development. Fortune comments on one dimension of that commitment: "What keeps them satisfied in St. Paul is the knowledge that anyone who invents a new product, or promotes it when others lose faith, or figures out how to mass-produce it economically has a chance to manage that product as though it were his or her own business and to do so with a minimum of interference from above."

(The inventors of new product (champions) are provided with a) champion's support system . . . to act as a protector or buffer of some sort. At 3M one of the protectors is the *executive champion*. Invariably at that company, owing to its history of innovation, the executive champion is an ex-product champion himself, who behaved "irrationally," got shot at, was committed to something, and probably hung in there for ten or more years on some pet project of his own. But now, as the executive champion, he is there to protect the youngsters from premature intrusions from the corporate staff and to push them out of the nest when the time is right. As is so often the case, 3M has a homily or two to describe the executive championing process—for example, "the captain bites his tongue until it bleeds." It's a naval expression and it refers to a junior officer bringing a big ship alongside the dock for the first time. At 3M, it refers to the agonizing process of delegating to the youngsters the all-important activity of nurturing new products. The executive champion at 3M is not a "boss." He is a coach, a mentor. He is paid for his patience and his skill in developing other champions; he is James March's builder of snow fences.

The fundamental unit of support for the champion at 3M is the new venture team. It's a task force with some very special characteristics. The three most important: full-time indefinite assignment from various disciplines; volunteers; and staying power.

After a venture team is formed at 3M, it quickly comes to have full-time members from at least the technical area, manufacturing, marketing, sales, and perhaps finance. The

†SOURCE: Pages 224-234 from IN SEARCH OF EXCELLENCE by Thomas J. Peters and Robert H. Waterman Jr. Copyright © 1982 by Thomas J. Peters and Robert H. Waterman, Jr. Reprinted by permission of Harper & Row, Publishers, Inc.

team gets full-time members whether it needs them initially or not. The company knows this ritual is apt to be duplicative, especially early on when, say, only a third of a manufacturing person is needed. But they seem willing to pay the price of duplication to get committment. And only full-time assignment, the sensible 3M argument goes, lead to zealous committment.

Another marked spur to committment is that all team members are volunteers. Says a 3M executive, "The team members are recruited, not assigned. There is a very big difference. If I am the marketing person assigned to evaluate the technical guy's idea, in most companies with the usual incentives I can get myself off the hook by saying the idea is poor, by pointing out all the deficiencies . . . that just doesn't happen if I'm a volunteer team member."

Finally 3M supports venture team autonomy and staying power. It insists that the team stay together from early in the initiation phase to the eventual rollout. "They say," notes MIT's Edward Roberts, who has studied 3M for twenty years, "we commit to you as a group. You will move forward with the product into the market and benefit from its growth, so long as you meet our conventional corporate measures and standards of performance. In case you fail, we will give you a back-up committment to job security at the level of the job you left before you entered this venture." (The latter statement depicts another part of the support system: backing for good tries even if they fail.)

The reward system supports both the team and the individual. Everyone gets promoted as a group as their project moves along from hurdle to hurdle. The champion benefits as the group prospers, and vice versa. Here is Roberts again on the subject of the career progress of someone who is a part of a successful venture team:

"The individual involved in a new venture will have automatic changes in his employment and compensation categories as a function of sales growth of his product. He starts out, for instance, as a first-line engineer at the top or bottom of the salary range for that job. As his product enters the market he becomes a 'product engineer.' When annual sales volume hits $1 million, it will automatically become a full-fledged product, and his job title changes. His salary range changes, too, because he now has something selling at $1 million a year. When a product hits the $5 million mark, he passes the next threshold. He is now a 'product line engineering manager.' If the product reaches $20 million, it suddenly becomes an independent product department, and if he is the key technical person associated with it, he now becomes "manager of engineering or R&D for that department."

If you want to understand the culture that encourages entrepreneurial activities at 3M, as good a starting point as any is its value system, in particular, its "eleventh commandment." It is: "thou shalt not kill a new product idea." The company may slow it down. Or it may not commit a venture team. But it doesn't shoot its pioneers. As one 3M observer notes, the eleventh commandment is at odds with most activities in large corporations. Moreover, he adds, "If you want to stop a project aimed at developing a new product, the burden of proof is on the one who wants to stop the project, not the one who proposes the project. When you switch the burden from proving that the idea is good to the burden of proving that the idea is no good, you do an awful lot for changing the environment within the company with respect to the sponsorship of entrepreneurial people."

In order to reinforce the shared values clustered around autonomy, innovation, individual initiative, and entrepreneurship, the company's leadership celebrates its heroes—past and present. In our research, one of us sat down with a 3M executive and discussed the last few chairmen and key executives. Virtually without exception, each had a well-publicized championing success. Thus the whole of the top management team, and many of their predecessors, act as role models for the young in the organization. The would-be champion gains encouragement from the panoply of heroes' tales: don't kill ideas; scrounge; failure is OK; years and years are expected to pass before a raw idea makes it in the marketplace; and so on. For instance the tales of the legendary Richard Drew and his cohort John Borden are instructive to the young. Chairman Lewis Lehr relates it: "The salesmen who visited the auto plants noticed that workers painting new two-toned cars were having trouble keeping the colors from running together. Richard G. Drew, a young 3M lab technician, came up with the answer; masking tape, the company's first tape. In 1930, six years after Du Pont introduced cellophane, Drew figured out how to put adhesive on it, and Scotch Tape was born, initially for industrial packaging. It didn't really begin to roll until another imaginative 3M hero, John Borden, a sales manager, created a dispenser with a built-in blade."

This is a typical and surprisingly important vignette, for several reasons. First, it reinforces the close interaction between the company and customer. Second, it shows that the technician doesn't have to be the one who invents. Third, it demonstrates that 3M doesn't limit projects on the basis of potential market size, exactly because the first use (e.g., the first incarnation of Scotch Tape was as a narrow-use industrial fastener) is so often unrelated to eventual product potential. Serious students of innovation note this phenomenon time and time again, with virtually every kind of new product.

When champions win at 3M, they're feted in style. Says Lehr, "Fifteen to twenty or more times a year some new and promising project reaches a level of a million dollars in profitable sales. You may think that this does not get much attention . . . but it does. Lights flash, bells ring, and video cameras are called out to recognize the entrepreneurial team that is responsible for this achievement." Thus does the company encourage the twenty-eight-year-old engineer with bright ideas to step out and take risks.

3M's value system is also specific in indicating that virtually any idea is okay. "Because of 3M's diversity the conviction spreads easily that someone in 3M will be able to use almost anything," a commentator notes. The venerable story illustrating the point is of a failed ribbon material that became a failed plastic cup for brasieres that became the standard U.S. worker safety mask after the advent of the Occupational Safety and Health Administration (OSHA). And although the company does stick close to its coating and bonding technological base, it doesn't put any restrictions on the kinds of products it will accept. Roberts notes: "If the product idea can meet financial measures of growth, profitability, and the like, 3M is happy to have it whether or not it's in their dominant field of business." A different point of the same sort surfaced from another 3M executive: "We don't like the cash cow idea. It's the people with success traditions in successful divisions who best realize the potential of continuous innovation." 3M understands that very human truth that "success breeds success."

And failure is supported. Legend once more shows the way. Chairman Lehr preaches:

"We got into the business of making roofing granules for asphalt shingles because one worker persisted in trying to find a way to use reject sandpaper minerals. He was actually fired [apparently sometimes champions get nailed, even at 3M] because of the time and effort he spent on this. But he kept coming to work anyway. Our Roofing Granules Division today earns substantial revenue. The man responsible retired ten years ago as vice-president of the division. . . .
Shortly after World War II, we had a program to develop a bacterial skin barrier, called a surgical drape, for surgeons to use during surgery. The program was twice killed by senior management.[1] But continued persistence ultimately produced a successful drape and led the way toward our $400 million-a-year health care business today . . . we keep these stories alive and often repeat them so that any employee with an entrepreneurial spirit who feels discouraged, frustrated, and ineffective in a large organization knows that he or she is not the first one to face considerable odds . . . the freedom to persist, however, implies the freedom to do things wrong and to fail."

Those who stayed with it were celebrated. Another executive comments: "We don't kill ideas, but we do deflect them. We bet on people." And he adds, "You invariably have to kill a program at least once before it succeeds.

That's how you get down to the fanatics, those who are really emotionally committed to finding a way—any way—to make it work."

What does it all mean? Among other things, it means living with (managing) a paradox: persistent support for a possible good idea, but not foolish overspending because 3M, above all, is a very pragmatic company. It typically works this way: The champion, as his idea moves out of the very conceptual stage and into prototyping, starts to gather a team about him. It grows to, say, five or six people. Then, suppose (as is statistically the likely case) the program hits a snag. 3M will probably cut it back quickly, knock some people off the team. But as the mythology suggests, the champion—if he is committed—is encouraged to persist, by himself or perhaps with one co-worker, at, say a 30 percent or so level of effort. In most cases, 3M has observed that the history of any product is a decade or more long before the market is really ready. (A decade sounds like a long time, but formal study after formal study reveals that the average space between idea and commercial deployment in virtually any field, high or low technology, is ten to twenty years.) So the champion survives the ups and downs. Eventually, often, the market does become ripe. His team rebuilds.

"We have a belief that we have the capability of solving practical problems," says a 3M executive, and that's what 3M is: a company of practical problem solvers, be they salesmen or technical champions. It started that way. One analyst observes: "the obsession with invention dates from the company's origin. Several local investors bought a mine they thought contained valuable corundum, a very hard mineral used in high-grade abrasives. It turned out to be low grade. The investors concluded that the only way to survive was to come up with off-shoots that had high value added." Says Lehr, "The salesmen would go from smokestack to smokestack knocking on doors. But they didn't stop at the purchasing agent's office. They went into the back shop to talk to the boys and see what was needed that nobody was making." The salesmen became problem solvers; and the

salesman, with his technical buddy in tow, is still the keystone of the 3M strategy today.

3M is the first to recognize innovation as a numbers game. "Our approach is to make a little, sell a little, make a little bit more," says Robert M. Adams, vice president of R&D. One of his colleagues talks about "big ends from small beginnings. . . . Spend just enough money to get what's needed next to incrementally reduce ignorance. . . . Lots of small tests in a short interval. . . . Development is a series of small excursions . . . the odds on any one idea making it through to commercial fruition are approximately zero. . . . There is no limit on raw ideas." So the champions are all over the place experimenting, spending a little. Mostly, they fail. Yet some march through hurdle after hurdle; and a few go all the way.

3M provides funds for people who want to put together a group of any sort, from basket-weaving (literally) to solid state physics or micro-electronics. Moreover, the physical "campus" in St. Paul is a hive of pilot testing facilities. The ability to get an idea turned into tin and into a prototype quickly is remarkable. The users, too, are heavily involved in the product development process from its inception through rollout.

In early interviews at 3M, we heard that the average length of a new-product plan was about five pages and were amazed at such brevity. One of us commented on that finding in a speech. A 3M vice president was a speaker, too. He got up and, though generally supportive of our 3M analysis, said: "You're all wet on that one." We waited for the other shoe to drop: Did 3M have 200-page new product proposals like most of the companies we've worked with? He went on: "We consider a coherent sentence to be an acceptable first draft for a new-product plan."

It all works—champions, venture teams, informal communications, voluntary assignment of team members, support for failure, and the like—because of the incessant focus on keeping the bureaucracy limited. The same vice president added: "We don't constrain ourselves with plans at the beginning when ignorance is highest. Sure we plan. We put together meticulous sales implementation plans. But that's after we know something. At the very front end, why should we spend time writing a 250-page plan that tries to drive out ignorance before having first done some simple tests on customer premises or in a pilot facility somewhere?"

In a similar vein, 3M eschews the idea of a "minimum size" for a product. "Our experience," says one executive, "tells us that prior to entry into the market we don't know how to properly anticipate the sales growth of a new product. Consequently, we tend to make market forecasts after we've entered the market, not before." And the head of the New Business Ventures Division stated: "An NBVD product is never justified on the analytic case; it must be based on belief."

Looked at one way, *organization structure* at 3M isn't important. Roberts observes, "The 3M structure, if you just look at it on paper, doesn't seem to have anything that is terribly unique." And in even stronger language, a 3M executive put it, "Structural form is irrelevant to us."

But there are a number of traits, more or less structural, that are essential. First, despite a common set of technical disciplines that might lead others to a functional or matrix organization, 3M remains a radically decentralized business. It has forty or so divisions. Moreover, the name of the game is creation of new divisions; the forty is up from about twenty-five just a decade ago. Spinning things off rather than seeking higher sales volume for one's division is the time-honored (albeit unconventional) path to success.

That sort of flexibility goes much further, especially in relation to starting up. At 3M, suppose someone working in the product development group in a division comes up with an idea. He first does the normal thing: he goes to his boss to seek funding. Suppose his boss turns him down. Then the 3M magic starts. He goes to another division within his group. If he's turned down again, he goes next to another division within his group. He may be in the adhesives group, but it's not unusual for him to wander off to office products. Now if that group or some other doesn't have time for him, he goes to the court of last resort: the NBVD. That's where the really far-out stuff ends up.

How does 3M make an approach like this work? Simple: managers are given every incentive to do so. The fellow heading any group gets rewarded in part on the dollar amount of venture activity that he's funded from outside his group. The same rule is in force among division heads. Straightforward incentives are there pushing you to look any place to see an idea, and, if you're a buyer, to look any place to buy one. Concomitantly, the organization is flexible in shifting its people around. After a fellow in Group A sells an idea to a division manager in Group B, say, he moves on over.

There are some associated rules. For example, each division has an ironclad requirement that at least 25 percent of its sales must be derived from products that did not exist five years ago. It is truly remarkable, per conventional theory, that the target is laid on each of the over forty divisions (whether in high- or low-growth business).[2] Such targets in other companies are more commonly applied at the corporate level or at the group level; commitment suffers where it is needed most, at the division where something can be done about it. At 3M where the goal is always demanded at the divisional level, forty separate general managers, not five or ten, are out scrounging for new products.

But the most important notion, as we've said time and again, is that there aren't any one or two things that make it all work. Sure, the champion, the executive champion, and the venture team are at the heart of the process. But they succeed, when they do succeed, only because: heroes abound; the value system focuses on scrounging; it's okay to fail; there's an orientation toward nichemanship and close contact with the customer; there's a well-understood process of taking small, manageable steps; intense, informal communications are the norm; the physical setting provides plenty of sites for experimentation; the organizational structure is not only accommodating but highly supportive of 3M-style innovation;

and the absence of overplanning and paperwork is conspicuous, as is the presence of internal competition. That's about a dozen factors. And it's all of them functioning in
concert—over a period of decades—that makes
innovation work at 3M.

NOTES

1. The ribbon-to-[brassiere]-to-face-mask champion was likewise told to knock it off. He ended doing most of the product development work on the
case—at home.

2. This is a P&G trick as well. One former brand
manager notes: "The first thing they tell you is,
'Forget product life cycles and cash cows!' One of
the soaps has been reformulated over eighty times
and is thriving."

REFERENCE

Galbraith, J. "The Innovating Organization."
   Organizational Dynamics, Winter 1982, 5-25.

50

Culture:
A Complex and Subtle Language

Think about culture as a language: a language expressed through words, gestures, situations, interpersonal relations, and numerous conventions. We live culture exactly as we live language: by "speaking it" and "reading it"—in the way we talk, act, spend our time, relate to others, and so on.

This linguistic aspect of culture is expertly illustrated by E. T. Hall in his book The Silent Language, *and in the following excerpts from his* Harvard Business Review *article on how culture influences overseas business.*

As you read, think about how the ideas can help you understand differences in corporate culture within a given society, as well as the differences encountered in moving from society to society. Moving from one organization to another can have many parallels with moving to a foreign land!

Language of Time[†]

Everywhere in the world people use time to communicate with each other. There are different languages of time just as there are different spoken languages. The unspoken languages are informal; yet the rules governing their interpretation are surprisingly *ironbound*.

In the United States, a delay in answering a communication can result from a large volume of business causing the request to be postponed until the backlog is cleared away, from poor organization, or possibly from technical complexity requiring deep analysis. But if the person awaiting the answer or decision rules out these reasons, then the delay means to him that the matter has low priority on the part of the other person—lack of interest. On the other hand, a similar delay in a foreign country may mean something altogether different. Thus:

• In Ethiopia, the time required for a decision is directly proportional to its importance. This is so much the case that low-level bureaucrats there have a way of trying to elevate the prestige of their work by taking a long time to

[†]SOURCE: Reprinted by permission of the *Harvard Business Review*. An excerpt from "The Silent Language in Overseas Business" by Edward T. Hall (May-June 1960). Copyright © 1960 by the President and Fellows of the Harvard College; all rights reserved.

make up their minds. (Americans in that part of the world are innocently prone to downgrade their work in the local people's eyes by trying to speed things up.)

• In the Arab East, time does not generally include schedules as Americans know and use them. The time required to get something accomplished depends on the relationship. More important people get fast service from less important people, and conversely. Close relatives take absolute priority; nonrelatives are kept waiting.

In the United States, giving a person a deadline is a way of indicating the degree of urgency or relative importance of the work. But in the Middle East, the American runs into a cultural trap the minute he opens his mouth. "Mr. Aziz will have to make up his mind in a hurry because my board meets next week and I have to have an answer by then," is taken as indicating the American is overly demanding and is exerting undue pressure. "I am going to Damascus tomorrow morning and will have to have my car tonight," is a sure way to get the mechanic to stop work, because to give another person a deadline in this part of the world is to be rude, pushy, and demanding.

An Arab's evasiveness as to when something is going to happen does not mean he does not want to do business; it only means he is avoiding unpleasantness and is side-stepping possible commitments which he takes more seriously than we do. For example:

The Arabs themselves at times find it impossible to communicate even to each other that some processes cannot be hurried, and are controlled by built-in schedules. This is obvious enough to the Westerner but not to the Arab. A highly placed public official in Baghdad precipitated a bitter family dispute because his nephew, a biochemist, could not speed up the complete analysis of the uncle's blood. He accused the nephew of putting other less important people before him and of not caring. Nothing could sway the uncle who could not grasp the fact that there is such a thing as an *inherent* schedule.

With us the more important an event is, the further ahead we schedule it, which is why we find it insulting to be asked to a party at the last minute. In planning future events with Arabs, it pays to hold the lead time to a week or less because other factors may intervene or take precedence.

Again, time spent waiting in an American's office is a sure indicator of what one person thinks of another or how important he feels the other's business to be. This is so much the case that most Americans cannot help getting angry after waiting 30 minutes: one may even feel such a delay is an insult, and will walk out. In Latin America, on the other hand, one learns that it does not mean anything to wait in an outer office. An American businessman with years of experience in Mexico once told me, "You know, I have spent two hours cooling my heels in an executive's outer office. It took me a long time to learn to keep my blood pressure down. Even now, I find it hard to convince myself they are still interested when they keep me waiting."

The Japanese handle time in ways which are almost inexplicable to the Western European and particularly the American. A delay of years with them does not mean that they have lost interest. It only means that they are building up to something. They have learned that Americans are vulnerable to long waits. One of them expressed it, "You Americans have one terrible weakness. If we make you wait long enough, you will agree to anything."

Indians of South Asia have an elastic view of time as compared to our own. Delays do not, therefore, have the same meaning to them. Nor does indefiniteness in pinpointing appointments mean that they are evasive. Two Americans meeting will say, "We should get together sometime," thereby setting a low priority on the meeting. The Indian who says, "Come over and see me, see me anytime," means just that.

Americans make a place at the table which may or may not mean a place made in the heart. But when the Indian makes a place in his time, it is yours to fill in every sense of the word if you realize that by so doing you have crossed a boundary and are now friends with him. The point of all this is that time communicates just as surely as do words and that the vocabulary of time is different around the world. The principle to be remembered is that time has different meanings in each country.

Language of Space

Like time, the language of space is different wherever one goes. The American businessman, familiar with the pattern of American corporate life, has no difficulty in appraising the relative importance of someone else, simply by noting the size of his office in relation to other offices around him:

• Our pattern calls for the president or the chairman of the board to have the biggest office. The executive vice president will have the next largest and so on down the line until you end up in the "bull pen." More important offices are usually located at the corners of building and on the top floor. The relative rank of vice presidents will be reflected in where they are placed along "Executive Row."

• The French, on the other hand, are much more likely to lay out space as a network of connecting points of influence, activity, or interest. The French supervisor will ordinarily be found in the middle of his subordinates where he can control them.

Americans who are crowded will often feel that their status in the organization is suffering. As one would expect in the Arab world, the location of an office and its size constitute a poor index of the importance of the man who occupies it. What we experience as crowded, the Arab will often regard as spacious. The same is true in Spanish cultures. A Latin American official illustrated the Spanish view of this point while showing me around a plant. Opening the door to an 18-by-20-foot office in which seventeen clerks and their desks were placed he said, "See, we have nice spacious offices. Lots of space for everyone."

The American will look at a Japanese room and remark how bare it is. Similarly, the Japanese look at our rooms and comment, "How bare!" Furniture in the American home tends to be placed along the walls (around the edge). Japanese have their charcoal pit where the family gathers in the *middle* of the room. The top floor of Japanese department stores is not reserved for the chief executive—it is the bargain roof!

In the Middle East and Latin America, the businessman is likely to feel left out in time and overcrowded in space. People get too close to him, lay their hands on him, and generally crowd his physical being. In Scandinavia and Germany, he feels more at home, but at the same time the people are a little cold and distant. It is space itself that conveys this feeling.

In the United States, because of our tendency to zone activities, nearness carries rights of familiarity so that the neighbor can borrow material possessions and invade time. This is not true in England. Propinquity entitles you to nothing. American Air Force personnel stationed there complain because they have to make an appointment for their children to play with the neighbor's child next door.

Conversation distance between two people is learned early in life by copying elders. Its controlling patterns operate almost totally unconsciously. In the United States, in contrast to many foreign countries, men avoid excessive touching. Regular business is conducted at distances such as 5 feet to 8 feet; highly personal business, 18 inches to 3 feet—not 2 or 3 inches.

In the United States, it is perfectly possible for an experienced executive to schedule the steps of negotiation in time and space so that most people feel comfortable about what is happening. Business transactions progress in stages from across the desk to beside the desk, to the coffee table, then on to the conference table, the luncheon table, or the golf course, or even into the home—all according to a complex set of hidden rules which we obey instinctively.

Even in the United States, however, an executive may slip when he moves into new and unfamiliar realms, when dealing with a new group, doing business with a new company, or moving to a new place in the industrial hierarchy. In a new country the danger is magnified. For example, in India it is considered improper to discuss business in the home on social occasions. One never invites a business acquaintance to the home for the purpose of furthering business aims. That would be a violation of sacred hospitality rules.

Language of Things

Americans are often contrasted with the rest of the world in terms of material possessions. We are accused of being materialist, gadget-crazy. And, as a matter of fact, we have developed material things for some very interesting reasons. Lacking a fixed class system and having an extremely mobile population, Americans have become highly sensitive to how others make use of material possessions. We use everything from clothes to houses as a highly evolved and complex means of ascertaining each other's status. Ours is a rapidly shifting system in which both styles and people move up or down. For example:

• The Cadillac ad men feel that not only is it natural but quite insightful of them to show a picture of a Cadillac and a well-turned out gentleman in his early fifties opening the door. The caption underneath reads, "You already know a great deal about this man."

• Following this same pattern, the head of a big union spends an excess of $100,000 furnishing his office so that the president of United States Steel cannot look down on him. Good materials, large space, and the proper surroundings signify that the people who occupy the premises are solid citizens, that they are dependable and successful.

The French, the English, and the Germans have entirely different ways of using their material possessions. What stands for the height of dependability and respectability with the English would be old-fashioned and backward to us. The Japanese take pride in often inexpensive but tasteful arrangements that are used to produce the proper emotional setting.

Middle East businessmen look for something else—family, connections, friendship. They do not use the furnishings of their office as part of their status system; nor do they expect to impress a client by these means or to fool a banker into lending more money then he should. They like good things, too, but feel that they, as persons, should be known and not judged solely by what the public sees.

One of the most common criticisms of American relations abroad, both commercial and governmental, is that we usually think in terms of material things. "Money talks," says the American, who goes on talking the language of money abroad, in the belief that money talks the *same* language all over the world. A common practice in the United States is to try to buy loyalty with high salaries. In foreign countries, this maneuver almost never works, for money and material possessions stand for something different there than they do in America.

Language of Friendship

The American finds his friends next door and among those with whom he works. It has been noted that we take people up quickly and drop them just as quickly. Occasionally a friendship formed during schooldays will persist, but this is rare. For us there are few well-defined rules governing the obligations of friendship. It is difficult to say at which point our friendship gives way to business opportunism or pressure from above. In this we differ from many other people in the world. As a general rule in foreign countries friendships are not formed as quickly as in the United States but go much deeper, last longer, and involve real obligations. For example:

It is important to stress that in the Middle East and Latin America your "friends" will not let you down. The fact that they personally are feeling the pinch is never an excuse for failing their friends. They are supposed to look out for your interests.

Friends and family around the world represent a sort of social insurance that would be difficult to find in the United States. We do not use our friends to help us out in disaster as much as we do as a means of getting ahead—or, at least, of getting the job done. The United States systems work by means of a series of closely tabulated favors and obligations carefully doled out where they will do the most good. And the least that we expect in exchange for a favor is gratitude.

The opposite is the case in India, where the friend's role is to "sense" a person's need and do something about it. The idea of reciprocity as we know it is unheard of. An American in India will have difficulty if he attempts to follow American friendship patterns. He gains nothing by extending himself on behalf of others, least of all gratitude, because the Indian assumes that what he does for others he does for the good of his own psyche. He will find it impossible to make friends quickly and is unlikely to allow sufficient time for friendships to ripen. He will also note that as he gets to know people better, they may become more critical of him, a fact that he finds hard to take. What he does not know is that one sign of friendship in India is speaking one's mind.

Language of Agreements

While it is important for American businessmen abroad to understand the symbolic meanings of friendship rules, time, space, and material possessions, it is just as important for executives to know the rules for negotiating agreements in various countries. Even if they cannot be expected to know the details of each nations's commercial legal practices, just the awareness of and the expectation of the existence of differences will eliminate much complication.

Actually, no society can exist on a high commercial level without a highly developed working base on which agreements can rest. This base may be one or a combination of three types:

1. Rules that are spelled out technically as law or regulation.
2. Moral practices mutually agreed on and taught to the young as a set of principles.
3. Informal customs to which everyone conforms without being able to state the exact rules.

Some societies favor one, some another. Ours, particularly in the business world, lays heavy emphasis on the first variety. Few Americans will conduct any business nowadays without some written agreement or contract.

Varying from culture to culture will be the circumstances under which such rules apply. Americans consider that negotiations have more or less ceased when the contract is signed. With the Greeks, on the other hand, the contract is seen as a sort of way station on the route to negotiation that will cease only when the work is completed. The contract is nothing more than a charter for serious negotiations. In the Arab world, once a man's word is given in a particular kind of way, it is just as binding, if not more so, than most of our written contracts. The written contract, therefore, violates the Moslem's sensitivities and reflects on his honor. Unfortunately, the situation is now so hopelessly confused that neither system can be counted on to prevail consistently.

Informal patterns and unstated agreements often lead to untold difficulty in the cross-cultural situation. Take the case of the before-and-after patterns where there is a wide discrepancy between the American's expectations and those of the Arab:

• In the United States, when you engage a specialist such as a lawyer or a doctor, require any standard service, or even take a taxi, you make several assumptions: (a) the charge will be fair; (b) it will be in proportion to the services rendered; and (c) it will bear a close relationship to the "going rate."

You wait until after the services are performed before asking what the tab will be. If the charge is too high in the light of the above assumptions, you feel you have been cheated. You can complain, or can say nothing, pay up, and take your business elsewhere the next time.

• As one would expect in the Middle East, basic differences emerge which lead to difficulty if not understood. For instance, when taking a cab in Beirut it is well to know the going rate as a point around which to bargain and for settling the charge, which must be fixed before engaging the cab.

If you have not fixed the rate *in advance*, there is a complete change and an entirely different set of rules will apply. According to these rules, the going rate plays no part whatsoever. The whole relationship is altered. The sky is the limit, and the customer has no kick coming. I have seen taxi drivers shouting at the top of their lungs, waving their arms, following a redfaced American with his head pulled down between his shoulders, demanding for a two-pound ride ten Lebanese pounds which the American eventually had to pay.

It is difficult for the American to accommodate his frame of reference to the fact that what constitutes one thing to him, namely, a taxi ride, is to the Arab two very different operations involving two different sets of relationships and two sets of rules. The crucial factor is whether the bargaining is done at the beginning or the end of the ride! As a matter of fact, you cannot bargain at the end. What the driver asks for he is entitled to!

One of the greatest difficulties Americans have abroad stems from the fact that we often think we have a commitment when we do not. The second complication on this same topic is the other side of the coin, i.e., when others think we have agreed to things that we have not. Our own failure to recognize binding obligations, plus our custom of setting organizational goals ahead of everything else, has put us in hot water far too often.

People sometimes do not keep agreements with us because we do not keep agreements with them. As a general rule, the American treats the agreement as something he may eventually have to break. Here are two examples:

• Once while I was visiting an American post in Latin America, the Ambassador sent the Spanish version of a trade treaty down to his language officer with instructions to write in some "weasel words." To his dismay, he was told, "There are no weasel words in Spanish."

• A personnel officer of a large corporation in Iran made an agreement with local employees that American employees would not receive preferential treatment. When the first American employee arrived, it was learned quickly that in the United States he had been covered by a variety of health plans that were not available to Iranians. And this led to immediate protests from the Iranians which were never satisfied. The personnel officer never really grasped the fact that he had violated an ironbound contract.

Certainly, this is the most important generalization to be drawn by American businessmen from this discussion of agreements: there are many times when we are vulnerable *even when judged by our own standards*. Many instances of actual sharp practices by American companies are well known abroad and are giving American business a bad name. The cure for such questionable behavior is simple. The companies concerned usually have it within their power to discharge offenders and to foster within their organization an atmosphere in which only honesty and fairness can thrive.

But the cure for ignorance of the social and legal rules which underlie business agreements is not so easy. This is because:

• The subject is complex.

• Little research has been conduced to determine the culturally different concepts of what is an agreement.

• The people of each country think that their own code is the only one, and that everything else is dishonest.

• Each code is different from our own; and the farther away one is traveling from Western Europe, the greater the difference is.

But the little that has already been learned about this subject indicates that as a problem it is not insoluble and will yield to research.

Since it is probably one of the more relevant and immediately applicable areas of interest to modern business, it would certainly be advisable for companies with large foreign operations to sponsor some serious research in this vital field.

51

Corporate Culture and Core Values

Corporate culture is like a language. Yes, but it's also like — an iceberg.
- an onion
- an umbrella
- sticky glue

Management writers are fond of using many different metaphors to characterize how the culture of an organization serves as an integrating force, binding everything together.

As has been suggested (Resource 50), the experience of moving from one organization to another can be like moving between countries: the social realities can be so different that one can easily experience being a foreigner in a strange land. The differences between the daily realities of working for firms like Magna International (Resource 47), 3M (Resource 48), Tandem Corporation (Resource 54), Servicemaster (Resource 55), Apple Computer (Resource 57), McDonald's (Resource 77) (and the insurance companies, voluntary organizations, government departments, engineering, and other companies described in the cases in Part 3 of this Resourcebook) can be so great, that the transition from one to another may well be described as one of culture change, and at times, of "culture shock."

One of the easiest ways to grasp and "see" the nature of an organization's culture is to try to view it as if you are a visitor from a foreign land (try doing the exercise in Resource 16, or using the framework in Resource 85). As one tries to look at the organization with fresh eyes, one can see the intangible "social glue" that holds everything together: how the language, norms, values, rituals, myths, stories and daily routines form part of a coherent "reality" that lends shape to how and what people do as they go about their work.

In understanding this "social glue" (which like all glue sometimes does not stick as well as it might, producing a fragmented or divided "culture") other ways of thinking about culture may be appropriate.

For example, try thinking about the corporate culture as an iceberg. Recognize that what you see on the surface is based on a much deeper reality. Recognize that the visible elements of the culture may be sustained by all kinds of hidden values, beliefs, ideologies and assumptions—questioned and unquestioned, conscious and unconscious. As a manager, recognize that it may not be possible to change the surface without changing what lies below.

Or try thinking about the corporate culture as an onion. Recognize that it has different layers. Recognize that one can penetrate beneath the rituals, ceremonies and symbolic routines to discover inner layers of mythology, folklore, hopes and dreams that eventually lead to the innermost values and assumptions that lend meaning to the outward aspects of the culture. Recognize that to impact or change the culture in any significant way it is necessary to address and perhaps change the values that lie at the core.

Or try thinking about the corporate culture as an umbrella. Look for the overarching values and visions that unite, or are capable of uniting, the individuals and groups working under the umbrella. Recognize that one's ability to mobilize or change any organization may depend on finding the umbrella that can unite potentially divergent individuals, groups and sub-cultures in pursuit of a shared vision of reality.

Whatever one's favored metaphor—whether iceberg, onion, umbrella or sticky glue—it seems important to remember that there's more to corporate culture than meets the eye. Just as the culture of a country tends to be shaped and sustained by deeply held core values and beliefs, so too in the corporate world. Changing a corporate culture is not like changing a suit of clothes. One can change surface appearances, e.g. by giving the corporation a new image, introducing staff picnics, and by espousing new philosphies and beliefs. But to have significant and lasting impact, basic values also have to change.

REFERENCES

Deal, T.E., and A.A. Kennedy, *Corporate Cultures: The Rites and Rituals of Corporate Life.* Reading, MA, Addison-Wesley, 1982.

Frost, P.J., L.F. Moore, M.R. Louis, C.C. Lundberg, and J. Martin (eds.), *Organizational Culture.* Newbury Park, CA, Sage Publications, 1985.

Ouchi, W.G., and A.L. Wilkins, "Organizational Culture." *The Annual Review of Sociology,* 1985, 457-483.

Pondy, L.R., P.J. Frost, G. Morgan, and T.C. Dandridge (eds.), *Organizational Symbolism.* Greenwich, CT, JAI Press, 1983.

Smircich, L., "Concepts of culture and organizational analysis." *Administrative Science Quarterly,* 1983, 339-358.

52

Corporate Culture:
The Role of Stories†

Every organization has its own stories to tell. These communicate its origin, style, and core values, as well as the juicy tidbits that can lend color and life to daily routine.

In the following pages, Alan Wilkins of Brigham Young University explores the many roles that stories and story-telling can play in shaping corporate culture.

A concerned manager recently expressed dismay that many of the middle managers in his company really believed that top management followed the philosophy of "the employee can do no wrong." It seems that three years earlier a manager had written a formal complaint about an employee and put it in the employee's personnel file. The disgruntled employee complained directly to one of the corporate vice-presidents. The vice-president immediately went to the personnel office and ripped up the complaint before even conferring with the manager about the case.

The manager I spoke to was dismayed because, in almost three years with the company, he hadn't seen anything like this event repeated, and yet the story kept circulating. "Why is the story so powerful?" he asked. "Why do people continue to believe that what happened three years ago still is the way this company does things now?"

Stories are one of the most important sources of information, for people in organizations, about "how things are done around here." When told by several people, organizational stories may become the best way of passing on a distinctive competence or philosophy that is the key to a company's success. The following story from the Minnesota Mining and Manufacturing Company (3M) illustrates this point well.

At 3M the 11th commandment is: "Never kill a new product idea." This emphasis on innovation is supported by a story about the discovery of transparent cellophane tape. The story relates how an employee accidentally discovered the tape but was unable to get his superiors to buy the idea. Marketing studies predicted a relatively small demand for the new material. Undaunted, the employee found a way to sneak into the boardroom and tape down the minutes with his transparent tape. The board was impressed enough with the

†SOURCE: Alan Wilkins, *Exchange*, Fall 1981. Reprinted by permission of EXCHANGE, a publication of the Brigham Young University School of Management.

novelty to give it a try, and the cellophane tape was an incredible success.

Today's 3M employees thus are encouraged to be entrepreneurs, to try out new ideas in the marketplace rather than putting their trust in market forecasts.

Why Stories?

For the new employee, the organization is like a foreign culture—you have to learn how to fit in and avoid major blunders. When traveling in a foreign country, it is of course useful to have a map that shows you how to get from one place to another. However, avoiding social blunders and really understanding another culture requires a different kind of map—a social map. The new employee needs a social map that will point out the dangerous areas and the safe turf. Organizational stories are an important way to map this social territory.

Shortly after starting a job, the new employee learns that knowing certain ways of thinking and acting (we are a "conservative company," "look busy," "don't kill a new product idea") really are more important than knowing the formal rules.

One scholar has suggested that these different maps or ways of directing behavior can be categorized into three orders of control:

• First-order controls—direct control by a supervisor who tells an employee what to do.
• Second-order controls—more remote operating procedures deriving from standard operating procedures and organizational incentive systems or from an assembly-line layout.
• Third-order controls—control through directing the attention or assumptions of company employees.

An example of the subtlety of these third-order controls comes from the experience of a high-ranking personnel executive stationed for a time in the Far East. He and another manager were confronted one day with an emergency decision. They tried to get some help on a problem for which formal rules and official policies were inadequate, but were unable to get through. They sat down together, and the first question was, "Well, what would the company president do?" The personnel executive then recalled an experience he had heard the president relate and the conclusion the president had drawn. The president's example gave these men a sense of where to start and a basis on which to make a decision. They later found that top management agreed fully with their actions.

This kind of control works by restricting what decision makers consider relevant, defining the appropriate form of logical reasoning and the kinds of solutions that are acceptable.

Symbolism

Anthropologist Emile Durkheim claimed that shared symbols are necessary for cultural cohesion. Contemporary organizations also need to obtain some cohesion so that the various subunits cooperate for the good of the company. Stories like the one about the inventor of Scotch tape at 3M serve as symbols of an orientation and values that can unify participants from diverse organizational subunits.

Tom Peters of McKinsey & Company, Inc., a management-consulting firm, reported that in a study of 70 successful US companies the key common features were simple structure, avoidance of number-driven bureaucracy, and a focus on a "key business theme." Peters's study of successful executives in these companies suggests that managers have more control over their organizations through a simple overarching theme than through strategic planning, structural rearrangements, or organizational development efforts. Examples of such themes are Harold S. Geneen's "search for the unshakable facts" at ITT, Alden Winship Clausen's "laying pipe" (shorthand for anticipating and preparing for events) at Bank of America, John D. deButts's "the system is the solution" at AT&T, or Thomas V. Jones's "everybody at Northrop is in marketing."

A key business theme may be most useful as a third-order control when it is exemplified by shared stories. That is especially true when the stories are seen not as rules but as examples. An electronics company with widely shared stories exemplifying its managerial philosophy had much higher levels of commitment to the company and sense of community than a competitor with no such stories.

Stories as Scripts

Many stories become scripts that help employees learn about acceptable behavior or attitudes or what they can expect the organization to do in the future. They also provide a way to map the future, using the past as a guide. For example, most employees in a large West Coast electronics firm know the story about how the company avoided a mass layoff in the early 1970s when other companies in the industry laid off many employees. Instead of dismissing 10 percent of its employees, this company had everyone take a 10 percent cut in salary and had the employees work only nine out of ten working days.

This experience became known as the "nine-day fortnight" and apparently is used as a script by the company. In 1974 the company again was confronted with a drop in orders, and it went to the "nine-day fortnight" scheme for a short period. Today old-timers use this story to quiet the anxiety of concerned newcomers. The story is a script that employees use to predict the behavior of the company and that managers use to make decisions when layoff pressures mount.

Of course, not all stories will be as useful to the whole organization as they are to the people within the organization. Some stories teach participants how to beat the system. A top personnel officer told of how the current company president had made it to the top. The story goes back to the time when the president was an executive vice-president. This company faced a serious drop in orders due to a softening economy. The then-president had just left the country for a working vacation, and the ambitious executive vice-president took advantage of this opportunity to fly to the distant meeting of the board of directors and offer the directors an ultimatum. He announced that he had been offered the presidency of a competitor and planned to accept the offer unless the board made him president of the company. The then-president was a bright man but wasn't tough enough to make the kinds of decisions needed at the time. The board of directors discussed the ultimatum, eventually deciding in favor of making the then-president vice-chairman of the board in charge of research and development, and installing the executive vice-president as president.

This story symbolizes nicely the climate in this organization. It represents how many managers feel about their relationship to the company and teaches them some specific ways to protect themselves. But it is not conducive to a company culture where long-term innovation and cooperative development of ideas across the divisions can occur. Officials in this company complained to me on several occasions that they just couldn't seem to increase their sales. The story and its popularity in the organization suggest many of the reasons.

Among business stories, the most common themes have to do with the perceived relationship between an employee and the organization. When employees see that the organizational representatives are fair and have the interest of the employees at heart, the stories reflect that feeling. Such stories are used to pass on persuasively to newcomers the self-fulfilling prophecy that problems can be worked out. But when employees feel that they are mere "hands" and not whole "human beings," they tend to be cautious and share stories that helped them prepare for confrontation or escape.

An example of this idea comes from an experience reported by Dick Walton of Harvard Business School. He was studying a new plant start-up and found that numerous employees told him the same story when interviewed. Before the plant opened, managers and employees had met to draft a statement of principles that would guide their relationship. One of the most important of these principles was that employees and management would trust and treat one another as partners in the plant. This was symbolized by establishing an open cash box. Anyone could put in an IOU, borrow cash and then pay the box back within some period of time.

When the plant manager arrived at work one morning, he discovered that everyone was talking about an employee who had taken $60 from the cash box without leaving an IOU. Several people predicted that this would be the beginning of the end for the new trust policy. Three managers held a quick meeting and then called the employees together. The plant manager said he regretted that the money was gone and hoped it would be returned. He then pulled $10 out of his own pocket and said he wanted to contribute personally to replenishing the cash box. Several others quickly followed suit, and the trust policy was reconfirmed. The employees used the story to show that the management gave them a fair chance and that the idea of trust still was alive in their plant after the incident.

T. J. Watson, Jr., a past chief executive officer of IBM, claims that creating a successful, long-run company involves three steps:

• Start by describing your beliefs—what you feel are the important themes ("IBM means service") and values ("the dignity of the individual must be maintained").

• Incorporate those beliefs in programs, policies, organizational structure and incentive systems so that practice always is consistent with belief.

• Change the operating procedures whenever necessary to remain competitive while still being consistent with the beliefs. The important idea here is that the beliefs, not the programs, are enduring.

Managers ought to exemplify the values in many ways rather than launching a single major program. By pointing to the value rather than the programs, employees are able to adjust to changes that leave values intact. Managers who become sensitive to symbols and stories realize that they are managing meanings and not just numbers of bodies.

53

Transformational Leadership†

The leader of an organization exerts a major impact on corporate culture. His or her influence is rarely neutral!

In the following pages, Noel Tichy and David Ulrich discuss what James McGregor Burns (1978) has called "transformational leadership": leadership that can get beyond the problems of holding an organization together, to set it on a new course.

To revitalize organizations such as General Motors, American Telephone and Telegraph, General Electric, Honeywell, Ford, Burroughs, Chase Manhattan Bank, Citibank, U.S. Steel, Union Carbide, Texas Instruments, and Control Data—just to mention a few companies currently undergoing major transformations—a new brand of leadership is necessary. Instead of managers who continue to move organizations along historical tracks, the new leaders must transform the organizations and head them down new tracks. What is required of this kind of leader is an ability to help the organization develop a vision of what it can be, to mobilize the organization to accept and work toward achieving the new vision, and to institutionalize the changes that must last over time. Unless the creation of this breed of leaders becomes a national agenda, we are not very optimistic about the revitalization of the U.S. economy.

We call these new leaders transformational leaders, for they must create something new out of something old: out of an old vision, they must develop and communicate a new vision and get others not only to see the vision but also to commit themselves to it. Where transactional managers make only minor adjustments in the organization's mission, structure, and human resource management, transformational leaders not only make major changes in these three areas but they also evoke fundamental changes in the basic political and cultural systems of the organization. The revamping of the political and cultural systems is what most distinguishes the transformational leader from the transactional one.

One of the most dramatic examples of transformational leadership and organizational revitalization in the early 1980s has been the leadership of Lee Iacocca, the chairman of Chrysler Corporation. He provided the leader-

†SOURCE: Excerpted from "The Leadership Challenge—A Call for the Transformational Leader" by Noel M. Tichy and David O. Ulrich, SLOAN MANAGEMENT REVIEW, Fall 1984, pp. 59-68. Copyright © 1984 by the Sloan Management Review Association. All rights reserved; used by permission.

ship to transform a company from the brink of bankruptcy to profitability. He created a vision of success and mobilized large factions of key employees toward enacting that vision while simultaneously downsizing the workforce by 60,000 employees. As a result of Iacocca's leadership, by 1984 Chrysler had earned record profits, had attained high levels of employee morale, and had helped employees generate a sense of meaning in their work. . . . There are three identifiable programs of activity associated with transformational leadership.

1. Creation of a Vision.   The transformational leader must provide the organization with a vision of a desired future state. While this task may be shared with other key members of the organization, the vision remains the core responsibility of the transformational leader. The leader needs to integrate analytic, creative, intuitive, and deductive thinking. Each leader must create a vision which gives direction to the organization while being congruent with the leader's and the organization's philosophy and style.

For example, in the early 1980s at GM, after several years of committee work and staff analysis, a vision of the future was drafted which included a mission statement and eight objectives for the company. This statement was the first articulation of a strategic vision for General Motors since Alfred Sloan's leadership. This new vision was developed consistently with the leadership philosophy and style of Roger Smith. Many people were involved in carefully assessing opportunities and constraints for General Motors. Meticulous staff work culminated in committee discussions to evoke agreement and commitment to the mission statement. Through this process a vision was created which paved the way for the next phases of the transformation at GM.

At Chrysler, Lee Iacocca developed a vision without committee work or heavy staff involvement. Instead, he relied more on his intuitive and directive leadership, philosophy, and style. Both GM and Chrysler ended up with a new vision because of transformational leaders pro-

actively shaping a new organization mission and vision. The long-term challenge to organizational revitalization is not "how" the visions are created but the extent to which the visions correctly respond to environmental pressures and transitions within the organization.

2. Mobilization of Commitment.   Here, the organization, or at least a critical mass of it, accepts the new mission and vision and makes it happen. At General Motors, Roger Smith took his top 900 executives on a five-day retreat to share and discuss the vision. The event lasted five days not because it takes that long to share a one-paragraph mission statement and eight objectives, but because the process of evolving commitment and mobilizing support requires a great deal of dialogue and exchange. It should be noted that mobilization of commitment must go well beyond five-day retreats; nevertheless, it is in this phase that transformational leaders get deeper understanding of their *followers*. Maccoby acknowledges that leaders who guide organizations through revitalization are distinct from previous leaders and gamesmen who spearheaded managers to be winners in the growth days of the 1960s and early 1970s. Today, Maccoby argues:

The positive traits of the gamesman, enthusiasm, risk taking, meritocratic fairness, fit America in a period of unlimited economic growth, hunger for novelty, and an unquestioned career ethic. The negative traits for manipulation, seduction, and the perpetual adolescent need for adventure were always problems, causing distrust and unnecessary crises. The gamesman's daring, the willingness to innovate and take risks are still needed. Companies that rely on conservative company men in finance to run technically based organizations (for example, auto and steel) lose the competitive edge. But unless their negative traits are transformed or controlled, even gifted gamesmen become liabilities as leaders in a new economic reality. A period of limited resources and cutbacks, when the team can no longer be controlled by the promise of more, and one person's gains may be another's loss, leadership with values of caring and integrity and a vision of self-development must create the trust that no one will be penalized for cooperation and that sacrifice as well as rewards are equitable.

After transformational leaders create a vision and mobilize commitment, they must determine how to institutionalize the new mission and vision.

3. *Institutionalization of Change.* Organizations will not be revitalized unless new patterns of behavior within the organization are adopted. Transformational leaders need to transmit their vision into reality, their mission into action, their philosophy into practice. New realities, action, and practices must be shared throughout the organization. Alterations in communication, decision making, and problem-solving systems are tools through which transitions are shared so that visions become a reality. At a deeper level, institutionalization of change requires shaping and reinforcement of a new culture that fits with the revitalized organization. The human resource systems of selection, development, appraisal, and reward are major levers for institutionalizing change. . . .

What Qualities Do Transformational Leaders Possess?

So what does it take to transform an organization's technical, political, and cultural systems? The transformational leader must possess a deep understanding, whether it be intuitive or learned, of organizations and their place both in society at large and in the lives of individuals. The ability to build a new institution requires the kind of political dialogue our founding fathers had when Jefferson, Hamilton, Adams, and others debated issues of justice, equity, separation of powers, checks and balances, and freedom. This language may sound foreign to corporate settings but when major organization revitalization is being undertaken, all of these concepts merit some level of examination. At Chrysler, issues of equity, justice, power, and freedom underlay many of Mr. Iacocca's decisions. Thus, as a start, transformational leaders need to understand concepts of equity, power, freedom, and the dynamics of decision making. In addition to modifying systems, transformational leaders must understand and realign cultural systems.

In addition to managing political and cultural systems, transformational leaders must make difficult decisions quickly. Leaders need to know when to push and when to back off. Finally, transformational leaders are often seen as creators of their own luck. These leaders seize opportunities and know when to act so that casual observers may perceive luck as a plausible explanation for their success; whereas, in reality it is a transformational leader who knows when to jump and when not to jump. Again, Mr. Iacocca can be viewed either as a very lucky person or as the possessor of a great ability to judge when to act and when not to act.

REFERENCES

Burns, J. McGregor. *Leadership.* New York: Harper & Row, 1978.
Maccoby, M. *The Gamesman.* New York: Simon and Schuster, 1976.

54

The Tandem Corporation:
A Successful Corporate Culture?[†]

Here's a look inside Tandem: a computer firm that places a lot of emphasis on creating and sustaining a vibrant corporate culture:

The Tandem Corporation, one of Silicon Valley's most highly publicized companies, is a company whose president deliberately manages the "informal," human side of the business. Founded by four former Hewlett-Packard employees, Tandem has built a highly successful company by solving a simple problem: the tendency of computers to break down. By yoking two computers together in one mainframe, Tandem offers customers the assurance that they will always have computer power available. If one of the processors breaks down, the other will carry on.

"Tandem is saying something about the product and people working together. Everything here works together. People with people; product with product; even processor with processor, within the product. Everything works together to keep us where we are." The quotation is not from Jim Treybig, Tandem's chief executive officer. It came from one of Tandem's managers, and the same sentiment is echoed through the ranks of the employees:

"I feel like putting a lot of time in. There is a real kind of loyalty here. We are all working in this together—working a process together. I'm not a workaholic—it's just the place. I love the place."

"I don't want anything in the world that would hurt Tandem. I feel totally divorced from my old company, but not Tandem."

These employees seem to be describing an ideal corporation, one most managers would give their eyeteeth to create. And by most standards, Tandem is enormously successful. It is growing at the rate of 25 percent per quarter, with annual revenues over $100 million. The turnover rate is nearly three times below the national average for the computer industry. Tandem's loyal employees like their jobs and the company's product. They are led by a talented group of experienced managers, a group which so far has been able to handle the phenomenal growth of the company.

Only time will tell whether Tandem can maintain its pattern of high performance. While it is easy to attribute the success of the company to fast growth and lack of competition, other things at work internally at Tandem suggest an interesting rival explanation—that

[†]SOURCE: Excerpted from Terrence E. Deal and Allan A. Kennedy, *Corporate Cultures: The Rites and Rituals of Corporate Life*—Deal/Kennedy, *Corporate Cultures*, © 1982, Addison-Wesley Publishing Co., Inc., Reading, Massachusetts. Pages 8-13. Reprinted with permission.

the strong culture of Tandem produces its success. Here is how.

A Widely Shared Philosophy. Tandem is founded on a well-ordered set of management beliefs and practices. The philosophy of the company emphasizes the importance of people: "that's Tandem's greatest resource—its people, creative action, and fun." This ethic is widely shared and exemplified by slogans that everyone knows and believes in:

"It's so nice, it's so nice, we do it twice."

"It takes two to Tandem."

"Get the job done no matter what it takes."

"Tandemize it—means make it work."

The slogans are broadcast by T-shirts, bulletin boards, and word of mouth.

Top management spends about half of its time in training and in communicating the management philosophy and the essence of the company. Work is underway on a book that will codify the philosophy for future generations of workers at Tandem. "The philosophy is our future," one senior manager notes:

"It mostly tells the 'whats' and 'hows' for selecting people and growing managers. Even though everything else around here changes, I don't want what we believe in and what we want to change."

At Tandem the management philosophy is not an afterthought, it's a principal preoccupation.

The Importance of People. Tandem has no formal organizational chart and few formal rules. Its meetings and memos are almost nonexistent. Jobs are flexible in terms of duties and hours. The absence of name tags and reserved parking spaces suggests a less well-defined hierarchy than is typical in the corporate world. Despite this, the organization works and people get their jobs done.

What keeps employees off each other's toes and working in the same direction? One pos-

sibility is the unwritten rules and shared understandings. As one person put it: "There are a lot of unwritten rules. But there is also a lot of freedom to make a jerk out of yourself. Most of the rules are philosophical rules." Another is dispersed authority:

"The open door policy gives me access to anyone—even the president."

"Everyone here, managers, vice-presidents, and even janitors, communicate on the same level. No one feels better than anyone else."

Tandem seems to maintain a balance between autonomy and control without relying heavily on centralized or formalized procedures, or rigid status hierarchies.

Heroes: The President and the Product. Jim Treybig is a hero at Tandem, and his employees confirm it:

"Jimmy is really a symbol here. He's a sign that every person here is a human being. He tries to make you feel part of the organization from the first day you are here. That's something people talk about."

"The one thing you have to understand about the company—Treybig's bigger than life."

Treybig shares the hero's limelight with the Tandem Continuous 10 Computer—the backbone product of the company. The computer design is the company's logo and provides the metaphor for the "working together" philosophy.

"The product is phenomenal, everyone is proud to be part of it."
"When a big order was shipped, everyone in the plant was taking pictures. There were 'oh's' and 'ah's'. People were applauding. Can you believe it? For a computer."

Treybig and the computer share the main spotlight. But there are countless other heroes at Tandem—people whose achievements are regularly recognized on bulletin boards as "Our Latest Greatests."

Ritual and Ceremony.   Tandem is renowned for its Friday afternoon "beer-busts" which everyone attends. But the ritual does more than help people wind down after a busy work week. It serves as an important vehicle for informal communication and mingling across groups.

Tandem's emphasis on ritual, ceremony, and play is not confined to beer-busts, however. There is a golf course, exercise room, and swimming pool. Company-wide celebrations are staged on important holidays. These provide opportunities for employees to develop a spirit of "oneness" and symbolize that Tandem cares about employees.

Tandem's attention to ritual and ceremony begins in its personnel selection interviews. During the hiring process, potential employees are called back two or three times for interviews and must accept the position before salary negotiations take place. The interviews have been likened to an "inquisition." The message conveyed to prospective employees is "we take longer, and take care of people we hire— because we really care." The impact of this process is significant.

"They had me here for four interviews. That's about four hours, for a position of stock clerk. It was clear that they were choosy about the people they hired. That said something about what they thought I was. They thought I was good."

Treybig personally appears at each orientation to welcome new employees and to explain the company's motivation and commitment philosophy. His appearance reinforces the honor of being accepted to work at Tandem. It's no surprise that people at Tandem feel special—after all, they were made to feel that way before they were hired. Moreover, they feel special because the company and its product are special. And their feelings are expressed in an unusual display of loyalty and commitment to the company.

"My goals follow the company's. It's the company and I. I think that's pretty true of everyone. We all want to see it work. You have to have it all or don't have any of it."

Employees see their work as linked to Tandem's success:

"My job is important, and if I don't do it, Tandem doesn't make a buck."

Tandem is a unique company. And much of its success appears as intimately tied to its culture as to its product and marketplace position. The company has explicit values and beliefs which its employees share. It has heroes. It has storytellers and stories. It has rituals and ceremonies on key occasions. Tandem appears to have a strong culture which creates a bond between the company and employees, and inspires levels of productivity unlike most other corporations. Established heroes, values, and rituals are crucial to a culture's continued strength, and Tandem has kept them. The trick is in sustaining the culture so that it in turn drives the company.

Will Tandem's culture last? Although Tandem is neither big enough nor old enough to judge whether or not it will ultimately take a place in the annals of great American business, we think it is off to a good start. Indeed, other companies like IBM and P&G have already succeeded in sustaining and evolving culture over generations. These strong culture companies truly are the giants of American industry. Yet, their cultures began taking shape in a way that was very similar to Tandem.

55

ServiceMaster:
Combining Vision and Control†

ServiceMaster is one of America's most successful companies. Specializing in the provision of support services to health, educational, commercial, and industrial organizations—such as those relating to plant operations and maintenance, laundry, linen and janitorial services, materials management, and food service management—ServiceMaster has established an enviable record of growth, profit, and productivity. It frequently ranks among the best of the big companies in return on equity, with operating revenues exceeding $1 billion. It has set its sights on a figure of $2 billion for 1990.

One of the special characteristics of the company rests in how it has combined a quest for bottom-line efficiency with a set of corporate values that emphasize the importance of helping people—whether employees, customers, or the public at large. Every task that the company performs—whether polishing a floor or preparing a buffet meal—is meticulously organized. The company devotes considerable research to finding the best way of doing a job, often creating its own tools and materials, and ensures that employees are thoroughly trained, and motivated to achieve excellent results. In the following pages, ServiceMaster Chairman Kenneth T. Wessner explains how the company achieves its exceptional levels of performance by linking vision and control.

"Vision determines why. Controls determine how, when, where, with what, and through whom."

"The vision of your company must promise a benefit to them in order to be meaningful."

"Profitable growth is not an end in itself, but a means through which to achieve more visionary objectives."

"We need to redefine controls. Instead of a regulatory process, let us speak of building a team."

"Studies point out consistently that top performers are motivated by positive aspects of controls, not negative."

"Your personal dedication to the vision of your

†SOURCE: K. W. Wessner, "A Company Needs Vision as Well as Controls," *Management Review*, vol. 70, no. 8. Reprinted, by permission of the publisher, from MANAGEMENT REVIEW, August 1981 © 1981 American Management Association, New York. All rights reserved.

company is the basis on which employees judge the fairness of your controls."

How does a growing service business set management controls that will keep pace with business without threatening to extinguish the organization's entrepreneurial enthusiasm or commitment to personal service for each customer?

It may be argued that services cannot be treated like manufactured goods or that people who provide services cannot be managed with the same system of tight controls as production workers. On the other hand, one cannot expect to endure growth without some kind of accountability system. You may be able to achieve growth, as some companies have, by tapping into the rapidly expanding services market. But the question then becomes one of whether or not you will survive the growth you experienced.

The ultimate responsibility of management is survival, hence the dilemma for a growing service business.

• If you set rigid controls on the expanding delivery system, they may alter the atmosphere, the "package" surrounding the service "product," so that the product no longer is attractive to customers—or to the new employees required to make the expanding system work.

• If you pay little attention to controls, you may see the delivery of service become unprofitable or increasingly unwieldy and unreliable.

The solution to this dilemma lies in the interaction of two managerial elements: vision and control.

Vision determines why an organization is doing what it is doing. Controls determine how, when, where, with what, and through whom the enterprise is to accomplish its objectives. Successful management depends not simply on establishing these two elements, but on relating them in a way that each has an influence on shaping the other.

This interaction is especially important in a service organization. Unlike customers of a manufacturing concern, which competes on the basis of product comparison, the customer for a service most often will distinguish one provider from another on the basis of their differing management policies. From the customer's point of view, these management policies are seen in the way a service company understands and serves their needs.

In the health-care industry, for example, there is a great deal of emphasis currently on cost containment. But the deeper concern of most people in this field—whether administrators or medical professionals—is the quality of care provided the patient. The orientation of people in the health-care profession continues to be primarily one of compassion, of concern for people and caring for their needs.

A service organization that approaches this market with a cost-effective program, but no credible atmosphere of concern for people, will almost certainly provoke a negative response. It will have failed to project to customers a feeling that it is aware of what really motivates people in this field, how they perceive the work they are doing, what kind of help they feel they need in doing it.

In the excitement of rapid expansion, it is easy to confer the mantle of a vision on continued growth itself. On the surface, at least, a chorus of "We want to grow!" may seem to ring with enthusiasm. But is commitment to your own growth really visionary? Does it really project a commitment to the customer? Does it portray any sense of social responsibility beyond the narrow aim of making a profit? As attractive as this may be to prospective investors and career-minded employees, how attractive will this essentially self-centered theme appear to those who, by taking on your service, become dependent upon you? Or to those who are critics of free enterprise and advocate its close regulation—or elimination?

The customer and the community at large are concerned with their own needs, not yours. The vision of your company must promise a benefit to them in order to be meaningful to them. But it must do so in a way that is credible. It must indicate an awareness of the realities of business. "We'll do whatever it takes to please you" is not a vision, for example. It is advertising. As your customer knows, effort always implies cost. If you promise to spare no effort, therefore, who is to assume the cost? Will it appear in the price to the customer, in the profit to shareholders, in the pay to your employees, or in some residual social or environmental "cost" charged to the community around you? These are the business realities that must be reflected in your vision.

In my own organization, ServiceMaster Industries Inc., we feel that our corporate purpose—the why of our enterprise—is, in the broadest sense, to have an influence for good in our society, in our government, and in people's lives. To express this in words that are both visionary and realistic we have established four corporate objectives:

1. To honor God in all we do.
2. To help people develop.
3. To pursue excellence.
4. To grow profitably.

By working to accomplish these objectives, we feel we can exercise our responsibilities both externally, to our customers and the community around us, and internally, to our employees and shareholders. Our customers, as well as our employees and shareholders, will agree that it is essential to be profitable if we are to provide the services we have promised to deliver, the career opportunities for employees, and the return on investment made in our company.

We perceive profitable growth not as an end in itself, but as a means through which to achieve other, more visionary objectives. The pursuit of excellence, our third objective, is similarly viewed as a means to an end rather than an end in itself. Our first two objectives—to honor God and to help people develop—are indeed visionary. But they also are pragmatic in that we recognize how completely they depend on the company's profitable growth and sound management in order to be accomplished.

To be meaningful, vision cannot simply be talked about. It must be lived. It must be made an integral part of the enterprise. It must be incorporated into the lives—both professional and personal—of people throughout the organization. This is where sound management controls play their part.

Controls in a business organization have been defined as a formal system for:

- Establishing objectives
- Measuring and evaluating performance
- Taking action to improve performance

Another definition is that controls are a means of assuring that resources are obtained and used effectively to accomplish the organization's objectives.

Although these definitions have a utilitarian ring to them, they also emphasize the relentless and regulatory nature of controls. Like the governor on an engine, they seem intent on restraining the organization, rather than letting it "rev up" freely. Such definitions do not show much of the spirit of an enterprise that wants to build on a vision and grow at a substantial pace. Remember that the challenge is to find ways for visions and controls to influence each other. Where is the vision in these definitions?

To infuse controls with a vision we need to redefine what they are. Instead of emphasizing the regulatory process, let us speak of the process of building a team, the process of creating a sense of shared enterprise. Controls are not something to be legislated by top management. Instead they should be an expression of top management's leadership. The responsibility of management is not to get employees to toe the line or follow procedures, but rather to help them share in the vision of the company.

How can this be accomplished? One of the most important and effective control mechanisms for building teamwork is education and training. At ServiceMaster, for example, we invest a great deal of time and effort in education and training of people at every level of our company. The focus of this activity is not so much on what we want our people to do, but rather on what we want people to be.

Another essential element of team building for management control is planning. To build teamwork through planning the company must involve employees in determining both the future of the organization and what their own individual role is in achieving that future.

Our current planning process in Service-Master looks forward over the next 20 years. There are hundreds of people participating in this process. They represent every segment of the company and every level of management. The effect of this enlarged planning process is a sense of teamwork, a shared interest pervading our plans for the future.

Studies of the impact management controls have on a worker's quality of performance and level of job satisfaction show that three factors are involved in a successful control system:

First, controls must seek to make clear what the organization expects of the individual worker. Second, controls must be established in such a way that the workers feel some sense of influence and control over their work situation. Third, controls must include a formal and continuous evaluation in which the worker can expect rewards for good performance as well as corrective action for failure to meet expectations.

It would be a mistake to focus only on the negative, legislative aspects of this control process. It is counterproductive to stress only the expectations placed on the worker and the promise of corrective action for failure to meet those expectations. Yet this may be the implication most often drawn when the term "controls" is used.

What studies have pointed out consistently is that top performers are motivated by the positive aspects of the control process. Promise of reward is especially important as a motivating factor. But the degree of autonomy a person feels in deciding how to accomplish what is needed by the organization also plays a significant role in motivating top performance. People are motivated to the extent they

feel valued as members of the team, able to contribute creatively to achieving the vision.

Further, people are motivated to the extent to which their personal vision corresponds with that of the organization. This dynamic union of purposes between the individual and the organization cannot be legislated. People must be *led* to see the advantages of linking their personal goals with those of the company. How can such leadership be achieved? How does a manager begin to build a team?

The key lies in the effort of the leader to maintain personal and corporate integrity. As part of the initial process of establishing controls, it is necessary that you as a leader:

• Understand yourself. Know what your own values are and what purpose you see for your life.

• Understand your company, the requirements placed on you by its sense of values and purpose.

• Make sure these two elements are compatible.

Out of that compatibility will come a shared sense of vision and purpose that you as a leader can successfully communicate to your workers. You must share the dream. Your personal enthusiasm will attract others to join you in an exciting venture. It also will influence the way your employees respond to the controls you establish. Your personal dedication to accomplishing the vision of your company will be the basis on which your employees judge the fairness of your controls.

That dedication will not be simply to a job. If you are sincere in determining what you stand for, that dedication will become a way of life. The controls you will establish, in that case, will be no more and no less than the disciplines you have imposed on yourself in order to accomplish the vision. Rather than chafe under such controls, your employees will recognize these disciplines as a formula for achieving a level of success and self-realization similar to your own.

REFERENCES

"Servicemaster: Looking for New Worlds to Clean."
Business Week, 19 January 1987, 60-61.

Skolnik, R. "Marketing Cleanliness with Godliness."
S & MM, 5 December 1983, 34-37.

Wade, M. E. *The Lord Is My Counsel: A Businessman's
Personal Experiences with the Bible.* Englewood
Cliffs, NY: Prentice-Hall, 1966.

56

Life on the
Fast Lane at Datsun†

Japanese organizations have developed a reputation for their strong sense of corporate culture, particularly those aspects that unite and direct the organization toward achievement of common goals. The following article by John Junkerman provides an additional perspective, showing how exterior harmony may be accompanied by internal dissent, and how union power has been mobilized as a force supporting management control.

When the assembly line stops for the morning break at the Datsun plant in the town of Zama, one hour southwest of Tokyo, none of the workers puts down his tools. For a good two or three minutes into the break, the sound of impactors and clanging steel continues throughout the plant. A worker in tennis shoes and a baseball cap finishes attaching a bumper, turns to the next car on the line to fasten a license plate, then squeezes rubber trim around a rear window. Another worker stacks brake fluid reservoirs close to the line and fiddles with a troublesome fastener that has slowed his production during the morning's first stint.

The guide from the plant's public relations office is quick to point out this industrious behavior to the caravans of Western executives who come regularly to the Zama factory in search of the secret of success. The company has become adept at showing visitors what they long to see: an indefatigable work force whose primary goals are to boost productivity and to make the company No. 1.

Nissan Motor Company (official name of the corporation that manufactures Datsun cars and trucks) conceives of itself as something of an industrial Nirvana. "Quality through harmony . . . the unsung harmony of man and machine," exults one company film. Mutual trust between labor and management has created a "community full of vitality," declares Nissan's chairman, Katsuji Kawamata. "We don't use the term *worker* anymore," adds a company spokesperson. "Everyone is an employee of the company and a member of the Nissan family."

This "oneness" between labor and management is credited with making Nissan the third-largest vehicle manufacturer in the world—after General Motors and Toyota—and with making Japan the dominant force in the world auto industry. Japanese firms passed Detroit

---

†SOURCE: John Junkerman, "We Are Driven," *Mother Jones*, August 1982, pp. 21-23, 38-40; used by permission.

in the multinational road race in 1980, and they have left the rest of the world sputtering in the dust.

The dazzling performance of Japan's automobile industry (not to mention its electronics, steel and—more recently—computer industries) has created an army of converts among management consultants and business writers in the United States. Best sellers extol the art of Japanese management, and overnight experts command four-figure fees for teaching seminars on how to import the Japanese economic model.

But there is a dark side to the Japanese industrial miracle, a side that becomes easily apparent after talking with the harried workers on the Nissan shop floor. Over the past five years, Nissan has stepped up its vehicle output by 25 percent without hiring additional workers. The company has accomplished this astonishing feat by running the assembly line at a frenzied pace. "A few years ago we could talk, even joke around a bit on the line," comments one assembly worker. "Now if the manager sees you talking while you're working, he'll give you more work to do. The other night I saw a television documentary about an American auto plant," he added wistfully, "and the workers were smoking and waving at the camera. Here we don't have the margin to do that—we're driven to the wall." According to another line worker, "If you drop a bolt, you don't have time to pick it up. After all," he muttered, "this is Nissan; so there is no time to spare."

Nissan would prefer to think that its speedy assembly workers are motivated by a sense of loyalty and gratitude, which, in some cases, they undoubtedly are. More to the point, however, is the fact that the company and its union have joined together to create a powerful system of control and intimidation that mass-produces cooperative and efficient workers as reliably as the assembly line churns out subcompacts. Harmony and diligence at Nissan are the product of union and managerial policies that reward conformity, punish even the mildest dissent with wage discrimination

and ostracism from the work group, and—in extreme cases—contribute to ruthless persecution and violence. Both the union and management demand total participation and commitment to production from every Nissan employee.

It is this unique and eerie system of joint management-union control that explains why the workers at Nissan's Zama plant don't skip a beat when break time rolls around.

A stone monument stands just inside the main gate to the Nissan assembly plant at Oppama, on the south shore of Tokyo Bay, where the popular Bluebird (Datsun 810) is produced. It is adorned with two sculpted bluebirds and engraved with the words of a former union president, rendered in calligraphy by Nissan's chairman of the board: "It is necessary to insist on one's rights, and it is splendid to fight for that purpose," the labor official's words read. "But the 'bluebird' of happiness does not alight in the swamps of spite where the storms of struggle rage. . . . Mutual trust between labor and management is the wellspring and the pride of Nissan."

For nearly 30 years, the Nissan Labor Union has strived to keep the company's bluebird of happiness from flying away. The current union was established with company support in 1953, during Nissan's successful campaign to smash a more militant auto workers union. The Nissan Labor Union's founding slogan was: "Those who truly love their union, love their company. Wage increases shall derive from increasing productivity."

Ichiro Shioji heads the Nissan labor organization and also serves as president of the Confederation of Japanese Automobile Workers Unions (JAW), which represents the industry's 600,000 laborers. Shioji—who earns about $75,000 a year, owns a $200,000 yacht and drives a telephone-equipped Nissan President— is one of Japan's leading champions of cooperative unionism. Says Nissan chairman Kawamata, "Shioji is a man who conceives of things primarily from the perspective of management." So entwined has Shioji become with Nissan management since he took over the union in 1960 that he has been called "Nissan's other president."

Shioji's union in fact performs many of management's more distasteful tasks, including monitoring workers' performance and attitudes, punishing dissent and boosting workers' output. The union-directed productivity campaign, known as the Three P Movement, aims to raise *productivity* through the *participation* of the workers to bring about the *progress* of the company and society at large. Although the campaign has the specific goal of increasing productivity ten percent and reducing faulty parts 20 percent per year, its actual purpose is much broader: "More than the material results of increased productivity," union documents state, "what is important is whether each individual is productivity-minded, with a high union consciousness and a high social consciousness. It is a movement to improve morals."

The union's emphasis on attitude reflects a basic feature of Nissan worklife: it is not enough just to do one's job; Nissan workers have to believe in their work as well. Since a major portion of their paycheck hinges on their positive evaluation by supervisors, Nissan workers are under constant pressure to prove their commitment.

The primary mechanism for promoting productivity at Nissan is the quality control (Q.C.) circle. These small groups, organized on the shop floor to examine ways of improving product quality and manufacturing efficiency, have become the symbol of Japanese management throughout the world. Ostensibly a voluntary activity on the part of the workers, the groups are said to give each individual a sense of participation in management. Some 4,000 such groups have been organized at Nissan. Attendance in the Q.C. circles, which meet after work and during lunch, is not officially required; nonetheless, virtually all of Nissan's workers are involved in the groups—not to participate would reflect a lack of "productivity-mindedness."

The ideas that emerge from Nissan's Q.C. circles are of undisputed value to the company:

in 1980 alone they helped save the auto firm as much as $60 million. Whether or not the workers themselves benefit from this form of self-management, however, is debatable.

One assembly worker reports that during Q.C. circle meetings employees regularly perform simulated production tasks to devise ways of cutting time: "First we work one machine with the left hand, then another with the right; then we put one machine in front and another behind and work them simultaneously. Sometimes I feel like I'm involved in an experiment to determine how much a human being can stand."

One group decided that instead of knocking off early to clean up the shop and service the machines, they would do this maintenance after work hours. Since the Q.C. circles compete for company recognition and are afraid of being outdone by the others, this idea soon spread throughout the plant, and everyone began working an extra ten minutes a day. "Japanese workers aren't fools," says a square-jawed clutch assembler. "Everyone knows that it's strange to work without pay, but if you complain, you lose—it affects your pay and you won't get promoted."

Some Nissan laborers become so intent on winning company approval that they devise increasingly cosmetic suggestions and implement them on their own. For one such worker, the result was tragic. Sadamitsu Ada, a 50-year-old former miner from southern Japan, had found employment at Nissan's Oppama plant after his mine was shut down. He was eager to please. Last year, Ada suggested that a Danger sign be posted behind a drop-lifter, a machine that picks up painted auto bodies and transfers them to another line. While the machine was still operating (workers say that stopping machines is a taboo at Nissan), Ada climbed the safety barrier to install the sign. Before he could complete his mission, he was caught by the machine and crushed to death. According to interviews with workers, there has been a rash of similar accidents at Nissan: workers often try to repair or adjust a machine while it is still in operation to avoid halting production. "Both the company and the union bear responsibility for Ada's death," says one of his coworkers. "They have pushed the spirit of rationalization to the point where workers risk their lives for the sake of production."

It is not easy to pierce the shell that surrounds Nissan. Workers are reluctant to talk openly for fear that their words will be used against them; those who do talk ask not to be identified. When I arrange a meeting with Tsutumu Higashi (not his real name), an inspector from the Zama plant, at a nearby train station one evening, it is clear how pervasive this fear is. I follow him, ten paces behind, until we reach the privacy of his apartment, a two-room flat (the size of a one-car garage), where he lives with his wife and infant son. The precautions are necessary, Higashi tells me, because he has been followed home recently by a member from the plant. He once spoke against a union proposal at a shop-floor meeting and he has since been branded a radical and subjected to periodic surveillance.

"There's a pretense of 'family' at Nissan," Higashi says, "and workers are forced to put on a good face. The definition of the 'Nissan man' is one who is never late, never takes a day off and never complains. But the workers at Nissan don't depend on the company or on the union—they depend on themselves, on their own strength," he says, sipping a fresh cup of sake. We are sitting in his living room, which doubles as a bedroom—his futon mattresses are stacked to one side, leaving us little room to stretch out on the straw-mat-covered floor.

"Most workers won't even join the mutual-aid society," Higashi continues. "There's meaning and mutual aid even in a terrible union, and it only costs 100 yen [about 40 cents] a month. But it seems they don't trust people; they depend only on themselves. It really feels like I work in a desert, a shop-floor desert where all the workers are grains of sand—dry, unconnected. There's no sense of warmth, no shared humanity with the other workers."

When he began working for the auto company in 1970, says Higashi, there were a substantial number of young workers who resisted

the pressures to become "Nissan men." Many of them had been influenced by the student movements of the late '60s, and they brought demands for democracy into the factory. "But most of those with any consciousness quit," he recalls, "because they realized they couldn't stand working for that kind of company until retirement. Those who remain say, 'If I'm going to stay, I'll keep quiet and try to get promoted.' " Until about 1975, some 40 percent of Nissan's newly hired workers quit during their first year of employment, but in recent years this figure has fallen to ten percent because of the scarcity of other jobs.

There are still scattered signs of resistance at Nissan. One hears reports of small groups of dissidents—three or four workers at one plant, perhaps ten at another. One particularly bold group publishes an underground newspaper but prints just 15 copies. These are passed by hand to only the closest of friends. "The only time people say what they are really thinking is when they write on the toilet stalls," says an employee of a Nissan parts supplier.

What do the workers write? A brief inspection of one Nissan plant's bathroom stalls—not a designated stop on the official factory tour—would reveal a host of complaints. About assembly line speed-up: "This isn't a beer company—why are we increasing production at the height of summer? Hire more workers!" About the quality of cafeteria food: "Beware the revenge of those who eat!" And about the union: "A regular union—supports a union member who is fired. A good union—supports workers who are fired even if they aren't in the union. A bad union—takes the place of management and fires workers."

This last bitter scrawl is a reference to the sanctions taken by the union against a dissident group at the Atsugi Motor Parts Company, a Nissan subsidiary located outside of Tokyo. The "Atsugi Seven" are the most persistent and overt internal opposition Nissan has encountered in recent years. Since the early 1970s, this group of worker-activists has been speaking out on a wide range of issues—from the intense heat in the plant during the summer to the lack of democracy within the union. After suffering years of discrimination in wages and job assignments, five of the workers decided to sue the company and the union. In 1979, the company reached a settlement with the workers, giving them $100,000 in back pay. But the union wasn't satisfied: it pushed through a resolution at its annual convention to have the seven expelled from membership in the union shop—and thus from Nissan.

"We don't like to do things like that, but the other members at Atsugi threatened to circulate a petition if we didn't act," said a union spokesperson. "Those people take their orders from the Japan Communist party, and we have plenty of evidence to prove it." A Nissan official said: "For those people there is no consensus like we talk about here in Japan, so of course things are uncomfortable for them."

Things got more uncomfortable for them. In 1979, all of the Atsugi Seven were fired from their jobs. In January 1980, more than 200 union members were mobilized to attack them while they were distributing leaflets at a train station near the plant; five of the dissidents were hospitalized with injuries. The unionists who attacked them called them "termites" who were attempting to undermine the company.

"I like Nissan," says Masaharu Tsukamoto, one of the seven, as we sit in the group's small, cluttered storefront office. "I am proud of the cars we make, and I have confidence in them. That's a natural feeling for a worker to have . . . but I think it's strange for the union to demand to put the company in our hearts. I won't sell my soul to the company."

Indeed, there is much that is peculiar about the Nissan union. It has assumed primary responsibility for disciplining the work force, ferreting out dissidents and squashing opposition. "If there would happen to be someone who seeks to destroy the Nissan culture that we have forged together over the years, we must battle them without restraint," union president Shioji has said.

On the shop floor, members of the union's organizing committee watch vigilantly for signs of dissent. In the tenementlike dormitories attached to each of the factories, where young workers usually live for the first ten years of their work lives, members of the union's youth committee listen for complaints and report them back to the union office. When workers leave the dorms to enter company housing or to rent an apartment in town, there is a Nissan community organization—primarily a vehicle to mobilize support for the conservative, union-sponsored Democratic Socialist party—to monitor "Nissan culture" on the streets.

It does not take much to be labeled an enemy of the company, and it doesn't take long for Nissan workers to learn the consequences. Masao Kayama, an employee of Nissan Diesel, had the temerity to criticize the union's wage demand at a shop-floor meeting in 1974, at a time when Nissan was pushing for higher productivity and wage restraint in response to the first oil crisis. Kayama says he was promptly tagged a troublemaker and was cold-shouldered by his workmates. Workers in his shop refused to return his greetings and shunned him during breaks. Friends were warned that if they associated with him it would affect their wages and chances for promotion, just as it has affected Kayama: his pay is currently about $2,000 a year less than that of workers with equal seniority.

Exercising leverage over wages—a powerful weapon against dissent—is just one of the ways the Nissan union involves itself in what would be considered a management area in most industrialized countries. Another is promotions: the union reserves veto power over supervisory appointments, and virtually all production supervisors first serve as officers in the union before they are advanced. This type of clout is unusual even by Japanese standards. Most Japanese unions—such as the one that represents Toyota workers—play a much more passive role.

Lately the intimate relationship between Nissan's management and its union has come under some strain. Responding to criticism from business circles that Nissan had allowed its union officials too much power, corporate president Takashi Ishihara has mounted a concerted effort to reduce union influence. Among other steps, he has begun to limit Ichiro Shioji's access to the inner chambers of the corporation. While in the past Shioji was consulted about nearly everything—from model changes to corporate directors—talks with the union are now limited to wage negotiations.

Miffed at this treatment, Shioji has countered by making things difficult for Ishihara and openly threatens to oust him from power. The labor leader has gone so far as to call work stoppages, in one case shutting down the Oppama assembly line for a week after the accident in which Sadamitsu Ada was crushed to death.

While at first glance it might appear that the Ishihara-Shioji rivalry has suddenly converted the Nissan union to militancy, it is clear that the union's power is being used only to shore up its leadership, not to protect workers on the shop floor. Shioji continues to think, talk and act like a Nissan executive rather than a union president.

Last year the labor leader traveled to Mexico, where Nissan was building a new engine plant, to discuss "cooperative unionism" with a moderate union that is organizing the plant. Nissan has had a long-term dispute with a more militant union at its Mexican assembly plant, and Shioji's job was to prevent a similar situation from developing at the new factory. "It's our job," said the Nissan union president, "to cover for management and do the things they can't do themselves."

This spring, 120 leaders from auto workers unions throughout the world gathered in Tokyo—not to study the Japanese model, but to commiserate about the sorry state of their industry. Japan is the only major auto-producing nation that has not been shutting down assembly lines and laying off thousands of auto workers. The hardest hit, of course, has been the United States, where some 250,000 members of the United Auto Workers Union (UAW) are now jobless. Although the theme of the meeting was international solidarity, UAW President Douglas Fraser clearly wanted to put his Japanese union brothers on the hot seat.

Fraser's message to JAW officials was simple: Raise wages and cut work hours. The gap between Japanese and American auto workers' wages and benefits—estimated by General Motors at $8.95 an hour—was used earlier this year by G.M. and Ford to squeeze concessions from the UAW. "Of course, there is too wide a gap between us and Japan," Fraser told the conference. "But the way to correct this is to pull up the wages of underpaid Japanese workers—not to push down the wages of American workers."

Fraser's remarks were on target. Japanese auto workers' wages are low even by Japanese standards: they are about ten percent below the average wage in the Japanese steel and petro-chemical industries, for example. Despite the robust performance of Japanese auto-makers—Nissan alone chalked up $700 million in profits last year—JAW has not been pushing to catch up. And Japanese auto workers are not only underpaid—they are overworked too. As Fraser pointed out, Japanese workers put in about 300 more hours per year than their American counterparts.

The Japanese labor leaders gave Fraser a polite hearing but, according to UAW sources, told him—diplomatically—to mind his own business.

The other demand Fraser brought to Tokyo—for the Japanese to shift more vehicle production to the United States—may be eliciting a more favorable response. This is a natural demand for the UAW to make, considering that the Japanese have been selling more than two million cars and trucks per year in the United States without producing any on American soil. Now, Japanese investment is beginning to trickle in: both Honda and Kawasaki have begun operating motorcycle plants in the U.S.; Nissan is building a truck assembly plant in Tennessee; and Toyota and General Motors are discussing the possibility of reopening a moth-balled G.M. plant in California under joint management.

But the outcome of all this may not be exactly what Fraser had in mind. For with the Japanese manufacturing plants could come the Japanese labor model. In place of the UAW's adversarial unionism—which has won American auto workers a decent standard of living and protective measures against managerial caprice—could come Japanese-style labor-management "harmony."

Indeed, Japanese manufacturers are already digging in against the UAW. Honda fought hard with the union over union rights at its Ohio plant before the conflict was resolved in April. Kawasaki has so far succeeded in shutting the union out of its Nebraska factory, using tactics that have resulted in a series of unfair labor practice charges. And Nissan representatives have vowed to operate their Tennessee assembly plant in a "union-free environment" so that management can "deal directly with our employees."

Japanese automakers are not alone in pushing for the "Nissanization" of the American work force. Clearly, many U.S. business leaders feel the country's economic future lies in adopting some version of the Japanese labor model. Hundreds of speeches at corporate luncheons and articles in the business press all sing the praises of Japan's "productivity-minded" workers.

Ichiro Saga has a markedly different view. Saga, a sociologist at Tokyo University, has been studying Nissan labor relations for the past five years. He is acutely aware of the coercion and regimentation that underlie the Japanese industrial miracle. "The mere thought of Japanese labor relations being copied in other countries," Saga tells me, shaking his head, "is enough to fill us all with horror."

57

Apple Computer and the Politics of Change

The story of the rise of Apple Computer under the influence of Steve Jobs and Steve Wozniak is legendary in the annals of computer history. But both have now left the company. Wozniak resigned, feeling that Apple had "lost its soul," and Jobs was fired in 1985 on the recommendation of John Sculley, the professional manager he himself brought into the company.

The story has many dimensions, being a tale of how a company at different stages of development calls on different styles of management, of how the demands and styles of entrepreneurship can conflict with those of solid business management, and of how political conflicts can erode and reshape the culture and destiny of an organization.

The following Newsweek article clearly illustrates how these factors are intertwined.

SHOWDOWN IN SILICON VALLEY[†]

Sitting cross-legged on the floor, surrounded by five colleagues, Steve Jobs is starting over. He's doing what he likes best: war-gaming a new venture (tentative name: Next) with an eager group of smart young tekkies, mapping out strategy in hours of giddy talk, identifying potential problems but letting hope run wild. "Everyone wants to be involved in a start-up," says Bud Tribble, one member of Jobs's new team. "It's part of the dream." But this time it's a little different for Jobs. The seed money comes from the sale of $21 million in his own Apple Computer stock, not the sale of his used Volkswagen bus; and instead of huddling in Jobs's parents' garage, the company founders are sitting on an Oriental rug in Jobs's mansion in the hills above Silicon Valley. But the electricity of a start-up is there: Jobs's speech is

[†]SOURCE: From Newsweek, 30 Sept. 1985, "Showdown in Silicon Valley," pp. 46-57, © 1985, Newsweek, Inc. All rights reserved. Reprinted by permission.

animated, his manner confident. If occasionally a pained look flashes across his face, well, that is understandable. After all, Jobs, chairman of the board of Apple Computer, has just had to resign from the company he helped found.

Suddenly, a storm is brewing in Silicon Valley. The board of Apple Computer, accusing Jobs of betrayal, was debating whether to sue him. Even in an industry accustomed to nasty disputes over sudden departures and trade secrets, the showdown between Apple and Jobs has a special edge. For one thing, the two principals, Jobs and Apple president John Sculley, 46, had been close friends. Jobs recruited Sculley from PepsiCo in 1983, and the pair had quickly developed a relationship that was part brotherly, part father-son. But in recent months Sculley had decided that Jobs was hurting the company, and persuaded the board to strip him of power. Now it appeared that Jobs might be seeking revenge by setting out to compete with his own creation. For Apple the dispute could be a costly distraction from its efforts to recover from the current computer slump. And the prospect of a $2 billion company going to court to crush a tiny start-up threatened to chill the renegade enterprise spirit of America's premier industry.

The story of Apple Computer is not just another garage-to-gigabucks, brainstorm-to-burnout high-tech tale. It has become *the* success story of a generation: Two scruffy kids—whose most successful previous venture was selling equipment to make illegal telephone calls—combine some technical genius and marketing flair and spawn a billion-dollar company. The company, in turn, begets a multi-billion-dollar industry that for the moment, at least, seems capable of staving off both rust and the Japanese.

The two scruffy kids, though, have not survived. One, Steve Wozniak, the technical genius, in effect dropped out of the company several years ago. He finally severed all ties with Apple last February, complaining that the company had lost its soul. Jobs hung on longer, but his tenure is ending just as unhappily. In a series of interviews over three days, Jobs told his side of the story to NEWSWEEK'S Michael Rogers and Gerald C. Lubenow, "I'm not bitter, I'm not bitter," he says. But it is clear that his separation from Apple has been as painful as a divorce.

Jobs's fall began when Apple president John Sculley wrested control of the company from Jobs in a bitter struggle last spring. Sculley came to the conclusion that "we could run a lot better with Steve out of operations," he says. Jobs tended to value technological "elegance" over customer needs—a costly luxury at a time of slowing sales. And Jobs's intense involvement with the Macintosh project had a demoralizing effect on Apple's other divisions. But he was still chairman, and being kicked around by his own company was a shock. "The San Jose Mercury had as their banner headline, APPLE DEMOTES JOBS," Jobs recalls. "My family and everybody reads that. It's certainly not a fun thing to go through." Things would only get worse.

Jobs was exiled to an office in an auxil[i]ary building that he and his secretary nicknamed "Siberia." Sculley says he repeatedly tried to interest Jobs in research-and-development projects but that Jobs insisted on an operating position. That's not what Jobs remembers: he says he got no assignments and gradually found that important company documents no longer landed on his desk. He called every member of the executive staff to say that he wanted to be helpful in any way he could, and he made sure each had his home phone number. Few ever called back. "It was very clear there was nothing for me to do," he says. "I need a purpose to make me go."

He soon came to believe that he would find no purpose within Apple. In July, Sculley had told a meeting of security analysts that Jobs would have no role in the operations of the company "now or in the future." The message got through. "You've probably had somebody punch you in the stomach and it knocks the wind out of you and you can't breathe," says Jobs, recalling his reaction. "The harder you try to breathe, the more you can't breathe. And you know that the only thing you can do is just you've got to relax and you've got to trust that if you relax you'll start breathing again. That's how I felt all summer long . . . If I tried to figure out what to do or sort out my life or all that stuff, it was just like trying to breathe harder."

Thoroughly dispirited, Jobs went for a lot of long walks through the Stanford University campus and its magnificent eucalyptus groves. It wasn't until late August that he began to catch his breath. To collect his thoughts one day, he took up pen and paper—not computer —and began to write down the things that were important to him. Along with the development of the Macintosh, he listed three educational projects he had launched: Kids Can't Wait, Apple Education Foundation and the Apple University Consortium. Around that time, Jobs had a long lunch with Paul Berg, a Nobel Prize-winning geneticist at Stanford. Jobs wondered why computer simulations of Berg's long, expensive experiments could not be distributed for teaching purposes. Berg said that most universities didn't have the necessary computers and software. "That's why I started to really think about this stuff and get my wheels turning again," says Jobs.

He began meeting with a few friends from Apple to discuss a new education-oriented computer venture. They decided that Jobs should inform the board of their plans. At a Sept. 12 meeting Jobs told the board that he had considered entering politics, returning to school or launching a new firm, ultimately deciding to combine the latter two in some enterprise that was still nebulous. He mentioned that he would take some Apple people with him, but not so many as to disrupt the company. After the board discussed the matter in private, Sculley told Jobs that he would like him to remain on the board and that Apple might be interested in buying 10 percent of the new venture. Jobs says vice chairman (and co-founder, along with Jobs and Wozniak) A. C. (Mike) Markkula suggested Jobs and Sculley should discuss it further the next week.

That night Jobs and his collaborators met as a group for the first time. Present were Tribble, Apple controller Susan Barnes, engineers George Crow and Rich Page and educational-marketing manager Dan'l Lewin. They decided it would be best if they all resigned immediately and assured Apple there would be no further resignations. "We decided to cut the umbilical cord and go as a group so there wouldn't be one hit after another," says Barnes. Jobs met with Sculley early the next morning and gave him the names of the people who would be leaving. According to Jobs, Sculley took a quick look at the list and said nothing about it. He did ask Jobs about the other two points the board had raised. Jobs replied that the group was uncomfortable with the idea of committing 10 percent of their new company to Apple. And he said he had no intention of staying on the board. As they stood and shook hands, Sculley said he really hoped they could work together, and Jobs sensed a flicker of their old friendship.

Sculley tells a very different story of that encounter. "I was absolutely taken aback when Steve walked in and handed me the list," he says. Sculley says he complained to Jobs that he was taking key people, several of them from the crucial education division. The Apple board agreed. "The board felt they had been deceived," says Sculley. "He [had] said he would take a few low-level people not involved in anything Apple considered important." Apple's successful efforts in the educational market—largely inspired by Jobs—have been one bright spot during the current computer-industry slump. And while Jobs denies it, some experts agree that any computer he produced could well find itself in competition with the next generation Macintosh.

Last Tuesday Markkula issued a statement raising the prospect that Apple would sue Jobs or his new company for theft of proprietary secrets. Late that night Jobs drove to Markkula's home and delivered his letter of resignation. "We have tried to assure them that we have absolutely no plans to use any trade secrets or technology," says Jobs. "We can't tell [them] what we're going to do because we honestly don't know. What we want to do is come to some kind of acceptable parting with Apple so we can start our company." But

Sculley believes there's more to it than that. "We all understand [that breakaway start-ups are] part of the culture," he says. "But people felt this was Steve Jobs getting even, not just Steve Jobs going off to start something new."

This is one corporate clash with an intensely personal element. Early on, Jobs and Sculley enjoyed a remarkable friendship. Their closeness even provoked resentment among other top Apple executives, who referred to it as "the love affair." They spent many hours in conversation and took long walks in the woods together. "We talked two or three times a day," says Sculley. "He would call in the middle of the night. We finished each other's sentences." All that started to change last spring as the computer industry began to descend into its current slump. As Sculley sees it, Jobs's "ideas on how to sell into the office [market] didn't work and that put an incredible strain on the relationship." Sculley decided to remove Jobs from his operating position as head of the Macintosh division, and the board backed him. In late May, as Sculley was beginning a trip to China, Jobs made one final attempt to depose him, but the board remained loyal to Sculley. "We agreed then," says Sculley, "that we'd set our friendship aside."

The departure of Jobs left many Apple staffers reeling. "I had no idea Steve was forming a company," say William Campbell, executive vice president for sales and marketing. "Losing those people was a shock. But losing the chairman of the board was even more shocking." The process of replacing Jobs's recruits will cost the company valuable time. "The people who are really upset are at the vice-president level," according to one longtime Apple executive. "Their plans have really been upset. The rough estimate is delays of two to three months, due to bringing in new key people. They're the ones pushing for some kind of revenge." In some quarters, though, there is simply "a sense of relief that the other shoe has fallen," says the Apple veteran. So far there has been no sign of an exodus from the company by Jobs loyalists. . . .

From the comfortable distance of Wall Street, the bloody battle looked like a healthy jog around the park: the news of Jobs's resignation sent Apple stock up. "Most professional investors are happy to see Jobs out of Apple," said Don Sinsabaugh, a partner in Swergold Chefitz & Sinsabaugh. "He ruffled a lot of feathers on Wall Street with his brashness and self-confidence." More importantly, CEO John Sculley will now be able to run the company with a free hand.

There is a question, though, of whether the ordeal will dampen Apple's innovative flair. "It was really Steve's vision, his drive, his charisma, his relentless championing of the personal computer [that made Apple a success]," says venture capitalist Benjamin Rosen, chairman of Compaq Computer Corp., an Apple competitor. "When Jobs left active management last spring, there was concern that his change in roles would result in loss of spirit," says Barbara Isgur, an analyst with D.H. Brown & Associates. "But that doesn't seem to have happened." Isgur believes that while Apple may have lost a certain wild energy, it is now in a position to proceed "in a more deliberate fashion."

It will take more than hard work to get Apple back on track. For the immediate future, Apple can get by offering incremental improvements on its current lines. But over the long run it will need to dazzle the market with something sexy and new. "Their new-product release rate has slipped badly in the past two years," says Sinsabaugh.

In the business market, which accounts for 65 percent of all desk-top personal-computer purchases, Apple has been especially weak. Apple once dominated the business market by default. But it was slow to respond to the challenge of IBM's extraordinarily successful PC, introduced in 1981. In January 1984 Apple renewed its bid for the business community with the Macintosh. But the Mac had several crippling drawbacks as a business machine. Jobs's insistence that the Macintosh be easy to use made the machine's internal software complicated. That slowed the Mac down and limited its memory. It could not be customized, had little useful software and, worst of all, it was not IBM-compatible. The Mac has sold well to individuals but has not gained Apple the hoped-for access to the business market.

The flap has already had one negative side effect: it obscured the announcement this week of several significant upgrades in the Apple II, by far the company's most successful product. There may be a measure of mischievous satisfaction in that for Jobs—he has long been known to hate the Apple II, which he considers a "boring" and technologically clumsy machine. But Jobs may have hurt himself, too. "Steve really had the opportunity to show the business community that he had grown up," says Ida Cole, a former Apple employee and now vice president for applications software at Microsoft in Bellevue, Wash. "He didn't do that."

But for Steve Jobs, growing up has always been something of a problem. In many ways he is a child of the '60s. A college dropout, he journeyed to India in search of enlightenment. He stopped eating meat, and he still feels a kinship with the East: one of the things he admires about his Japanese competitors is that, like him, they "believe in the ultimate importance of the journey," not just specific goals. In the early days of Apple his sandals, long hair and beard alarmed a number of potential investors. His mansion is almost monastic: he sleeps on a mattress on the floor. Most characteristically '60s of all, however, is his devotion to youth, which comes through in his determination to produce educational products. That the drama in his life now revolves around control of a billion-dollar corporation and not kitchen duty in a commune is merely testament to his drive.

Jobs was also a child of Silicon Valley; both he and Wozniak grew up there. Like the rest of the valley, he was deeply influenced by two conservative businessmen who couldn't have been further from the '60s in style: Dave Packard and Bill Hewlett. At the company they built, Hewlett-Packard, human values commanded the same respect as profits—and HP

has plenty of both. Jobs was exposed to HP early on. During his freshman and sophomore years of high school he attended lectures at HP every Tuesday night, along with about 20 other students. They got thrilling glimpses of the future at technology's cutting edge. "I think it is fair to say there wouldn't have been an Apple if there hadn't been a Hewlett-Packard and if Hewlett-Packard hadn't had the values that included caring and nurturing the young people in technical directions," said Jobs.

While proficient, Jobs was never really a technical star. In the early days of Apple it was Wozniak who came up with the technical innovations that made the Apple II the first practical "computer on a circuit board." Jobs's contribution was conceptualizing what the machine ought to be able to do—and what it should look like. Jobs coaxed money out of investors, cajoled suppliers to extend credit, encouraged Wozniak to keep trying. Most of all, he was a visionary, sensing that personal computers could be attractive not just to nerdy hobbyists, but to everyone. "My motivation was to make a showoff product to take down to the computer club," says Wozniak. "Jobs's was to make a product and sell it."

Those qualities were essential to a start-up, but it has been harder for Jobs to find an outlet for them in a more developed organization. As Apple grew larger—and it did so with astonishing speed—Jobs began to lose his sense of purpose. Launching the project to develop the Macintosh in 1982 was a way of returning to his roots. "The Macintosh team was what is commonly known now as intrapreneurship," he says. "A group of people going in essence back to the garage, but in a large company." For Jobs it meant the chance once again to be directly, intimately—and dictatorially—involved in every aspect of a new product.

Like any strong leader, Jobs has alienated many friends. One casualty was Wozniak, who maintains an oddly mixed view of his partner in history. For one thing, he does not think Jobs can be trusted to give a straight answer. "Even in personal conversations with the guy," says

Wozniak, "you could never really tell what he was thinking. You might ask him a yes-or-no question, and the answer said 'no' to anyone who heard it but really means 'maybe yes, maybe no'." And Wozniak believes Jobs always put his own interests ahead of anyone else's. "Aside from not being able to trust him," he says, "he will use anyone to his own benefit." Yet Silicon Valley is still filled with people who would love to work for Jobs. He gets a daily stream of letters, phone calls, even people who call at the gates of his house bearing letters requesting an audience.

Idolatry can be subversive. As Silicon Valley publicist Regis McKenna sees it, Jobs suffered from the way people deferred to him. "I've told him that people were not honest with him," says McKenna, who has been involved with Apple since the early days. "[He needed people to say,] 'No, Steve, that isn't the way the world works'." People encouraged him to go into politics, for example, telling him he could be a senator or even president. But Jobs has never even registered to vote, an act of benign neglect that would surely hinder any political career. Data-processing managers, who are responsible for buying computers for large companies, would tell Jobs that they admired him for refusing to conform to the standards set by IBM. But when it came time to put in their purchase orders, they played it safe, going with Big Blue.

As the Macintosh project unfolded, it began to appear that Jobs was listening only to himself. For one thing, he did not provide the Mac with a letter-quality printer, an essential for any computer aimed at the office market. "There was no in-house cynic to stand up to Steve Jobs and say, 'It's incredibly stupid to sell a business machine that doesn't support a letter-quality printer'," says Tom Warrick, a Washington lawyer and president of a large Apple users' club who has recently visited the company. Jobs also refused to put a fan inside any Apple computer. Fans, he has said, are required to correct inelegant design. But without a fan, no hard-disc drive can be included in the machine, a further drawback for business

users. Jobs's obsession created problems within the company, too. To protect his pet Macintosh, which was aimed at the office market, he refused to allow the company to advertise the Apple II as a business computer. Finally, he estranged himself from Apple staffers who worked for other divisions.

As McKenna sees it, the rift between Jobs and Sculley ultimately stems from the sudden, dramatic change in the marketplace in the last two years. No longer can a company simply hope to dazzle customers with gee-whiz gadgetry or innovations. Companies must go to the customers first, finding out what their needs are and what kinds of computers can solve their problems. "Apple designed and built computers like a consumer-products company," says McKenna. "But there's been a very rapid change. The [personal computer] market is more like the traditional computer marketplace." That makes IBM's service-oriented approach and its careful consideration of how new products fit into the existing family of products more effective. "Ironically, it was John Sculley, with his background in consumer products, who realized that," says McKenna. "Steve, the one with the technical background, didn't recognize that soon enough."

Like Jobs, Silicon Valley has been experiencing growing pains. As technology has grown more sophisticated, the costs of starting a new firm have soared and the freewheeling process of entrepreneurship has become institutionalized. "If you want to start a company now," says Jobs, "there are companies that help you start a company." And slowly, executives from outside the computer industry, like Sculley, have begun taking charge of technology companies. Jobs understands that the switch to a more professional kind of management may be necessary for a large business. But there is danger in that. "To me," he says, "Apple exists in the spirit of the people that work there and the sort of philosophies and purpose by which they go about their business." He believes that may be his greatest legacy. "If I'm a million miles away and all those people still feel those things and they're still working to make the next great personal computer, then I will feel that my genes are still in there. If Apple just becomes a place where computers are a commodity item and where the romance is gone . . . then I'll feel I have lost Apple."

And so at 30, Jobs is starting over. He carries an extraordinary burden: he may have already authored his greatest work. But he is still driven, and he believes he has a responsibility to keep working. "If I just . . . went and laid on the beach the rest of my life—which I couldn't do anyway—that would send a pretty ridiculous message to people who are thinking about starting their own companies, thinking about risking everything they have on an idea," Jobs says. He is also pretty sure he can pull off something spectacular. "I did it in the garage when Apple started, and I did it in the metaphorical garage when Mac started," he says. "So I have a certain degree of confidence that I can do that again." No one who knows Steve Jobs would expect anything less.

58

Politics at Work†

Whenever individuals or groups find themselves in situations where their in-
terests diverge, some kind of politicking almost always results. In the following
pages, Vic Murray and Jeff Gandz explore executive opinions about the nature
of organizational politics, and give some tips about what can be done to manage
more effectively in politicized situations:

"That was strictly a political decision, Charlie, and you know it!"

"This is the most political department I've ever worked in."

"Just sit tight; to bring that subject up now would be politically unwise."

For years people have talked to each other about office politics, political decisions, and political people at work. During coffee breaks or lunch hours, politics in the workplace holds its own as a conversation piece with such perennial favorites as sex and sports. In books, movies, and T.V. a sure-fire plot shows the political machinations of evil senior executives destroying the hero, or some naive, amiable klutz outfoxing the cynical bigwigs at the top.

Considering that politics is so commonplace in everyday conversation and popular culture, it is remarkable how little serious study has been undertaken by people interested in life in complex organizations. In the thousands of books on business management, reference to politics is rarely made. When it is mentioned,

it is usually dismissed as a nasty abnormality which competent executives should try to eliminate from their organizations. In the cool, rational world of executive decision making, politics is taboo.

Maybe one of the reasons why politics in the workplace has not been systematically studied is that "politics" has many meanings and refers to many different behaviors. We thought, therefore, that the best place to start a study of the subject would be to gather and analyze information from a sample of working people about what *they* mean when they talk about workplace politics. On the assumption that a lot of workplace politics gets played and talked about at the management level, we began by writing 590 alumni of the MBA and BBA programs of a large eastern Canadian university. This group is predominantly young (between 25 and 40), male, and upwardly mobile. Its members hold positions ranging from supervisor to president, and they work in organizations of all kinds: large, small, government, and

†SOURCE: Excerpted from Victor Murray and Jeffry Gandz, "Games Executives Play: Politics at Work," *Business Horizons*, Indiana University, December 1980, pp. 11-23; used with permission.

business. We sent them a questionnaire about workplace politics and asked them to tell us a story about an actual situation which was a "good example of workplace politics in action." In all, 428 people returned the questionnaire and, of these, 132 took the trouble to provide illustrative stories. We wanted to know:

- What issues do people feel are most influenced by "political" considerations?
- Which people in the organization are most commonly seen as "political?"
- What do people actually do when they are seen as engaging in politics at work?
- How did our sample of managers feel about the politics they perceived going on around them?
- What kinds of people are more likely than others to see politics going on around them?

Finally, we wanted to develop some practical suggestions to answer two questions: First, what can the average manager do to get rid of a pervading feeling among his subordinates and colleagues that "all the decisions around here are political," or at least to change "crooked" politics to "open" or "honest" politics? Secondly, how do managers in a genuinely negative political climate survive or even thrive in it?

Political Issues at Work

In virtually all the stories our managers told us, politics was perceived when people were believed to be trying to advance or protect their own self-interests in the face of actual or potential opposition from others in the organization. The basic sources of this opposition were twofold: from supervisors or subordinates, or from colleagues. This gives us two basic types of politics: vertical and horizontal.

The vertical politics category is by far the most common because there are so many subcategories within it. By far the most common was that of favoritism or bias in promotions, transfers, and dismissals. The majority of these stories told of perceived "injustice" when people better qualified on the usual "rational"

grounds were passed over in favor of friends of the person doing the promoting. This case is typical.

Favoritism in Promotion

A new manager was brought in as the heir-apparent to the treasurer. A super-clerk attached herself to this person. When he was placed in charge of stock investments, she was made a stock analyst. Soon the heir became treasurer and clashed with the stock portfolio manager and appointed the former clerk to take his place. The treasurer and his new portfolio manager have been seen in a hotel together.

The new portfolio manager was an incompetent stock analyst and has been a disaster as a portfolio manager. She has not been fired even though her predecessor was.

Promotions are only one outcome in a long sequence of dealings between superiors and subordinates in which each tries to impress the other with his or her competence, or conversely, tries to avoid being blamed for failure. One of the more extreme examples of this kind of "look good/avoid blame" interaction is the following story of a department manager. Not only did he act the sycophant to his bosses, he insisted that his subordinates toady to him in the same manner.

Look Good/Avoid Blame

A particular department manager in my organization is ambitious to a fault. His approach to his job is such that he plays politics constantly and his employees must too if they are to survive in his department without unusual pressure being thrust upon them.

For example, the information sent to this manager's senior executive is interesting in that everything positive is overemphasized and anything negative is totally ignored unless it is impossible to do so. Everything is for effect.

Many of his employees who are unsatisfied in their work dare not ask for a transfer to another department as this would be tantamount to insulting him and could easily mean that individuals would be blackballed. [Similarly], if one disagrees too often he is labelled as a nonsupporter, and one learns that he should fall into line if he wishes to be truly trusted—and on it goes.

The converse of the person who seeks to look good by avoiding blame is the person who seeks advancement by drawing attention to himself like a high wire artist. In the next case, the ambitious manager takes the "high-risk gamble" by pushing to head up a high-profile special project that attracted top management attention and brought him valuable contacts.

The High Risk Gamble

The general manager was young (40-45), ambitious, and wanted to be noticed; however, his department (line engineering) was responsible for low-profile, production-type functions while all the "super star" projects were handled by staff departments (with equally young and ambitious executives). Rather than attempt to shine in his own field, he took on a risky, expensive, and highly innovative research project. The internal selling job to obtain financing and authorization provided an excellent stage in itself and, once underway, the project became as important for itself. It was significantly long term. This meant that the managers on it were evaluated on their performance in conducting the research rather than on the end effect of the research in increasing revenues. Three of the six managers directly associated with the project (including our hero) were promoted during the project although the project as a whole ended up a failure.

Finally among the forms of vertical politics we have a typical, old-fashioned, power struggle between a subordinate and his superior. In this example, an executive vice-president attempts to depose his boss, the president, by means of an end-run to the final authority, the board of directors.

The Power Struggle

This happened in a cyclical industry [temporarily] depressed. The board of directors was selected on the basis of their prestige, not their ability to contribute to policy making. Involved were:

a) The president—a dynamic entrepreneur with imagination and a host of friends in the industry. His biggest fault was that he was extremely democratic and totally uninterested in lobbying for support at board level.

b) The executive vice-president—an able financial person with poor rapport within the organization but extremely talented at lobbying for support among powerful and influential members of the board.

The executive vice-president tried to fight one of the president's policies and eventually forced a showdown at board level. He lost by one vote and was ousted from the job.

When we examine the stories for illustrations of the other major form of activity, that of horizontal politics, three basic sub-categories reveal themselves. The most daring and unusual we called "The Entrepreneurial Capture" in which a major effort is made to secure authority for a new project or function.

Entrepreneurial Capture

A very major contract was about to be awarded to my company: the VP marketing, who has personally been responsible for it for several years, considered that a company VP ought to be named program manager to show just respect to the program. The natural choice was the VP engineering division but these two were political enemies. So the VP marketing laid a plan to ensure that he would become VP of a newly formed division to handle the contract. The execution of this took about six months and was very political in its strategy. It entailed getting his own executive director of sales renamed VP sales (to take his place), then the buildup of dedicated staff under him while the program was still embryonic. Then —when people woke up—there was a group, doing a job with a VP reporting direct to the president. All that was necessary was to formalize that which already existed! A new division was born.

The second type is less risky but appears to be more common. This is the situation in which a supplier of a service and its user(s) cannot balance the supply-demand equation. In the sample case, this conflict [led] the user unit to try to sever its dependence on the supplier by creating its own supply. In other instances the user will seek to absorb and control the supplier instead.

Border Clash

A management information systems (MIS) group was established to handle the company's data processing needs. The director of this group allocated resources on the basis of financial payoff. A marketing administration group found that although they had many worthy projects for the MIS group, they would not get done because of other, better justified, projects from other areas.

The marketing administration manager used his political power to rally marketing executives together. His strategy was to show the poor service of the MIS group and thus justify his solution which was to use his own people for MIS work. He convinced his own higher management of the benefits of better service and got his own MIS group within marketing.

The MIS head then rallied the rest of the organization against the successful marketing administration group. Since the administration group was getting service that others weren't, the MIS head argued that this was done at the expense of the other department heads.

The result was that the marketing administration group's data processing expertise has been absorbed by MIS. In another organization a similar problem ended with the decentralization of the MIS group. The difference was politics (who one rallies to meet the opponent).

Finally, by far the most common form of horizontal politics is that which arises over the simple matter of deciding who should have how much in the way of money, equipment, staff, or other resources. Whenever there is not enough to go around, a conflict over allocation is almost inevitable.

Scarce Resource Competition

In a budget presentation of all departments in a local community college, one head made a very pious and long presentation outlining the very deep cuts to be made in his area. The rest were moved by his presentation and a portion of his funds were restored.

Following the meeting, the head asked for feedback on his "performance" from a small group of his staff who were also at the meeting. All were unanimous in awarding full marks for presentation, piety, general dishonesty, and success of the game plan.

Later, in a priority ranking capital budget exercise, each of ten members of equal rank posted their first-ranked item. This was followed by group discussion and group consensus upon the number one rank. One member received no support at all during the first fifteen or sixteen rounds. His sin was twofold: (1) his insistence on ranking funds for furnishing his own office higher than funds for improving teaching facilities; (2) his general attitude of superiority prior to the session which bred resentment among the rest of the group.

Without any verbal communication or actual collusion, the entire group lined up to "punish" the offender. Not only did the action serve to deny him any funds, but it served everyone else's end.

These basic types of vertical and horizontal politics were the most common ones mentioned (in well over half the stories received), but the stories also included many minor varieties of politics that are by no means uncommon. For example, 33 percent of our managers thought that politics frequently played a role in how much people were paid, salary levels being influenced as a result of a superior's unreasonable ethnic, gender, or other prejudices. Some 28 percent also felt there was "politics" in some of the hiring decisions in their organizations. In almost all these cases, "politics" is seen to arise when managers depart from the code of pure "business rationality" which emphasizes cost/benefit efficiency and effectiveness in achieving organizational goals.

Who Is Most Political?

Turning from what gives rise to politics to who is involved, the evidence from our study was quite clear. It seems that the higher your position, the more others will believe that you are involved in politics; 87 percent of our respondents felt that upper management would be "moderately" or "highly" involved in politics while only a third felt that blue collar workers would be so involved. "Middle management" (department heads, division managers, etc.) were perceived to be almost as politically involved as upper management, while white collar employees, the technical and professional staff, and first-level management fell in between.

We also tried to look at which management functions are more likely to be seen as politically involved. For example, are people in sales seen as more political than people in accounting? It turns out, however, that people see politics mostly in their own areas and don't notice it too much elsewhere. As a result, they tend to report that politics is most common in their own area and in whatever departments or sections they deal with.

What Is Political Behavior?

The briefest definition of workplace politics is simple: the pursuit of self-interest at work in the face of real or imagined opposition. Thus, to know for sure how much politics is going on one would have to get inside the head of those being studied and learn their motives and perceptions. Most people have neither skill nor the opportunity to do this, yet they nevertheless reach conclusions about others' motives by making inferences from observations of the others' outward actions.

We wanted to find out which actions were most likely to be seen as politically motivated. Judging from the stories we obtained there appeared to be two basic kinds of political behavior: Conflictful Maneuvering and Blatantly Self Advancing/Protecting Actions.

Conflictful maneuvering is that which those on the scene can see as being directed against the opposition of someone else. There are two types of conflictful behaviors, overt and covert. For example, in the story of the clash between the executive VP and his president the showdown at the board level represents a case of overt or "out-front" conflict, as does the story of the marketing manager setting up his own MIS group. Conversely, the following cases illustrate the more covert side of conflictful maneuvering.

Covert Maneuvering at the Top

My company is part of a worldwide multinational organization with the head office in Europe. It is very decentralized at the operational level. Two independent service companies had evolved in one marketplace (North America), one in the U.S., and one in Canada. Strong rivalry developed.

The Canadian president was senior to the U.S. president and was given nominal control of the two companies. The U.S. manager was a European national, close to the parent company's executive. He tried to retain his independence by controlling vital technical information and generally by trying to avoid the influence of the Canadian president.

The Canadian company developed a new area of technical expertise independently. The Canadian president lobbied to have a similar service set up in Europe and was successful. He then arranged a 'stick and carrot' situation to force the U.S. manager's transfer to head up the new organization.

The new European company has had difficult marketing problems and it appears that it will probably be absorbed into the parent company's 'Engineering Technical Centre.'

The U.S. operation is now, for all practical purposes, a subsidiary of the Canadian company, with a new docile manager, picked up by the Canadian president. Manipulation was the thread in this five-year saga.

Covert Politics at the Bottom

A fellow who worked in a department with myself and three other fellows was extremely dissatisfied with the work he was doing and his personality became abrasive, sarcastic, etc. He wanted to transfer to another area to work in a more glamorous type of endeavour. He was an excellent analyst, however, and our boss did not want to give him up.

As I knew most of the people in the area he wanted to move to, I arranged for him to meet these people at a luncheon and he took over from there to sell himself. Within our department, the four of us shifted our workload such that the bulk of the tasks assigned to the fifth individual were purely administrative.

When the issue of losing the disgruntled analyst was brought up to the boss again, he approved the transfer as he felt he could lose this particular person with minimum loss in overall performance.

In the first case, the Canadian president subtly undermined the U.S. president's position without the latter being aware of it until too late. In the second case a covert operation had to be mounted by colleagues to put the analyst in the position to get the transfer he wanted. It is impossible to know what was really going on in the minds of the key people in these stories. The important point is that their actions were *defined* as being political.

In contrast to conflict, the second dominant type of political action was that which was viewed as being too obviously "for" oneself. This behavior takes the form of either aggressively putting oneself forward or, conversely, being overly cautious and defensive in avoiding blame and risk to one's status. For example, the young general manager who sought out the new project was seen as blatantly self-advancing.

Occasionally, of course, extreme political behavior is perceived as a result of someone combining both Conflictful Maneuvering and Blatant Self-Advancement/Protection. The community college department head managed to put on a calculated performance to protect his own budget while later participating as a competitor to reduce another's share of the resources. . . .

What to Do About It?

There is no question that there are devious, scheming, cynical people in organizations who really do plot to gain purely selfish ends with no thought at all to the success of the organization or the harm done to their opponents. In that sense, politics is "real" and not simply the distorted figment of a frustrated employee's imagination. On the other hand, studies of high-level business decision making suggest that many issues are generally complex and ambiguous. When several highly persuasive alternatives to complicated problems are available, managers are bound to conflict with those above, below, and beside them and do so with the genuine conviction that their approach is truly best for the whole organization. While some interpret their conflicts as politicking behavior, others do not.

The problem for the dedicated executive is how to minimize the tendency of others to perceive events as the outcome of "bad politics" when in fact they are simply the result of honest differences of opinion. From our interviews with managers and the conclusions of other students of management effectiveness, the following steps are suggested:

• The executive must be sensitive to the possibility revealed in our study that subordinates may see things as political which the executive does *not* see as political. In other words the first step is to be able to recognize when a negative political climate exists.

• Perhaps the main conclusion to be drawn from our study is that well motivated employees tend to be less likely to perceive politics in their work settings. Autonomy, responsibility, diversity, challenge, and full and honest feedback on performance often go hand-in-hand with a nonpolitical view of the decision-making process.

• The above general conclusion means the executive must seek to delegate authority, provide adequate support and resources to allow subordinates the necessary freedom to achieve objectives, provide variety and challenge in assignments to subordinates, and avoid the notorious pitfalls that go with evaluating performance. These include the tendency to use power to force acceptance of objectives, to define the measuring devices unilaterally and unfairly, and to use the evaluation as a way to tell how badly a person failed rather than as an indicator of a problem which needs to be mutually solved. "Feedback" under these circumstances will provoke the worst kind of political response of all.

• Recall that the perception of negative politics isn't entirely in the eye of the beholder but may be based on the executive's own actions as Conflictful Maneuvering or Blatantly Self Advancing/Protecting. Since conflict is inevitable in management, the perceptions of it depend on how it is handled. The more the executive follows the basic steps in conflict management, the less negative politics will be seen. This means:

• Get disagreements out in the open as soon as possible rather than let them fester and grow; look for areas of agreement first, building a positive base from which to tackle contentious issues; identify and concentrate on "superordinate goals" (those ends which the parties have in common) at all times and refer to them when discussing the pros and cons of various alternatives. The aim is to find that solution which comes closest to satisfying the general good and the particular special interests. When emotions flare, as they are bound to do, try to talk them out rather than act them out. This means saying "I feel angry because . . ." rather than "You stupid numbskull, where did you get that idiotic idea?"

• Finally, avoid covert operations. Even the RCMP and CIA have been found out too often and in the hands of amateurs the risks are too high. One slip-up and the manager's reputation for trustworthiness is ruined for all time: the label of "machiavellian," once applied, is almost impossible to dislodge.

Surviving at Work

Consider now the situation of the innocent victim of what appears to be a poisonous political climate. Again, the first step to take is that of trying to be brutally honest. Just as the boss must become aware of that which is viewed as political by others in order to deal with it, so must the "victims" face up to the possibility that their interpretation of events is putting a political cast to them which may never have been intended by those involved. The temptation to impute malicious motives to those on the winning side of an honest conflict is great and must be the first thing the "victim" should confront.

Once victims are convinced that a genuine negative political climate exists, there are three basic options: flight, fight, and capitulation. The one most commonly followed by those who can manage it is flight. What this means in practice is that the better people who are most able to get jobs elsewhere leave the organization, thereby creating a vicious circle in which the "losers" remain behind and lapse into an increasingly greater state of apathy or fear.

The second most commonly followed path is "capitulation": if you can't lick 'em, give in. Among those who are relatively powerless to mount political counterattacks against opponents and engage in such delightful pursuits as character assassination, sabotage, hidden agendas and the like, the usual response is "cover your ass." What this boils down to is making sure that they follow all rules, get all orders in writing (always keeping a copy for their own files), and engage in absolutely no original or creative initiatives for fear that they may fail and the initiator will be used as the scapegoat. The net effect of all this of course, is the creation of the classic mouldy, red-tape ridden bureaucracy.

There are two basic approaches to fighting: "fight fire with fire" and the "expose."

To fight politics with politics is perhaps the more human tendency, akin to hitting back when one is hit first. Aside from a devious, cynical mind, there is one major resource needed for this approach to succeed: power. Power comes through the exclusive control of resources (knowledge, funds, material goods) which others need. With power one can acquire allies, and all successful political schemes need strategically placed allies to lend support to the endeavor. It behooves the budding organizational politician, therefore, to concentrate particularly on building a network of "friends" and "favor-owers" in all parts of the organization below, laterally, and especially above. There are enough popular books on the distasteful subject of how to use others for selfish ends that we need not go into that here.

The best and most difficult response to living in a negative political climate is that of the expose. A certain recklessness is involved because one can get hurt in the process. The procedure, however, is straightforward. It consists of gathering evidence, as much as possible, of the bias, the irrationality, the glaring self-serving nature of the politician's actions, laying it before whatever authorities can take action to correct the situation, and trusting them to act honorably.

The study of politics in the workplace has really just begun. Until now it has been a term with no clear meaning used primarily by people upset by results of conflict in the organization. In the future more effort must be devoted to exploring further what conditions are associated with leading people to define their work situation as negatively political and what impact such a definition has on the organization's effectiveness and the quality of working life.

59

Some Sources of Organizational Conflict

Conflict is a familiar feature of life in an organizational society: It is always latent in situations where interests collide, and becomes manifest when people begin to perceive and act upon their different ideas, aims, and aspirations.

Organization theorists generally draw distinctions between *perceived conflict*, where parties rightly or wrongly see a divergence of interests; *felt conflict*, where parties experience tension, hostility, anger, fear, or mistrust; and *behavioral conflict*, where parties act to advance or defend their interests in ways that may range from passive resistance, through various kinds of subtle confrontation and maneuvering, to outright hostility (Filley, 1975, Pondy, 1967).

Though conflict may be entirely personal or a product of how people perceive a situation, having no substantial basis in fact, more often than not it is the product of tensions associated with the structure of organized situations, for example:

- Scarcity of financial and other valued resources creates conflict around the process of allocation, for example, through budgets (Pondy, 1964).
- The differentiation of tasks and roles often places people in competitive win-lose situations, for example, in work inspection systems (Litterer, 1966).
- Hierarchical relations, for example, between superior and subordinate, often create conflicts around control and the reaction to control.

- Differences in status may create barriers to communication or provide the basis for feelings of inequity that create friction (Litterer, 1966).
- Patterns of interdependence may make one group critically dependent on another (Thompson, 1967) within the context of situations where priorities are not shared; for example, A may be dependent on B for a particular service that A does not see as being important and does not wish to provide.
- Scheduling priorities may be at variance.
- The roles and objectives allocated to different individuals may be in direct conflict with each other.
- Eiements of a person's role may be internally inconsistent; for example, an inspector or auditor may be required to act as both a watchdog and friendly adviser to those with whom he or she interacts.

Each conflict episode in an organization may be just part of an ongoing system of relations where the aftermath of one conflict provides the context for another. Perceptions, actions, and the characteristics of the situation in which the conflict is set all combine to influence the way conflict develops.

REFERENCES

Filley, A. C. *Interpersonal Conflict Resolution.* Glenview, IL: Scott Foresman, 1975.

Litterer, J. A. "Conflict in Organizations: A Re-Examination." *Academy of Management Journal*, 1966, 178-86.

Pondy, L. R. "Budgeting and Intergroup Conflict in Organizations." *Pittsburgh Business Review*, 1964.

Pondy, L. R. "Organizational Conflict: Concepts and Models." *Administrative Science Quarterly*, 1967, 296-320.

Thompson, J. D. *Organizations in Action.* New York: McGraw-Hill, 1967.

60

A Perspective on Conflict Management

Conflict may perform many functions in an organization:
It can

—energize
—encourage self-evaluation
—stimulate adaptation
—stimulate innovation
—improve the quality of decision making
—serve as a release valve and maintain the status quo

Over the years, numerous organization theorists have devoted considerable attention to finding ways of promoting constructive conflict as a management tool.

For example, Dave Brown (1983) has suggested that managers can intervene in at least three ways, for example,

1. by changing perceptions:
   - such as through the use of symbolism and the management of meaning;
   - by redefining interests, such as by introducing some form of superordinate goal or by encouraging new patterns of rivalry or cooperation;
   - by changing understandings of interdependencies and relationships; and
   - by influencing and modifying feelings, stereotypes, and general processes of enactment.

2. by changing behaviors:
   - by manipulating patterns of reward and punishment;
   - by training individuals to recognize and deal with conflict resolution, and by improving bargaining, negotiation and team-building skills; and
   - by changing interpersonal dynamics.

3. by changing structures:
   - such as by redesigning roles and interdependencies;
   - by creating rules that set new contexts for conflict resolution or arbitration;
   - by introducing third parties to act as mediators or process consultants;
   - by creating integrative roles or new interface mechanisms; and
   - by establishing consultative groups and other modes of participation to act as early warning systems.

Table 60.1 (Brown, 1983, 234) illustrates how these approaches can be used to manage situations where there is either too much conflict, or too little conflict.

REFERENCE

Brown, L. D. "Managing Conflict among Groups." In *Organizational Psychology*, edited by D. A. Kolb, I. M. Robin, and J. McIntyre, 225-37. Englewood Cliffs, NJ: Prentice-Hall, 1983.

TABLE 60.1

Area of Concern	General Issue	Strategies for Too Much Conflict	Strategies for Too Little Conflict
Attitudes	Clarify differences and similarities	Emphasize interdependencies	Emphasize conflict of interest
	Increased sophistication about intergroup relations	Clarify dynamics and costs of escalation	Clarify costs and dynamics of collusion
	Change feelings and perceptions	Share perceptions to depolarize stereotypes	Consciousness-raising about group and others
Behavior	Modify within-group behavior	Increase expression of within-group differences	Increase within-group cohesion and consensus
	Train group representatives to be more effective	Expand skills to include co-operative strategies	Expand skills to include assertive, confrontive strategies
	Monitor between-group behavior	Third-party peacemaking	Third-party process consultation
Structure	Invoke larger system interventions	Refer to common hierarchy	Hierarchical pressure for better performance
	Develop regulatory contexts	Impose rules on interaction that limit conflict	Deemphasize rules that stiffle conflict
	Create new interface mechanisms	Develop integrating roles of groups	Create "devil's advocates" or ombudsmen
	Redefine group boundaries and goals	Redesign organization to emphasize task	Clarify group boundaries and goals to increase differentiation

61

Decision Making in
Conflict Situations

Approaches to decision making where the parties are obviously at odds may be approached in different ways. Roy Lewicki (1985) has distinguished between three approaches: one based on competitive "win-lose" processes (distributive bargaining), another based on trying to find "win-win" solutions (integrative bargaining), and a third based on coalition building.

Lewicki describes the essentials of each approach in the following way:

1. Distributive Bargaining[†]

Group members may attempt to use a distributive bargaining strategy—assuming that the group decision will be made by a fundamentally competitive, win-lose process, and that they must behave competitively in order to have the group accept their preferred solution. As a result, they may employ any or all of the following tactics:

• State their preferred solution as a "demand," and take a "hard line" position;
• Selectively reveal only the information which supports their preferences;
• Refuse to compromise or make concessions toward the preferred solutions of others, instead insisting that it is the responsibility of others to make concessions;
• Threaten to walk away if demands are not met;

• Suggest overt or covert rewards or punishments for others if they go along or refuse to go along with one's own preferences;
• Make covert "side deals" and bargains with others in exchange for their support;
• Engage in offensive behavior designed to coerce or intimidate other group members;
• Attempt to dominate the discussion;
• Attempt to control the agenda of the meeting—what is discussed, when it is discussed, what information may be introduced, etc.

2. Integrative Bargaining

Group members may also attempt an integrative bargaining strategy, assuming that the group decision will be made by a fundamentally cooperative win-win process as the group searches for the optimal solution to the prob-

[†]SOURCE: Roy Lewicki, *Decision-Making in Conflict Situations*, National Institute for Dispute Resolution, 1985; used by permission.

lem. As a result, they may employ any or all of the following tactics.

• State their preferences as elements which the group should consider in diagnosing the problem and developing solution options;

• Share information about their preferences and the reasons that these preferences are important to them;

• Ask questions to learn more about others' preferences and needs, and the ways that these are similar or different to one's own;

• Willingly contribute to the search process to identify solution options which satisfy the preferences and needs of all group members;

• Help test solution options to determine whether they meet the needs of all parties, and whether they are practical and implementable;

• Determine whether there are objective standards for selecting among alternative options to determine which one is optimal.

3. Coalition Building Strategies

Finally, group members may attempt a coalition-building strategy. This strategy attempts to create a "consensus" by building a majority of group members who agree to support one another's position. Group members who discover that they are of like-minds may tacitly or explicitly agree to join together in pursuing their common objective. As the pairs form, individual preferences and priorities are compromised, modified and reshaped into a collective perspective that all coalition members can endorse. Thus, group consensus emerges from a "snowballing" of explicit or tacit exchanges, sometimes fleeting and nonverbal in nature, between pairs of group members. Once one or more coalitions have formed, they will attempt to exert collective influence to pressure the remaining group members to join up and to adopt the prevailing viewpoint. If there is one dominant coalition, remaining group members will experience pressures toward conformity and unanimity. If there is more than one coalition, the larger coalitions may attempt to overwhelm the smaller one, or the coalitions may use whatever power tactics are available to them.

Pressures on group members to change their point of view will be affected by the announced standard that the group will use to make its decision. If the group will make the decision by a consensus, influence pressures will continue until one coalition believes it can determine the outcome. Minority members who do not support the majority viewpoint are likely to be ignored or rejected. In contrast, if complete unanimity is required, influence efforts and tactics will be directed at all group members to adopt a common perspective and/or endorse a common decision.

62

Managing Intergroup Conflict

Many strategies have been developed for analyzing and handling conflicts between groups. In the following pages, Eric Neilsen identifies a range of behavioral, structural, and attitudinal approaches:

METHODS OF CONFLICT RESOLUTION[†]

Let us consider some of the tactics which can be used for coping with conflict. There are literally an infinite number of ways in which one might go about stopping or reducing a particular pattern of intergroup conflict, but they all probably can be placed at some point along a continuum which represents different combinations of two basic approaches—halting the conflictful behavior itself without regard to changes in attitude, on the one hand, and changing the attitudes of the protagonists so that they no longer see anything to fight about, on the other. [See Figure 62.1.]

Physical Separation

Physically separating the conflicting groups has the distinct advantages of preventing more damage from being done and of preventing the creation of further rationales for fighting based on what happens in combat itself. If the intervening party is sufficiently strong, it is something which can be done quickly. The tactic may be especially helpful where the groups in conflict are not highly interdependent or where the intervening party does not rely on their active cooperation with each other in order to secure some desired output. One of the tactic's disadvantages is that it may require continuous surveillance to keep the parties separate, especially if tempers are hot and energy levels high. Also, the tactic does not encourage the members of the conflicting groups to change their attitudes toward one another. On the contrary, lack of new objective information about an opponent encourages a group's members to reinforce their negative attitudes through unchecked fantasy building. Most important, the tactic is of little use to those who rely on the active cooperation between the conflicting groups for getting some job done. For them it is at best a stopgap measure, a way

[†]SOURCE: Excerpted from Eric E. Neilsen, "Understanding and Managing Intergroup Conflict," in *Managing Group and Intergroup Relations*, edited by J. W. Lorsch and P. R. Lawrence, pp. 334-39. Homewood, IL: R. D. Irwin, 1972; used by permission.

EXHIBIT 62.1 Strategies for Resolving Intergroup Conflict

Behavioral Solution   *Attitudinal Change Solution*

1	2	3	4	5	6	7

1. Separate the groups physically, reducing conflict by reducing the opportunity to interact.
2. Allow interaction on issues where superordinate goals prevail and decision-making rules have been agreed to beforehand.
3. Keep groups separated but use as intergrators individuals who are seen by both groups as justifying high status for the job, possessing personal attributes consistent with both groups' ideals, and having the expertise necessary for understanding each group's problems.
4. Hold direct negotiations between representatives from each group on all conflictful issues, in the presence of individuals who are seen as neutral to the conflict and who have personal attributes and expertise valued by both groups.
5. Hold direct negotiations between representatives from each group without third-party consultants present.
6. Exchange some group personnel for varying periods of time, so that contrasting perceptions and the rationales for them are clarified through day-to-day interaction and increased familiarity with the other group's activities, and then attempt direct negotiations after returning members have reported to their groups.
7. Require intense interaction between the conflicting groups under conditions where each group's failure to cooperate is more costly to itself than continuing to fight, regardless of how the other group behaves.

of preventing further damage until some other tactic can be devised.

Limited Interaction

Reducing interaction to issues where superordinate goals exist and where decision-making rules have been agreed to, offers the advantage of getting some joint work done, but its utility depends upon whether the areas in which the protagonists are willing to cooperate, if any, are of any use to those in a position to impose this solution. Continued surveillance is also likely to be necessary, since the protagonists might easily make use of the available opportunities for communication for further attacks. The tactic may be of considerable use in situations where the interdependence between the two groups is clearly defined and stable over time, and where the joint decisions involved are generally routine. The tactic is least advantageous where the groups need to cooperate on a variety of issues or where areas requiring cooperation shift frequently and new decision-making procedures must continuously be established. Like the first tactic discussed,

this one does little to encourage attitudinal change either, so that the basic motivation to fight may remain indefinitely or be redirected in a more damaging direction.

Using Integrators

Using as integrators individuals who are seen by both groups as possessing high legitimate status, high expertise, and a constellation of personal attributes consistent with group ideals, creates the advantage of allowing the conflicting parties to coordinate each other's activities on a variety of issues while making it unnecessary for them to interact with each other directly. Thus it can be used in conjunction with a policy of physical separation, or with a policy where some interaction is permitted on routine issues. Lawrence and Lorsch have shown that this tactic is typically used by firms which need to maintain high levels of coordination among functional groups with clearly different work orientations. For instance, in some segments of the plastics industry, the production task is highly certain, the research task highly uncertain. As discussed earlier, this kind of situation promotes intergroup conflict. These authors found that in organizations where the men who were assigned the task of coordinating the research and production units were rated high by both in terms of expertise and legitimate power, the quality of relations between these groups was better and their firms on the whole economically more effective than in those firms where the integrators did not have these characteristics. Some research done by this author indicates that the possession by integrators of commonly valued personal attributes—education, business background, personal style—can play a similarly important role. While studying relations among departments in two small firms, he found that coordination between pairs of departments was considerably better where the integrators possessed personal attributes valued by both groups, even in cases where ratings of power and expertise would have indicated no differences in their quality of integration.

One major difficulty in executing this tactic is finding the golden men who fit all the requirements. Many firms simply may not have the resources or the sophistication to do so. Also, as with the previous two tactics discussed, this approach does not encourage attitudinal change. In some cases—where job demands require differences in orientation—this may be an important advantage. Where this is not the case, though, the tactic is obviously less desirable.

Third-Party Consultants

One tactic which represents something of a balance between attempts at attitudinal change on the one hand and the direct stopping of conflict behavior on the other, involves the use of direct negotiations between representatives of the warring parties in the presence of a third-party consultant whose advice and actions are valued by both groups.

The negotiating activity itself encourages the clarification of assumptions and the exploration of each party's motives—in essence a clear confrontation of differences. Thus, it sets the stage for new learning to take place. The presence of the third party, if the latter's opinions and counsel are sufficiently valued, inhibits lapses into name calling or other emotional outbursts and, in general, acts as a deterrent against further overt conflict behavior. If the third party is sufficiently skilled, he can also guide the negotiations in ways that tend to create the best results, e.g., sequencing differentiation and integration phases, keeping tensions at a moderate level, lending his status to a weaker party so that a balance of power is obtained and issues of ultimate influence do not get in the way of the confrontation process.

Negotiations without Consultants

Bringing representatives together for negotiations without a third party present involves greater risk of further conflict. There is no one there to keep tempers under control. But one can argue that if the need to resolve differences is sufficiently important to both parties, the agreements under this condition might involve even more attitudinal change and acceptance. The participants are doing all the work themselves and thus the experience is more intense. The key to making this tactic work, of course, is one of making the motivation to resolve the conflict so strong that the negotiators are willing to work their way through the issues in spite of the mistakes they are likely to make without a third party present. One method for creating such motivation is to make the need to cooperate crucial for each negotiator, regardless of what the other party does. For instance, if each negotiator's failure to cooperate is likely to result in losses either to himself or his group that are nearly equal or slightly greater than anything the other party can do to him, cooperation in and of itself becomes important and he is likely to be more flexible in his demands. An example of this would be a situation in which both groups were in danger of being dispersed or reorganized by a powerful third party, e.g., top management, if their fighting continued, and thereby of suffering the same fate either one would if it were to lose control over its activities to the other. The relative strengths of the need to cooperate on the one hand and the need to meet group demands on the other must not be too disparate; otherwise agreements might be made simply for the sake of survival and no real differences aired. But if this disparity can be prevented, the tension created by attempting to serve two needs simultaneously can result in considerable attitudinal change.

Exchanging Members

One problem with negotiations of the sort where only representatives of the protagonists are involved is that agreements made at the bargaining table may be interpreted as a betrayal by those group members who have not taken part in the negotiations and who therefore have not been subjected directly to the strains of having to come to an agreement. Even where notions of betrayal do not arise, members may interpret a new agreement as a behavioral requisite only, caused by prevailing circumstances, and not encouraging them to change their minds about anything. One way of setting the stage for more pervasive attitudinal change is to have the warring groups exchange some of their members for sufficient lengths of time to let them become familiar with how the other group operates, what kinds of problems it faces on a day-to-day basis, and how its rank and file explain their own ideals, statuses, norms, and the like.

The exchanged individuals then return to their own groups and, as accepted members who have not been working under the strain of negotiations, are possibly in a better position to communicate these data to their cohorts than would potentially suspect representatives. These data can then be used both during and following negotiations to evaluate the agree-

ments made and encourage greater acceptance of them.

The tactic has some noteworthy disadvantages. It takes time, perhaps more than an intervening party thinks he can afford. It takes sophistication since an astute social analysis is a prerequisite. It requires the voluntary cooperation of both parties. Each group must be willing to give up some of its members. The exchanged members must be encouraged to gather their data objectively. Temporary outsiders must be responded to positively and provided with honest discussions of how one's group works and what its members actually believe. A visiting individual who is isolated or given poor data will probably hinder successful negotiations at a later date. Finally, the data visitors gain, even if honest and accurate, may possibly serve to convince one or more of the groups that they really do want to fight with the other or that agreements made later do not represent a change in attitude. Thus, a major risk is involved.

On the positive side, exchange of this sort can clear up important misconceptions, indicate to each party where the most fruitful negotiations might take place, and ultimately result in permanent attitude change so that the sources of conflict cease to exist. If the latter occurs, the intervening party or anyone relying on cooperation between the two groups no longer has to worry about the possibility of conflict or continue to invest his energies in preventing its occurrence.

Because of its disadvantages, this tactic is rarely used, if ever, in connection with major institutional disputes, such as those between labor and management. But, it is used by firms to prevent or reduce conflict between members of different functional departments. For instance, numerous firms in industries that require close coordination between production and applied research departments require newcomers in each department to work for a time in the other to gain a greater familiarity with the problems the members of the latter face.

Multilevel Interaction

At the other end of the continuum from the reduction of conflict through physical separation is the encouragement of intense interaction among many or all of the members of opposing groups. Like the previous two tactics, an essential ingredient in its use is the development of a set of conditions under which the failure of each group to cooperate will result in major costs to itself, regardless of what the other group does. This situation, if an intervening party can create it, ideally forces an open confrontation of differences followed by basic attitudinal change. Besides the fact that, like all negotiations, it takes time, the main disadvantage of this tactic is that the requisite conditions may be hard to create and to maintain for the period it takes for the issues to be resolved. Whole groups are involved and not just a few negotiators whose behavior and status can be closely surveyed. Members of opposing forces are likely to start out by making peace in terms of norms of action while maintaining their negative attitudes. In some cases, only time and shared experience can open up the way for the development of positive emotional bonds. If the intervening party is unable to maintain the reward structure as described above on a continuous basis, even if the lapse in these conditions is only momentary, one or both of the protagonists might seize the opportunity to attack and set the process back several steps. The possibility also exists that, if differences are strong enough, some of the protagonists may choose to incur the cost of refusing to cooperate and resolve the situation by leaving the group or being forced to leave. The intervening party has to accept this possibility and take into account his manpower needs and resources in the process. . . .

63

Rational for Whom?[†]

Organizations are often defined as groups of people who come together to pursue a common goal. But more often than not, goals diverge as much as they converge, making the rationality of the overall organization no more than an elusive ideal.

Beneath the collective irrationality, however, organizations are often operating in a way that is eminently rational from the standpoint of the individuals, groups, and coalitions directly involved. In the following, Jeffrey Pfeffer presents two excellent illustrations:

Two examples illustrate how difficult it is to talk of rationality in real organizational decision-making situations. One is the construction of the Bay Area Rapid Transit System (BART). This is a well-publicized major effort to construct a new, modern, efficient transportation system for the San Francisco Bay Area. More complete histories of this system can be found in Homburger (1967) and Wolfe (1968). For the present, it is sufficient to note the following (1) the initial planning committees instrumental in planning for BART were dominated by companies that stood to benefit either directly from the work of the project or indirectly through their positions in real estate or their possible involvement as underwriters of the BART financing; (2) the appointed board of directors was generally unfamiliar with the engineering and technical aspects of the project; (3) the largest donors to the Citizens for Rapid Transit, the group that advertised in favor of the special bond election to finance BART in 1962, were the Bank of America, Wells Fargo, Crocker Bank, Tudor Engineering, Bechtel, Westinghouse Electric, Bethlehem Steel, Kaiser Industries, Perini Corporation (real estate), Westinghouse Air Brake, the Downtown Property Owner's Association, and Parsons, Brinckerhoff, Quade, and Douglas (engineering consulting) (Wolfe, 1968); (4) Parsons, in a joint venture with Tudor and Bechtel, was retained as the engineering consultant for system design and construction, with an open-ended fee arrangement which climbed from its initially expected $47 million to over $120 million; (5) BART was completed years late, at a cost of $1.6 billion rather than the originally estimated figure of about $900 million.

Our question is: Was this a rational organizational process, effective in serving its intended

[†]SOURCE: Reprinted from J. Pfeffer, *Organizational Design* (Harlan Davidson, Inc., Arlington Heights, IL: 1978), pp. 9-12, by permission of the publisher.

goals? It should be obvious that the answer to this question is very much dependent on where in the coalition one is. From the perspective of a taxpayer, burdened with both a special sales tax increment and property tax increments as well, many aspects of the system were not rational or effective. From the perspective of the contributors to Citizens for Rapid Transit, all of whom have enriched themselves enormously from the contracts involved in the construction, the project was both successful and rational. Indeed, the higher the costs and the greater the difficulties, the better for Bechtel and its joint venture associates, which could make fees designing the system, and would make additional fees fixing it when it did not work. The moral: What looks like irrational behavior, leading to inefficiency, is only irrational to those not profiting from the extra revenues generated.

Our second example involves the allocation of faculty positions to subject area groups within, say, a school of business. Further, let us assume that class enrollments are the only factor to be considered. Here, you might expect, is a computational decision situation if there ever was one. After all, a student is a student, and we can all count students and faculty. But, does an undergraduate student count the same as an M.B.A., or an M.B.A. the same as an advanced M.B.A. taking an elective, or a Ph.D. student? Is a course taught by an instructor the same as one taught by an assistant professor, or one by a full professor? And, how about students who take the courses from other departments? How should they be weighted in determining resource needs by the various subject areas? It is probably the case that in any real situation, the resource-allocation implications are altered greatly, depending upon how these weights are assigned. And while it is true that there are facts—the number of students of what types, and the composition of the faculty—it is far from a computational procedure to determine how varying students should be counted for purposes of allocating resources, although once the weightings are assigned, the actual decision-making appears to be routine. Here is an instance in which there is ostensible agreement on the criterion, allocating positions based on teaching loads, and there is plenty of objective data, and even so, the possibility remains of conflict and influence being associated with the decision.

It is difficult to think of situations in which goals are so congruent, or the facts so clearcut that judgment and compromise are not involved. What is rational from one point of view is irrational from another. Organizations are political systems, coalitions of interests, and rationality is defined only with respect to unitary and consistent orderings of preferences.

REFERENCES

Homburger, Wolfgang S. "Case Study: San Francisco Bay Area Rapid Transit Planning and Development." In *Urban Mass Transit Planning*, edited by W. S. Homburg. Berkeley: University of California, Institute of Transportation and Traffic Engineering, 1967.

Wolfe, Burton, H. "Bart Probe." *Bay Guardian*, 18 June, 30 Aug., 1 Nov., and 24 Dec. 1968.

64

Powerless Power?

Chief executives are often viewed as extremely powerful people. But they are also dependent on others. In the following pages, David Calabria explores the paradox of the CEO's role in a way that generates many insights on the nature of interpersonal power.

CEOs AND THE PARADOX OF POWER†

Chief executive officers have a power problem. They possess considerable formal authority, yet a survey of nearly 400 CEOs showed that one in three reported worrying several times a year about being abruptly removed from office.[1] These apprehensions seem to be well founded. In 1977, two-thirds of all large American companies were headed by chief executives who had been in office less than seven years.[2]

This high turnover rate has one cause—the inability to solve the paradox of power. On paper the CEO is all-powerful; in reality he or she is often powerless, sometimes because of incompetence, but more often because he or she is undermined by traps inherent in the ways his or her work is organized. Fortunately, these traps can be identified and avoided.

Powerlessness stems from the one characteristic that separates management from other professions—dependence.[3] The existence of dependence in the modern corporation is quite ironic. Rational bureaucracies were created to eliminate the arbitrary and unpredictable whim of rulers, but other forms of dependence were, in turn, created by the bureaucracies. In a bureaucracy, the division of labor precludes any individual from having within his or her domain all the skills or people he or she needs to succeed. The scarcity of money, raw materials, property, and other supplies fosters reliance on people who control these resources. As the president of a major bank said, "Everyone has power until they try to use it. Then you see how real the power is. I appear to have it, but it is impossible to act unilaterally."[4]

Dependence is a fact of management life and this fact creates both traps and opportunities. On the one hand, vulnerability results from dependence. Chief executives are themselves controlled by the power relationship. They

†SOURCE: David C. Calabria, "CEOs and the Paradox of Power," *Business Horizons*, January-February, 1982, pp. 29-31; used with permission.

must give orders that will be obeyed, justify personal whim on impersonal and collective grounds, and act on their promise to reward or punish.[5] Subordinates can withhold compliance from the CEO either directly or indirectly, thereby threatening and controlling the careers and influence of the chief executive.

On the other hand, dependence encourages CEOs to acquire power. "Everyone up there is vulnerable, but they are more vulnerable because all those below them are competing hard to be in their slots. So he has to devote an enormous amount of his time to power consolidation," says Dr. Jonas Kohler, a New York psychiatrist.[6] Furthermore, David McClelland has shown that subordinates who have powerful bosses reward them with high morale and performance.[7] Power is the antidote to dependence. It enables the CEO to extricate himself or herself from organizational traps.

Three Traps

Becoming powerful and staying that way is no easy task. The very nature of CEOs' work contains three formidable traps, any one of which could render them powerless. Step one in avoiding entrapment is being able to identify the pitfalls.

• The credibility of the CEO is under constant threat. The chief executive is charged with assuring the future of the corporation. Planning for the future is an uncertain business and the best strategic plans can be undermined by changes or conditions in the environment over which the CEO has no control, such as OPEC, inflation, or constituency pressures. The way in which CEOs react to these threats will determine whether their credibility is augmented or diminished.

Credibility grows when the chief executive responds to the challenges of the marketplace with innovative ideas and organization which visibly improve the viability of the company. This type of response is especially important when external conditions affect the corporation adversely.

CEOs become trapped when they respond to threatening conditions with retrenchment, that is, focusing on short-term fluctuations and results, delegating less and overseeing the work of subordinates more closely, and defining accomplishment as nailing down details. Frederick Fox and Barry Staw have found that the trapped CEOs can be thought of as the ones who are most likely to increase rather than decrease their commitment to previously chosen policy and most likely to become inflexible in their defense of such positions.[8]

When chief executives abandon long-range goals, they give up opportunities for building credibility, thereby rendering themselves powerless. Subordinates respond to this state of affairs by withdrawing their respect, loyalty, and commitment.

• CEOs often are out of contact with important information. Ironically, this loss of contact can be triggered by coping successfully with the first trap. As CEOs insulate themselves from detail and routine work, they put greater distance between themselves and the daily action which indicates the corporation's success or failure in the marketplace.

In place of direct access to data, chief executives rely on the reports of subordinates. Even under the best conditions, these reports are distortions of reality. Too often the worst conditions prevail and these reports are influenced by the unwillingness to bear bad news and power moves by political alliances.

Cut off from information and unsure of the allegiance of subordinates, the CEO feels lonely. "Many CEOs attempt to offset the loneliness by finding an alter ego, a confidant or two, with whom he can let his guard down. The result, in all too many cases, is that he builds a team of sycophants, loyal, usually innocuous staff members, with whom he frequently eats and pretests his ideas and proposals. Unfortunately, while realistically he seeks a measurable response, all he gets is often too-willing approval. Unless he recognizes it for what it is, it works against him. Carried to its extreme—as happens many times—the certain conclusion is disappointment for him and sometimes even disaster for the company and its employees."[9]

Fortunately these problems are also solvable. CEOs can identify their data needs and arrange for direct access to these data, thereby reducing dependence on subordinates and their biases. Chief executives can take a small risk and choose a management team composed of people with different backgrounds, experiences, and ideas, who are willing to challenge a CEO's thinking, thereby avoiding the "whatever-you-say" syndrome. Finally, CEOs can negotiate a workable interpersonal contract with each team member. Such contracts evolve through a series of stages; if subordinates see the chief executives' judgments as decisive and credible, the CEOs' influence on the subordinates exceeds even their positional power.[10]

When chief executives do not have independent sources of information and a diverse but trustworthy management team, they invite isolation, dependence, and powerlessness.

• CEOs are increasingly under attack by pressure groups, called "stakeholders." They represent a major challenge to business decision making, because they want to be part of the process. Their interests and motivations are long term and cannot be ignored. As Dr. Eugene Jennings comments, "Today the chairman as CEO increasingly is involved personally in promoting his company's cause in the arena of public opinion. His ability to persuade dissident stockholders, consumer activists, and even disgruntled employees of his worthiness to maintain his position of power will determine his degree of effectiveness and ultimately his tenure in office."[11]

There is a growing literature on this subject, advising CEOs in their conduct of external relations. Briefly, the literature proposes doing homework before taking on pressure groups, opening up and maintaining communications with these groups, and negotiating mutually beneficial outcomes. More and more corporate business is subject to public scrutiny. CEOs who

can enter the public arena and win the support of the constituencies they find there will acquire power and influence far beyond that associated with their formal position. If, however, CEOs cannot successfully develop public support for their companies, they will feel powerless and out of control.

Finding an Ally

Chief executives are powerful people, yet their hold on their power is fragile. They occupy the most powerful position in the corporation, yet they can be made powerless by traps inherent in their office. They can survive these organizational traps but they need help. Although it seems unlikely at first glance, the person who can often provide this assistance is the chief personnel officer.

For their part, chief executives can liberate personnel officers from conditions which limit their power and careers: being excluded from making many significant human resource decisions, having their authority undercut by superiors, having their work go unrecognized, being a staff rather than a line manager, handling only routine personnel matters, working only on predictable tasks, having short career ladders, and avoiding organizational politics.

In return, personnel officers can help CEOs avoid the traps of their office by providing the following services.

• Provide access to employment data which the CEO can use to assure the board of directors that the corporation has a work force which will successfully respond to the challenges of the marketplace and forestall affirmative action litigation.

• Set up a flow of information to the CEO which will enable him or her to know whether the corporation has the management personnel to meet its product, market, and financial goals.

• Enable the CEO to adapt to new social and personal values emerging in the corporation and the marketplace.

- Role play with the CEO decisions that may negatively affect the careers, status, or power of key subordinates.
- Assist the CEO in tracing out the extent to which different directors and officers command key resources of the organization.
- Bring different power centers together, through diplomacy, to resolve conflicts in order that the corporation may survive.
- Put together a handbook the CEO can use to do political analysis to avoid palace coups.
- Use knowledge of competencies and political alliances of employees to let the CEO know on whom to rely.
- Recruit management personnel with skills needed by the corporation and the CEO.
- Keep the CEO up to date on the research about power in management and organizational politics.

Being a chief executive will undoubtedly remain an exciting, but precarious, occupation. Understanding the traps inherent in the office of CEO and forging an alliance with the chief personnel officer can add significantly to the security and tenure of the chief executive.

NOTES

1. Survey conducted by John Arnold, Execu-Trak Systems (reported in *Boston Globe*, 19 August 1977).
2. Isadore Barmash (New York: Lippincott, 1978), 111.
3. Leonard R. Sayles, *Managerial Behavior: Administration in Complex Organization* (New York: McGraw-Hill, 1964).
4. "Life at the Top: The Struggle for Power," in *Life in Organizations*, ed. Rosabeth Moss Kanter and Barry A. Stein (New York: Basic Books, 1979), 4.
5. "Life at the Top," 7-8.
6. Barmash, *The Chief Executives*, 56.
7. David McClelland and David Burnham, "Power Is the Great Motivator," *Harvard Business Review*, March-April, 1976, 102.
8. Frederick Fox and Barry Staw, "The Trapped Administrator: Effects of Job Insecurity and Policy Resistance on Commitment of a Course of Action," *Administrative Science Quarterly*, September 1979:449-71.
9. Barmash, *The Chief Executives*, 19.
10. John Gabarro, "Socialization at Top: How CEOs and Subordinates Evolve Interpersonal Contracts," *Organizational Dynamics*, Winter 1979.
11. Barmash, *The Chief Executives*, 117.

65

Gender and Corporate Politics

In September 1980, Mary Cunningham was promoted to the role of vice president at Bendix Corporation at the age of 29. She was the youngest woman to hold such a post with such a major corporation. Just a week later, she resigned after rumors about an affair with Chairman William Agee (who she married in June 1982) made national headlines. In the following pages, Gail Sheehy tells part of the story: a story which raises the question of whether female executives stand a fair chance in today's corporate world.

THE CRASH OF A CORPORATE WOMAN†

Mary Cunningham used to leave the executive suite of Bendix Corp. after her usual 14-hour working day, crawl into bed with a big briefcase and make notes for a book she was writing on management styles. She also wrote out her life plan.

Her 20s would be for finding her weaknesses.

Thirties would be for developing credentials and becoming financially independent.

And her 40s would be the time to start jockeying for real power.

There was no room in this plan for love, she realized.

I could not love thee Dear so much
Lov'd I not power more.

Mary Cunningham was 28, just one year out of Harvard Business School, yet she had already risen to the vice-presidency of the 88th largest industrial company in the United States. She wanted more.

She wrote out 200 pages of career planning with four potential avenues to follow. All led to public service. Not surprising. Her childhood models had been moral crusaders: Dag Hammarskjold, Gandhi. The disappointment of her adolescence was to discover she couldn't be a priest.

†SOURCE: Excerpted from Gail Sheehy, "The Crash of a Corporate Woman," *Toronto Star*, 18 and 19 October 1980, pp. 91-92, and pp. D1 and D2. Reprinted with permission—The Toronto Star Syndicate.

Compelling Fantasy

Yet ever since she was a little girl, Cunningham had the sense: "I'm in preparation; some day I'll be called upon to do something really significant in the world."

Could there be a more compelling corporate fantasy?

A bright and beautiful executive, close confidante of Bendix chairman William Agee, sharing the company JetStar with him, her strawberry blonde hair ablaze in the sun at 30,000 feet, his feet up and his shirt open as they discussed their crusade to revolutionize Big Business.

Bill Agee and Mary Cunningham. They were one of the most glamorous and dynamic management teams in the United States, and they flew together across the country all last summer with close to a billion dollars to spend, stockpiled from the sale of other divisions of the company.

Bill Agee and Mary Cunningham. Their goal was to retrofit Bendix Corp. and make it a high-technology leader in the 21st century.

So accelerated was everything about this 42-year-old chairman and the meteoric rise of his closest adviser that when it all fell apart last week, all North America took notice.

For two weeks, ever since Agee called his company's executives together in Detroit's Cobo Hall and publicly denied that Mary Cunningham's rapid promotion had anything to do with a romance between them, the case had made headlines. After offering to take a leave of absence because of the "false innuendos," she was given a vote of confidence by the board of Bendix. Then, abruptly, she resigned—leaving behind a host of questions:

Sabotaged by Envy

Where does this leave men and women of the future who would aspire to a close working relationship at the top? Were Agee and Cunningham sabotaged by envy and brought down by ageism, sexism and corporate conservatism?

Is Mary Cunningham just a clever corporate game player? Or is she something more?

The irony of the situation was summed up by a top executive who knew of the intensely religious background that had molded Cunningham's missionary zeal.

"If Mary Cunningham was trying to capture anything from Bill Agee it wasn't his heart—more likely she wanted to save his soul."

What follows is an exclusive account of the rise and sudden deceleration, and recent recovery, of Mary Cunningham's rocket to success.

* * *

Mary Cunningham came across the radar screens of the corporate recruiters like a comet. Everyone who interviewed her had the same impressions. "She's brilliant." "She's intimidating." "She's aggressive." "She's beautiful, too!" And everyone wanted to know the same thing. "What drives her?"

Teams of interviewers picked through her brain that spring of 1979 before she graduated with breathtaking credentials. She was a Phi Beta Kappa philosophy graduate from Wellesley College, and then one of 30 out of 800 business school students elected to Harvard's Century Club as leaders of tomorrow. In her second year there she took a course overload, carried a job, created an exam review program for first-year business students, and sailed out with honors at age 27.

A team from Salomon Brothers went over her meticulously and concluded she was "awesomely motivated." But they couldn't figure out why. "Does money motivate you?" they tried. "Would anything keep you working until one in the morning?" Definitely, she said. "What is it you are really trying to accomplish?" they kept asking.

"One day I will have something to say," she replied. "I'm not ready to say it yet."

It made Mary Cunningham smile. They couldn't slot her. Couldn't say. "Oh yes, you must be from Darien." Recruiters found her background, well, quaint . . . Hanover, New Hampshire, no money or family connections, drawn toward philosophy from an early age, and what was this about being raised by a mother and a substitute father who was a monsignor?

Offers from the financial world started at $47,000. Cunningham kept them all dangling. Try as they might, none of them could figure out what make her *fly?*

Money wasn't what she had on her mind. Lord, no, what she wanted was to do good. . . .

Mary Cunningham met Bill Agee in his suite at the Waldorf Astoria hotel in New York in 1979.

She was being screened by the top corporate recruiters in the country, and she was surprised when the relaxed, handsome man in shirtsleeves and no tie opened the door. His mouth broke out of the clefted brackets on either side and into an infectious grin.

"Are you Mary Cunningham?"

"Yes."

"I'm Bill Agee, chairman of Bendix Corp. How would you like to be my executive assistant?"

She kept her cool. "Well, let's see how we get along."

Intense Talks

The scheduled hour interview stretched into four hours of intense discussion during which each tried to take the measure of the other's mind. He asked what she was all about.

"I want to go out there into the murkiest part of human nature and force myself to deal with it," she explained. "I have to admit that what also excites me is competing and making acquisitions and seeing my team win."

The young king of Bendix delighted in her solemnity. The moral crusader Cunningham saw him as potentially unique among captains of industry: He, too, seemed to care about more than money and titles. Only 31 when he was elevated to financial vice-president of Boise Cascade, he was heralded as a genius.

"He had continued his wunderkind romp at Bendix. When Mike Blumenthal left as chairman to take a cabinet post as U.S. Secretary of Treasury, Blumenthal tapped Agee, then 38, to take his place. Now at the pinnacle of success, Agee could afford to ask, "What is my moral responsibility to speak out on the issues?"

Something moved in Cunningham. They were both energetic, aggressive, driven individuals with animated minds that leapt easily from the specific to the conceptual. She could do astonishing things with this man.

Over spring vacation Cunningham sat for three days trying to coax her husband into commenting on the Bendix offer. Howard "Bo" Gray had come far in business for a black man of 39, but he had never seen anything like the rush being given Cunningham. He refused to comment.

"But you're part of the decision," Cunningham pleaded. Already they had been separated for two of their three years of marriage while she went through Harvard Business School. Joining Bendix in Michigan would mean leaving him in New York.

"This is your career," Gray said. "I want you to choose."

On the third day Cunningham said she had made her decision. She went into the bedroom and closed the door and called Bill Agee. When she came out Gray said, "You look really peaceful. You chose Bendix, didn't you?"

Turned Down

"No, I just turned Bill Agee down.'

Gray rolled that surprise around in his mind for 10 minutes. Cunningham had given him a signal that he was very important in her life: "Acting that out isn't going to tell me anything more than you've just told me," he said. "Call Agee back and take it."

For the first three months at Bendix, Cunningham studied her boss' management style. From her arrival at the office every morning at 6 until she left at 8 or 9 or 10 at night, she observed his moves microscopically.

Bill Agee didn't know it but he had hired himself an angel. She wrote all his speeches. She prepared testimony for him to give in Washington. She wrote a first-rate chairman's letter for the annual report. She became Bill Agee's alter ego in the outside world.

By last December she had moved into strategy at Bendix. Then into acquisitions. Agee and Cunningham agreed on the short-term financial orientation for Bendix as well as on a long-term push into high technology. Their minds were almost "frighteningly compatible."

The chairman found in Cunningham something few men at the top have. A friend. And a perceptive confidante. Most senior executives have no real friends at all, and if their wives function as confidantes it is not in the finely tuned way Agee and Cunningham played adversaries.

By January, Cunningham had to face the reality that her marriage was finished. Gray was standing on the sidelines of her career and cheerleading. She wanted to look up to a man who was achieving even more than she—only then could there be mystery. There was no transition from Bo Gray as "husband" to Bo as "friend" which, Cunningham realized, said it all. Cunningham's religion remains the most important thing in her life. Bill Agee was the third in a series of taboo men whom she could love only with the celibate perfection of one chosen for higher purpose. The first was the priest who had helped raise her; the second was her black husband. Cunningham was not unaware by now of the defense her unconscious mind had favored. It is called sublimation.

Everyone needs defenses and sublimation is much healthier than most. It is a form of desexualization. The person's unallowable instincts are channeled into work or altruistic acts, or sexual abstinence itself, thereby relieving reproach from one's conscience. Mary Cunningham was delighted to find that Bill Agee was a world-class sublimator himself.

Describe Her Boss

Last June, after a year at Bendix, Cunningham tried to describe her boss and why she had decided to stay. For the first time in her life she couldn't put her words together.

"He is intellectually honest, he has courage and takes risks and has a flawless value system . . ." Then Cunningham simply let rip with a truth she held to be self-evident: "He is the finest human being I've ever met."

That same June the chairman wanted to promote Mary Cunningham to vice-president for corporate and public affairs. That would make her the most senior female executive in the whole company—at 28.

"I'll be a target on your back," she warned him.

He insisted. Bill Agee wanted to be a trailblazer in bringing bright women into senior management and promoting for merit along the fast track.

"How clear is your reputation?" Cunningham asked him again, just as she had during their first interview.

"Mine's flawless," he said.

"Mine's flawless, too," she said.

She took the promotion.

Warnings about appearances began to reach Cunningham last summer. The most vocal was Nancy Reynolds, an older woman who had lost her singular status as the top female executive when Cunningham was put in over her as vice-president in charge of the national affairs department Reynolds had headed. Don't be seen in public with Bill Agee, she said, don't go to conventions or social-business dinners with him. Or you'll be sorry.

Cunningham confessed her fear to Agee: "I have the sense I'm approaching a cliff . . . there's some magnetism drawing me toward a dead end . . . forces that have been at work throughout history cannot handle women in upper-middle management, let alone being the closest confidante of the chairman."

Bill Agee said there was nothing to worry about. But the gossip about them had begun. . . .

On the last Monday in September at 4 o'clock in the afternoon, Mary Cunningham sat in her room at New York's Waldorf Astoria hotel. She could not eat. Every so often she stepped into the bathroom to vomit. Her career was on the block because of rumors linking her romantically with her boss. Her fate had to be decided by a "jury" of board members.

The immediate burst of controversy surrounding her promotion five days before, at 29, to one of the highest ranking women executives in American industry had prompted her boss, Bendix chairman Bill Agee, to defend her rise as based strictly on performance.

The next morning, Thursday, Sept. 25, the Detroit Free Press quoted Agee telling an employees' meeting: "I know it has been buzzing around that Mary Cunningham's rise in this company is very unusual and that it has something to do with a personal relationship we have. It is true that we are very close friends and she's a very close friend of my family. But that has nothing to do with the way that I and others in this company evaluate performance. Her rapid promotions are totally justified."

Fallen Status

Mary was on her way to the Detroit airport when she opened the paper and saw herself, like some sort of fallen statue, in pieces all over the front page. A few hours later she joined Bill Agee in a meeting in San Francisco. A message was slipped to her, saying the story had gone out over the AP wire and even crossed the Dow-Jones tape. Tomorrow it would get news play all over the country: "Bendix Chairman Denies Rumors."

Mary pulled a sheet of paper out of her notebook. In longhand she wrote out her immediate response: "I unilaterally and unconditionally offer my resignation."

Corporations take to the limelight of scandal the way moles take to fresh air. Mary sensed she would become an overnight freak. The culture simply wasn't ready for her yet. Too brilliant, too ambitious, too young, too pretty—as well as a woman. She wouldn't be able to function at this crucial moment in the $4-billion company's history with anything like the performance level she would expect from herself.

Her only choice was to move fast, she thought —"unilaterally" so the company wouldn't fake the brunt of appearing to have panicked and asked for her resignation; "unconditionally" so that Bill Agee wouldn't look as though he had left his protege in the lurch.

It was envy that did Mary Cunningham in.

REFERENCE

Cunningham, Mary. *Powerplay: What Really Happened at Bendix.* New York: Ballantine, 1984.

66

Game-Playing and the Psychodynamics of Organizational Life

There is often a deeper psychological basis to the events and activities decorating day-to-day routine. In the following pages, Jack Weber examines the games that managers play in their interactions with others.

GAMES MANAGERS PLAY†

Do you sometimes blame other people or departments for your own mistakes? Do you know someone who takes on more responsibilities than he or she can handle or who feels and looks harried? Do you know people who repeatedly procrastinate on important projects or arrive late to meetings and invite criticism from superiors? If these situations sound familiar, then you or others may have been engaging in a recurring pattern of dysfunctional behavior colloquially known as a "game."

As with Monopoly or checkers, people start playing psychological games in childhood. Children learn to manipulate their parents to elicit the attention they can't get by asking directly. Thus, the boy who asks his father to play baseball and is refused may moments later provoke his sister to fight. Dad then breaks up the quarrel with unnecessary force and the little boy cries. Mom intervenes, criticizes the father, and provides the children with a snack. Each time the pattern recurs, reinforcement takes place, and through a process of social learning, the child unconsciously learns to pick fights or break rules when he feels neglected.

Indeed, it is asserted that the patterns of behavior developed in the context of dependency during childhood become archetypes for subsequent authority relationships such as those between managers and subordinates in organizations. Learning to identify games and their underlying hidden agendas can provide the basis for more productive, satisfying, and growthful relationships.

†SOURCE: R. Jack Weber, "Games Managers Play," reprinted with permission from Darden School of Business Administration, University of Virginia.

Game Roles

When people engage in games, they unconsciously act out roles of Persecutor, Rescuer, or Victim. In the situation described above, the boy's invitation to his father is apparently direct, nonmanipulative, and free of games. Having failed, however, he initiates a game by Persecuting his sister who plays Victim by exaggerating the actual transgression. Father rushes to Rescue his daughter (who could handle her own problems) and ends up Persecuting his son by slapping him. Shifting to the Victim role, the little boy screams for his mother who Persecutes the father and Rescues her son by fixing him chocolate milk.

As the boy grows and becomes the general manager of a subsidiary and his achievements go unrecognized by the home office, he unconsciously repeats his childhood scenario by missing targets and turning in reports late, and is finally reprimanded by his boss. The boy-turned-manager angrily leaves the office early and complains about his superior to his wife who agrees with him and fixes him a drink. And although the actors have changed since childhood and he gets a double martini rather than chocolate milk, the game roles and dynamics are essentially unchanged.

It is important to note that game role behavior is nonproblem-solving, avoids responsibility, and results in bad feelings or otherwise fails to satisfy the underlying need. Thus, the boy's attack on his sister does nothing to identify other alternatives for playing ball or for getting his father's attention. Similarly, the manager's poor performance, criticism of his superior, and double martini do nothing to solve the original problem of inadequate recognition.

The three roles and their dynamic relationship may be represented in the form of the Game Triangle [Exhibit 66.1]. The Persecutor (P), Rescuer (R), and Victim (V) roles are connected in the diagram to indicate that games involve two or more roles and that people frequently switch roles during the course of one game or may play different roles in different games. However, most people have a favorite game role and tend to favor associates that behave in ways that permit them to play that role.

EXHIBIT 66.1 The Game Triangle

Each of these roles is described in greater detail below together with some of the principal games associated with each role.

Persecutor Games

The person in the role of Persecutor manipulates others to feel badly through blaming, shaming, ridiculing, bullying, threatening, criticizing, nitpicking, belittling, mocking, and so on. People playing Persecutor use one-up language laced with imperatives and judgments such as "you ought to know better!," "how could you be so stupid?," "you'll never learn!," and so on. The verbal statements may be accompanied by an accusing or threatening pointed finger, arms folded across one's chest, eyes rolled upward, a furrowed brow or frown, and loud, punitive, or condescending voice tones. The underlying feeling is anger or contempt and the underlying assumption is that others ought to be perfect or otherwise behave in ways consistent with the Persecutor's grandiose expectations. Specific examples include NIGYSOB and Blemish, two games that are described below.

Now I've Got You, You SOB (NIGYSOB). The "NIGYSOB" player tries to make other people feel bad to cover up his own negative feelings. He criticizes others excessively when they violate his standards or expectations, . . . frequently unrealistic or ambiguous. The psychological "payoff" for the Persecutor is a justification for feeling self-righteous and angry, an avoidance of intimate or authentic relationships with others, and an escape from his own underlying low self-esteem.

Case Example

Professor Corsini teaches finance in a major M.B.A. program. One day, in the middle of a case discussion that Corsini felt was not going very well, he noticed that Susan Morris was covertly whispering and smiling to her neighbor. Corsini imagined that the students were laughing about how poorly his class was going and he punitively snapped: "Miss Morris, what are *your* thoughts?" Miss Morris apologetically admitted that she hadn't followed the prior discussion. Rather than giving her enough information to respond, Corsini gave her an icy stare and turned to another student.

"NIGYSOB" can be avoided by negotiating clear, mutual expectations and achievable goals, by providing or acquiring the information and resources necessary to succeed, and by ongoing problem-solving.

Blemish. The "Blemish" game player criticizes insignificant flaws in performance rather than rewarding major successes. The "Blemish" player also Persecutes by constantly looking for minor gaps in logic rather than trying to understand the bigger picture. "Blemish" players experience an uncontrollable need to correct and find fault with others.

Case Example

Sydney Rogers asked a young marketing manager to evaluate his company's marketing strategy on their major product lines. When the subordinate submitted his detailed report, Rogers circled a couple of minor substantive and typographical errors in red pencil and wrote in red on the cover sheet: "Rewrite!"

Managers who play "Blemish" covertly invite their subordinates to concentrate on the in-consequential aspects of their jobs and to try to do everything perfectly without regard to priority. Subordinates also tend to develop feelings of inadequacy and resentment.

Victim Games

People in the role of Victim feel helpless or inadequate to solve their own problems or achieve their own goals when in fact they are not. The person playing Victim manipulates others to Rescue or Persecute by complaining, whining, bitching, agitating, getting sick, procrastinating, making mistakes, apologizing, and so on. The person playing Victim differs from a real victim (such as someone who is drowning) in that the Victims's helplessness is imaginary. The Victim also frequently does not ask for the help or support he or she needs, rejects advice or help when others offer it, and does not work at identifying and solving his or her problems.

People in the role of victim use language such as "I don't know" (when they really do), "I can't do it" (when they really could), "I can't stand it" (when they are), "I've tried everything" (when they have lots of other options), "It wasn't my responsibility" (when it was), "I didn't do it" (when they did), and so on. Frequently this kind of verbal behavior is accompanied by slumped or dejected postures, depressive voice tones, pouting or helpless facial expressions, and downcast eyes.

Kick Me. "Kick Me" players unconsciously provoke potential persecutors to criticize, condemn, punish, or otherwise put them down. They always seem to be getting into trouble and ask themselves "Why does this always happen to me?" The payoff to the game is a feeling of inadequacy and an opportunity to ask someone for sympathy.

Case Example

Karl Glasser is an account executive at a New York bank. Karl always seems to have more than he can get done. But while Karl efficiently processes paper work concerning his clients and other departments in the bank, he always seems to put off reports requested by his immediate superior. In fact, his boss frequently has to ask Karl a second time for important reports, which irritates Karl's boss and leaves Karl feeling guilty. Karl also plays "Kick Me" by frequently arriving late to meetings.

The game can be stopped by negotiating clear contracts with the potential player, by providing recognition or positive "strokes" for achieving commitments, and by withholding negative strokes or criticism for his or her mistakes.

If It Weren't for You. The basic theme of this game is that "there is someone else who keeps me from doing what I really want to do." The payoff of the game is to avoid doing something that one deeply fears.

Case Example

Earl Wilson worked for a major public accounting firm in New York City. He hated the bureaucracy of the large organization almost as much as the two hours a day he spent in commuting from Westchester. He griped about his situation constantly to friends on the train and talked repeatedly about his desire to return to the midwest to start his own firm. When asked why he didn't leave, he said that his wife was afraid that they wouldn't make it. Over time he became increasingly bitter towards his wife and complained to a broader circle of people that "If it weren't for Nancy, I would get out of New York."

The game can be broken up by granting the player permission to do what he or she claims to want to do. In the example above, if the wife would have said, "Go ahead and make a crack at your own business," the husband's underlying fears would be revealed and he could no longer hold his wife responsible.

Ain't It Awful. As the name suggests, "Ain't It Awful!" involves protracted complaining about some aspects of one's life or work. The

covert message is a plea for sympathy that the Victim usually rejects on the grounds that the situation is hopeless. The payoff is a feeling of hopelessness or despair.

Case Example

John Wickenden was in the first year of a demanding two-year M.B.A. program, and every few days John would wile away two or three hours with a classmate at a local coffee house bitching about the work load and various professors. When they had finished, both would feel even worse than when they started.

The problems that are the source of the material for "Ain't It Awful" are frequently exaggerated or imaginary. But even when they are serious and authentic, the situation is a game because it does not lead to problem-solving nor to an improvement in the player's life or work situation.

The game can be stopped by shifting the topic, by asking the person what has been going well in his or her life, or by engaging the person in an exploration of ways that they might improve their situation.

Why Don't You? Yes, But. In this game the initiator solicits advice from another on a decision or problem and then rejects any suggestions offered.

Case Example

Dick Pfeiffer, a first-year M.B.A. student, had recently flunked his accounting midterm exam and had gone to talk to his faculty advisor, a professor of marketing. Dick asked his advisor's advice, but when the professor suggested that he ask his accounting professor for help, Dick replied, "Yeh, but he is awfully busy and I really don't want him to know how much trouble I'm having." The advisor then suggested that Dick ask one of his classmates to help, to which Dick replied, "Yes, but they already have enough of their own work to do."

The professor next suggested that Dick hire a part-time tutor from the student tutoring agency, to which Dick replied, "Yes, but I don't really have the money." The professor quickly informed the student that there were long-term, low-interest loans available for such purposes and the student responded that "Yes, but I already have a lot of loans and I wouldn't want to get into any more debt." By this time the advisor was experiencing a lot of frustration and politely told the student that he had an important meeting to go to.

In organizational life a "Yes, But" player presents a personal or work-related problem in such a way that his superior or other potential Rescuer is induced to offer advice. When the superior offers a possible solution to the problem, the subordinate responds by saying "Yes, but . . ." and adds information that renders the advice redundant, gratuitous, or presumably unworkable. On the surface, the situation appears to be a direct and straightforward request: "Here is a problem. Do you have any ideas on how I can solve it?" However, if the person is playing "Yes, But" there is also a covert message that belies that "If you try to give me advice, I'll find fault with every suggestion."

The game ends in an exasperated silence that ensues after the superior has offered several solutions and has run out of ideas or is frustrated. This tells the subordinate that he has won the game. It also demonstrates that the boss is inadequate and reinforces an early childhood decision that "parents are dumb."

If the superior above had suspected the beginning of a game, his first response to the request for information above might have been to say: "Sounds like a tough problem. What ideas have you thought about?" This approach also has the advantage of strengthening the subordinate's capacity to solve his or her own problems. Even if the subordinate did accept the superior's advice or solution it is still the superior's solution and he or she is responsible for its success or failure. As such, solving other people's problems is also a set-up for "See What You Made Me Do." Finally, it is important to understand that bosses can initiate the game by inviting "participation" in decisions

when they have strong feelings about the preferred outcome.

Rescuer Games

A manager Rescues when he helps someone who does not want help, someone who does not need help, or someone who is not helping himself. A manager Rescues when he meddles in other's decisions, underestimates other's abilities, or fails to require people to carry their share of the work load.

A manager who Rescues may deny his own needs, delegate too little, work too hard, and become a Victim when others take advantage of his generosity and concern. Or he may shift to persecutor when others whom he "helped" do not respond by helping themselves.

A manager who Rescues secretly believes that others cannot solve their own problems and that others will grow through his making decisions for them or through his giving them advice. He may also believe that others will be destroyed if confronted with their inadequacies or otherwise given straight information. The Rescuer perpetuates dependence.

People playing the Rescuer role appear helpful and use language such as "Sure, I'd love to do it" (when he really hates to do it), "Let me do it for you" (when the other person hasn't asked for help), "If I were you, I . . ." (When the other person is capable of making the decision), and so on. Nonverbally, Rescuing behavior is frequently accompanied by sympathetic or supportive voice tones, encouraging head nodding, or consoling pats on the back.

Harried. The "Harried" player in his effort to be loved and approved by everyone takes on everything that comes down the pike, agrees to do things he really doesn't want to do, and seeks out more things to do even when he is already grossly overloaded. He agrees with all of his superior's criticisms and accepts all of his subordinates' demands. Eventually his performance suffers and he blames it on having too much to do, feigning that he had no control over his decisions to accept each new responsibility.

I'm Only Trying To Help You. In this game the player offers advice to someone who hasn't asked for it or who really doesn't want to change. The "client" takes the advice but returns and reports that the suggestion did not have the desired effect. The player who offered the unwanted advice feels inadequate, privately thinks "Nobody ever does what I tell them," and offers new advice.

Case Example

A first-year M.B.A. student went to one of his instructors, Professor Patsy, and confided that another first-year student, David Maxey, was not speaking in any of his classes and might "flunk out" due to poor participation. While Professor Patsy knew that Maxey wasn't speaking in his own class, he was unaware that it was a broader problem for Maxey.

Professor Patsy sought out David Maxey and invited him to his office. Patsy told Maxey that he had a problem, and after listening to Maxey's somewhat unrelated personal problems for two hours, advised Maxey to change seats and prepare a few "key points" to make in each class.

Two weeks later Maxey still hadn't opened his mouth and Patsy called Maxey in again for more coaching. Another week passed and Maxey quit school, informing the Dean's Office that there was "unreasonable pressure" to participate and that the emphasis on quantity of participation was "sophomoric."

People who receive unsolicited and unwanted advice or help in making decisions can stop this game by telling the player that they will ask for help when they need it. Likewise, people who initiate this game and other Rescuing games can learn to say no without feeling guilty, can reserve their help and advice for people who take the initiative to ask for it, and can contract with the people with whom they live and work to take responsibility for asking for help when they need it.

Beyond Games

Why do people play games? After all, why would someone repeatedly show up late to class or to meetings when they know their superior values punctuality?While the complete explanation for the self-defeating quality of games is beyond the scope of this paper, the simple explanation is that "people need strokes to survive" and that "negative strokes are better than no strokes." To a child, to be yelled at may be preferable to being ignored. And unfortunately, the patterns developed in childhood tend to persist in organizational life even when they fail to produce satisfying outcomes.

Eric Berne once observed that the question is not *"Do* I play games?" but *"What* games do I play?" The challenge then is to learn to identify and stop your own games, to refuse to buy into others' games, and to find honest and assertive ways to get the strokes you need.

67

Groupthink:
The Problems of Conformity†

Many organizations know that they face problems in managing conflict. But agreement, consensus, and conformity can create problems too.

In the following pages, Irving Janis identifies the phenomenon of "groupthink," and points to some of the factors that sustain it in practice.

"How could we have been so stupid?" President John F. Kennedy asked after he and a close group of advisors had blundered into the Bay of Pigs invasion. For the last two years I have been studying that question, as it applies not only to the Bay of Pigs decision-makers but also to those who led the United States into such other major fiascos as the failure to be prepared for the attack on Pearl Harbor, the Korean War stalemate and the escalation of the Vietnam War.

Stupidity certainly is not the explanation. The men who participated in making the Bay of Pigs decision, for instance, comprised one of the greatest arrays of intellectual talent in the history of American Government—Dean Rusk, Robert McNamara, Douglas Dillon, Robert Kennedy, McGeorge Bundy, Arthur Schlesinger Jr., Allen Dulles and others.

It also seemed to me that explanations were incomplete if they concentrated only on disturbances in the behavior of each individual within a decision-making body: temporary emotional states of elation, fear, or anger that reduce a man's mental efficiency, for example, or chronic blind spots arising from a man's social prejudices or idiosyncratic biases.

I preferred to broaden the picture by looking at the fiascos from the standpoint of group dynamics as it has been explored over the past three decades, first by the great social psychologist Kurt Lewin and later in many experimental situations by myself and other behavioral scientists. My conclusion after pouring over hundreds of relevant documents—historical reports about formal group meetings and informal conversations among the members—is that the groups that committed the fiascos were victims of what I call "groupthink."

"Groupy." In each case study, I was surprised to discover the extent to which each group displayed the typical phenomena of social conformity that are regularly encoun-

†SOURCE: Excerpted from Irving L. Janis, "Groupthink," *Psychology Today*, November 1971, pp. 271-79. Reprinted with permission from Psychology Today Magazine, copyright © 1971 (APA).

tered in studies of group dynamics among ordinary citizens. For example, some of the phenomena appear to be completely in line with findings from social-psychological experiments showing that powerful social pressures are brought to bear by the members of a cohesive group whenever a dissident begins to voice his objections to a group consensus. Other phenomena are reminiscent of the shared illusions observed in encounter groups and friendship cliques when the members simultaneously reach a peak of "groupy" feelings.

Above all, there are numerous indications pointing to the development of group norms that bolster morale at the expense of critical thinking. One of the most common norms appears to be that of remaining loyal to the group by sticking with the policies to which the group has already committed itself, even when those policies are obviously working out badly and have unintended consequences that disturb the conscience of each member. This is one of the key characteristics of groupthink.

1984. I use the term groupthink as a quick and easy way to refer to the mode of thinking that persons engage in when *concurrence-seeking* becomes so dominant in a cohesive in-group that it tends to override realistic appraisal of alternative courses of action. Groupthink is a term of the same order as the words in the newspeak vocabulary George Orwell used in his dismaying world of *1984*. In that context, groupthink takes on an invidious connotation. Exactly such a connotation is intended, since the term refers to a deterioration in mental efficiency, reality testing and moral judgments as a result of group pressures.

The symptoms of groupthink arise when the members of decision-making groups become motivated to avoid being too harsh in their judgments of their leaders' or their colleagues' ideas. They adopt a soft line of criticism, even in their own thinking. At their meetings, all the members are amiable and seek complete concurrence on every important issue, with no bickering or conflict to spoil the cozy, "we-feeling" atmosphere.

Kill. Paradoxically, soft-headed groups are often hard-hearted when it comes to dealing with outgroups or enemies. They find it relatively easy to resort to dehumanizing solutions—they will readily authorize bombing attacks that kill large numbers of civilians in the name of the noble cause of persuading an unfriendly government to negotiate at the peace table. They are unlikely to pursue the more difficult and controversial issues that arise when alternatives to a harsh military solution come up for discussion. Nor are they inclined to raise ethical issues that carry the implication that *this fine group of ours, with its humanitarianism and its high-minded principles, might be capable of adopting a course of action that is inhumane and immoral.*

Norms. There is evidence from a number of social-psychological studies that as the members of a group feel more accepted by the others, which is a central feature of increased group cohesiveness, they display less overt conformity to group norms. Thus we would expect that the more cohesive a group becomes, the less the members will feel constrained to censor what they say out of fear of being socially punished for antagonizing the leader or any of their fellow members.

In contrast, the groupthink type of conformity tends to increase as group cohesiveness increases. Groupthink involves nondeliberate suppression of critical thoughts as a result of internalization of the group's norms, which is quite different from deliberate suppression on the basis of external threats of social punishment. The more cohesive the group, the greater the inner compulsion on the part of each member to avoid creating disunity, which inclines him to believe in the soundness of whatever proposals are promoted by the leader or by a majority of the group's members.

In a cohesive group, the danger is not so much that each individual will fail to reveal his objections to what the others propose but that he will think the proposal is a good one, without attempting to carry out a careful, critical scrutiny of the pros and cons of the alternatives. When groupthink becomes dominant, there also is considerable suppression of deviant thoughts, but it takes the form of each person's deciding that his misgivings are not relevant and should be set aside, that the benefit of the doubt regarding any lingering uncertainties should be given to the group consensus.

Stress.   I do not mean to imply that all cohesive groups necessarily suffer from groupthink. All ingroups may have a mild tendency toward groupthink, displaying one or another of the symptoms from time to time, but it need not be so dominant as to influence the quality of the group's final decision. Neither do I mean to imply that there is anything necessarily inefficient or harmful about group decisions in general. On the contrary, a group whose members have properly defined roles, with traditions concerning the procedures to follow in pursuing a critical inquiry, probably is capable of making better decisions than any individual group member working alone.

The problem is that the advantages of having decisions made by groups are often lost because of powerful psychological pressures that arise when the members work closely together, share the same set of values and, above all, face a crisis situation that puts everyone under intense stress.

The main principle of groupthink, which I offer in the spirit of Parkinson's Law, is this: *The more amiability and esprit de corps there is among the members of a policy-making ingroup, the greater the danger that independent critical thinking will be replaced by groupthink, which is likely to result in irrational and dehumanizing actions directed against outgroups.*

Symptoms.   In my studies of high-level governmental decision-makers, both civilian and military, I have found eight main symptoms of groupthink.

1. *Invulnerability.* Most or all of the members of the ingroup share an *illusion* of invulnerability that provides for them some degree of

reassurance about obvious dangers and leads them to become over-optimistic and willing to take extraordinary risks. It also causes them to fail to respond to clear warnings of danger.The Kennedy ingroup, which uncritically accepted the Central Intelligence Agency's disastrous Bay of Pigs plan, operated on the false assumption that they could keep secret the fact that the United States was responsible for the invasion of Cuba. Even after news of the plan began to leak out, their belief remained unshaken. They failed even to consider the danger that awaited them: a worldwide revulsion against the U.S.

A similar attitude appeared among the members of President Lyndon B. Johnson's ingroup, the "Tuesday Cabinet," which kept escalating the Vietnam War despite repeated setbacks and failures. "There was a belief," Bill Moyers commented after he resigned, "that if we indicated a willingness to use our power, they [the North Vietnamese] would get the message and back away from an all-out confrontation. . . . There was a confidence—it was never bragged about, it was just there—that when the chips were really down, the other people would fold.". . .

2. *Rationale.* As we see, victims of groupthink ignore warnings; they also collectively construct rationalizations in order to discount warnings and other forms of negative feedback that, taken seriously, might lead the group members to reconsider their assumptions each time they recommit themselves to past decisions. Why did the Johnson ingroup avoid reconsidering its escalation policy when time and again the expectations on which they based their decisions turned out to be wrong? James C. Thomson, Jr., a Harvard historian who spent five years as an observing participant in both the State Department and the White House, tells us that the policymakers avoided critical discussion of their prior decisions and continually invented new rationalizations so that they could sincerely recommit themselves to defeating the North Vietnamese. . . .

3. *Morality.* Victims of groupthink believe unquestioningly in the inherent morality of their ingroup: this belief inclines the members to ig-

nore the ethical or moral consequences of their decisions. . . .

4. *Stereotypes.* Victims of groupthink hold stereotyped views of the leaders of enemy groups: they are so evil that genuine attempts at negotiating differences with them are unwarranted, or they are too weak or too stupid to deal effectively with whatever attempts the ingroup makes to defeat their purposes, no matter how risky the attempts are. . . .

5. *Pressure.* Victims of groupthink apply direct pressure to any individual who momentarily expresses doubts about any of the group's shared illusions or who questions the validity of the arguments supporting a policy alternative favored by the majority. This gambit reinforces the concurrence-seeking norm that loyal members are expected to maintain. . . .

6. *Self-censorship.* Victims of groupthink avoid deviating from what appears to be group consensus; they keep silent about their misgivings and even minimize to themselves the importance of their doubts. . . .

7. *Unanimity.* Victims of groupthink share an *illusion* of unanimity within the group concerning almost all judgments expressed by members who speak in favor of the majority view. This symptom results partly from the preceding one, whose effects are augmented by the false assumption that any individual who remains silent during any part of the discussion is in full accord with what the others are saying. . . .

8. *Mindguards.* Victims of groupthink sometimes appoint themselves as mindguards to protect the leader and fellow members from adverse information that might break the complacency they shared about the effectiveness and morality of past decisions. At a large birthday party for his wife, Attorney General Robert F. Kennedy, who had been constantly informed about the Cuban invasion plan, took Schlesinger aside and asked him why he was opposed. Kennedy listened coldly and said, "You may be right or you may be wrong, but the President has made his mind up. Don't push it any further. Now is the time for everyone to help him all they can." . . .

Products. When a group of executives frequently displays most or all of these interrelated symptoms, a detailed study of their deliberations is likely to reveal a number of immediate consequences. These consequences are, in effect, products of poor decision-making practices because they lead to inadequate solutions to the problems under discussion.

First, the group limits its discussions to a few alternative courses of action (often only two) without an initial survey of all the alternatives that might be worthy of consideration.

Second, the group fails to reexamine the course of action initially preferred by the majority after they learn of risks and drawbacks they had not considered originally.

Third, the members spend little or no time discussing whether there are nonobvious gains they may have overlooked or ways of reducing the seemingly prohibitive costs that made rejected alternatives appear undesirable to them.

Fourth, members make little or no attempt to obtain information from experts within their own organizations who might be able to supply more precise estimates of potential losses and gains.

Fifth, members show positive interest in facts and opinions that support their preferred policy; they tend to ignore facts and opinions that do not.

Sixth, members spend little time deliberating about how the chosen policy might be hindered by bureaucratic inertia, sabotaged by political opponents, or temporarily derailed by common accidents. Consequently, they fail to work out contingency plans to cope with foreseeable setbacks that could endanger the overall success of their chosen course.

Support. The search for an explanation of why groupthink occurs has led me through a quagmire of complicated theoretical issues in the murky area of human motivation. My belief, based on recent social psychological research, is that we can best understand the various symptoms of groupthink as a mutual effort among the group members to maintain self-esteem and emotional equanimity by providing social support to each other, especially at times when they share responsibility for making vital decisions. . . .

Pride.   Shared illusions of invulnerability, for example, can reduce anxiety about taking risks. Rationalizations help members believe that the risks are really not so bad after all. The assumption of inherent morality helps the members to avoid feelings of shame or guilt. Negative stereotypes function as stress-reducing devices to enhance a sense of moral righteousness as well as pride in a lofty mission.

The mutual enhancement of self-esteem and morale may have functional value in enabling the members to maintain their capacity to take action, but it has maladaptive consequences insofar as concurrence-seeking tendencies interfere with critical, rational capacities and lead to serious errors of judgment.

68

Some Unconscious
Aspects of Organization

Organizations always have an unconscious dimension.

The following three vignettes illustrate this in different ways.

In the first, Larry Hirschhorn presents a perspective on the bureaucratic approach to organization, emphasizing how procedures and rules may act as an unconscious defense against anxiety: a powerful reason why these rules are often so difficult to change.

In the second vignette, Abraham Zaleznik and Manfred Kets de Vries illustrate how unconscious preoccupations may have influenced Henry Ford I's management of the Ford Motor Company. And in the third—a series of vignettes— Manfred Kets de Vries and Danny Miller provide a description of five different types of "neurotic organizations."

The ideas and examples presented in each case have a common message, encouraging us to understand that the structural, cultural, political, and other day-to-day aspects of organization may be shaped, sustained, and perhaps destroyed by unconscious concerns and preoccupations of the people involved.

BUREAUCRACY AS A SOCIAL DEFENSE†

Critics of the bureaucratic process charge that it alienates people by separating them from an organization's goals and purposes. Senior managers monopolize the policy-making process by dividing up the work between those who think and those who do. This division of labor, in turn, creates a technically efficient work flow. But, such critics suggest, in the absence of broad participation, senior managers pursue narrow and often dysfunctional goals, and act

†SOURCE: Themes of this excerpt are developed in greater detail by Larry Hirschhorn, *The Workplace Within: Psychodynamics of Organization Life*, MIT Press, Cambridge 1988.

irrationally despite the technical apparatus at their disposal. In Mannheim's (1940) terms, the organization, while technically rational, lacks substantive rationality.

A psychoanalytic critique offers a different perspective. Isabel Menzies's (1960) theory of the social defenses suggests that bureaucratic processes *contain anxiety* rather than promote efficiency or monopolize control. In her classic example, nurses wake patients up to take a pill, even when it is better to let them sleep, to depersonalize their relationships to patients and so contain the anxiety of working with people who might die. The procedure, waking patients up at a pre-specified hour, is reified, enabling nurses to project their anxiety into it. As fixed rules increasingly govern action, people lose touch with the purposes of their behavior. The more they project their anxiety into the rules, the less are they in touch with the reality of their work. Failing to think about the purposes of their behavior they increasingly engage in rituals rather than activities. Thus they behave thoughtlessly not because the division of labor prevents them thinking, but because they wish to contain the anxiety of working itself. They collude in their own thoughtlessness.

Decision rituals in government agencies also exemplify the workings of a social defense. In one agency I consulted to, employees used a *concurrence chain* to develop policies or make decisions. A manager wrote a document proposing a decision or policy and then circulated it to all the other managers on the chain. If they agreed with the document, they signed it; if not, they effectively vetoed it by refusing to sign. The document writer then had to negotiate with each person who did not sign until everyone on the chain approved. Feeling politically exposed people on the chain were cautious in signing any document. On the other hand, feeling burdened and overworked they did not read any document unless it was being put through the concurrence chain. This meant that a manager who wanted attention for *any* idea had to put it through the chain. Most of management's thinking and communication

was thus organized by the chain. Managers began to think like lawyers. They scrutinized documents and [paid] undue attention to wording, fearing that if they signed they might be liable for some mistake later.

The decision process was thus grossly inefficient. Managers could not get an informal hearing for their thinking, nor could they collaborate with a group of colleagues in developing ideas. Both important and insignificant decisions were forced through the chain, leading managers to feel overworked and ineffective. At the same time, since the document writer had to negotiate with each signer separately, final decisions reflected preferences that minimally satisfied everyone, though rarely pleasing anyone. Decision quality degraded. Yet by distributing decision making and accountability over the entire agency the concurrence chain *helped managers deny the primary anxiety of making decisions.* Managers behaved as members of a firing squad, in which everybody shoots but no one knows whose bullet killed the victim. No single person felt accountable and at risk. By depersonalizing the decision process, making it inefficient, and degrading the quality of decisions, managers could feel calm.

As these two examples suggest, in a bureaucratic process the work is technically irrational, procedures detach people from purposes because they are erected to contain anxiety, and workers and managers may very well collude to erect such defenses. Complaints about paperwork and meaningless procedures in bureaucratic settings belie people's willingness to collude in their own alienation.

Finally, in bureaucratic settings, *social* relationships at work are paradoxically often quite pleasant precisely because *work* relationships are ritualized and depersonalized. In one utility with which I worked, higher level managers did not delegate authority to those below. They held subordinates responsible for correctly executing procedures ("in processing a work order, fill out the following forms") rather than producing results ("income net of work order expenses for your unit should be X dollars"), and checked their actions by reviewing numerous reports. Subordinates, not feeling accountable for results, experienced little anxiety and so liked their superiors and peers. They felt good about the people around them. They called the company a "family," precisely because the actual work was depersonalized. Standing outside a chain of delegation, subordinates never had to face the risks nor experience the pleasure that comes with proving that they could be trusted to manage the company's resources for particular ends.

Substituting procedures and paper controls for delegation and trust, bureaucracies depersonalize the work relationship while personalizing the non-work ties. People can't bring their feelings and thoughts to their roles. By sanctioning what Bion calls "the flight from work," the bureaucratic process can persist despite its inefficiency.

REFERENCES

Mannheim, K. *Man and Society in an Age of Reconstruction.* London: Routledge & Kegan Paul, 1940.

Menzies, Isabel. "A Case Study in the Functioning of Social Systems as a Defense against Anxiety." *Human Relations* 13 (1960): 95-121.

POWER AND THE CORPORATE MIND:
Henry Ford I††

One of the fascinating dramas in the history of industrial management is the life of Henry Ford and his development of the Model T and the assembly line. Ford was determined to gain complete control of all aspects of the manufacture and sale of his car. That he nearly succeeded testifies to his genius. That he also failed indicates the limits of his capacity to translate fantasy into reality. There was a rather strange quality to Ford's human relationships. Compare, for example, his attachment to Harry Bennett with his relationship to his own son, Edsel. Harry Bennett came from a shady background in Detroit; he had associated with gangsters and thugs. By contrast, Edsel was a sensitive, well-educated man who was averse to using aggressive tactics in his dealings with other people. Bennett took the lead in Ford's strike-breaking activities, encouraging sabotage and spying on employees even remotely suspected of disloyalty to Ford. Ford developed a very close relationship with Bennett, but he rejected and humiliated his son. When the Ford Motor Company found itself in trouble because of its antiquated organization and product line, Edsel attempted to remedy the situation by making proposals for new methods of organizing the company and for the development of new product lines. Ford cruelly rejected his son's help and seemed to draw ever closer to Bennett, whose advice and suggestions only fed Ford's paranoid and distrustful thoughts.

Common-sense observation of Ford's relationship to subordinates fails to explain his perverse attachment to an aggressive and devious man and his simultaneous rejection of his constructive and well-meaning son. But this bizarre and self-defeating attachment is part of a compulsion to defend oneself against unconscious objects that are represented in the self.

††SOURCE: Excerpted from Abraham Zaleznik and Manfred Kets de Vries, *Power and the Corporate Mind,* Boston: Houghton Mifflin, 1975, pp. 91-93, 96-97; used by permission.

Individuals attach themselves to real objects who meet the requirements of fantasy. The fantasies include opposing images of what is good and bad in relationships of power, love, and dependency. Ford could not resolve his attachment to his parents; he carried a legacy of anger toward them. He split his perceptions of parents, just as he created split images in his relationship to subordinates. At a conscious level, he idealized his mother and hated his father. His father, in effect, became the carrier for the negative reactions of a dependent child to a powerful parent; his mother reflected what he idealized but probably never realized. The split images of loving and hating parents and of good and bad sons were the precursors of his reactions to Harry Bennett and Edsel Ford. By projecting these split images on to them, he was able to create a drama in the real world by unfolding images of his past. In this way, Ford attempted to excise the hostile images that he was unable to put away or to heal. His acceptance and overvaluation of Harry Bennett as the angry, aggressive, harsh side of himself enabled Ford to regulate his anxiety over being rejected and cast out. Bennett also acted out for Ford the side of himself that wanted revenge on siblings and on others who came between himself and his parents. Edsel Ford, who represented the image of the good, loving son, had to be rejected and dealt with harshly, because this tender and loving self reflected Ford's own wishes for a close relationship to his father, which he also unconsciously feared. Closeness to his father was a source of anxiety because it involved unconscious homosexual impulses. Unable to tolerate these impulses, he had to reject and cast aside his son. Ford prevented himself from accepting and using the help offered to him. . . .

We can also look to Henry Ford to understand more fully how reality enters into the play of individual attachment to fantasy. One of the legends about Henry Ford, backed by significant fact, is that he remained completely attached to the Model T, for him the instrument of perfection. When subordinates attempted to show him that new market conditions made the Model T less than the ideal car, Ford resisted their suggestions. On one occasion, when Ford returned from a trip abroad, subordinates brought him into a room to see a mock-up of a new car that could replace the Model T. Ford walked around the car, inspecting it, and then tore it apart with his hands. He refused to entertain any possibilities that the perfect product of his imagination was no longer acceptable in the real world. Ford carried his attachment to the Model T to such an extent that competitors, like General Motors, gained positions in the market that threatened the very existence of the Ford Motor Company. How can one explain this irrational attachment to an inanimate object? The explanation lies in the investment of inanimate objects (as a substitute for people) with meaning from self-images. The car carried symbolic content for Henry Ford. It signified a particular attachment to him, a method of reconstituting his relationship to his father. In this sense, the car became a transitional object, defending him against the loss of his father. Ford built the car for the farmer. It was to be simple in design. Above all, it had to be designed so that the farmer could maintain the car independently (and so that it was serviceable over the rough roads that the farmer generally had to travel). Ford's father was a farmer (an occupation that Ford consciously rejected). The car became the link to his father and the past. Ford paid a price for this link; he lost objectivity about the car's purpose and mutability, and diminished his capacity to be a father to his son.

NEUROTIC STYLES AND ORGANIZATIONAL DYSFUNCTIONING†††

Things began to change radically at Stevens Corporation after it was acquired by Pyrax International. Pyrax was a rapidly expanding conglomerate making new incursions into a number of vastly different industries. It had had a striking growth record, but its profits were already beginning to level off when it bought Stevens. Pyrax was run by Alex Herzog, a vain, ambitious, and domineering entrepreneur who was the founder, prime mover, and, many thought, the tyrant-in-chief. He drove his employees ruthlessly, arrogated the lion's share of decision-making power, and was noted for his boldness and audacity in acquiring firms larger than Pyrax itself. Herzog, a self-made man, had as his main objective to run a powerful and gigantic enterprise. By the zealous pursuit of growth through acquisition, he had gone a long way toward achieving his dream, incurring massive amounts of long-term debt in the process. Mounting interest rates were already starting to threaten Pyrax when it acquired Stevens.

Before the acquisition, Stevens was almost as large as Pyrax. It operated as a component and replacement parts manufacturer in the heavy equipment field. Stevens was a lively firm whose product innovations had produced a respectable growth rate and whose manufacturing economies had given it the highest rate of return on equity in the industry. The president, David Morse, was devoted to balancing innovation with efficiency and growth with financial strength. Stevens' products were known for their excellent quality.

Things soon began to change after the acquisition. Herzog disliked having strong managers in charge of *his* companies. He insisted on making all the major decisions at Stevens even though he knew nothing about the industry. He kept Stevens' top executives busy supplying him with trivial information and questioned —even scolded—them when they failed to consult him in deciding things. Morse rapidly became disenchanted with the situation. He quit after a final confrontation with Herzog during which the latter insisted on several misplaced cost-cutting measures that would ultimately damage product quality. It became more and more apparent that, in Stevens, Herzog simply saw a cash cow to finance his grandiose expansion plans.

The departure of Morse allowed Herzog to install Byron Gorsuch, one of his divisional controllers, as chief executive at Stevens. Gorsuch, a diminutive, shy, and insecure bureaucrat, knew little about Stevens' markets. His expertise lay in his ability to follow Herzog's directives to the letter. At Stevens he never took any initiatives. All managerial guidance had to come from Pyrax. Stevens' managers were forced to play a purely advisory role. As Herzog and Gorsuch generally failed to heed their advice, the most competent managers left. The more imaginative managers, those with initiative, were fired. The remaining personnel were passive and fearful; they simply did what they were told. Anxious about job security, they slavishly adhered to the rituals laid down by Herzog and the Pyrax Systems Department. Strategic issues and adaptation were ignored. Things just drifted along and the firm soon began to stagnate. Market share and profitability declined, as did real growth in sales.

The situation was not helped by recent events at Pyrax. The stubborn, grandiose Herzog and his staff had become enmeshed in still more ambitious, and ultimately more disas-

†††SOURCE: Excerpted from Manfred Kets de Vries and Danny Miller, *The Neurotic Organization*, San Francisco: Jossey Bass, 1984, pp. 15-40; used by permission.

trous, acquisitions. They were too busy to recognize the danger signs at Stevens and too ignorant of its markets to be able to do much about them. The depressive, passive group of managers at Stevens were too insecure to undertake any decisive measures to address the problem.

Both Pyrax and Stevens are examples of what we have called "neurotic organizations"— troubled firms whose symptoms and dysfunctions combine to form an integrated "syndrome" of pathology. Just as numerous symptoms combine to indicate a human disorder, similar patterns of strategic and structural defects often point to an integrated organizational pathology. Pyrax can be described as a *dramatic* company whose bold, grandiose leader caused the firm to overextend its financial and managerial resources. Stevens became a *depressive*, lethargic firm whose decline was due to strategic stagnation. In both firms the personalities of the top managers, Herzog and Gorsuch, were strongly reflected in the problematic strategies, structures, and managerial cultures. What surprised us in our experiences in organizations is that several types of organizational neuroses recur with such remarkable regularity. The same pathologies keep occurring again and again. . . .

We have identified five very common neurotic styles, well established in the psychoanalytic and psychiatric literature: paranoid, compulsive, dramatic, depressive, and schizoid. Each style has its specific characteristics, its predominant motivating fantasy, and its associated dangers. Table [68.1] presents an overview of the salient characteristics of each neurotic style.

In the following descriptions of organizational pathology we shall see how each of these styles strongly parallels the strategic behavior, culture, structure, and environment of a number of failing or borderline companies. Some of the firms are still successful, but their rigidity seems to contain at least the seeds of failure. To reiterate a major point: each of these organizational types has many characteristics that stem from its dominant neurotic style—that is,

the shared inner world of the organization's dominant coalition. These characteristics not only appear to derive from the same source but are mutually supportive. . . .

The Paranoid Organization. In the paranoid organization, managerial suspicions (see Table [68.1]) translate into a primary *emphasis on organizational intelligence* and controls. Management information systems are very sophisticated in their methods of scanning the environment and controlling internal processes. The environment is studied to identify threats and challenges that may be leveled by government, competitors, and customers. Controls take the form of budgets, cost centers, profit centers, cost-accounting procedures, and other methods of monitoring the performance of internal operations. Top managers are suspicious and wary about people and events both inside and outside the firm. The elaborate information-processing apparatus is a product of their desire for perpetual vigilance and preparedness for emergencies. . . .

The following example of a paranoid firm is taken from our consulting experience. Paratech, Inc., was a semiconductor manufacturer run by its two founders, who had originally worked for a much larger electronics firm that did a good deal of top-secret defense contracting. Three factors contributed to the founders' paranoid behavior. The first was an episode at the defense contractor in which Soviet spies had made off with designs of great value. The second was a competitor that regularly beat Paratech to the marketplace with products that Paratech had first conceived. Finally, there was a high rate of bankruptcy in the industry.

The founders took all kinds of precautions to prevent their ideas from being stolen. They fragmented jobs and processes so that only a few key persons in the company really understood the products. They very rarely subcontracted any work. They also paid employees very high salaries to give them an incentive to stay with the firm. All three of these precautions acted to make Paratech's costs among the highest in the industry.

TABLE 68.1 Summary of the Five Neurotic Styles

Key Factor	Neurotic Style				
	Paranoid	Compulsive	Dramatic	Depressive	Schizoid
Characteristics	Suspiciousness and mistrust of others; hypersensitivity and hyperalertness; readiness to counter perceived threats; overconcern with hidden motives and special meanings; intense attention span; cold, rational, unemotional	Perfectionism; preoccupation with trivial details; insistence that others submit to own way of doing things; relationships seen in terms of dominance and submission; lack of spontaneity; inability to relax; meticulousness, dogmatism, obstinacy	Self-dramatization, excessive expression of emotions; incessant drawing of attention to self; narcissistic preoccupation; a craving for activity and excitement; alternating between idealization and devaluation of others; exploitativeness; incapacity for concentration or sharply focused attention	Feelings of guilt, worthlessness, self-reproach, inadequacy; sense of helplessness and hopelessness—of being at the mercy of events; diminished ability to think clearly; loss of interest and motivation; inability to experience pleasure	Detachment, noninvolvement, withdrawnness; sense of estrangement; lack of excitement or enthusiasm; indifference to praise or criticism; lack of interest in present or future; appearance cold, unemotional
Fantasy	I cannot really trust anybody; a menacing superior force exists that is out to get me; I had better be on my guard	I don't want to be at the mercy of events; I have to master and control all the things affecting me	I want to get attention from and impress the people who count in my life	It is hopeless to change the course of events in my life; I am just not good enough	The world of reality does not offer any satisfaction to me; my interactions with others will eventually fail and cause harm, so it is safer to remain distant
Dangers	Distortion of reality due to a preoccupation with confirmation of suspicions; loss of capacity for spontaneous action because of defensive attitudes	Inward orientation; indecisiveness and postponement; avoidance due to the fear of making mistakes; inability to deviate from planned activity; excessive reliance on rules and regulations; difficulties in seeing "the big picture"	Superficiality, suggestibility; the risk of operating in a nonfactual world—action based on "hunches"; overreaction to minor events; others may feel used and abused	Overly pessimistic outlook; difficulties in concentration and performance; inhibition of action, indecisiveness	Emotional isolation causes frustration of dependency needs of others; bewilderment and aggressiveness may result

235

The founders also pursued other dysfunctional strategies that reflected their paranoia. First, the cyclicality of the markets made them financially conservative in an industry known for its rewards to risk takers. For example, Paratech spent too little on R&D relative to the competition and hence was slow to develop new products. As a result, the paucity of "innovator profits" made Paratech's margins among the lowest in the industry. Second, the founders carefully scanned the environment to see what the competition was up to. Unfortunately, they waited too long for the market's reaction to the competitor's products before making the decision to imitate. The delay was very costly, as markets for high-technology products saturate very quickly. Third, Paratech did not want to be left out of any segment of the market or to be overly dependent on any one sector. Therefore it diversified. But this spread it a bit too thin. The firm was unable to develop sufficient distinctive competenc[i]es to stay on the leading edge of any one market. All these tendencies squeezed Paratech's profit margins. Paratech became one of the least successful firms, even when the industry was booming.

The Compulsive Organization. The compulsive firm is wed to ritual. Every last detail of operation is planned out in advance and carried on in a routinized and preprogrammed fashion. Thoroughness, completeness, and conformity to standard and established procedures are emphasized. These are central tendencies manifested by the organization structure, decision-making processes, and strategies of the compulsive firm.

The organization of the compulsive firm is a bit like that of the paranoid firm. There is an emphasis on *formal controls* and information systems to ensure that the organizational machine is operating properly. However, a crucial difference between paranoid and compulsive organizations is that, in the latter, controls are really designed to monitor internal operations, production efficiency, costs, and scheduling and performance of projects. The paranoid firm, in contrast, places more emphasis on monitoring *external* environmental conditions. . . .

The Minutiae Corporation was a classically compulsive firm. It was dominated by David Richardson, its founder and its chief executive officer for the past twenty years. The firm manufactured roller bearings for railroad cars. It was generally accepted that Minutiae's bearings, though costlier than the competitors', were easily the best available. They had been designed by Richardson himself, a mechanical engineer of great ability. He made sure that the bearings were manufactured to extremely precise specifications. Minutiae's quality control procedures were the tightest and most sophisticated in the industry. The machines were always kept in excellent repair. The firm's strategy strongly emphasized selling a very durable, high-quality product, and for many years this strategy paid off well. Indeed, Minutiae became the largest firm in the industry.

Over the past five years, however, smaller firms in the industry had begun to pioneer the use of new materials in their bearings. They were able to produce rather high-quality bearings for a fraction of the cost of the old products and thus could lower their prices. Richardson steadfastly refused to adopt the new material and its related technology, having found out about its somewhat inferior wearing qualities. The new material's softness made it easy to machine and therefore extremely economical for use in manufacturing, but this softness reduced bearing durability by 20 percent compared with the old material. Minutiae's product now became *twice* as expensive as the competition's, and it lost market share as a result. Richardson's obsessive attention to a few elements of product quality caused him to ignore his product's overall attractiveness relative to the competition. Minutiae's strategy was focused too narrowly to allow it to survive in a changing environment.

The Dramatic Firm. Dramatic firms live up to their name in many respects: They are hyperactive, impulsive, dramatically venturesome, and dangerously uninhibited. Their decision makers live in a world of hunches and impressions rather than facts (see Table [68.1]) as they address a broad array of widely disparate projects, products, and markets in desultory fashion. Their flair for the dramatic causes top echelons to centralize power, reserving their prerogative to independently initiate bold ventures. . . .

We can take another disguised example from our consulting experience. Ken Lane, with the help of several investment-banker friends, bought a faltering fire equipment company and converted it into Lane Corporation. Lane's first task was to turn the failing company around. This he did brilliantly by reorienting the marketing strategy to take advantage of several growing markets. He pruned away the less attractive product lines, fired many of the less promising managers, and was left with a fairly profitable company after eighteen months. The bankers were impressed, and Lane was exhilarated by his successes. It was time, he thought, to go on to bigger and better things.

With his newly acquired capital he began to buy up firms in related industries, using the same methods as before to turn them around and improve their performance. His continued success motivated him to move still further afield, to acquire companies in unrelated industries. Because his past growth record had boosted the price-earnings multiple of his firm's stock, he could, by exchanging shares, purchase new firms at a fairly reasonable price. Lane's past record as a turnaround specialist made him eager to purchase cheap companies that were in a lot of trouble.

The pace of acquisition soon quickened, and Lane began to buy firms in industries he was not very familiar with, firms that were much sicker than he realized. He now found himself the leader of a large, diversified, complex, and rapidly expanding company. Still, he continued to make all the key decisions himself. It was *his* company and *his* strategy, so he would take the credit for its achievements. The group of staff experts he had recruited were there only to iron out the details. He felt free to ignore their advice and usually did. Time pressures,

resulting from Lane's wish to boldly run the firm by himself, forced him to make decisions quickly and impulsively. As he did so, his errors multiplied. His constant quest for new acquisitions forced him to neglect the problems of existing operations. Profits began to fall precipitously. Eventually, the investment bankers, weary of Lane's grandiose pursuits, forced him to leave the scene. They had to sell off many of the firm's new divisions at a loss just to keep Lane Corporation afloat.

The Depressive Organization. Inactivity, lack of confidence, extreme conservatism, and a bureaucratically motivated insularity characterize the depressive organization. There is an atmosphere of extreme passivity and purposelessness. Whatever does get done is that which has been programmed and routinized and requires no special initiative. The organization thus acquires a character of automaticity. . . .

The general outlook is one of pessimism. Yesterday's products and markets become today's, not so much because of an explicit policy of risk avoidance or conservatism as from a lethargy or blindness to strategic matters. Managers are focused inward. They do not receive or process much information about the external environment. Most of their time is spent working out minor details and handling routine operating matters. Decisions are avoided and much procrastination occurs. In fact, any outside observer would say that the firm seems to be in a catatonic state. Instead of an effort to adapt, to grow, or to become more effective, we see mainly inactivity and passivity.

The authors have observed a number of instances of this kind of behavior in organizations, particularly in certain firms taken over by conglomerates. In one case, after the departure of the previous top decision maker, an executive with entrepreneurial inclinations, the firm was subjected to a new style of management. The parent company introduced detailed new control procedures, many of which were irrelevant to that type of business. A new marketing strategy was forced on the company, which might have been appropriate for the parent firm but was totally out of place in the market served by the subsidiary. This lack of understanding on the part of the parent eventually stifled initiative and induced apathy among the key executives, who felt that they had very little control over the firm. A number of the most capable eventually left to take up more challenging positions in less restrictive firms. After a lengthy period of stagnation and financial losses, the parent sold off the crippled subsidiary.

Another depressive firm we dealt with was run by Roderick Kent, who was in his early sixties. He had taken over his father's dairy company at thirty-five and had been running it ever since. Very little had changed in the Sealed Fresh Company since the early days. The same production techniques were being used, very similar products were being sold, and the identical geographical area was being served—in the same way. For the last few years Kent had been given to working a twenty-five-hour week. He focused only on minor details such as revising product labels, raising prices to keep up with costs, and presiding over the retirement ceremonies of his employees. Kent's health was not very good, and of late he had been looking for someone to buy the business. Few firms were interested, as the Sealed Fresh Company was behind the times: It had old equipment, served a declining market, and had an undistinguished product line. Sales had been growing very slowly; profit margins were below average and falling, and losses were becoming much more frequent.

The vice-president of marketing had been urging Kent to change the product mix to emphasize products with growing popularity, such as "all natural" ice cream and fruit-flavored yogurts. She also thought it would be wise to go after more rapidly growing segments of the market and to make greater efforts to land more lucrative wholesale sales contracts. Kent discouraged all these projects as too costly or risky. In reality, he just did not want to make his job or his life any more complicated. The firm just continued to amble along, functioning like a poorly maintained machine and sus-

tained mainly by momentum. Gradually competitors took more and more good business away from Sealed Fresh, leaving it with a doubtful group of customers.

The Schizoid Organization. The schizoid organization, like the depressive one, is characterized by a *leadership vacuum.* Its top executive discourages interaction because of a fear of involvement. Schizoid leaders experience the world as an unhappy place, populated by frustrating individuals (see Table [68.1]). Perhaps because of past disappointments, they believe most contacts may end painfully for them. Consequently, they are inclined to daydream to compensate for a lack of fulfillment. In some organizations the second tier of executives will make up for what is missing from the leader with their own warmth and extroversion. This complementarity among executive personalities can sometimes overcome certain deficiencies of the leader. Frequently, however, the schizoid organization can become a political battlefield. Members of the second tier see in the withdrawn nature of the top executive an opportunity to pursue their own needs. . . .

The divided nature of the organization thwarts effective cross-functional (and, where relevant, interdivisional) coordination and communication. Information is used more as a power resource than as a vehicle for effective adaptation. Very real *barriers* are erected *to prevent the free flow of information.* But this is not the only shortcoming of the information system. Another is the absence of environmental scanning. The focus is internal—on personal political ambitions and catering to the top manager's desires. Second-tier managers find it more useful to ignore objective environmental phenomena that might reflect poorly on their own past behavior or might conflict with the wishes of the detached leader.

The Cornish Corporation was a political battlefield for two of its second-tier managers. It was a ladies' apparel manufacturer run by Selma Gitnick. Gitnick had been a very successful manager, but the suicide of her daughter and her recent divorce had turned an already withdrawn individual into a recluse. She rarely left her office or had other managers visit her there. Instead, everything was done through written memos. In a firm that required rapid adaptation to a dynamic and uncertain fashion market, this slowdown in communications caused serious difficulties.

Gitnick reserved the right to make all important final decisions herself; but she was very difficult to reach, and she had been very imprecise in allocating responsibilities and authority to the second-tier managers. These factors required the managers to make most decisions. But because they were unclear about

TABLE 68.2 Strengths and Weaknesses of the Five Organizational Styles

Style	Potential Strengths	Potential Weaknesses
Paranoid	Good knowledge of threats and opportunities inside and outside the firm Reduced market risk from diversification	Lack of a concerted and consistent strategy—few distinctive competences Insecurity and disenchantment among second-tier managers and their subordinates because of the atmosphere of distrust
Compulsive	Fine internal controls and efficient operation Well-integrated and focused product-market strategy	Traditions embraced so firmly that strategy and structure become anachronistic Things so programmed that bureaucratic dysfunctions, inflexibility, and inappropriate responses become common Managers discontent owning to their lack of influence and discretion; stifling of initiative
Dramatic	Creates the momentum for passing through the start-up phase of a firm Some good ideas for revitalizing tired firms	Inconsistent strategies that have a very high element of risk and cause resources to be needlessly squandered Problems in controlling widespread operations and in restoring their profitability Rash and dangerous expansion policies Inadequate role played by second tier of managers
Depressive	Efficiency of internal processes Focused strategy	Anachronistic strategies and organizational stagnation Confinement to dying markets Weak competitive posture due to poor product lines Apathetic and inactive managers
Schizoid	Second-tier managers share in strategy formulation; a variety of points of view may be brought to bear	Inconsistent or vacillating strategy Issues decided by political negotiations more than facts Lack of leadership Climate of suspicion and distrust, which prevents collaboration

their own and everyone else's decision-making authority and responsibilities, each decision involved a power struggle.

The design people believed they could make the final choice of designs. They began to clash frequently with the head of the marketing department, who accused the design personnel of incompetence and claimed he could veto any of their design decisions. Each department head had written to Gitnick, complaining about the other and asking for a final decision. Git-nick was ambiguous in her reply, essentially instructing the managers to give each other full cooperation. As a result, the bickering (and vetoing) continued, and the consequent delays allowed competitors to purchase the best designs. Moreover, Cornish was two months late with its new line—which was to prove disastrous for sales.

Table [68.2] gives an overview of the strengths and weaknesses of each organizational neurotic style.

69

Hooked on Work†

Many people "love" their work. Sometimes the extent of the loving takes the form of a disease. In the following pages, Anne Wilson Schaef and Diane Fassel argue that work can be addictive, and that organizations actually foster the addiction.

When workaholics are most "into" their disease, they feel most alive, even though it may be killing them. Workaholism is the most socially acceptable addiction because it is so socially productive.

The organization has ways of enhancing its centrality in [workers'] lives. It does it primarily through benefits, bonuses, and tenure. We are not opposed to benefits and retirement packages for workers. We believe that benefits are important and necessary and that too few workers have adequate benefits. The issue is not benefits per se but the way the organization uses them to stay central in the lives of workers and to prevent workers from moving on and doing what they need to do.

The addictive organization promotes workaholism. It loves it as the "cleanest" of addictions. Unlike drug— or alcohol—addicted people, workaholics rarely miss a day (they just drop dead). Like good adult children of alcoholics and co-dependents, workaholics can be counted on to go the extra mile; they rarely let you down.

As we began recognizing the addictive process in organizations, we started to share our observations with those who attended our workshops and training groups. Frequently a discernible hush would fall over the group, and as we described the characteristics of addicts and co-dependents in the work place, people's eyes would light up, heads would nod, and looks of recognition would cross their faces. By the end of our discussion, people would be saying, "You've described where I work. I feel as if you've been in there with me."

For years we had observed, studied, worked with, and experienced personally the effects of addiction on individuals and on families. We initially believed the organization was just another context in which addictive behavior occurred. Then, about a year ago, we began to realize we were seeing something in addition to the organization as a setting for addictive behavior. We were also seeing that in many instances the organization itself was the addictive substance. This realization provided an entirely new perspective on the addictive organization and resulted in our moving to another level of understanding of both addictions and organizations.

Anything can be addictive when it becomes so central to a person that life feels impossible without it. We recognized that for many the work place, the job, and the organization were

†SOURCE: Excerpted from "Hooked on Work" from THE ADDICTIVE ORGANIZATION by Anne Wilson Schaef and Diane Fassel. Copyright © 1988 Anne Wilson Schaef and Diane Fassel. Reprinted by permission of Harper & Row, Publishers, Inc.

the central focuses of their lives. Because the organization was so primary in their lives, and because they were totally preoccupied with it, they began to lose touch with other aspects of their lives and gradually gave up what they knew, felt, and believed.

One of the major ways the organization functions as an addictive substance is through the promise it makes and holds out to every employee. The purpose of such a promise in the addictive system is to take people out of the here and now. This process moves the person from what he knows and encourages him to look outside the self for answers, security, and a sense of worth.

The organization holds lots of promises. It promises that you will get ahead. It promises power, money, and influence. It promises that you will be a nice guy or gal if you perform in certain ways. If you live up to what the company promotes, you may even be liked and "belong."

Almost all the promises of the organization are linked to the promises of the society. They are the same: power, influence, and money—the good life as defined by popular culture and advertising. This is seductive.

The promise of the good life keeps us actively focused on the future in the belief that even if things are not so good now, they will get better. The future orientation of the promise in the organization prevents us from looking at the present, functioning in the system, and seeing the system for exactly what it is: addictive. People often feel mired in organizations. Rather than acknowledging their feelings, they find it easier to look forward to the weekend, a vacation, or retirement. By continuing to present us with the promise, the organization remains central in our lives, in control of our present, "hooking" us into an addictive relationship with the organization, the promiser.

Some organizations promise things people long for in their families and have never gotten, like recognition, approval, social skills, and caring. "We are one big happy family here," a software executive said of his company. "We socialize on Friday nights. We play ball to-gether. We know each other's spouses. We help each other out." "Oh," we responded, "and what do you do when someone doesn't want to socialize or gets out of line?" "They don't stay around long," said the executive.

This was an organization where the best-adjusted employees were the ones who had come from dysfunctional homes and were willing to let the company become their families. Those who had no family came to believe that family consisted of the types of activities promoted in the organization. They let this model feed back into their primary families. Those who did not feel so comfortable being taken in by the wide arm of the corporation, whose spouses and children resisted company picnics and wearing company T-shirts, always felt uneasy, usually did not readily move up in the company, or left.

Those who looked to the company and believed it was a family were hooked by a very seductive promise indeed. For what kind of a family can the organization possibly be?

It is the kind of family where membership is dependent on playing by rather rigidly defined rules and behaving according to established norms. Acceptance in the corporate family is won by learning the right thing to do and doing it (just as it is in the additive family). The main thing learned about family from the promise of the organization is that membership is conditional upon not being yourself, upon not following your own path. The other lesson learned is to keep attuned outside yourself, to be constantly vigilant about what you need to do to stay in the company's good graces and win approval.

Another area where we see the organization's promise operating is in its mission and goals. All organizations have a mission; it is their public statement for why they exist. Presumably all employees are oriented toward the accomplishment of the mission. Companies with unclear missions often flounder helplessly because they have no sense of why they exist or the meaning of their work.

Although we have worked with numerous types of organizations, we find those in the helping professions—hospitals, schools, agencies, churches, and community organizations—have the most difficulty with the promise of the mission. The reason many people are attracted to the helping professions is that they identify with, and sincerely believe in, the stated goals of the organizations they join, as well as with the professions with which they are identified. Often, however, what they are committed to and what they experience are quite different.

Let us use as an example a group of *nurses* with whom we once worked in a large metropolitan hospital. At one point, it became clear that the nurses were confused and angry about their work. Since this confusion and anger appeared to relate to the discrepancy between what they thought they should be doing and what they were actually doing, we asked them what the stated goals of the hospital were. The goals they listed were concerned with promoting health and wellness, being responsive to the needs of the people, providing high-quality health care, and developing new forms of healing. The nurses all felt comfortable with these goals. We then asked them to list the unstated goals of the hospital. These goals turned out to be saving the city money, being the vehicle for the political advancement of hospital administrators, upholding the reputation of the hospital, and increasing federal funding.

Inevitably, the accomplishment of the unstated goals was how they spent most of their time. They had joined the hospital to support the stated goals, yet in reality they spent most of their time working toward the unstated goals. They were confused, frustrated, and angry, because they had been promised something that was a con. The power of the promise is that it seems possible—just possible enough to keep people hooked.

Addicts are consummate con artists. Initially their deceptive statements look good to others; unfortunately, they usually end up conning themselves as well. They come to believe their own lies. The promise of the mission has similar qualities. The very fact of *having* goals frequently can be enough to con employees into

believing that everything is all right with the organization. The mission is like a household god. As long as it is in its shrine, the organization is protected, even if what the organization is doing is at odds with the stated mission.

When organizations function as the addictive substance, it is in their interest to keep promoting the vision of the mission, because as long as the employees are hooked by it, they rarely turn their awareness to the discrepancies. They choose to stay numb in order to stay in the organization. The mission is a powerful source of identification for workers. It is a type of philosophical orientation that appeals to their values. Through the mission they find a link between themselves and the organization.

In addition to the mission, there are other, more concrete processes by which employees stay hooked into the company. These are the processes by which the organization keeps itself central in the lives of its employees. Loyalty and the benefits of loyalty are other paths to the organization's becoming an addictive agent, or "fix."

There is nothing inherently wrong with being loyal to an organization, nor with being a dedicated employee. In fact, this kind of orientation is essential for a good working relationship. Loyalty to the organization becomes a fix, however, when individuals become preoccupied with maintaining the organization. When loyalty to the organization becomes a substitute for living one's own life, then the company has become the substance of choice. The organization itself has ways of enhancing its centrality in workers' lives. It does this primarily through such means as benefits, bonuses, and tenure.

We are not opposed to benefits and retirement packages for workers. We believe that benefits are important and necessary and that too few workers have adequate benefits. The issue is not benefits per se but the way the organization uses them to stay central in the lives of workers and to prevent workers from moving on and doing what they need to do. When the benefits become a controlling factor in a person's life, the organization becomes the addictive agent. It is when the organization is willing to take advantage of the worker's dependence and not be competitive with other work places for the worker's loyalty and creativity that the organization functions as the addictive agent.

Many of the people we interviewed are completely burned out at their work. They may be sick or aging or simply unable to be creative in their field any longer. Most want to be doing something else. When we challenge them to explore other opportunities, they respond that they cannot afford it. We should not miss the real message here: They also cannot afford to take the risk of being fully alive.

Benefits encourage dependency. In cases where workers lose all benefits when they leave a company, the company is burdened with people who are often counterproductive because they do not want to be in the organization but are afraid to leave. In order to stay, they have to become not dead and not alive—zombies. The organization has become the addictive agent.

As with any addictive substance, the organization's benefits and bonuses become the controlling factor in the lives of employees. Getting one's fix becomes primary. We have an acquaintance who works in the highly competitive photocopier field as a sales representative. His company offers substantial rewards in the form of bonuses, parties, and eventually vacations. Our friend laughingly says that he sometimes finds himself selling customers products he knows they do not need in order to meet personal and team quotas.

We know that addicts will stop at nothing to get a fix. Their behavior also becomes increasingly more self-centered and personally immoral. This kind of incentive program encourages similar behavior. The rewards become primary, and the individual's ethics begin to recede into the background. This is what it means to be out of touch with one's personal morality and one's spirituality. It is what Alcoholics Anonymous (AA) means by moral deterioration. The organization becomes the source of moral deterioration as it makes itself indispensable to its employees through the structure of benefits, bonuses, and tenure.

70

The Destructive Side of
Technological Development†

*Western society has a love affair with technology. Yet its technology frequently
solves problems in ways that just create new ones. The process of development
is a two-edged sword and is often carried along in a kind of runaway feedback
loop bringing tangible short-run benefits at the expense of long-term problems.
The threat of industrial pollution to human health and the long-term viability
of our planet is an obvious example.*

*In the following pages, John McKnight tells the story of John Deere and the
Bereavement Counselor, inviting us to reevaluate our relations with our technology,
and to understand the potentially destructive side of progress.*

Only eleven years ago, E.F. Schumacher star-
tled western societies with a revolutionary
economic analysis that found "Small Is Beautiful." His book concluded with these words:
"The guidance we need . . . cannot be found
in science or technology, the value of which
utterly depends on the ends they serve; but it
can still be found in the traditional wisdom of
mankind."

Because traditional wisdom is passed on
through stories rather than studies, it seems
appropriate that this lecture should take the
form of a story.

The story begins as the European pioneers
crossed the Alleghenies and started to settle the
Midwest. The land they found was covered
with forests. With incredible effort they felled

the trees, pulled the stumps and planted their
crops in the rich, loamy soil.

When they finally reached the western edge
of the place we now call Indiana, the forest
stopped and ahead lay a thousand miles of the
great grass prairie. The Europeans were puzzled by this new environment. Some even
called it the "Great Desert." It seemed untillable.
The earth was often very wet and it was
covered with centuries of tangled and matted
grasses.

With their cast iron plows, the settlers found
that the prairie sod could not be cut and the
wet earth stuck to their plowshares. Even a
team of the best oxen bogged down after a few
yards of tugging. The iron plow was a useless
tool to farm the prairie soil. The pioneers were

†SOURCE: John L. McKnight, "John Deere and the Bereavement Counselor," The Fourth Annual Schumacher Lecture, New
Haven, Connecticut, October 27, 1984; used by permission.

stymied for nearly two decades. Their western march was halted and they filled in the eastern regions of the Midwest.

In 1837, a blacksmith in the town of Grand Detour, Illinois, invented a new tool. His name was John Deere and the tool was a plow made of steel. It was sharp enough to cut through matted grasses and smooth enough to cast off the mud. It was a simple tool, the "sod buster" that opened the great prairies to agricultural development.

Sauk County, Wisconsin is the part of that prairie where I have a home. It is named after the Sauk Indians. In 1673, Father Marquette was the first European to lay his eyes upon their land. He found a village laid out in regular patterns on a plain beside the Wisconsin River. He called the place Prairie du Sac. The village was surrounded by fields that had provided maize, beans and squash for the Sauk people for generations reaching back into the unrecorded time.

When the European settlers arrived at the Sauk prairie in 1837, the government forced the native Sauk people west of the Mississippi River. The settlers came with John Deere's new invention and used the tool to open the area to a new kind of agriculture. They ignored the traditional ways of the Sauk Indians and used their sod-busting tool for planting wheat.

Initially, the soil was generous and the farmers thrived. However, each year the soil lost more of its nurturing power. It was only 30 years after the Europeans arrived with their new technology that the land was depleted. Wheat farming became uneconomic and tens of thousands of farmers left Wisconsin seeking new land with sod to bust.

It took the Europeans and their new technology just one generation to make their homeland into a desert. The Sauk Indians who knew how to sustain themselves on the Sauk prairie land were banished to another kind of desert called a reservation. And even they forgot about the techniques and tools that had sustained them on the prairie for generations unrecorded.

And that is how it was that three deserts were created—Wisconsin, the reservation, and the memories of a people.

A century later, the land of the Sauks is now populated by the children of a second wave of European farmers who learned to replenish the soil through the regenerative powers of dairying, ground cover crops and animal manures. These third and fourth generation farmers and townspeople do not realize, however, that a new settler is coming soon with an invention as powerful as John Deere's plow.

The new technology is called "bereavement counseling." It is a tool forged at the great state university, an innovative technique to meet the needs of those experiencing the death of a loved one, a tool that can "process" the grief of the people who now live on the Prairie of the Sauk.

As one can imagine the final days of the village of the Sauk Indians before the arrival of the settlers with John Deere's plow, one can also imagine these final days before the arrival of the first bereavement counselor at Prairie du Sac. In these final days, the farmers and the townspeople mourn at the death of a mother, brother, son or friend. The bereaved is joined by neighbors and kin. They meet grief together in lamentation, prayer and song. They call upon the words of the clergy and surround themselves in community.

It is in these ways that they grieve and then go on with life. Through their mourning they are assured of the bonds between them and renewed in the knowledge that this death is a part of the past and the future of the people on the Prairie of the Sauk. Their grief is common property, an anguish from which the community draws strength and gives the bereaved the courage to move ahead.

It is into this prairie community that the bereavement counselor arrives with the new grief technology. The counselor calls the invention a service and assures the prairie folk of its effectiveness and superiority by invoking the name of the great university while displaying a diploma and certificate.

At first, we can imagine that the local people will be puzzled by the bereavement counselor's claims. However, the counselor will tell a few of them that the new technique is merely to *assist* the bereaved's community at the time of death. To some other prairie folk who are isolated or forgotten, the counselor will offer help in grief processing. These lonely souls will accept the intervention, mistaking the counselor for a friend.

For those who are penniless, the counselor will approach the County Board and advocate the right to treatment for these unfortunate souls. This right will be guaranteed by the Board's decision to reimburse those too poor to pay for counseling services.

There will be others, schooled to believe in the innovative new tools certified by universities and medical centers, who will seek out the bereavement counselor by force of habit. And one of these people will tell a bereaved neighbor who is unschooled that unless his grief is processed by a counselor, he will probably have major psychological problems in later life.

Several people will begin to use the bereavement counselor because, since the County Board now taxes them to *insure* access to the technology, they will feel that to fail to be counseled is to waste their money, and to be denied a benefit, or even a right.

Finally, one day, the aged father of a Sauk woman will die. And the next door neighbor will not drop by because he doesn't want to interrupt the bereavement counselor. The woman's kin will stay home because they will have learned that only the bereavement counselor knows how to process grief the proper way. The local clergy will seek technical assistance from the bereavement counselor to learn the correct form of service to deal with guilt and grief. And the grieving daughter will know that it is the bereavement counselor who *really* cares for her because only the bereavement counselor comes when death visits this family on the Prairie of the Sauk.

It will be only one generation between the time the bereavement counselor arrives and the community of mourners disappears. The counselor's new tool will cut through the social fabric, throwing aside kinship, care, neighborly obligations and community ways of coming together and going on. Like John Deere's plow, the tools of bereavement counseling will create a desert where a community once flourished.

And finally, even the bereavement counselor will see the impossibility of restoring hope in clients once they are genuinely alone with nothing but a service for consolation. In the inevitable failure of the service, the bereavement counselor will find the desert even in herself.

There are those who would say that neither John Deere nor the bereavement counselor have created deserts. Rather, they would argue that these new tools have great benefits and that we have focused unduly upon a few negative side effects. Indeed, they might agree with Eli Lilly whose motto was, "A drug without side effects is no drug at all."

To those with this perspective, the critical issue is the amelioration or correction of the negative effects. In Eli Lilly's idiom, they can conceive of a new drowsiness-creating pill designed to overcome the nausea created by an anti-cancer drug. They envision a prairie scattered with pyramids of new technologies and techniques, each designed to correct the error of its predecessor, but none without its own error to be corrected. In building these pyramids, they will also recognize the unlimited opportunities for research, development, and badly-needed employment. Indeed, many will name this pyramiding process "progress" and note its positive effect upon the gross national product.

The countervailing view holds that these pyramiding service technologies are now counterproductive constructions, essentially impediments rather than monuments.

E. F. Schumacher helped clarify for many of us the nature of those physical tools that are so counterproductive that they become impediments. From nuclear generators to supersonic transports, there is an increasing recognition of the waste and devastation these new physical tools create. They are the sons and daughters of the sod buster.

It is much less obvious to many that the bereavement counselor is also the sod buster's heir. It is more difficult for us to see how service technology creates deserts. Indeed, there are even those who argue that a good society should scrap its nuclear generators in order to recast them into plowshares of service. They would replace the counterproductive *goods* technology with the *service* technology of modern medical centers, universities, correctional systems and nursing homes. It is essential, therefore, that we have new measures of service technologies that will allow us to distinguish those that are impediments from those that are monuments.

We can assess the degree of impediment incorporated in modern service technologies by weighing four basic elements. The first is the monetary cost. At what point does the economics of a service technology consume enough of the commonwealth that all of society becomes eccentric and distorted?

E.F. Schumacher helped us recognize the radical social, political and environmental distortions created by huge investments in covering our land with concrete in the name of transportation. Similarly, we are now investing 12% of our national wealth in "health care technology" that blankets most of our communities with a medicalized understanding of well being. As a result, we now imagine that there are mutant human beings called health consumers. We create costly "health making" environments that are usually large windowless rooms filled with immobile adult bicycles and dreadfully heavy objects purported to benefit one if they are lifted.

The second element to be weighed was identified by Ivan Illich as "specific counterproductivity." Beyond the negative side effect is the possibility that a service technology can produce the specific inverse of its stated purpose. Thus, one can imagine sickening medicine, stupidifying schools, and crime-making corrections systems.

The evidence grows that some service tech-nologies are now so counterproductive that their abolition is the most productive means to achieve the goal for which they were initially established. Take for example the experiment in Massachusetts where, under the leadership of Dr. Jerome Miller, the juvenile correction institutions were closed. As the most recent evaluation studies indicate, the Massachusetts recidivism rate has declined while comparable states with increasing institutionalized populations see an increase in youthful criminality.

There is also the unmentionable fact that during doctor strikes in Israel, Canada and the United States, the death rate took an unprecedented plunge.

Perhaps the most telling example of specifically counterproductive service technologies is demonstrated by the Medicaid program that provides "health care for the poor." In most states, the amount expended for medical care for the poor is now greater than the cash welfare income provided that same poor population. Thus, a low-income mother is given $1.00 in income and $1.50 in medical care. It is perfectly clear that the single greatest cause of her ill health is her low income. Nonetheless, the response to her sickening poverty is an ever-growing investment in medical technology —an investment that now consumes her income.

The third element to be weighed is the loss of knowledge. Many of the settlers who came to Wisconsin with John Deere's "sodbuster" had been peasant farmers in Europe. There, they had tilled the land for centuries using methods that replenished its nourishing capacity. However, once the land seemed unlimited and John Deere's technology came to dominate, they forgot the tools and methods that had sustained them for centuries in the old land and created a new desert.

The same process is at work with the modern service technologies and the professions that use them. One of the most vivid examples involves the methods of a new breed of technologists called pediatricians and obstetricians. During the first half of this century, these technocrats came, quite naturally, to believe that the preferred method of feeding babies was with a manufactured formula rather than breast milk. Acting as agents for the new lactation technology, these professionals persuaded a generation of women to abjure breast feeding in favor of their more "healthful" way.

In the 1950s in a Chicago suburb, there was one woman who still remembered that babies could be fed by breast as well as by can. However, she could find no professional who would advise that she feed by breast. Therefore, she began a search throughout the area for someone who might still remember something about the process of breastfeeding. Fortunately, she found one woman whose memory included the information necessary to begin the flow of milk. From that faint memory, breastfeeding began its long struggle toward restoration in our society. These women started a club that multiplied itself into thousands of small communities and became an international association of women dedicated to breastfeeding: La Leche League. This incredible popular movement reversed the technological imperative in only one generation and has established breastfeeding as a norm in spite of the countervailing views of the service technologists.

Indeed, it was just a few years ago that the American Academy of Pediatrics finally took the official position that breastfeeding is preferable to nurturing infants from canned products. It was as though the Sauk Indians had recovered the Wisconsin prairie and allowed it once again to nourish a people with popular tools.

The fourth element to be weighed is the "hidden curriculum" of the service technologies. As they are implemented through professional techniques, the invisible message of the interaction between professional and client is, "You will be better because I know better." As these professional techniques proliferate across the social landscape, they represent a new praxis, an ever-growing pedagogy that teaches this basic message of the service technologies. Through the propagation of belief in authoritative expertise, professionals cut through the social fabric of community and sow clienthood where citizenship once grew.

It is clear, therefore, that to assess the purported benefits of service technologies they must be weighed against the sum of the socially distorting monetary costs to the commonwealth, the inverse effects of the interventions, the loss of knowledge, tools and skills regarding other ways and the anti-democratic consciousness created by a nation of clients. Weighed in this balance, we can begin to recognize how often the tools of professionalized service make social deserts where communities once bloomed.

Unfortunately, the bereavement counselor is but one of many new professionalized servicers that plow over our communities like John Deere's sodbusting settlers. These new technologists have now occupied much of the community's space and represent a powerful force for colonizing the remaining social relations. Nonetheless, the resistance against this invasion can still be seen in local community struggles against the designs of planners, parents' unions demanding control over the learning of children, women's groups struggling to reclaim their medicalized bodies, and in community efforts to settle disputes and conflicts by stealing the property claimed by lawyers.

Frequently, as in the case of La Leche League, this decolonization effort is successful. Often, however, the resistance fails and the new service technologies transform citizens and their communities into social deserts grown over with a scrub brush of clients and consumers.

This process is reminiscent of the final British conquest of Scotland after the Battle of Culloden. The British were convinced by a history of repeated uprisings that the Scottish tribes would never be subdued. Therefore, after the Battle, the British killed many of the clansmen and forced the rest from their small crofts into the coastal towns where there was no choice but to emigrate. Great Britain was freed of the tribal threat. The clans were decimated and their lands given to the English Lords who grazed sheep where communities once flourished.

My Scots' ancestors said of this final solution of the Anglo Saxon, "They created a desert and called it freedom."

One can hear echoes of this understanding in today's social deserts where modern "Anglo Saxons" declare the advantages of exiled client-hood describing it as self-fulfillment, individual development, self-realization, and other mirages of autonomy.

Our modern experience with service technologies tells us that it is difficult to recapture professionally occupied space. We have also learned that whenever that space is liberated, it is even more difficult to construct a new social order that will not be quickly [co-opted] again.

A vivid current example is the unfortunate trend developing within the hospice movement. In the United States, those who created the movement were attempting to detechnologize dying—to wrest death from the hospital and allow a death in the family.

Only a decade after the movement began, we can see the rapid growth of "hospital-based hospices" and new legislation reimbursing those hospices that will formally tie themselves to hospitals and employ physicians as central "care givers."

The professional [co-option] of community efforts to invent appropriate techniques for citizens to care in community has been pervasive. Therefore, we need to identify the characteristics of those social forms that are resistant to colonization by service technologies while enabling communities to cultivate and care. These authentic social forms are characterized by three basic dimensions: They tend to be *uncommodified, unmanaged,* and *uncurricularized.*

The tools of the bereavement counselor made grief into a *commodity* rather than an opportunity for community. Service technologies convert conditions into commodities, and care into service.

The tools of the *manager* convert communality into hierarchy, replacing consent with control. Where once there was a commons, the manager creates a corporation.

The tools of the *pedagog* create monopolies in the place of cultures. By making a school of

every-day life, community definitions and citizen action are de-graded and finally expelled.

It is this hard working team—the service professional, the manager and the pedagog—that pull the tools of "community-busting" through the modern social landscape. Therefore, if we are to re-cultivate community, we will need to return this team to the stable, abjuring their use.

How will we learn again to cultivate community? It was E.F. Schumacher who concluded that "the guidance we need . . . can still be found in the traditional wisdom." Therefore, we can return to those who understand how to allow the Sauk prairie to bloom and sustain a people.

One of their leaders, a Chief of the Sauk, was named Blackhawk. After his people were exiled to the land west of the Mississippi, and his resistance movement was broken at the Battle of Bad Axe, Blackhawk said of his Sauk prairie home: "There, we always had plenty; our children never cried from hunger, neither were our people in want. The rapids of our river furnished us with an abundance of excellent fish, and the land, being very fertile, never failed to produce good crops of corn, beans, pumpkins and squashes. Here our village stood for more than a hundred years. Our village was healthy and there was no place in the country possessing such advantages, nor hunting grounds better than ours. If a prophet had come to our village in those days and told us that the things were to take place which have since come to pass, none of our people would have believed the prophecy."

But the settlers came with their new tools and the prophecy was fulfilled. One of Blackhawk's Wintu sisters described the result: "The white people never cared for land or deer or bear. When we kill meat, we eat it all. When we dig roots, we make little holes. When we build houses, we make little holes. When we burn grass for grasshoppers, we don't ruin things. We shake down acorns and pinenuts. We don't chop down trees. We only use dead wood. But the white people plow up the ground, pull down the trees, kill everything.

The tree says, 'Don't. I am sore. Don't hurt me!' But they chop it down and cut it up.

The spirit of the land hates them. They blast out trees and stir it up to its depths. They saw up the trees. That hurts them . . . They blast rocks and scatter them on the ground. The rock says, 'Don't. You are hurting me!' But the white people pay no attention. When (we) use rocks, we take only little round ones for cooking . . .

How can the spirit of the earth like the white man? Everywhere they have touched the earth, it is sore."

Blackhawk and his Wintu sister tell us that the land has a Spirit. Their community on the prairie, their ecology, was a people guided by that Spirit.

When John Deere's people came to the Sauk prairie, they exorcised the prairie Spirit in the name of a new God, technology. Because it was a God of their making, they believed they were Gods.

And they made a desert.

There are incredible possibilities if we are willing to fail to be Gods.

REFERENCES

Illich, I. *Tools for Conviviality*. London: Fontana/Collins, 1973.

Schumacher, E. F. *Small Is Beautiful*. Paris: Contratemps/Le Seuil, 1979.

71

Unfolding Contradictions?

Japan has established itself as one of the most successful industrial nations, outperforming most major competitors on the international stage. Yet success itself brings many problems. In the following pages, Japanese management consultant Kenichi Ohmae highlights some of contradictions currently facing the country.

CASH-RICH JAPAN HEADING FOR A FALL[†]

Many economists say that the United States today is in a situation alarmingly similar to that of 1929. But Japan, far more than the United States, is close to plunging into a depression that, with double-digit unemployment, could severely strain a society that counts lifetime employment as a virtual right of citizenship.

Real estate prices provide one of the more obvious signs of Japan's troubles and rising social pressures. A few years ago, many U.S. baby-boomers despaired of ever owning their own homes because prices seemed to be rising so fast. But most of them managed to buy their starter houses, begin families and move ahead. Not so in Japan.

By the time a young couple in Japan is ready to settle down, a home is probably beyond their reach. Real estate prices in Tokyo have risen an average of 300 per cent in the past 2½ years.

As a result, Japan is creating a new proletariat —people with little hope that they will possess any property in their lifetime.

Japan is also creating many millionaires. Until recently, the country was 90 per cent middle class. It was a happy, growth-oriented nation. Today, there is a growing polarization between those who invested in their education and now rent small apartments and those who own and speculate with property.

While, thanks to the yen-dollar exchange rate, Japan has the highest per capita gross national product in the world ($18,000), living standards for most Japanese have improved little. To enjoy the same standard of living as a U.S. couple, a Japanese couple would have to spend an average of 35 per cent more—twice as much to maintain cars and 50 per cent more on utilities and food.

[†]SOURCE: "Dark Clouds Over Japan's Economy," by Kenichi Ohmae, *New York Times*, July 29, 1987. Copyright 1986/87 by the New York Times Company. Reprinted by permission.

And the brilliance of Japan's economic progress could fade as quickly as it appeared. North Americans tend to think that all Japanese industries are competitive, but this is far from true. Japan is about to face, by any standard set in developed countries, widespread unemployment. Add up all the employees in Japanese industries that are strong worldwide—automobiles, machinery, electronics and steel—and they amount only to 7 per cent of the workforce. The others work in less competitive and sometimes protected industries.

Today's unemployment rate in manufacturing of about 3 per cent will climb by 2 percentage points as a result of increased imports, assuming the current exchange rate continues. Reduced exports will likely add another 2.5 percentage points to the unemployment rate, raising the over-all rate in the manufacturing sector to 7.5 per cent. If Japan were to reduce rice and other agricultural trade barriers, unemployment could reach 13 per cent.

Ironically, one of the country's biggest problems is that it has too much money. Individual savers generate more than $1 billion a day, while companies pile up about $500 million day. This money once financed plants and facilities, but no longer. Japan's industrial overcapacity has created tensions internationally, and Japanese companies are not building plants at home. The excess cash can no longer be absorbed in the Japanese stock market, where the average price-earnings ratio is already 80 (compared with about 20 for Standard & Poor's 500). Even Japanese golf-course memberships, which are traded like seats on a stock exchange, now cost $100,000 to $2 million.

How can Japan avert a depression, renew investment and replace the lost jobs? It could build a service industry comparable to that of the United States and move into high-tech sectors. But these are no panaceas, as Americans have learned in recent years. Japan must try something else, however, because the vision and determination that guided Japanese investments over the past three decades is gone.

Clearly, the stimulative measures proposed by Prime Minister Yasuhiro Nakasone will not be enough. The $35 billion he promised he would spend to stimulate consumption in Japan may look promising, but keep in mind that as much as 80 per cent of that money will disappear in real estate. That's because most government investments in infrastructure begin with land purchases. Sellers of land will then take that money to the stock exchange and further inflate share prices. Or the money will cycle back to the foreign-exchange markets and further aggravate speculation there. Today, of the $1.6 billion generated daily, as much as $790 million goes to the foreign-exchange market or similar speculative areas.

That is Japan's Catch-22. Plenty of money—but nowhere to invest it except in more money. Companies have so much money they are building foreign-exchange trading floors instead of adding production lines, reasoning that it is better to make money with money than to make profitless products that cause retaliation and resentment abroad.

The situation is not hopeless, however, Japan has its fundamental lessons to learn from the United States. First, it must deregulate. Thousands of intrusive regulations strangle Japanese consumers. The Ministry of Transportation, perhaps the champion regulator, has more than 2000 regulations, including such rules as a mandatory $650 auto inspection every two years. In the United States, if a person wants to move, he simply rents a U-Haul truck or trailer. Not in Japan. The Japanese have to get a license to use a trailer. Of course, they have to have a driver's license, too. Those cost a tidy $2000. Along with the high cost of housing, regulations are the primary reason Japanese are rich only on paper. One of Japan's first steps toward improving the standard of living is to remove them. But it takes many years to take power away from government.

Like the United States, Japan is making the fundamental mistake of liberalizing its markets in a piecemeal fashion. Creeping up on closed markets and opening them a few at a time kills the wrong industries for the wrong reasons.

For example, if the Japanese biscuit market were opened, local companies would be destroyed by imports from Denmark and elsewhere. Japanese biscuit-makers would be handicapped by the high cost of regulated domestic wheat. On the other hand, if Japan liberalized wheat markets, it could keep the biscuit-bakers working. They are, in fact, efficient and competitive manufacturers. By opening manufacturers to competition while protecting raw-materials producers, Japan destroys the wrong people. Japan has done this too often in response to the complaints of foreign exporters.

Unfortunately, all this takes time, and time is growing exceedingly short. In fact, Japan may be facing a vicious cycle. Its continuous trade imbalances will result in a stronger yen, which will lead to higher unemployment. The corresponding shortfall of tax revenue will restrict Government spending, causing a contraction of domestic demand. That will force companies once again to resort to export markets. Their efforts to exploit foreign markets will result either in the closing of those markets or larger trade imbalances and an even stronger yen. Within this spiral, speculation in foreign exchange will live a life of its own, divorced from the economy, until it leads to an economic breakdown.

72

The Bhopal Disaster

In December 1984, the world was rocked with news of the worst industrial disaster of all time. Union Carbide's pesticide plant at Bhopal had leaked a cloud of toxic gas, killing and maiming thousands of men, women, and children and destroying a whole community. The accident stands as a metaphor expressing some of the worst aspects of the relationship between man and technology in the modern world.

In the following pages Time *and* Newsweek *writers explore how much of modern industry is poised on a knife's edge, where controlled success can easily change to unmitigated chaos.*

A TRAGIC GAS LEAK OFFERS A PARABLE OF INDUSTRIAL LIFE†

In *Specimen Days* Walt Whitman created a terrible picture of the proximity of human progress and human frailty by describing the U.S. Patent Office when it was used as a hospital during the Civil War. There the dead and dying soldiers lay on cots surrounded by the latest inventions of the day, high shelves packed with gleaming instruments devised to ensure the world's safety and advancement. India provided some specimen days last week. On Monday the death toll was 410. On Friday, more than 2,500. By the weekend, numbers had no meaning any more, since no one could tell how many of the citizens of Bhopal who managed to survive the leaking toxic gas would eventually be counted among the dead. Something went very wrong at the Union Carbide pesticide plant. Human progress came up against human frailty. The air was poisoned, and the world gasped.

It was, in fact, the world's tragedy that occurred in Bhopal, not only because one saw fellow mortals stricken but because the industrialized society has created a shared fragility. The sources of enhancement are also the sources of fear and peril—all the chemical

†SOURCE: Roger Rosenblatt, "All the World Gasped," *Time*, 17 December 1984, p. 127. Copyright 1984 Time Inc. All rights reserved. Reprinted by permission from TIME.

plants, nuclear power plants and other strangely shaped structures concocting potential salvation and destruction in remote and quiet places. The citizens of Bhopal lived near the Union Carbide plant because they sought to live there. The plant provided jobs, the pesticide more food. Bhopal was a modern parable of the risks and rewards originally engendered by the Industrial Revolution: Frankenstein's wonder becoming Frankenstein's monster.

Not that it was an abstract lesson that we watched all week, as mothers rocked blinded children in their arms and old men convulsed in their hospital beds. The pictures were all too real. More human frailty was on display than human progress. Odd how little it takes to pick up the facts involved in so sudden a catastrophe—to learn all about "methyl isocyanate," and how the pressure built up in a storage tank too rapidly for the "scrubber" to neutralize the gas that escaped into the atmosphere. Even a tragedy becomes a moment in technology, as

if we feel compelled to advance knowledge at the same time we experience shock and grief. But acquiring information also serves as a deflection of feeling. In the long run we remember people like ourselves, drowned in the air by an enemy that was supposed to be an ally.

If the world felt especially close to Bhopal last week, it may be because the world is Bhopal, a place where the occupational hazard is modern life. History teaches that there is no avoiding that hazard, and no point in trying; one only trusts that the gods in the machines will give a good deal more than they take away. But the problem is not purely mystical either. If social advancement lies in something as lethal as methyl isocyanate, it only argues for handling with the greatest care. After this tragedy is out of the news, and the lawsuits are filed, and the dead cremated, things ought to be made considerably safer than they were before Bhopal. Human progress, human frailty. Ashes float in the air near the pesticide plant.

COULD IT HAPPEN IN AMERICA?[††]

Residents of Institute, W.Va., were used to something funny in the air that caused hacking coughs and sometimes stripped the paint off cars. Old-timers affectionately called Union Carbide's big Institute plant "Uncle John's," and its foul odor, "the smell of jobs." The news that more than 2,500 people in India had been killed by methyl isocyanate (MIC)—a chemical made at the plant as well—came as a shock. Union Carbide halted MIC production there last week. But at a town meeting Tuesday night, one man demanded that residents be issued gas masks; another said the poison was so deadly that

masks wouldn't help. "I dreamed about it all night long," said Sylvia Parker, a retired social worker. "My immediate concern is that what happened in India doesn't happen here."

That same cloud of concern wafted through communities all across the nation in the wake of the Bhopal tragedy. Chemical-industry experts hastened to say that a similar calamity was unlikely here, since most U.S. facilities are not so dependent on unskilled labor and have far more sophisticated emergency-warning systems. Last month, when a small amount of MIC spilled at a plant run by FMC Corp. in Mid-

[††]SOURCE: "Could it Happen in America?" From NEWSWEEK, 12/17/84. © 1984 Newsweek, Inc. All rights reserved. Reprinted by permission.

dleport, N.Y., 500 schoolchildren and staffers were evacuated in 35 minutes with no serious injuries. In fact, the chemical industry has the best safety record of any U.S. industry. But the potential for danger is enormous. "We have nothing to be comforted by just because we're living in an advanced industrial society," said safety expert Anthony Mazzocchi of the Workers' Policy Project. "On the contrary, we are at greater risk because we have more toxic plants here."

Tests: The dimensions of the potential risk are staggering. An estimated 6,000 U.S. facilities make possibly hazardous chemicals. There are approximately 180,000 shipments by truck or rail every day in the United States of everything from nail-polish remover to nuclear weapons. More than 60,000 chemical substances are in use—and federal regulators don't even know how many pose health dangers. The 1976 Toxic Substances Control Act—TOSCA—requires that *new* chemicals be reviewed before they go on the market. But only 20 percent of those already in use have been tested even to minimal standards, according to the National Research Council. Federal disposal regulations do not even classify carbamates—the group of pesticides that use MIC during manufacture—as hazardous waste. That means, says Richard Fortuna of the Hazardous Waste Treatment Council, that "they can be discarded like orange peels."

What's more, responsibility for preventing a Bhopal-like disaster falls between the cracks in the federal bureaucracy. The Labor Department's Office of Safety and Health Administration (OSHA) periodically inspects facilities to ensure that accidents don't harm workers. The Environmental Protection Agency coordinates cleanups of some types of accidents. But EPA was only last month given the authority to regulate underground storage tanks such as the one that leaked in Bhopal. It has not begun to count such tanks, let alone determine what is in them. It will be three years before EPA proposes safety regulations—longer if its budget is cut further. In the meantime, "we've got no regulations and no enforcement," says EPA hazardous-waste expert Hugh Kaufman. "The only reason we haven't had a release with the same disastrous effect is that we've been lucky."

Chemical-industry officials insist it is far more than luck—that they police themselves far more thoroughly than federal regulations ever could. The industry is "obsessed with safety, because of the nature of the product," says Geraldine Cox of the Chemical Manufacturers Association. Because accidents do happen, chemical handlers go to great lengths to minimize the dangers, and many are reviewing their safeguards in the wake of the Bhopal tragedy. "Never say never," says Pat Goggin of Dow Chemical in Midland, Mich., which staged a mock "release" of chlorine gas two weeks ago to test its leak-detection and community-warning procedures.

Some chemical firms use elaborate computer models to gauge the likely paths of accidental releases. One such model, made by SAFER Emergency Systems in California, not only senses that a leak has occurred, but monitors its rate, concentration and toxicity, evaluates weather conditions and displays the anticipated cloud on a computer screen along with the degree of danger for anything in its path. The system can even dial phone numbers and play a recorded warning message—all within five minutes after the leak is detected.

Whistles: But emergency precautions vary widely from plant to plant. In Institute, Union Carbide officials had discussed evacuation plans with a nearby college and a local center for the handicapped. But many residents said they had no idea what to do in case of an accident—nor had many seen a letter that plant spokesmen claimed was sent to residents every year since 1975 outlining the plant's emergency programs.

If they had, they might still be confused. According to the letter, two three-second blasts of the plant's whistle means a fire or medical emergency; three three-second blasts means a gas release; two-second blasts every three seconds for two minutes means a major disaster, with two-second blasts every 30 seconds until the danger has passed. (Last year, when a valve broke on a chemical barge moored at the plant and a neighborhood had to be evacuated at 3 a.m., most people were sleeping with the windows closed and never heard the whistle.) Instructions for what to do next are equally confusing: if the wind is blowing favorably, stay put. If the wind is blowing toward you from the plant, evacuate "by going crosswind." "In some cases, you can see the fumes as a white cloud," the letter added. "However, this is not always the case so don't depend on your eyes."

The very fact that anything so lethal was made nearby stunned many Institute residents. People in Woodbine, Ga., were also surprised to learn that MIC is used at a Union Carbide plant there. Institute plant spokesman Dick Henderson said the company did inform residents—via a newspaper story in 1952. "Do you want an update every six months that we're still making it?" he asked. "For years, we used to tour people around the plant, then interest died down."

Communities elsewhere are pressing for more information about the chemicals next door. Manufacturers are resisting, on the ground that disclosing specific names and quantities will reveal trade secrets—and the Reagan administration sympathizes. One of its first acts was to withdraw a Carter administration proposal that all toxic chemicals in the workplace be identified. In defiance, 21 states have passed their own right-to-know laws, but OSHA has moved to pre-empt those with a new rule requiring that substances be labeled *only* generally as "hazardous." A district court in Newark is set to rule this week on New Jersey's effort to keep its law, which also forces firms to file lists of their chemicals with local safety authorities. "I don't want an orange sign that says 'Danger', says Rick Engler of the Philadelphia Area Project on Occupational Safety and Health. "I want to know what the real hazards are."

Areas like New Jersey pose particular hazards because of the dense concentration of chemical facilities. And though few U.S. plants abut crowded shantytowns like Bhopal, some are upwind of large population centers. "All of Niagara County is a trouble spot," says Peter Slocum of the New York state Department of Health. "Those who live in Staten Island live in constant peril of New Jersey." Last October, a derivative of the insecticide malathion escaped from an American Cyanamid tank in Linden, N.J., blanketing a 20-mile area with noxious fumes that drove 100 people to hospitals. Last month there were two more minor chemical releases in the direction of New York City from plants located in Linden.

The prospect of evacuating large sections of any major city is the stuff of nightmares—and most are alarmingly unprepared. The area around the Houston Ship Channel has the nation's highest concentration of petrochemical installations, yet the city has no plan for coping with an accident like the natural-gas explosion that killed 452 in Mexico City last month. Given Houston's chronic traffic congestion and lack of industrial zoning, "evacuation isn't the answer," says city public-health director James Haughton. "It isn't a possibility. It doesn't even seem like a hope. . . . There would be total chaos." A major chemical disaster would also quickly overwhelm available medical facilities. As it is, most physicians aren't trained to deal with toxicological problems. "I don't know of *any* hospital in the Houston area that specializes in chemical injuries," Haughton says. "We don't even know how many burn units there are."

The potential hazards are also mobile. Given the vast amounts of hazardous cargo crisscrossing the nation, accidents could happen anywhere—in rural areas far from the nearest hospital or in congested urban areas. Every day, some 4,000 trucks barrel along Houston's freeways from one petrochemical plant to another. In 1976, a tank truck went off an elevated freeway, exploded and released 19 tons of anhydrous ammonia, killing seven people. In 1947, a French ship loaded with ammonium nitrate exploded at a dock in Texas City, near Galveston, destroying a Monsanto plant and everything else within blocks. A second ship loaded with the same material exploded 16 hours later. In all, 565 people were killed and more than 2,000 injured.

The Texas City disaster prompted vast improvements in transportation-safety measures. Last year there were only eight deaths and 191 injuries in 5,671 reported "incidents" involving shipments of hazardous material—a remarkable record, considering traffic-accident rates over all. The Department of Transportation requires that the contents of every load be identified with a numerical code—MIC's is 2480—visibly posted on the truck or rail car, and every police and fire vehicle supposedly carries the DOT's Emergency Response Guidebook which identifies the substance and accident procedures. But there are few federal rules governing shipment routes, and DOT has overruled some local restrictions—on the ground that they simply exported the hazards to neighboring areas.

Big Fear: The transport trucks and rail cars that carried MIC from Institute to Woodbine stopped rolling last week. Company officials said they might close the Georgia plant, which uses MIC to manufacture the pesticide Temik,

until the cause of the Bhopal disaster is found. In Institute, though the plant was no longer making MIC, it was using up 600,000 pounds of the substance on hand, turning it into the pesticide Sevin at a rate of 11,000 pounds per hour. Gov. Jay Rockefeller ordered the state Air Pollution Control Commission to monitor the plant 24 hours a day until the MIC was gone. Ten state agencies were investigating plant safety along with OSHA officials. Some plant workers, meanwhile, were ambivalent. Said one: "I make $620 a week and I don't want to talk about it."

Other Institute residents did give voice to their other big fear: that repercussions from the Bhopal tragedy might put Uncle John's out of work, along with the 1,400 people he employs. The 150 products made at the Institute plant, some pointed out, find their way into everything from shampoo to floor wax; Sevin was airlifted into Egypt one year to save the cotton crop. Experts elsewhere said that many of the victims in India would not have been alive at all if not for chemicals that increased food supplies, reduced the incidence of malaria and improved sanitation. Judged against such benefits, the risks of chemical accidents seem more acceptable. But there is clearly room for improvement in reducing them.

73

The Not-Enough World of Work†

Many people hate their work, or find themselves socially crippled and demeaned by this aspect of their lives. In the following pages, sociologist Alvin Gouldner presents a penetrating analysis of how organizations use the parts of people that are useful to them, ignoring the rest. The paper presents an insightful and scathing critique of this waste of human life, and the problems it creates for individuals and society, inviting us to reflect on some of the most basic ethics and values shaping the corporate world.

The quality of work in industrial society, like several other realms there, is not quite what it seems. (Or perhaps the trouble is that it is exactly what it seems.) The world of work is, on the one side, a familiar world of mundane meanings and routine encounters, a hammer and saw, a button and switch, a mix together and assemble world, a pound and shilling and a buy and sell world, a Monday through Friday world—a perfectly ordinary, everyday world. That, on the one side; but there is also another.

Cached within the self-contained shell of industrial affluence of power, and of seemingly settled meaning, there is another, inner world —a not-enough world. We may glimpse it in some of the comments made: this not-enough world, says the toolmaker, is 'the fundamentally alien world of machines' . . . . It is, remarks the town planner, a world of 'interest and energy evaporated'; it is also, asserts the store-

man, a place where there is a lack of 'those things that make men human—a certain dignity, a measure of equality and above all . . . self-respect.' For many in modern industrial society, for the member of parliament no less than the coalminer, the world of work then is one of human insufficiency or of downright failure in the midst of technological triumph, of personal confusion in the midst of detailed organizational blueprints. Men's resistance to work is ingenious and ancient and the complaints about it are familiar and traditional. . . .

In industrial society, with its complex division of labour and its confining occupational specializations, no man is responsible for any object, but only for a function of it. We buy things from persons who know (or care) little about how they work, have them maintained by servicemen who know only a bit more, and these objects were made in the first place not by any one man who could see and understand

†SOURCE: Excerpted from "The Unemployed Self" by Alvin Gouldner in *Work*, vol. 2, pp. 346-65, edited by Ronald Fraser (Penguin Books, 1969), copyright © New Left Review, 1967, 1968; used by permission.

them as a whole. In the passage from the largely agricultural and craft economy, in which the maker of things commonly sold them, to an industrial and commercial one, we have created a mountain of objects that no one has made, that few can maintain, that fewer still know much if anything about, even though surrounded by them daily in homes and work places. The 'alien world of machines' is only a special case of the alien world of objects in industrial society. We commonly know little or nothing about how these objects work, and content ourselves with knowing what they are supposed to do, that is with their supposed usefulness.

Our orientation toward most objects then is, in the first place, concerned with their usefulness and, in the second, when there is a plethora of objects to choose from, with their design, appearance or decoration. In referring to this ordering or priority of standards, it is not my intention to denigrate aesthetic criteria, but only to suggest the place they have in contemporary society. For most of us, decorative considerations are secondary to, and are made within a framework of, utilitarian concerns. Indeed, this is why they are deemed decoration rather than art. So pervasive and powerful are standards of utility that even conceptions of true or fine art—as distinct from decoration—are commonly formulated with reference to them, often entailing a polemical emphasis on pure form. Art, that is, is negatively defined; it is that which does *not* serve a practical use or does not have an instrumental significance.

In large reaches of our society, but particularly in its industrial sector, it is not the man that is wanted. It is, rather, the function he performs and it is the skill with which he performs it for which he is paid. If a man's skill is not needed, the man is not needed. If a man's function can be performed more economically by a machine, the man is replaced. This has at least two obvious implications. First, that opportunities for social participation in the industrial sector are contingent upon a man's imputed usefulness, so that in order to gain admission

to it—and the rewards it brings—people must submit to an education and to a socialization that early validates and cultivates only selected parts of themselves, that is, those that are expected to have subsequent utility. Secondly, once admitted to participation in the industrial sector, men are appraised and rewarded in terms of their utility as compared with that of other men.

Both processes have, of course, one common consequence, namely, they operate as selective mechanisms, admitting some persons and some individual talents or faculties, while at the same time excluding still others, thereby roughly dividing men and their talents into two pools, those useful and those not useful to industrial society. So far as men are concerned, the not useful may constitute the unemployed or unemployables, the aged, unskilled, unreliable or intractable. Much the same selective inclusion and exclusion occurs so far as the attributes of individual persons are concerned. The useless qualities of persons are, at first, either unrewarded or actively punished should they intrude upon the employment of a useful skill. In other words, the system rewards and fosters those skills deemed useful and suppresses the expression of talents and faculties deemed useless, and thereby structures and imprints itself upon the individual personality and self.

Correspondingly, the individual learns what the system requires; he learns which parts of himself are unwanted and unworthy; he comes to organize his self and personality in conformity with the operating standards of utility, and thereby minimizes his costs of participating in such a system. In short, vast parts of any personality must be suppressed or depressed in the course of playing a role in industrial society. All that a man is that is not useful will somehow be excluded, or at least not be allowed to intrude, and he thereby becomes alienated or estranged from a large sector of his own interests, needs and capacities. Thus, just as there are unemployed men, there is also the unemployed self. Here, then, in the exclusions of self fostered by an industrial system oriented towards utility, is a fundamental source of the sense of a life wasted which is so pervasive, even if muffled, in an industrial society. For the excluded self, while muffled, is not voiceless and makes its protest heard. That it also takes its revenge upon its betrayer is illustrated, with sad but poetic justice, in the personal life of the ascetic prophet of time and motion studies, F. W. Taylor, who spent his days creating a hellish efficiency and who spent his nights propped up, perpetually stricken with insomnia and nightmares.

A central problem confronting a society organized around utilitarian values is the disposal and control of 'useless' men and of their useless traits. So far as useless men are concerned, various strategies of disposal may be noted. They may, for example, be ecologically separated out and extruded into spatially distant locales where they are not painfully visible to the useful. They may be placed, as American Indians were, on reservations; they may come to live in ethnic ghettos, as American Negroes do; or, if they have the means to do so, they may choose to live in benign environments as in communities for the aged in Florida; they may be placed in special training or retraining camps, as with certain unskilled and unemployed American youth, often Negro; or again, they may be placed in prisons or in insane asylums following routine certification by juridical or medical authorities.

A transition to a welfare state implies a greater involvement of the state in the planning for and in the management of disposal strategies. In some part, the growth of the welfare state means that the disposal problem is becoming so great and complex that it can no longer be left to the informal control of market or traditional institutions. Increasingly, the welfare state's disposal strategies seek to transform the sick, the deviant, and the unskilled into 'useful citizens,' and to return them to 'society' after periods of hospitalization, treatment, counselling, training or retraining. It is this emphasis upon the reshaping of persons which differentiates the welfare state's disposal strategies from those earlier employed, which tended

to cope with the useless primarily by custody, exclusion and insulation from society. The newer strategies differ from the old in that they are, in the long run, self-financing, for the aim is to increase the supply of the useful and to diminish that of the useless. . . .

That workers in modern industrial societies express a sense and a fear of a life wasted testifies in some part, I would suggest, to the gradual attenuation of the problem of exploitation—at least in these societies—and to the fact that the increased provision of elemental needs may have now permitted the surfacing of a problem at the root of our industrial system, that of human uselessness; a human uselessness generated not only by hard times but during work and by employment itself. Increasingly, the problem of exploitation is giving way to the problem of uselessness. The bitter truth seems to be that the current militancy of American Negroes is less a product of their exploitation than of their growing uselessness in an increasingly automated economy. One can bargain and negotiate and thus affect the terms and conditions of exploitation; but one can only grow desperate and overtly rebellious in the face of a sense of growing uselessness. For when men are not wanted at all, when they have little or nothing that they can give which is deemed useful, then they can only turn to the generation of hostilities—in short, the production of cost-increasing protest—to have their needs met.

In earlier stages of industrialization the central problem of the working class was the achievement of the basic requisites for both individual survival and, also, of family maintenance and thus of the stable incomes necessary for these. Among those sections of the working classes in the advanced industrial nations whose real incomes have historically improved, what abides in working-class discontent with work seems to be nothing less than the most fundamental of discontents, the unemployed self's sense of life wasted. To this degree, the discontents of the working class merge increasingly with those of an increasingly bureaucratized middle-class and white-collar group. From this standpoint, then, it would be expected that the character and the intensity of modern class-conflicts or alliances will be changing radically.

The malaise of modern industrial society, then, derives from the fact that it relates to men and incorporates them primarily as utilities useful for performing functions, that it has no commitment toward the talents or needs of men except as they are useful in the production of marketable objects or services. It pays for a man's skills but everything else he is, or has, or wants, is—within the context of producing objects or services—subordinated to their efficient employment.

Disturbing though it is, the sense of a life wasted is commonly expressed, at least by workers who have participated in the growing affluence or who have experienced steady employment, with cloudy pathos rather than sharp polemic. When verbalizable at all, it is voiced with an almost shy diffidence. One reason for this is that many are afraid to see the full dimensions of the problem clearly. They may glimpse it, but are not sure that they can believe what they see. Moreover, there is no institutional or organizational framework within which men can openly communicate this view of the industrial world to one another, and might thereby validate their sense of its

reality. For unions, after all, limit and confine the range of the freely discussable, even among their own members, to that which is contractually relevant. To this extent they are participants in the repressive process.

And most politically powerful socialist parties have largely accepted the premises of a repressive utilitarianism, particularly as they come to power and equate national productivity with national power and security. The unemployed self, then, still largely tends to be a latent rather than a manifest social problem, a festering but suppressed problem, and a not yet well focalized and publicly voiced grievance. The wasted life is the big secret that everyone suspects but that all are embarrassed to discuss and may, therefore, remain thankfully uncertain about. Central to the repression of this problem is that, first, men often feel it was ever thus, that not very much can be done about it now or in the future, that it is best not to dwell on the insoluble and, secondly, the further sense that the utilitarian arrangements that stunt their lives are somehow fundamentally legitimate. Men today can often no more imagine that it is possible that things might be otherwise than could the greatest philosophers of antiquity imagine a world without slaves. In other words, most workers believe in the validity of the very arrangements that waste their lives. . . .

PART III

Cases and Exercises

The materials in this section have been specially designed to help develop skills in organizational analysis. The exercises invite one to reflect on personal experience in an unusual way. The cases present details about organizational episodes and situations open to multiple interpretations. Can you "read" the significance of the information provided in these cases and develop some overall evaluation, for example, along the lines discussed in Chapter 10 of *Images of Organization?*

In writing the cases emphasis has been placed on communicating essential information and ideas in a clear and straightforward manner. Most are just a few pages long. Yet they get to the center of major issues and problems. The identities of all the organizations featured in the cases have been completely disguised. Some are based on events occurring in Fortune 500 companies. Others are based on smaller companies. But the format of presentation is the same; essential information about real events distilled and presented in the context of a situation that is easy to understand. The cases illustrate important organizational dynamics found in many different types of organizations in different sectors of the economy. In learning how to analyze these cases, one can develop important insights on organizational life generally.

74

American Football:
A Case of Mechanistic Organization?

Here's an exercise for sports fans.

Observe a game of American football and try to understand the organizational principles through which the game is organized. For example:

1. In what ways are the principles of classical management theory and the theory of bureaucracy evident in the team's organization?

2. In what ways do Taylor's five principles of scientific management (*Images of Organization*, p. 30) apply? Identify as many detailed examples as you can.

3. To what extent is the organization of the team "political"?

4. To what extent and in what ways can the team be understood as a kind of corporate culture?

5. To what extent can the team be understood as a learning system?

6. What other ideas about organizations do you think may apply?

75

Charlie Chaplin's *Modern Times*

View the first 13½ minutes of this movie.

Treat it as a case study to be "read" and analyzed and address the following questions:

1. How do *you* "read" the main message that Chaplin and his colleagues are trying to convey?

2. What are the main organizing principles evident in the organization for which Charlie is working?

3. What parallels do you see between the situation presented in *Modern Times* and modern manufacturing enterprises?

4. Do you think that modern organizations have learned the lessons presented in this movie?

76

Eagle Smelting†

The Eagle Smelting Company has a number of smelting and refining operations in various sites across North America. The firm usually ships its finished product—aluminum ingot of various qualities—directly from its smelters to its customers, heavy industry manufacturers around the world.

Eagle's Northtown smelter is just outside a small port town on the Pacific coast. Raw materials are brought in by ship to the all-weather harbor and unloaded at the company dock, which is linked to the smelter by a private railroad. The railroad relays the raw materials to the smelter, where they are processed, returned to the dock as finished product, and shipped out. Any breakdown in the railway is a very serious matter, as it can disrupt both production and shipping schedules. Also important to the smelter's operation is the firm's fleet of land vehicles, which are, for the most part, maintained on-site. To keep all this machinery in repair, the company has a full-time crew of mechanics and a well-equipped machine shop, capable of fabricating most needed parts.

Don Macrae, a professional engineer, is the plant manager. Macrae, 53, has been with the company for 24 years. He was plant engineer for 4 years before being named plant manager.

The current plant engineer is John Holt, also a professional engineer. Holt, 36, has been with Eagle for 13 years. He was transferred to the Northtown smelter when Macrae became plant manager 18 months ago.

Holt is responsible for all engineering-related activities at Northtown, and is therefore involved in a variety of tasks, both at the plant and the nearby town site. Sometimes his work takes him even farther afield. One of his responsibilities is the plant's machine shop, but only a fraction of his time is actually spent there.

Ed Smith, a master mechanic, is foreman of the machine shop. Under him are three trainees, a half dozen semi-skilled workers, and five fully qualified mechanics. The machine shop operates regular daytime hours, except when overtime work becomes necessary. Job requests are usually submitted to the shop by section heads, and requests are often supported by drawings or lists of specifications. Smith assigns tasks each day, but usually the work itself requires only a minimum of supervision.

One sunny Friday morning in June, events at Northtown got off to a bad start. The smelter's locomotive broke down while carrying a "rush order" to the dock. The breakdown was reported to dock captain Luke Hardy just as he was leaving for the "morning conference," a short daily meeting with the plant engineer and the plant manager, held to discuss and deal with routine operational problems. Hardy raised the matter immediately when the meeting began. Holt, after hearing details, realized a part would have to be fabricated, and promised delivery of it by 1:45 that afternoon.

†SOURCE: Adapted from a case "The Highlands and Islands company" of unknown origin by an anonymous author.

Allowing for proper installation, this timing meant that the locomotive would be running again in time to catch the final shipment of the day.

The arrangement called for swift action, but Holt was confident that his target could be achieved even though special problems were involved in the fabrication of the required part. The special lathe needed for the job had recently become unreliable. While still functioning well at low RPMs, it tended to vibrate badly when operated at normal or high speeds. This vibration made precision work difficult and would, Holt feared, soon ruin the machine itself. The service representative from the manufacturer was due to visit the smelter to repair this lathe the following week, and Holt had hoped to keep it out of service until then. The present emergency, of course, made its use unavoidable. He felt, however, that the job could be done satisfactorily at low speed without risk to the machine and thus did not raise the problem for fear of lengthening the meeting.

As the job was urgent, Holt decided to leave the meeting early, and went straight to the machine shop to get work on it started. Foreman Smith, having made his daily work assignments, was over at the payroll department looking into a complaint by his mechanics that too much was being deducted from their paychecks for the company's pension plan. Knowing that Smith was likely to be there a while, Holt decided that the work being done by Lee Curtis, one of the senior mechanics, was not urgent, and assigned Curtis to the job.

Curtis, a fully qualified mechanic and one of the most experienced and skilled men in the shop, had at one time been considered for the post of machine shop foreman. However, Macrae and Holt both preferred Ed Smith, another excellent mechanic who, at 48, was just a few years younger than Curtis. At first, Curtis had taken the missed promotion badly, but he soon seemed to settle down and accept the situation.

In assigning the priority job to Curtis, Holt specified that the machining should be done at a low speed. Curtis knew the machine well and had in fact reported the problems in operating the lathe just two weeks before. Holt was thus quite confident that Curtis could do a high-quality job, as he had on so many other "rescue operations" in the past.

After giving Curtis his directions, Holt left the machine shop to attend to his other duties. Most Friday mornings these took him to Northtown, where it was his custom to stop by his bank to deposit his weekly paycheck, and sometimes do a little shopping for the weekend. He felt free to do this as he often started early and worked late into the evening without overtime when his job required.

In the late morning, Macrae, on one of his frequent walks through the smelter, happened to stop by the machine shop. Seeing that Curtis was at work on the locomotive part, he stopped at his work station, where he discovered that Curtis was operating his machinery at low speed.

"Where's your foreman?" asked Macrae.

Curtis said he didn't know.

"How about Mr. Holt?"

Curtis replied that he didn't know where he was either. Macrae muttered to himself, told Curtis to speed the job up, and hurriedly took off for his office.

Holt returned to the machine shop a little after noon, and dropped in on Smith, who, after returning from the Payroll Department and making a rapid tour of the machine shop, had gone straight to his office to deal with a backlog of paperwork. Holt explained the trouble with the locomotive, and after a brief conversation they decided to visit Curtis's workstation to check on progress. The lathe was vibrating badly, and making an unpleasant whining sound. The part being tooled by Curtis was obviously not going to meet the required specifications.

"You knew the lathe shouldn't be run at this speed," said Holt in a fury. "You've messed up this job on purpose. You're fired." Turning to the foreman he told him to make arrangements for Curtis's severance pay and to see that some-one else took over the priority job. He then returned to his office.

A few minutes later, Smith sought him out there and told him that he was not justified in firing Curtis.

"He speeded up the job because Macrae ordered him to," explained the foreman. "He says Macrae is the boss, and he did what he was told."

Holt, on hearing this explanation, strode over to Macrae's office and burst in without knock-ing. "The machine shop's my area of respon-sibility," he shouted. "By sticking your nose in this morning you've ruined the rush job on the locomotive part and probably scrapped an ex-pensive lathe to boot. If that's the way you run things here, then I quit."

"You're right," Macrae shouted back. "That locomotive job was a top priority, so why weren't you or Smith overseeing it? Was it in danger of interfering with your personal busi-ness? I know your Friday morning routine! I accept your resignation."

Discussion Question

How would you explain the situation de-scribed in this case?

77

A Visit to McDonald's

Bob and his wife Joan are driving down to the Maritimes for their summer vacation. It's late in the morning, and the young couple are on the Nova Scotia throughway, headed up toward Cape Breton Island. The scenery is new and exciting, and their home seems a long way away.

It's noon, so they decide to eat a fast lunch in the next town they come to. Accordingly, a few miles later they exit the throughway, wondering where should they go? But the question is answered for them almost as soon as it has arisen, for at the bottom of the exit ramp is a familiar sign, a gold arch on a red background. "McDonald's—Straight Ahead One Mile," it reads.

McDonald's! Hamburgers! French fries! "Why not eat at McDonald's," Bob suggests. "After all, we don't know where else to go, or what their food's like."

"Sure," Joan agrees. "I could use a good cheeseburger, maybe even a Big Mac."

About a mile further on is a large shopping mall, and at the far end of its parking lot the golden arches of McDonald's are plainly visible.

Bob and Joan enter the restaurant, walk down the center aisle between uniform rows of spotlessly clean tables, and examine the menu that is posted behind and above the service counter. Exactly the same menu as the one back home! They make their selections quickly and approach the counter.

"What can I get you?" inquires the counter girl, smiling at them.

"Two Big Macs, two small fries, and two large root beers to go please."

The girl punches the order into her cash register and looks up. "Will there be anything else sir?" she asks.

Bob looks at his wife, who shakes her head. "Er, no. Thanks anyway."

Not at all put out, the girl hits a key on her register to total up the sale and states the amount in a clear voice. Bob gives her a ten-dollar bill.

"Ten dollars," she says, counting out the correct change and giving it to Bob before putting the bill in her cash drawer. Change delivered, she turns to assemble the order.

Joan, meanwhile, has been watching the other members of the staff at their various tasks—one taking a new batch of French fries from the cooking oil, another loading burgers into their special boxes, a third bustling from table to table, cleaning as he goes.

"They certainly are efficient," she remarks.

"They're trained to be." Bob smiles. "I worked for McDonald's one summer when I was in college. Do you know, they actually managed to make an efficient cook out of me! Of course I didn't start as a cook. You have to work up to that."

Joan shakes her head in disbelief. "But you're hopeless in the kitchen."

"Yeah, but the trick was, here everything was done for you. The patties were premade, all the same size so you didn't have to guess. And there was even a timer you set, so that the burgers were cooked for exactly the right length of time. Anyone could do it." In his mind's eye, Bob sees again the kitchen in which he cooked, his fellow workers waiting for the burgers to come off the grill so they can be dressed with just the right amount and mix of condiments, put in buns and delivered to the counter people. "A hundred and seventy to a hundred and eighty sandwiches per gallon," he mutters to himself.

"What?"

Bob smiles. "I said, 'a hundred and seventy to a hundred and eighty sandwiches per gallon.' That's how many servings of Big Mac sauce the manual says you should get from a jar of the stuff. Let me see . . . twenty-four to twenty-eight sandwiches per pound of lettuce. One hundred and eleven to one hundred and thirty-five slices per pound of pickles. Mustard, now that was a hard one to control—you were allowed anywhere from forty-two hundred to seventy-four hundred servings per gallon! I learned all the regulations 'cause I thought I might want to be a manager one day. There's a whole book of regulations for McDonald's you know. It tells you absolutely everything you need to know to run an outlet. I mean everything! Why, the manual even gives you a special chore for each day of the year. July 25, clean the potato peelers, November 2, check up on snow removal contract, April 7, have parking lot repainted. I don't remember the exact dates of course, but that was the general idea."

By now the server is getting their drinks. "Watch," says Bob. "She'll fill the cups with ice up to the bottom of the arches on their sides."

And that is exactly what the server does.

"How did you know?" asks Joan.

"Easy. It's in the manual. Everything is. I know how that girl was trained, for example. First she was given a guided tour of the store. Then she watched videotapes, showing how typical McDonald's jobs are done. Then she worked with a trainer for about ten hours. Right now she might be on probation for this workstation—the counter, that is. At the end of two months, if she gets a good evaluation,

she can advance to another station."

Joan laughs. "You make it sound really well thought out."

"You're right! Each position has a very definite set of jobs, and you have to learn them all before you can go on to the next station. Of course, you're evaluated at each station in terms of efficiency, as well as for your manner, grooming, and so on. Eventually, when you've learned all the stations, you're promoted to crew trainer. From there, you work up to crew chief, then part-time manager, manager trainee, and so on."

"OK then," asks Joan, "what's that station over there?" She points to where a neat-looking teenager, probably a high school student is working busily.

"That's the bun station. The person at that station loads buns into the toaster, which incidentally has an automatic setting to make sure the buns are cooked just so. When a batch is cooked, he'll take them over to the dressing station."

"I'm impressed," admits Joan. "It must be hard, making sure all these stations put out just the right amount of buns or hamburgers or whatever at just the right time."

"That's the manager's job," explains Bob. "He has to make sure the place runs according to plan."

Now their order is being placed into the bag that the counter person has placed ready for this moment. In go the Big Macs, each in its distinctive package. On top of them, two bags of French fries, each filled to precisely the same level. Finally the drinks go in, and the bag is folded with a double fold. "Thank you," says the counter girl, handing the bag to Bob and giving the couple a wide, sincere smile. "Come again."

"Does the manual say she has to fold the bag twice?" asks Joan as they leave the restaurant.

"It sure does," replies Bob. "You've got the picture."

Joan glances at her watch as they get into their car. The whole experience has taken just a couple of minutes. During those minutes, she has totally forgotten that she is a thousand miles from home, so familiar is the restaurant they have visited.

Soon they are back on the throughway and the smell of hot food fills the car. Bob bites into his Big Mac. "Perfect every time!" he says with satisfaction.

Discussion Questions

1. In what ways does a McDonald's retail outlet resemble a machine?

2. Why do you think that the firm has been so successful?

3. Are there any similarities in organization between McDonald's and other successful franchising systems? If so, what are they? Can we begin to generalize the principles of franchise design?

78

Judging the Degree of Fit
Between Organization and Environment

Many of the cases in this section of the Resourcebook *can be analyzed using the contingency approach discussed in Resource 32.*
  The following sheets can be used to plot your analysis.

Plot your analysis on the following chart:

1. How stable is the organization's environment?

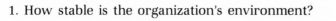

1	2	3	4	5

2. What kind of strategy is being employed?

1	2	3	4	5

3. What kind of technology is being used?*

1	2	3	4	5

4. What are the principal employee motivations?*

1	2	3	4	5

5. How is the organization structured?*

1	2	3	4	5

6. What kind of managerial style is being used?*

1	2	3	4	5

*This analysis should be applied to each of the principal departmental or other groupings within the organization.

Plot your analysis on the following chart:

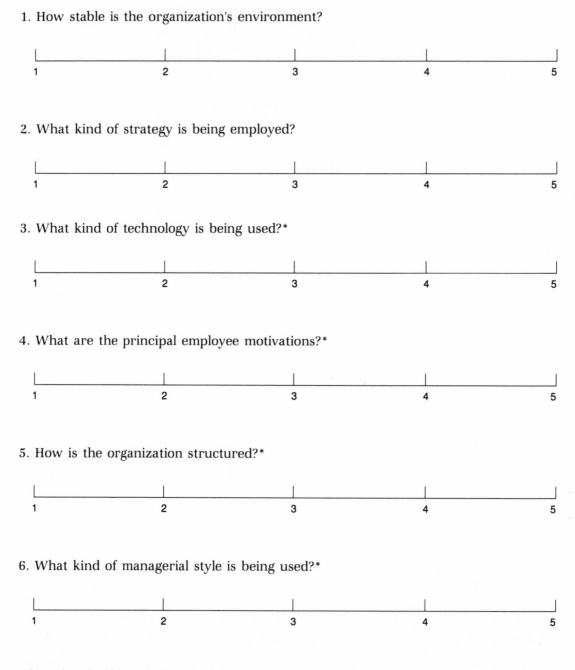

1. How stable is the organization's environment?

| 1 | 2 | 3 | 4 | 5 |

2. What kind of strategy is being employed?

| 1 | 2 | 3 | 4 | 5 |

3. What kind of technology is being used?*

| 1 | 2 | 3 | 4 | 5 |

4. What are the principal employee motivations?*

| 1 | 2 | 3 | 4 | 5 |

5. How is the organization structured?*

| 1 | 2 | 3 | 4 | 5 |

6. What kind of managerial style is being used?*

| 1 | 2 | 3 | 4 | 5 |

*This analysis should be applied to each of the principal departmental or other groupings within the organization.

Plot your analysis on the following chart:

1. How stable is the organization's environment?

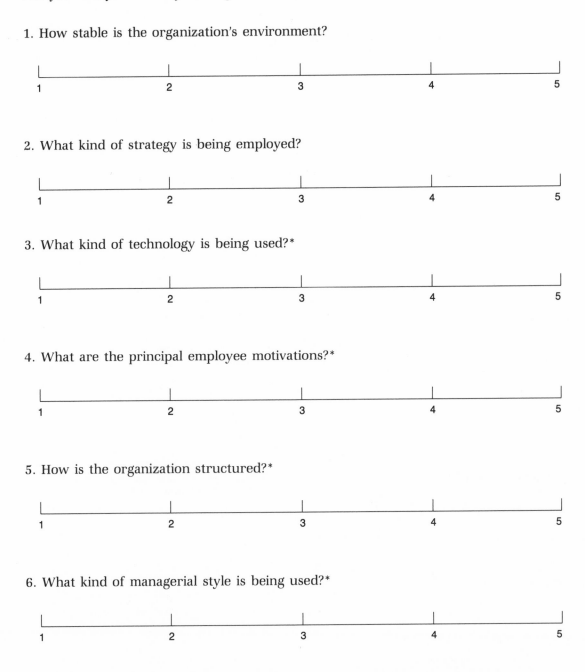

```
1              2              3              4              5
```

2. What kind of strategy is being employed?

```
1              2              3              4              5
```

3. What kind of technology is being used?*

```
1              2              3              4              5
```

4. What are the principal employee motivations?*

```
1              2              3              4              5
```

5. How is the organization structured?*

```
1              2              3              4              5
```

6. What kind of managerial style is being used?*

```
1              2              3              4              5
```

*This analysis should be applied to each of the principal departmental or other groupings within the organization.

79

The Paradoxical Twins:
Acme and Omega Electronics†

Part 1[1]

In 1955, Technological Products of Erie, Pa., was bought out by a Cleveland manufacturer. The Cleveland firm had no interest in the electronics division of Technological Products and subsequently sold to different investors two plants which manufactured printed circuit boards. One of the plants, located in nearby Waterford, Pa., was renamed Acme Electronics and the other plant, within the city limits of Erie, was renamed Omega Electronics Inc. Acme retained its original management and upgraded its general manager to president. Omega hired a new president, who had been a director of a large electronics research laboratory, and upgraded several of the existing personnel within the plant.

Acme and Omega often competed for the same contracts. As subcontractors both firms benefited from the electronics boom of the early 1960s and both looked forward to future growth and expansion. Acme had annual sales of $10 million and employed 550 people. Omega had annual sales of $8 million and employed 480 people. Acme was consistently more effective than Omega and regularly achieved greater net profits much to the chagrin of Omega's management.

Inside Acme

The president of Acme, John Tyler, credited his firm's greater effectiveness to his managers' abilities to run a "tight ship." He explained that he had retained the basic structure developed by Technological Products because it was most efficient for high volume manufacture of printed circuits and their subsequent assembly. Tyler was confident that had the demand not been so great, its competitor would not have survived. "In fact," he said, "we have been able to beat Omega regularly for the most profitable contracts thereby increasing our profits." "Acme's basic organization structure is shown in Exhibit [79.1]. People were generally satisfied with their work at Acme; however, some of the managers voiced the desire to have a little more latitude in their jobs. One manager characterized the president as a "one-man band." He said, "while I respect John's ability, there are times when I wish I had a little more information about what is going on."

Inside Omega

Omega's president, Jim Rawls, did not believe in organization charts. He felt that his organization had departments similar to Acme's but he thought the plant was small enough that things

†SOURCE: Reprinted by permission from THE DYNAMICS OF ORGANIZATION THEORY: ENVIRONMENTAL IMPACT ON ORGANIZATIONAL PERFORMANCE (2nd edition), by John F. Veiga and John N. Yanouzas; pp. 120-25. Copyright © 1984 by West Publishing Company. All rights reserved.

EXHIBIT 79.1 Acme Electronics Organization Chart

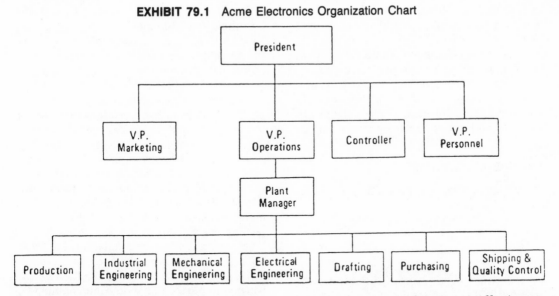

such as organization charts just put artificial barriers between specialists who should be working together. Written memos were not allowed since, as Jim expressed it: "The plant is small enough that if people want to communicate they can just drop by and talk things over." Other members of Omega complained that too much time was wasted "filling in" people who could not contribute to problems and solutions. As the Head of the Mechanical Engineering Department expressed it: "Jim spends too much of his time and mine making sure everyone understands what we're doing and listening to suggestions." A newer member of the Industrial Engineering Department said, "When I first got here, I wasn't sure what I was supposed to do. One day I worked with some mechanical engineers and the next day I helped the shipping department design some packing cartons. The first months on the job were hectic but at least I got a real feel for what makes Omega tick." Most decisions of any significance were made by the management team at Omega.

Discussion Questions

1. How would you describe the management systems utilized by Omega and Acme? What factors led you to this conclusion?

2. How can you explain Acme's effectiveness in contrast to Omega's? What factors might change it?

Part 2

In 1966, new integrated circuits began to cut deeply into the demand for printed circuit boards. The integrated circuits (I.C.) or "chips" were the first step into micro-miniturization in the electronics industry. Because the manufacturing process for I.C.'s was a closely guarded secret, both Acme and Omega realized the potential threat to their future and both began to seek new customers aggressively. In July 1966, one of the major photocopier manufacturers was looking for a subcontractor to assemble the memory unit for their new experimental copier. The projected contract for the job was estimated to be $5 to $7 million in annual sales. Both Acme and Omega were geographically close to this manufacturer and both had submitted highly competitive bids for the production of one hundred prototypes. Acme's bid was slightly lower than Omega's; however, both firms were asked to produce one hundred units. The photocopy manufacturer told both firms that speed was critical because their president had boasted to other manufacturers that they would have a finished copier available by Christmas. This boast, much to the designer's dismay, required pressure on all subcontractors to begin prototype production before final design of the copier was complete. This meant that Acme and Omega would have at most two weeks to produce the prototypes or delay the final copier production.

Discussion Questions

1. Which firm do you think will produce the best results? Why?
2. How will each firm handle the job?

Part 3

Inside Acme

As soon as John Tyler was given the blueprints (Monday, July 11, 1966), he sent a memo to the Purchasing Department requesting them to move forward on the purchase of all necessary materials. At the same time, he sent the blueprints to the Drafting Departments and asked that they prepare manufacturing prints. The Industrial Engineering Department was told to begin methods design work for use by the Production Department foremen. Tyler also sent a memo to all department heads and executives indicating the critical time constraints of this job and how he expected that everyone would perform as efficiently as they had in the past. On Wednesday, July 13, Purchasing discovered that a particular component used in the memory unit could not be purchased or shipped for two weeks because the manufacturer had shut down for summer vacations. The Head of Purchasing was not overly concerned by this obstacle because he knew that Omega would face the same problem. He advised Tyler of this predicament who in turn decided that Acme would build the memory unit except for the one component and then add that component in two weeks. Industrial

Engineering was told to build this constraint into their assembly methods. On Friday, July 15, Industrial Engineering notified Tyler that the missing component would substantially increase the assembly time if it was not available from the start of assembly. Mr. Tyler, anxious to get started suggested he would live with that problem and gave the signal to go forward on the assembly plans. Mechanical Engineering received manufacturing prints on Tuesday, July 12 and evaluated their capabilities for making the chassis required for the memory unit. Because their procedure for prototypes was to get estimates from outside vendors on all sheet metal work before they authorized in-house personnel to do the job, the Head of Mechanical Engineering sent a memo to the Head of Drafting requesting vendor prints be drawn up on the chassis and that these prints then be forwarded to purchasing who would obtain vendor bids. On Friday, July 15, Mr. Tyler called the Head of Mechanical Engineering and asked for a progress report on the chassis. He was advised that Mechanical Engineering was waiting for vendor estimates before they moved forward.

Mr. Tyler was shocked by the lack of progress and demanded that Mechanical Engineering begin building those "damn chassis." On Monday, July 18, Mr. Tyler received word from the Shipping Department that most of the components had arrived. The first chassis were sent to the Head of Production who began immediately to set up an assembly area. On Tuesday, July 19, two Methods Engineers from Industrial Engineering went out to the production floor to set up the methods to be used in assembly. In his haste to get things going, the Production Foreman ignored the normal procedure of contacting the Methods Engineers and set up what he thought would be an efficient assembly process. The Methods Engineers were very upset to see assembly begin before they had a chance to do a proper layout. They told the foreman they had spent the entire weekend analyzing the motions needed and that his process was very inefficient and not well-balanced. The Methods Engineers ordered that work be stopped until they could re-arrange the assembly process. The Production Foreman refused to stop work. He said, "I have to have these units produced by Friday and already I'm behind schedule."

The Methods Engineers reported back to the Head of Industrial Engineering who immediately complained to the plant manager. The Plant Manager sided with the Production Foreman and said "John Tyler wants these units by Friday. Don't bother me with methods details now. Once we get the prototypes out and go into full production then your boys can do their thing." As the Head of Industrial Engineering got off the phone with the Plant Manager, he turned to his subordinates and said, "If my boss doesn't think our output is needed, to hell with him! You fellows must have other jobs to worry about, forget this one." As the two Methods Engineers left the Head Industrial Engineer's office, one of them said to the other, "Just wait until they try to install those missing components. Without our methods, they'll have to tear down the units almost completely."

On Thursday, July 21, the final units were being assembled although the process was delayed several times as Production waited for chassis from Mechanical Engineering to be completed. On Friday, July 22, the last units were finished while John Tyler paced around the plant. Late that afternoon, Tyler received a phone call from the head designer of the photocopier manufacturer who told Tyler that he had received a call on Wednesday from Jim Rawls of Omega. He explained that Rawls's boys had found an error in the design of the connector cable and taken corrective action on their prototypes. He told Tyler that he checked out the design error and that Omega was right. Tyler, a bit overwhelmed by this information told the designer that he had all of the memory units ready for shipment and that as soon as they received the missing component, on Monday or Tuesday, they would be able to deliver the final units. The designer explained that the

design error would be rectified in a new blueprint he was sending over by messenger and that he would hold Acme to the delivery date on Tuesday.

When the blueprint arrived, Tyler called the Production Foreman in to assess the damages. The alterations in the design would call for total disassembly and the unsoldering of several connections. Tyler told the foreman to put extra people on the alterations first thing on Monday morning and try to finish the job by Tuesday. Late Tuesday afternoon the alterations were finished and the missing components were delivered. Wednesday morning, the Production Foreman discovered that the units would have to be torn apart again to install the missing components. When John Tyler was told this he "hit the roof." He called Industrial Engineering and asked if they could help out. The Head of Industrial Engineering told Tyler that his people would study the situation and get back to him first thing in the morning. Tyler decided to wait for their study because he was concerned that tearing apart the units again could weaken several of the soldered contacts and increase their potential rejection. Thursday, after several heated debates between the Production Foreman and the Methods Engineers, John Tyler settled the argument by ordering that all units be taken apart again and the missing component installed. He told Shipping to prepare cartons for delivery on Friday afternoon. On Friday, July 29, fifty prototypes were shipped from Acme without final inspection. John Tyler was concerned about his firm's reputation so he waved the final inspection after he personally tested one unit and found it operational. On Tuesday, August 2, Acme shipped the last fifty units.

Inside Omega

Jim Rawls called a meeting on Friday, July 8, that included department heads to tell them about the potential contract they were to receive. He told them that as soon as he received the blueprints, work could begin. On

Monday, July 11, the prints arrived and again the department heads met to discuss the project. At the end of the meeting, Drafting had agreed to prepare manufacturing prints while Industrial Engineering and Production would begin methods design. On Wednesday, July 13, at a progress report session, Purchasing indicated a particular component would not be available for two weeks until the manufacturer reopened from summer vacation shutdown. The Head of Electrical Engineering suggested using a possible substitute component, which was made in Japan, containing all of the necessary characteristics. The Head of Industrial Engineering promised to have the Methods Engineers study the assembly methods to see if the unit could be produced in such a way that the missing component could be installed last.

The Head of Mechanical Engineering raised the concern that the chassis would be an obstacle if they waited for vendor estimates and advised the group that his people would begin production even though it might cost more. On Friday, July 15, at a progress report session, Industrial Engineering reported that the missing component would increase the assembly time substantially. The Head of Electrical Engineering offered to have one of his engineers examine the missing component specifications and said he was confident that the Japanese component would work. At the end of the meeting, Purchasing was told to order the Japanese components.

On Monday, July 18, a Methods Engineer and the production foreman formulated the assembly plans and production was set to begin on Tuesday morning. On Monday afternoon, people from Mechanical Engineering, Electrical Engineering, Production, and Industrial Engineering got together to produce a prototype just to insure that there would be no snags in production. While they were building the unit, they discovered an error in the connector cable design. All of the engineers agreed after checking and rechecking the blueprints, that the cable was erroneously designed. People from Mechanical Engineering and Electrical Engineering spent Monday night redesigning the cable and on Tuesday morning, the Drafting

Department finalized the changes in manufacturing prints. On Tuesday morning, Jim Rawls was a bit apprehensive about the design changes and decided to get formal approval. Rawls received word on Wednesday from the head designer of the photocopier firm that he could proceed with the design changes as discussed on the phone. On Friday, July 22, the final units were inspected by Quality Control and then they were shipped.

Discussion Questions

1. How can you explain the differences between what happened at Acme and Omega?
2. What do you predict will happen to the final contract? Why?

Part 4

Retrospect

Ten of Acme's final memory units were ultimately defective while all of Omega's units passed the photocopier firm's tests. The photocopier firm was disappointed with Acme's delivery delay and incurred further delays in repairing the defective Acme units. However, rather than give the entire contract to one firm, the final contract was split between Acme and Omega with two directives added: (1) maintain zero defects, and (2) reduce final cost. In 1967, through extensive cost cutting efforts, Acme reduced its unit cost by 20 percent and was ultimately awarded the total contract.

Discussion Questions

1. How can this turnabout be explained?
2. If you were to counsel the presidents of Acme and Omega, what advice would you give each one concerning future survival?

NOTE

1. The case, though an old one, is very relevant for understanding the problems of many modern organizations. This case was developed with material gathered from the two firms by Dr. John F. Veiga. All names and places have been disguised.

80

Scholar Educational Products Inc.

Scholar Encyclopedias was founded in 1913 by Charles Farnley, a retired teacher, who thought that a good, low cost, easy to read, popular encyclopedia should be available to any family that wanted one.

After considerable work, Farnley and some of his academic friends managed to assemble a useful product, and with the help of an efficient printing firm, a small but hardworking sales team and liberal credit terms, soon began to make Scholar Encyclopedias into a prosperous company.

Scholar eventually branched out into related educational products such as "alphabet" coloring books, spelling games for grade school students, and kiddy blackboards. Although the encyclopedias remained the firm's financial mainstay, these other products also contributed to the company's profits. The Company changed its name to Scholar Educational Products in 1959, to give a more accurate view of its range of interests.

In the early 1980s, Scholar, although larger and more formally organized, still had strong links with the style and tradition set in Farnley's day. A hard-driving door-to-door sales network, easy credit terms, and low prices combine to make the firm's products well known among families with school-age children.

Scholar shares the household encyclopedia market with two similar firms. By common though informal agreement they do not engage in "head on" competition, and each enjoys a very regular and unchanging market share.

In 1985 Scholar decided to "prepare for the future" and formed a small "New Products Development" department, hiring Cindy Winton, a young executive with an excellent record in the educational products market as its head.

In 1986, at the Department heads meeting which traditionally preceded the Annual Sales Banquet, Winton was to give her first presentation. Somewhat to her chagrin she was last on the agenda, and it was with impatience that she waited for the previous speaker to finish his presentation.

"We've held our own in sales, and maybe even picked up a few dollars over last quarter," concluded Rick Fisher, head of the Eastern Sales Division. "I think you'll all agree that that's not bad, given the recession. Of course, we're hoping for an even better performance next quarter. And that's the story on sales."

There was a ripple of applause. When it subsided the Executive Vice-President of Scholar, Bruce Bilkowski, and a former head of its sales force, turned to Winton. "Well Cindy," he said jovially, "why don't you wrap things up by telling us what the NPD Department's done for the bottom line this quarter?"

Winton smiled politely at what she hoped was a joke as she rose and looked around the table. "As you all know," she began, "New Product Development usually doesn't contribute to this quarter's bottom line, or even to next quarter's, but to the bottom lines of periods several years down the road. These last few months we've been working on an exciting product which should really catch on if we can market it well."

Winton went on to outline the products her department had been investigating—a line of educational software designed to be used in conjunction with the encyclopedia—but as she concluded her presentation she could see that most of the Department heads were not impressed.

"Very interesting," remarked Bilkowski unenthusiastically when she had finished. "We all look forward to hearing more about the product as your ideas progress." He looked around the table. "If there's nothing else I think we can all adjourn until the Sales Awards Banquets tonight."

The executives trickled out of the meeting room and Winton went off to the hotel bar to meet Peter Trant, the second in command of her Department.

"I just don't get these people," Trant railed when he heard of the lukewarm description the new product had received. "The company needs new products like this one if it's going to stay competitive. Everyone knows that the whole educational products industry is going to get turned upside down by computers and TV over the next few years. Scholar will never survive if it relies on the same old stuff year after year."

"I know, I know," Winton agreed dolefully. "But somehow the message just doesn't get through. All anyone can think about is boosting sales, especially encyclopedia sales. New gimmicks, give-aways, promotions, they'll work for a while, but eventually the market is going to change."

"I suppose I can see how the company got this way," Trant admitted. "After all, it's done well just on its encyclopedias alone for about sixty years now. And its other products sell pretty well too."

"That's all well and good," said Winton. "But if it wants to survive for another sixty years, it had better get on the ball. Why, by the turn of the century I'll bet you kids aren't even going to need encyclopedias at home—if they want information they'll hook into the library on their computers."

"You're right," Trant agreed morosely. "But try and tell the Sales Division that!"

Several months later Winton received a memo from Bilkowski, informing her that the NPD's educational software program was to be canceled because, in the words of the memo, "projections indicated that the product would not become profitable quickly enough to justify the scale of investment required."

Winton was deeply disturbed by this turn of events, as all indications were that the product line would become extremely profitable three to five years down the road. She requested an appointment with Bilkowski and received one the following week, upon his return from a regional sales meeting.

Bilkowski was in a fine humor when the day of the meeting arrived. "Sales are up again in the West," he told Winton happily. "It looks like we're headed for a record year."

"I'm delighted to hear it," replied Winton. "But how long can Scholar keep on turning a profit if the educational industry changes and we don't change with it?"

"Aha," replied Bilkowski. "I know what the problem is; you're still upset about the decision to kill the software project. Now don't get me wrong, it looked like a good idea, and it reflected well on your department. But Scholar can't really afford to take risks on new products like that. And after all, why should we? We're doing very well, just carrying on doing what we've been doing for sixty years."

"Sixty years ago, or even six years ago, people weren't buying home computers for their kids," Winton replied. "And sixty years ago there wasn't such a thing as educational television. I'm not saying that encyclopedias won't continue to sell, but they may not be the number one educational tool they've been in the past."

"Parents don't change much," Bilkowski said soothingly. "Nor do kids. I think our market's pretty secure one way or another. You development people have good imaginations—that's why Scholar hired you—but don't let them run away with you."

The interview concluded on this note, and Winton returned to her own office in a thoughtful mood. It seemed to her that Scholar was sacrificing long term stability for short term gain, but she was not sure how to make management see her point.

After a few weeks of hard work she and her staff came up with a product that Winton felt sure would gain acceptance. The product was a series of tape cassettes which provided self guided instruction to grade-school children in a game format. Keyed for use with the Scholar encyclopedia, the cassette series scored very well on preliminary tests.

Initially the product was opposed by the Sales Department, which felt that it represented too much of a departure from the firm's traditional product area. However as it was cheap to produce and distribute the cassette series was accepted for test marketing by Scholar, and within a short period had become a small but consistent money maker. The NPD received a congratulatory note from Bilkowski, and Winton even received a small bonus at year's end.

Encouraged by this success, the NPD went on to develop several new products based on what Winton felt were the "up and coming" technologies in education. During this time another company developed and marketed a product very similar to the educational software first developed by the NPD. The product sold extremely well, a fact which Winton pointed out to Bilkowski in a terse memo.

None of the new products were accepted by Scholar, although the department frequently received special commendations in the internal newsletter. After two years in the position and only a single product accepted, Winton was beginning to have grave doubts about the firm's ability to change with the times.

Discussion Questions

1. How would you describe the corporate strategy adopted in this company?

2. How could Cindy Winton have been more successful in getting her proposals accepted?

3. To what extent is it possible to turn Scholar Educational Products into an innovation-oriented company? How can this be done?

4. What are the requirements for successful corporate innovation?

5. Do you know any other companies that are in the same position as Scholar?

81

The Changing Structure of
Financial Services†

The financial services industry is changing as the result of many forces converging, interacting and amplifying one another. Computers and communications technology are paving the way for the "globalization" of financial markets. The new global market place is forcing global deregulation at the national level, a trend which can be seen in every major financial centre in the world. Deregulation is prying open the door to a flood of new competitors, which in turn has stimulated a wide array of new inter-organizational strategic alliances among financial institutions. These strategic alliances are the genesis of a new species of organization, operating more like networks than traditional control hierarchies. All of the above has resulted in a need for increased collaboration among nation states to coordinate their economic policies to a degree never seen before.

In the 1960s and early 70s, the financial services sector could be divided into a well defined and neatly compartmentalized set of financial institutions. Each type had a more or less exclusive core function and each marketed a specialized range of services. Competition occurred between firms within major industry groups. Direct competition between groups, such as between banks and insurance companies, was not a salient feature in the development of the financial system. Even had individual financial institutions wanted to compete with other groups, most Organization for Economic Cooperation and Development (OECD) countries had developed very stable regulatory environments which allowed little room for inter-group rivalry.

In the late 1970s and 1980s, most OECD countries began shifting from the pattern of a highly structured set of specialized non-competing industry groups to a fluid field of diverse competitors and overlapping functions. Regulatory systems which had enjoyed and maintained remarkable stability in most OECD countries found themselves caught in a rising competitive tide with no clear means of containing the emerging "financial services sector" within existing legislative and regulatory frameworks.

The changes began gradually. Marginal regulatory changes and an increasing degree of market saturation increased the desire and opportunity for expanded business scope. As the tempo of marginal changes accelerated, it became increasingly clear that pressure was mounting for widespread structural change. Signs of breakdown began to appear, with an alarming increase in the number of bankruptcies among financial institutions. Significant distinctions between types of institution remain, but the notion of discrete industry functions is already history. The evolving financial services sector is intensely competitive and inhabited by a variegated population, most of

†SOURCE: A case prepared by Glen Taylor, Faculty of Administrative Studies, York University, Toronto, September, 1987.

whom are highly diversified financial and non-financial conglomerates, operating in an increasingly deregulated environment.

For the major traditional industry groups—securities brokers, commodities dealers, insurance companies, pension funds, banks, and near banks such as trust companies and credit unions—the turmoil in financial services has blurred industry identities. Intense competition between these major industry groups as well as with emerging groups has broken down the economic and regulatory barriers between them. Firms evaluate their own distinct and varied competence before carving out new competitive positions on a "level playing field," where competition and blurring of the boundaries between groups is not only allowed, it is becoming a question of survival.

Technology as Catalyst

Technology is playing a major role in the emerging financial services sector, with financial institutions now being among the most sophisticated users of new information technology. Computers and communications technology have changed the economics of managing financial information and opened up entirely new means of providing more accessible, cost effective and individualized services.

Customers can move funds from one account to another, into stocks and bonds, or use a credit card by directly entering their transactions into financial computers. Banks and other financial institutions around the world have rapidly transformed themselves to live in an electronic environment. Many firms are in the process of developing new services for the increasingly computer-knowledgeable clientele they serve, such as computer-based financial advising centres and one-stop financial supermarkets.

• In February 1977, the second largest bank in the world, Citibank, began installing Citicard Banking Centers. Three years later these Centers were handling six million transactions a month. At first the Centers were seen as glorified vending machines. But the power to access the computer of your bank and perform transactions at any time of night and day is proving to be more than that.

• New technology is changing the ordinary credit card into an information storage and retrieval device. The latest wrinkle is an ordinary sized credit card, made by SmartCard International, which in addition to financial transactions includes such exotic features as an internal display screen; credit/debit retailing; security access, personal, medical and other records; foreign currency conversion; language translation; electronic phone books and autodialing; and micro-radio capabilities.

• Insurance companies have developed new "products" on the basis of new computer technology. In the late 1970s inflation was seriously undermining the appeal of traditional life insurance. New computers and software enabled insurance companies to launch new insurance concepts like "universal life" with highly flexible savings and investment features. Computers made it possible to redesign their savings function based on short term investments and variable instead of the traditional fixed returns to policy-holders.

New Market Entrants

With technology acting as a catalyst, new non-deposit-taking entrants such as department stores, retail chains, oil companies, data-processing agencies, television and telephone companies are becoming a major competitive factor. Among its main attractions, financial services is seen as a potentially very profitable and fast growing sector of the "information economy."

Deregulation, or at least gaps in existing legislation, are enabling some new entrants to gain a competitive advantage over established competitors.

• In the U.S. new entrants in the banking business such as Sears have taken full advantage of out-of-date financial legislation. Banks in the United States are subject to either unit banking, limited branching or statewide branching legislation. Building on its vast retailing network and the widespread use of its credit cards, Sears has been able to create a "national banking system" without actually being a bank. The new Sears slogan is "from socks to stocks."

• In Canada, mutual life insurance companies are prohibited from owning non-insurance companies. Stock insurance companies can not only be purchased by non-financial companies, they can be used to create "upstream" holding companies to diversify into other segments of the financial services sector.

The Metamorphosis on Wall Street

In the midst of the new level playing field, securities brokers have played a leading role in positioning themselves to meet new competitive challenges and opportunities. As early as the 1940s, Wall Street securities brokers began to expand their market from merely underwriting new stock issues to tapping the savings market of the American hinterland by selling securities on commission. Since then, the securities industry has been rapidly diversifying from its core functions of underwriting, brokerage, own account trading, and commercial paper. By the end of the 1970s securities firms were moving into territory which had been the exclusive preserve of the banks, insurance companies and commodities traders. Securities dealers began offering banking services such as cash management accounts, credit cards, corporate advice, and money market funds. They sold insurance related products such as equity based insurance policies and tax shelters. Then they moved into stock option business, interest rate futures and commodity trading commissions.

• By the early 1980s Merrill Lynch had expanded to provide banking and investment banking services, handling as much as 67% of United States corporate financings. It also sponsors a major credit card, holds billions of dollars in accounts subject to demand checking and generates two-thirds of its income from interest. In addition, Merrill Lynch generates revenue from option trading, investment banking, insurance income and real estate sales through its own sales force of 5000 realtors. In the words of Mr. Walter Wriston, the bank of the future is here today.

Merger Mania

In the early 1980s the lure of Wall Street securities dealers began to pull insurance companies into cross-ownership relationships. The biggest customers for securities and related services are also the biggest customers for insurance. The flexibility of the securities industry, the rich capital base of the insurance industry, their common customer base, their joint expansion of computer related services, and the advantages offered by the large professional sales of the insurance industry combined with the upscale marketing capacity of the securities dealers, all combined to create a seemingly irresistible mutual attraction. With the Prudential Insurance purchase of Bache, a prominent securities dealer, the way was paved for new ownership patterns. But the new relationships were not always fruitful.

• After several years the expected "synergy" had not yet materialized. Three years after acquiring Bache in 1981 for $385 million it posted a loss of $58 million in the first six months of 1984.
• Sears Roebuck and Company experienced similar difficulties with their acquisition of the securities dealer Dean Witter Reynolds Inc. which has also suffered losses.
• Equitable Life, the third largest U.S. life insurer acquired DLJ for $432 million in cash on Nov. 5, 1984. Equitable has tried to avoid the supposition of synergy, believing instead that there is likely very little real synergy to be had and only at a price in time and effort. DLJ was chosen because it only deals with institutional investors and would have nothing to do with Equitable's existing distribution system.

• Restrictions in Canada have prevented similar acquisitions. When Prudential bought Bache the acquisition of Bache Canada by Prudential was blocked.

The New "Financial Supermarkets"

Geographic restrictions such as those that apply to interstate banking in the United States and those that separate Provincial and Federal responsibilities in Canada have been swept aside. Nor does the cost of a bricks and mortar system of bank branches continue to present a barrier to entry. In an electronic banking environment the "branch" concept is being replaced by transaction machines on the one hand, and by full service "financial supermarkets" on the other hand.

• In 1985 the largest of the British investment banking groups in London, Charterhouse J. Rothschild, owned and controlled a merchant bank; a venture buyout company; a portfolio investment company; several industrial companies in concrete, wallcovering, civil engineering, etc.; a securities brokerage; and asset management company for wealthy individuals; a life insurance company; a mutual fund; and a metals trading company. The broad range of activities is not unusual in London, which is rapidly deregulating. Nor is the age of the company, which was formed in 1983.

• London's relatively small merchant bankers and traders have been joined by some of the world's largest. In 1984, Aetna Insurance bought 40% of Samuel Montagu merchant bank and Prudential-Bache negotiated a joint venture with James Caspel. At the same time Merrill Lynch stepped up its presence in London, and Citibank bought into Vickers da Costa. Commenting on the growing presence of the large and more diversified American institutions, one London observer commented that it was "like inviting elephants to a tea party."

• Laurentian Group of Montreal, a Provincially incorporated mutual life insurance company, created an upstream holding company in order to invest in a variety of related financial undertakings, and to raise capital by selling stock in the holding company while the "parent" mutual company retains control. Laurentian's diversification includes a wide array of investments and affiliations—Imperial Life; Laurentian Financial Services; Laurentian Investment Management; Brooks Securities; Anglo-Permanent Corporate Holdings; La Societe Commerciale de Reassurance of France; SCDR Investments; Laurier Life; Montreal City & District Savings Bank; Credit Foncier; F.I.C. Fund (real estate); Le Groupe Palas of Luxembourg; Dillon, Read & Co.; Geoffrion, and Leclerc Inc.

• The Trilon Corporation, owned by the Bronfman Family, established an upstream holding company after acquiring London Life, the largest life insurer in Canada, and a large part of Royal Trustco. Trilon is one of the largest and best known of the new conglomerates in financial services.

Strengthening the Safety Net

Beyond the glamour and excitement of new market entrants, technologies, and more sophisticated services, there are cracks appearing in the emerging financial services sector. Concerns are being raised about concentration of ownership, powerful conglomerates with managing both financial and non-financial holdings, self-dealing, and a general erosion of the stability and confidence which we had grown to expect from our financial institutions.

• Bank failures in the United States jumped from an average of 10 per year in the 1970s, to 42 in 1982, 48 in 1983 and 63 in 1984. Contrary to some expectations, lower inflation rates and deregulation did not restore bank profitability as many had predicted. Borrowers in the real estate and energy industries had severe problems in adjusting to lower prices. Heated competition among financial institutions for deposits pushed many into risky loan positions. Loans and investments made as hedges against inflation when rates were moving up turned out to be albatrosses as inflation rates dropped off.

• In 1983, Continental Illinois wrote off $626 million in bad loans, taking it to the brink of insolvency. It was eventually rescued with a Federal U.S. government transfusion of two billion dollars.

• Two regional Canadian banks failed in 1985—The Canadian Commercial Bank and the Northland Bank. Despite initial attempts to bail the Canadian Commercial Bank out of its difficulties, a move which cost Canadian taxpayers several hundred million dollars, it proved impossible to save either bank. Testimony at the Estey Commission set up to investigate both failures indicated that the banks had been insolvent for two years before they failed. This and 17,000 pages of related testimony has created real concern that the supervision and management of financial institutions is out of control.

The regulation of financial institutions came under close scrutiny in the early 1970s. Major government commissions of inquiry were established in the United States (the Hunt Commission), Britain, France, Germany, Australia and South Africa. As market forces leaped over or went around existing legislative barriers, these governments and others found themselves unprepared to play a leading role in shaping the financial services sector, able to react to the open barn door only after the horse was out. What these commissions all came to recognize was that under the combined influence of such factors as new technology, international banking, saturated markets and new entrants, the financial services sector was jumping from its quiet and well protected market environment into an era of intense no-holds-barred competition. As one Capital Hill observer put it "Our banking laws are out of breath and trying to catch up with the market place."

Summary

Competition in a growing number of industries is being redefined in terms of the global market place. Competition in global industries calls into question traditional ways of understanding organizations and the inter-organizational domains in which they operate. New relationships are emerging between firms in formerly separate industries, as well as new forms of relationships between organizations in the same industry. Traditional forms of industry regulation are breaking down as government policies which reflect a purely national focus are swept aside by the new realities of global competition. New forms of international cooperation among governments are emerging, and regulatory systems are being overhauled to reflect a global outlook.

Discussion Questions

1. What are the organizational obstacles preventing some firms from coming to grips with the challenges and changes occurring in global industries?

2. Given the challenge of building more flexible organizations while integrating more complex technological systems, what new management competencies are likely to become central to competition in global industries?

3. The concept of business strategy has been based on the idea of being able to "define the business" in terms of products offered and markets served. Is this an adequate concept of strategy in global industries? How else might organizations conceptualize their position in global industries?

4. Organizations have traditionally dealt with the uncertainties of the market place by growing larger to exert a greater degree of influence on their environment. Should the strategy of large scale organization be reversed to compete in more turbulent global markets?

5. What does the case tell us about environmental turbulence, and the scope for developing "collective strategies" to manage that turbulence?

6. What links do you see between the developments occurring in financial services, and the population ecology view of organizations?

82

Organizations Often
Obstruct Learning†

In an article on the management of innovation, Jay Galbraith illustrates some of the pathologies of modern organization with the following case study:

The organization in question is a venture that was started in the early seventies. While working for one of our fairly innovative electronics firms, a group of engineers developed a new electronics product. However, they were in a division that did not have the charter for their product. The ensuing political battle caused the engineers to leave and form their own company. They successfully found venture capital and introduced their new product. Initial acceptance was good, and within several years their company was growing rapidly and had become the industry leader.

However, in the early 1970s Intel invented the microprocessor, and by the mid-to-late seventies, this innovation had spread through the electronics industries. Manufacturers of previously dumb products now had the capability of incorporating intelligence into their product lines. A competitor who understood computers and software introduced just such a product into our new venture firm's market, and it met with high acceptance. The firm's president responded by hiring someone who knew something about microcomputers and

some software people and instructing the engineering department to respond to the need for a competing product.

The president spent most of his time raising capital to finance the venture's growth. But when he suddenly realized that the engineers had not made much progress, he instructed them to get a product out quickly. They did, but it was a half-hearted effort. The new product incorporated a microprocessor but was less than the second-generation product that was called for.

Even though the president developed markets in Europe and Singapore, he noticed that the competitor continued to grow faster than his company and had started to steal a share of his company's market. When the competitor became the industry leader, the president decided to take charge of the product-development effort. However, he found that the hardware proponents and software proponents in the engineering department were locked in a political battle. Each group felt that its magic was the more powerful. Unfortunately, the lead engineer (who was a co-founder of the

†SOURCE: Jay R. Galbraith, "Designing the Innovative Organization," *Organizational Dynamics*, Winter 1982, pp. 5-25; used by permission.

firm) was a hardware proponent, and the hardware establishment prevailed. However, they then clashed head-on with the marketing department, which agreed with the software proponents. The conflict resulted in studies and presentations, but no new product. So here was a young, small (1,200 people) entrepreneurial firm that could not innovate even though the president wanted innovation and provided resources to produce it. The lesson is that more was needed.

As the president became more deeply involved in the problem, he received a call from his New England sales manager, who wanted him to meet a field engineer who had modified the company's product and programmed it in a way that met customer demands. The sales manager suggested, "We may have something here."

Indeed, the president was impressed with what he saw. When the engineer had wanted to use the company's product to track his own inventory, he wrote to company headquarters for programming instructions. The response had been: It's against company policy to send instructional materials to field engineers. Undaunted, the engineer bought a home computer and taught himself to program. He then modified the product in the field and programmed it to solve his problem. When the sales manager happened to see what was done, he recognized its significance and immediately called the president.

The field engineer accompanied the president back to headquarters and presented his work to the engineers who had been working on the second-generation product for so long. They brushed off his efforts as idiosyncratic, and the field engineer was thanked and returned to the field.

A couple of weeks later the sales manager called the president again. He said that the company would lose this talented guy if something wasn't done. Besides, he thought that the field engineer, not engineering, was right. While he was considering what to do with this ingenious engineer, who, on his own had produced more

than the entire engineering department, the president received a request from the European sales manager to have the engineer assigned to him.

The European sales manager had heard about the field engineer when he visited headquarters, and had sought him out and listened to his story. The sales manager knew that a French bank wanted the type of application that the field engineer had created for himself; a successful application would be worth an order for several hundred machines. The president gave the go-ahead and sent the field engineer to Europe. The engineering department persisted in their view that the program wouldn't work. Three months later, the field engineer successfully developed the application, and the bank signed the order.

When the field engineer returned, the president assigned him to a trusted marketing manager who was told to protect him and get a product out. The engineers were told to support the manager and reluctantly did so. Soon they created some applications software and a printed circuit board that could easily be installed in all existing machines in the field. The addition of this board and the software temporarily saved the company and made its current product slightly superior to that of the competitor.

Elated, the president congratulated the young field engineer and gave him a good staff position working on special assignments to develop software. Then problems arose. When the president tried to get the personnel department to give the engineer a special cash award, they were reluctant. After all, they said, other people worked on the effort, too. It will set a precedent. And so it went. The finance department wanted to withhold $500 from the engineer's pay because he had received a $1,000 advance for his European trip, but had turned in vouchers for only $500.

The engineer didn't help himself very much either; he was hard to get along with and refused to accept supervision from anyone except the European sales manager. When the president arranged to have him permanently transferred to Europe on three occasions, the engineer changed his mind about going at the last minute. The president is still wondering what to do with him.

Discussion Question

Why is this organization encountering so many barriers to learning and innovation?

83

Product X†

Several years ago the top management of a multibillion dollar corporation decided that Product X was a failure and should be disbanded. The losses involved exceeded one hundred million dollars. At least five people knew that Product X was a failure six years before the decision was taken to stop producing it. Three of those people were plant managers who lived daily with the production problems. The other two were marketing officials who realized that the manufacturing problems were not solvable without expenditures that would raise the price of the product to the point where it would no longer be competitive in the market.

There are several reasons why this information did not get to the top sooner. At first, the subordinates believed that with exceptionally hard work they might turn the errors into successes. But the more they struggled, the more they realized the massiveness of the original error. The next task was to communicate the bad news upward so that it would be heard. They knew that in their company bad news would not be well received at the upper levels if it was not accompanied with suggestions for positive action. They also knew that the top management was enthusiastically describing Product X as a new leader in its field. Therefore, they spent much time composing memos that would communicate the realities without shocking top management.

Middle management read the memos and found them too open and forthright. Since they had done the production and marketing studies that resulted in the decision to produce X, the memos from the lower-level management questioned the validity of their analysis. They wanted time to really check these gloomy predictions and, if they were accurate, to design alternative corrective strategies. If the pessimistic information was to be sent upward, middle management wanted it accompanied with optimistic action alternatives. Hence further delay.

Once middle management was convinced that the gloomy predictions were valid, they began to release some of the bad news to the top—but in carefully measured doses. They managed the releases carefully to make certain they were covered if top management became upset. The tactic they used was to cut the memos drastically and summarize the findings. They argued that the cuts were necessary because top management was always complaining about receiving long memos; indeed, some top executives had let it be known that good memos were memos of one page or less. The result was that top management received fragmented information underplaying the intensity of the problem (not the problem itself) and overplaying the degree to which middle management and the technicians were in control of the problem.

Top management therefore continued to

†SOURCE: Excerpted from C. Argyris and D. Schon, *Organizational Learning: A Theory of Action Perspective*. Argyris/Schon, *Organizational Learning*, © 1978, Addison-Wesley Publishing Co., Inc., Reading, Massachusetts. Pages 1-2. Reprinted with permission.

speak glowingly about the product, partially to assure that it would get the financial backing it needed from within the company. Lower-level management became confused and eventually depressed because they could not understand this continued top management support, nor why studies were ordered to evaluate the production and marketing difficulties that they had already identified. Their reaction was to reduce the frequency of their memos and the intensity of their alarm, while simultaneously turning over the responsibility for dealing with the problem to the middle-management people. When local plant managers, in turn, were asked by their foremen and employees what was happening, the only response they gave was that the company was studying the situation and continuing its support. This information bewildered the foremen and led them to reduce their concern.

84

Arnold:
The Paradox of Creativity†

What an abrupt way of starting a day!

Arnold had arrived quietly in his freshly pressed grey flannel suit, and was now being asked to take off his jacket, roll-up his sleeves, untie his tie, and sit on a cushion on the floor in a room with ten other colleagues. It's brainstorming day!

—"Go crazy, ARNOLD!"
—"Let go!"
—"Be creative today!"
—"Be innovative!!!"

For years, Arnold had been the perfect company man, adapting to the corporate philosophy, resolving organizational problems by referring to the file containing problem-solving alternatives. But, today he is being asked to forget his files and to think "laterally," something that has never been asked of him before, and something that was never really valued in his business training.

Discussion Questions

1. Is Arnold confronted by a "double-bind" where two contradictory messages are being sent at the same time?

2. Arnold has been trained for years to conform with the corporate rules. How can he now acquire the mindset that will allow him to "let go" and be truly creative?

3. Can one approach creativity with a philosophy that "anything goes," or does creativity need to be channeled to meet the organization's interests? Is there a paradox here?

4. How can business schools and management programs help their participants unleash their creative power?

---

†SOURCE: "Arnold: The Paradox of Creativity," contributed by Isabelle Landry, an MBA student at York University, Toronto; used by permission.

85

Understanding the Culture of Your Organization

The culture of an organization is encoded in the images, metaphors, artifacts, beliefs, values, norms, rituals, language, stories, legends, myths, and other symbolic constructs that decorate and give form to the experience of everyday life.

Think about an organization with which you are familiar.

How would you describe its culture?

Try to be systematic in your analysis by identifying systematic examples of the symbolism in use:

—What are the principal *images or metaphors* that people use to describe the organization?

_____

_____

_____

—What *physical impression* does the organization and its artifacts create? Does this vary from one place to another?

_____

_____

—What kinds of *beliefs and values* dominate the organization? (officially . . ., unofficially . . .)

_____

_____

_____

—What are the main *norms* (i.e., the dos and don'ts)?

_____

_____

_____

—What are the main *ceremonies and rituals* and what purposes do they serve?

_____

_____

_____

—What *language* dominates everyday discourse (e.g., buzzwords, cliches, catch phrases)?

_____

_____

—What are the dominant *stories or legends* that people tell? What messages are they trying to convey?

_____

_____

_____

—What *reward systems* are in place? What "messages" do they send in terms of activities or accomplishments that are valued, and those that are not?

_____

_____

_____

—What are the favorite topics of *informal conversation?*

_____

_____

_____

—Think of three *influential people:* In what ways do they symbolize the character of the organization?

_____

_____

_____

—Are there identifiable *subcultures* in the organization? How are they differentiated? Are they in conflict or in harmony?

_____

_____

_____

—What *impacts* do these subcultures have on the organization? What functions do these groupings serve for their members? Is the overall effect on the organization positive or negative?

_____

_____

_____

86

Perfection or Bust

Design Inc., a successful commercial art studio, is the brainchild of its founder/owner, Bill Klee. Its motto, which hangs on a hand-lettered sign in the reception area, is also Klee's personal motto: Perfection Or Bust!

Design Inc. was started by Klee in 1979. I'm not interested in launching just another commercial art studio, Klee told his industry colleagues. I want to found an academy, where talented young artists and designers can perfect their skills. To work at Design Inc. will be a privilege, because I'm not offering people jobs, I'm offering them a unique educational experience!

And because Klee, a well-known figure in the industry, had a reputation as a perfectionist, his aspirations were taken seriously in most quarters.

Klee's approach to potential staff members was highly unorthodox. Instead of promising recruits high salaries and tempting bonus packages, he stressed the rigors of the job. "You won't make as much money with us as you would somewhere else," he told one lettering specialist, "and you won't be working in a fancy office with a high-fashion receptionist and inch-thick carpeting. But you will be doing the most satisfying job you've ever done in your life, because I demand perfection, and I know that you won't settle for anything less yourself!" The lettering expert, duly impressed, accepted Klee's offer some days later and over the next several months other promising recruits followed his lead. In this way, Klee was able to put together in short order a talented and en-thusiastic team of graphic artists and designers.

Potential clients were treated to a similar sales pitch. We have no frills at this studio, Klee told one prospect, sitting him down in an uncomfortable, hard-backed chair in his austere office. If you want luxury, or if you want someone to hold your hand, then go someplace else. But if you want quality, the best commercial art work in this city, if not in this whole country, then you've come to the right place.

In a matter of months, Design Inc. had carved itself a prosperous niche in the commercial art industry. The staff, enthusiastic to start with, became even more entranced by Klee's vision of perfection as time went on. True, they weren't making as much as their colleagues in more orthodox firms, but they had an ideal to pursue, and their intangible rewards went far beyond mere money. At least this is what most of them argued, when socializing with their better-paid colleagues. Sometimes these conversations became quite acrimonious, and some long-standing friendships actually suffered. Employees of other firms did not take kindly to the idea that they were content with mediocrity. On the other hand, the employees of Design Inc. were not pleased when the superiority of their work was called into question by outsiders, especially as its superiority was difficult to demonstrate in any absolute fashion. "Who says your work is so great?" became a common question, to which the common reply evolved: "Our work must be better because we take it more seriously."

As time went on, it became increasingly common for the employees of Design Inc. to spend much of their leisure time together, discussing work-related matters and reaffirming, within the family circle as it were, their commitment to excellence within their field. Many of Klee's turns of phrase—"no compromise with mediocrity," "the best or bust," "perfection is our only concern"—became part of most staff members' vocabulary.

It isn't surprising that Design Inc. employees worked long hours, coming in early and leaving late. Klee was everywhere at once, advising on layout, suggesting new creative approaches for one piece of work, consulting on the choice of color and typeface for another. Things that would be done three or four times at another studio—reviewing artwork for example—might be done as many as a dozen times or more at Design Inc., as workers agonized to get every last detail of a project right. No stone was left unturned in the staff's pursuit of excellence. These hours cut even more into the social lives of the employees, throwing them more and more into each others' company.

About 18 months after Design Inc. was established, its top layout artist, forced to choose between his career at Design Inc. and his family, left the firm for another job. His departure was handled smoothly, a party being held to send him off.

Klee stepped into his position until a replacement could be found. Advertisements were put in the paper, and the word was passed along the industry grapevine. In line with the all for one and one for all philosophy of Design Inc., it was decided that every staff member should have a say in the selection of the new recruit. After all, as Klee put it, we'll probably be spending more time with whomever we hire than with our families! Everyone agreed that the new recruit would have to be enthusiastic about Art Inc's training mission, and would have to demonstrate an unswerving commitment to perfection in his or her work.

A large number of qualified people applied, but somehow none of them seemed exactly to fit the bill. One had a young family and expressed doubt about his ability to work every weekend if need be. A second was passed over because one employee felt that she wasn't a team player. Another was rejected because several staff members felt he just didn't have the right attitude. After several months, all the candidates had been interviewed, and all had been rejected for one reason or another.

During this time, Klee, because of his additional responsibilities, had begun to neglect his training mission. The studio continued to function, but as a business and not as an academy. Everyone agreed, however, that this situation was temporary. Design Inc. would become a training ground again as soon as it got a new layout person. . . .

In his private moments, Klee occasionally wondered if his studio was quite what he had wanted it to be. It seemed to him that something of his dream had been lost. He did not have a great deal of spare time in which to philosophize, however. Furthermore, the firm was doing well financially, and so, as owner, Klee found a certain consolation in the healthy state of his firm's balance sheet.

About a year after the layout artist took another job, he dropped by to visit his former colleagues. He found Klee still filling in for him. The staff still spoke of dedication to excellence and insisted that the day when Design Inc. again became an academy was close at hand. The visitor sensed a certain hollowness in their bluff statements, however. It seemed to him that employees were less certain of their mission and less confident about the future than they let on.

The layout position was never readvertised, and no new candidates were ever interviewed. Most of the original staff are still with the firm, however, which turns a respectable profit each year.

Discussion Questions

1. Does Design Inc. have a strong sense of corporate culture?

2. Is the firm a success?

3. If not, explain the reasons.

87

The Creation and Destruction of the Order of Maria Theresa[†]

Charles V ruled over an empire in which the sun did not set. This created fantastic communications problems for the officials of the Crown in the remote overseas possessions. They were supposed to carry out faithfully the imperial orders reaching them from Madrid, but often they could not, because the directives were issued in crass ignorance of the local situation or arrived weeks if not months after being decreed, by which time they were largely obsolete. In Central America this dilemma led to a very pragmatic solution: "Se obedece pero no se cumple" (One obeys but does not comply). Thanks to this recipe, the Central American possessions flourished, not because but in spite of the imperial orders from the Escorial. Two centuries later this expedient was awarded official recognition under the reign of Empress Maria Theresa through the establishment of the Order of Maria Theresa. . . . With refreshing absurdity it was reserved exclusively for officers who turned the tide of battle by taking matters into their own hands and actively disobeying orders.

Paul Watzlawick
(*The Invented Reality*)

Five summers ago I began work as a gas station attendant for Petroco, a large petroleum refiner with gas stations located primarily in the Northeast and North Central United States. Beginning work during mid-July, I worked in both part-time and full-time capacities until June of the following summer.

During this time there were two different managers. The first, Maria Theresa, had worked there for several months prior to my arrival, and lasted until she requested a transfer in mid-May. The second manager, Vincent MacMurdo, took over at that time and continued after I had left. Both of these managers held a bachelor's degree and had had some previous managerial experience. They had been assigned to this particular station because they had done an especially good job on their previous job assignments, and because the high volume of business made the station something of a proving ground for managers on the rise within the company. However, despite sharing a certain managerial competence, the two managers were as different as day and night.

Maria, for her part, deliberately operated in ways which circumvented the regulations laid down in the operations manuals. Instead of focusing on the letter of the law and enforcing orthodoxy, she sought instead to forge a sense of comradery and friendship. Her willingness to bend or disregard the rules was greatly appreciated, by both myself and others, and as a result her attempt to forge a sense of comradery was largely successful.

This sense of comradery was expressed through four channels: among the crew members, between the crew and Maria Theresa, between the crew and the customers, and in a peculiar way, between the crew, Maria and the district manager. The expression of the

[†]SOURCE: This case was contributed by Brian Duke, who is currently working toward an M.S. in accounting at the University of Massachusetts at Amherst; used by permission.

crew's comradery manifested itself during every work day, during which one crew member always helped out another, whether by "jumping" a dead battery, doing a little auto repair, or just running over to the Golden Arches for coffee. For example, during one January day my battery died of natural causes and when we attempted to jump it, we shorted the other car's electrical system. Where a lesser crew might at that stage have given up, the day crew instead rallied and repaired the short and began making phone calls and illegal trips to the junkyard. The results were soon 1) a used but serviceable battery, and 2) the necessary electrical parts and wires. In time, the favors were returned.

The second channel of comradery—between the crew and Maria—existed and prospered largely due to Maria's readily apparent concern for the crew. She would often show up early in the morning with coffee and donuts for the morning crew, or late in the evening with pizza for the evening crew. Her extra efforts on the crew's behalf were reciprocated whenever Maria needed an extra body because a crew member could not make his/her allotted shift. An indication of the loyalty which we felt for Maria is given by the fact that crew members would frequently *volunteer* to work another eight hour shift if Maria was going to be short. (The extent of this willing sacrifice can perhaps only be appreciated by those having spent 16 hours standing on concrete!)

The third channel of comradery, between crew members and customers, is perhaps best illustrated by the time a couple's car ran out of gas and sputtered to a stop about 1/4 mile from the station. When they asked to borrow the telephone we refused permission—letting a customer use the pay phone inside the station was expressly forbidden, since the safe was inside.[1] However, as we did so, we also offered to push their car the 1/4 mile uphill to the station. In what was soon to be an oft repeated story, the result was that we were generously rewarded for our efforts with a $15.00 tip and a standing ovation from the several cars waiting patiently in the parking lot.

The coup de grace came when the manager of the neighboring McDonald's sent over a complimentary round of cokes as a sign of approval. Interestingly, such behavior was completely against Petroco rules, which forbade employees to leave the station without managerial approval. Maria—who was not there at the time—gushed with superlatives when she eventually heard the story.

The final expression of comradery came about through the peculiar relationship between Maria, the crew and the district manager. The district manager was a well groomed M.B.A. devoted to enforcing the rules and regulations. One way he did so was to periodically spy on the crew members by parking in the shopping center across the road. However, we always knew he was coming before he "unexpectedly arrived" because of Maria's early warning system that she had established with other managers. While Mr. Bond was in our midst we were always on model behavior, following Petroco guidelines to the letter; after he left the station we returned to "normal." Naturally, the district manager knew something was going on, but because Maria consistently set new all-time-sales-records, while simultaneously maintaining average "shortages," he never investigated thoroughly. The crew, having a low tolerance of spies, was not about to inform him otherwise.

* * *

During the month of April, Maria began contemplating a move to a smaller station closer to her home in Connecticut. Although our particular station offered her greater prestige, she had begun to miss the community of her family and friends. When an opportunity to move arose in mid-May, Maria initially refused, to the crew's delight. Eventually, however, she reconsidered and accepted the opportunity to manage closer to home. We were an aggrieved crew which greeted Vincent MacMurdo.

Vince, for his part, operated by the book in a no-nonsense attempt to establish discipline and order. Where Maria fostered comradery,

Vince deliberately attempted to foster individual accountability. That a new manager had arrived was quickly driven home to the crew when a crew member was fired for being $2 short for 3 days' work. When an irate crew member demanded to know what the hell Vince thought he was doing, Vince responded by reading from the operations manual. Quoth he, "An employee shall be fired if s/he is $10 short for the month; or is $5 short for the week; or is $1 short for 2 days; or is $.75 short for 1 day." During the first two weeks of Vince's tenure, 3 people were fired for coming up short. When the crew protested that Maria had never done it that way, Vince responded by saying he was not Maria—the crew readily agreed!

The implementation of rule and order extended well past the area of shortages, fundamentally altering the way in which the crew operated. Previously the work crew had consisted of four attendants, one responsible for each island of gas pumps (three in all), and one floating assistant. Under this arrangement, the assistant was free to help wherever needed and the other attendants, if they were free, also helped out. Those helping out would pump gas, wipe windows, check oil and collect the money for the person being helped, and would then give the money to the person assigned to the island at the earliest convenience.

Vince deliberately destroyed the system, arguing that if the "helpers" decided to pocket the money, then the person being helped would be fired for someone else's theft. However, his initial instructions to cease and desist were ignored, as the crew members insisted on trusting one another. Eventually, however, Vince laid down the law: anyone collecting money for anyone else would be fired. When a new employee was actually fired for collecting money, the "helper" system ceased. In its place a system emerged where each attendant strayed less and less from his/her "own" island, attending to cleaning and sweeping instead of "helping." In this way, individual accountability was implemented.

However, the main change was in the rela-

tionship between the manager, crew and district manager. Where Maria had worked with, but around, the Petroco's rules, Vince adopted them as his own. An immediately noticeable effect was that the district manager was around much more than formerly, and most importantly, his pending arrival was not announced to the crew. Thus, his spying missions began to pay off, which only encouraged him to make even more spying missions, as he was beginning to uncover the sins he had long suspected.

One result of this was a reversal of the crew's long standing concern to help customers. For instance, I began to rigorously enforce the injunction about not pumping gas into running cars (which infuriated people). Although they might plead that their battery was dying, I held the company line. When they told me that if their car did not start, then I would have to jump them, I responded that it was against company policy. One time when a customer could not get his car started, Vince not only refused to let him use the phone, but called a tow truck himself.

It is important to emphasize that it was not only the crew who reacted to the destruction of the order of Maria Theresa. Customers also reacted, at first by complaining, and then by never returning. About this time strange things began to happen. For example, one night after I refused to pump regular gas into an unleaded tank, the driver of the van I had been arguing with suddenly gunned his engine—and narrowly missed me as I leaped out of the way. Then, even as this story was making the rounds, a woman crew member was run over and injured by a customer who "didn't see her." "Accidents" like these just continued to happen: first, several crew members were hurt moving boxes of pump parts; second, another employee suffered an injury that kept her out of work several months, and third, another crew member was suddenly out on workman's compensation after getting hit by a car door. Then when the bottom had apparently been reached, a woman crew member simultaneously quit and stole several hundred dollars while leaving.

* * *

The Saturday Night Massacre

In addition to this accident spree, during Vince's first two months at the station, several major, negative business events occurred. First, the sales volume of the station sharply declined. Second, despite Vince's rigorous application of Petroco's shortage policy, shortages reached new heights. And third, the district manager reported to Vince that crew service to customers was well below Petroco's standards. Confronted with these blossoming problems, and obvious crew hostility (one crew member he had fired had promised to come back and "discuss" it further), Vince and the district manager settled on a final solution: fire the Order of Maria Theresa. And one by one, the crew was fired, until there were only two of the Order left.

At this time Vince was looking for an assistant to help him keep tabs on the crew, and the choice came down to the two of us, as we were by far the most experienced crew members. The other remaining member was a local high school graduate who, although disliking Vince (his description: "the east end of a west bound horse"), was nevertheless willing to work for him. My position was simple: if nominated I will not run, if elected I will not serve.

Unsurprisingly, I was eventually fired.

So ended the Order of Maria Theresa.

Note

1. We were in fact supposed to deny having a phone, despite the fact that the phone rang outside for all to hear.

Discussion Questions

1. How would you characterize Maria's approach to management?

2. Which managerial style was better suited for running the service station—Maria's or Vince's? Why?

3. If you were a senior executive with Petroco and learned the full details of this case, how would you respond? Would you try to change company policy on the management of service stations?

88

Sink or Swim:
Reflections on a Corporate Training Program

David Hall is 30 years old and now occupies a middle management position with a large company in the automobile industry. He holds an M.B.A., and has had several positions with various organizations over the last ten years.

A few years ago, he obtained a job with a large electronics firm, and as part of his training was required to go through a corporate training program along with other recruits to the sales force of the organization.

The experience for David was a very traumatic one, and, as a result, he decided to quit the organization.

The following pages present his personal account of how he saw the company putting its recruits through the "corporate mill," communicating its core values and identifying those trainees best suited to its needs, but trampling on many values that David believed to be important. The way in which the program "fell apart" makes many of its underlying principles very visible.

I was hired by Comco in 1980 and began the training programme in May. To call it rigorous is an under-statement. It was an experience that will never be forgotten by those who participated. It convinced me that Comco is an immoral company. I resented the excessive workload and the mental stress to which we were subjected. Comco created human suffering in order to further its own ends. To me, this is immoral.

The training programme is designed for salesmen and technical support staff. It started with a six week term at the regional office. We were introduced to computers and communications systems and the rudiments of accounting and sales techniques. This phase was really a preparation for the second phase of the program, held at Comco's training center in Houston, Texas.

The time in Houston represented my first experience with an all-encompassing training environment. We lived in company townhouses, ate at the company cafeteria, and spent all of our non-sleeping hours at the complex. Our schedule was extremely structured with little free time. Those six weeks, living under such controlled circumstances, were very traumatic.

The third phase of the programme (weeks 13-19) was held back at the regional office. We were introduced to further information and ideas about computer systems and communications software. By now I was becoming aware of some aspects of Comco and its employees. Established members were in awe of the company and its achievements, and identified with it very closely. They respected "Comco", themselves, and each other and saw the results of their collective efforts in a constant string of corporate triumphs. Much of the same kind of respect was instilled during the training programme.

After phase three, we returned to Houston for the next phase (weeks 20-26). This was the most difficult section of the programme and, from a company standpoint, the most important. For this was the phase when Comco bombarded its recruits with its norms and values. One was taught respect—respect for co-workers and management, respect for customers, and respect for "Comco." Respect for co-workers stemmed in large part from their common struggle through the training programme. Mutual respect forms the basis of the company sales team.

The team concept is crucial for the company's success, because no single person is capable of solving all problems that may arise. People must relate to each other, so the "team" atmosphere is all-important. Naturally, teamwork was emphasized during phase four, and individualism and the "do it yourself" attitude was blatantly discouraged. I was asked: "If you were the top draft choice in the National Football League, would you choose to join a losing club and be the star, or a winning club and be a member of a team of stars?" The question was rhetorical: Comco was a winning club.

In phase four other company norms and values were taught. We were shown how to dress the company way, to act the company way, and to speak the company way. The methods were often quite subtle. It was my first experience with such indoctrination tactics, so I think I was particularly vulnerable. Now, in retrospect it seems obvious. But back in phase four we were only aware of the huge workload and the rigid daily schedule.

Phase four was organized like a Comco sales office, with a "Branch Manager," 6 "Unit Managers," and just under 50 "Sales People" (students).

The Branch Manager was responsible for the class's performance, which was based on students' grades and an appraisal of the class "spirit," meaning the extent to which it conformed with company norms and values.

"Branch Managers" were Comco employees who were ostensibly on the way to being Sales Managers. They are sent to Houston on six month to three year assignments, but the motives for their assignment are capricious. Assignment to Houston is viewed as a negative career move or a punishment. In fact, many students believed that Houston was simply a dumping ground for "losers." Certainly, there was great pressure on Branch Managers to perform well in Houston, so as to minimize its impact on their career and personal life. The evaluations that s/he received from students were at least as important as the students' grades were to them. For all concerned, therefore, phase four was an extremely pressure-filled experience.

When I arrived in Houston for phase four, I was intent on completing the program and looked forward to a career at Comco. My class was a little livelier than it had been in phase two. There were six former college football players in it. They had all been together in phase two and had grouped together to help each other through. Now in phase four they were more confident and vocal. I enjoyed the effect of their presence; it broke down some of the formality and rigidity of the program. Their [comradery] was infectious and one guy, Joe, had us all laughing during that first meeting.

Our phase four manager was a short, fat and balding guy named Jeff Bowes. He had no sense of humor and appeared very serious. Our loud class intimidated him. He had little physical presence; any of the six ex-footballers could have picked him up with one hand. The jocks immediately referred to Bowes as "the Wimp

Factor." After the first meeting, they joked: "I knew this was going to be easy, but with the Wimp Factor it'll be a piece of cake!"

The situation made Bowes nervous. He tried to make himself appealing to the jocks by being humorous and by acting with machismo. It did not quite work. Most of us, taking the jocks' lead, began to poke fun at Bowes behind his back. He was an uninspiring leader, personally weak. To all of us he became either "The Wimp" or "The Waterboy."

Right from day one, the workload was incredible. Every day we had at least one major examination or sales call, two major product assignments and seven hours of intense lectures. In the first week, we had 95 hours of scheduled work.

First thing in the morning, Bowes would come in and lead the class in singing songs. Some were company rah-rah songs while others were simple humorous songs. The Comco "fight song" was popular as was "Row, row, row your boat." Unit Managers put on skits and told jokes in front of the class. One of the regular skits involved the on-going saga of Tim and Jack in "Selling the South." Tim and Jack were Southerners who wore overalls, confederate caps and no shirts, socks or shoes. Tim played a Comco salesman (he wore a tie), and Jack played a Southern customer (no tie). A typical dialogue ran something like this:

Jack: "Y'all wanna sell me a computer—whatta they do?"
Tim: "They help you count stuff."
Jack: "I can't count."
Tim: "Neither can I, I'll buy one—where do I sign?"
Jack: (Hands him one of Tim's contracts, Tim signs it.)
Tim: "Well, see yu later, good luck in selling them thar things." (Jack walks out with Tim's papers and brochures.)
Tim: "Something's wrong here."

There was another series of skits involving muppets trying to be Comco salesmen. They, too, poked fun at the Comco selling experience. Morning exercises sometimes included

humorous movies as well. All in all, it was a pleasant way to start off the day. We yelled along with the skits. We laughed and cheered. If the exercises were particularly good, or particularly bad, we would end them by throwing waste paper at the actors. The jocks were informal judges: if it was time for a waste paper storm, they would start chanting, "uga, uga, uga, uga . . ."

Sometimes I would have trouble joining in the comic atmosphere. I really felt like a fool singing "Home on the Range," standing beside my desk in a three piece suit. I was usually silent when others yelled, "Movie, movie," or "Tim and Jack, Tim and Jack," to express their preference. It seemed absurd for grown men to be playing children's games. Bowes noticed my attitude problem. Sometimes he would make me sing a song alone. In the first week I had to sing "God Save the Queen." Six other Canadians joined me; the Americans didn't know if it was patriotism or cynicism.

The singing and skits had a serious purpose. They allowed the students to get back at the company for all the work it was putting them through. Without such "recreation," the tense and exhausted students would present the Manager with a volatile situation. Finally, it allowed the Branch Manager to promote corporate goals and consolidate his own power. It was his job to define the reality of phase four as "a challenge"; the most difficult, but rewarding, experience of a lifetime.

Bowes always tried to supplement the skits with his own injections of enthusiasm. He would enter the class, bubbly and enthusiastic, saying: "Hello class 80-B, how are we? We're number one—we're number one!" Bowes would also lead the songs and introduce the skits: "Tim and Jack thought they'd share some selling tips—take it away Tim and Jack—yeah, Tim and Jack." Somehow, Bowes did not quite pull it off. Maybe it was his physical appearance, or maybe his high squeaky voice, but in any case he was still "The Wimp" to us.

Following the songs and skits were the awards presentations. The top three performers from the previous day's examinations and sales calls were called to the front of the class to sign a large piece of paper, affixed to the wall—the "Wall of Fame." At the end of each week, the top performing units, as well as the worst, are recognized. At the end of week one, our class had a low rating so a meeting was called. Bowes was very serious. He reiterated how important the ratings were. He was obviously quite anxious; his own cumulative rating was a reflection of his units' ratings. Bowes tried to erase some of the divisiveness of competition by urging the class to "raise the roof" in applause for the winners, and show the other classes what spirit, [comradery] and bravado is "all about." Grateful for the tension release, we shouted and applauded like crazy.

In spite of Bowes' talk, the atmosphere became more and not less competitive in week two. There was at least one graded situation per day. The passing grade was 80%. At the beginning of week one, most of us were pulling off 90s. By the end of week two, however, we had dropped to about the 80% borderline.

If a student is failing, s/he could be "sent home." The instructor waits until the individual is alone, then takes him or her to an isolated spot, mentions the failed exams or failed sales calls (on video tape), and convinces him or her to leave. It they withdraw voluntarily they may be given a chance to repeat the program at a later date; if not, they are told that their ticket has already been purchased and that their poor performance at Houston has been relayed to their home office. Certainly, attitude plays a large part in the determination of who is sent home. I noticed that some poor performers survived phase four because of their attitude and in spite of their grades.

Once a student leaves, the class is told that "John told us that he would like to go back to L.A. and brush up on his computer programming and give this another shot! Good for John! That's the Comco spirit!" The "sending home" process reeked of hypocrisy but it showed that Comco could be a brutal, as well as a fair, employer.

The pressure to work harder and avoid being sent home became almost unbearable towards the end of week two. We realized that by sending someone home Bowes could raise our unit's rating and help his cumulative rating stand. This knowledge drove us into a competitive frenzy. People did not come together to help others in trouble as was usually the case in other classes. In fact, the opposite happened. Cliques formed on the basis of relative class standing. The "losers" were those near the bottom of the class. They were a despondent, tired and depressed group. When together, they would try to console one another and blame their shortcomings on Bowes, "Comco," or the Company's brainwashing process. They even had their own song: "Another one bites the dust" by the rock group "Queen." When it was played on the intercom they would dance and sing. It was an expression of their solidarity and contempt for their situation.

"Winners" were those in the top quartile of the class. If a "loser" tried to intrude on their lunchtime discussions, he was made to feel unwelcome. "Winners" were aware of the importance of attitude. They thought that associating with a "loser" could have a negative impact. "Winners" looked upon their training as a positive experience. They figured that though phase four was a difficult challenge, it was surmountable and that its completion would provide them with rewards and opportunities. They looked forward to a bright future as Comco's sales people or systems engineers. The winners numbered 10 to 15 in week three.

Besides the "winners" and the "losers" there were a few "non-affiliates." Non-affiliates either had sympathies with one group but grades that put them in the other, or they just didn't want to be associated with any group. I was a "non-affiliate." I was doing well in the program but I had a definite, and widely acknowledged, attitude problem. I hated the rigidity of the programme and the excessive workload demands put on us by Comco. It [bred] selfishness. I was intrigued by the "Winners" who accepted the programme's hardships as part of a legitimate process simply because they were winning. The "losers" moaned and groaned, but they did not act. They clung to the belief that they could be winners too.

At the end of week two, the jocks decided that the workload was unrealistic and put the blame on Bowes. The jocks had two spokesmen, Joe and a guy named Bob Roberts. They tried to drum up support. The "losers" were easily persuaded but the "winners" and "non-affiliates" were less enthused. They feared the consequences of confronting Bowes, yet saw possible benefits in such action, so they remained passive. There were two power sources in our class: Bowes who had the formal power, and the jocks who had always held informal power. A "show down" was imminent.

Our marks were setting a record low in week three and word got around that our class had a potential "attitude problem." The tension mounted as many refused to sing in the mornings or sat in silence during skit time. Soon, complaints about the workload, "Comco" and Jeff Bowes became audible. As a result, Jeff panicked.

One day in the middle of week three, Bowes came into the classroom raging about the "conspiracy" against him and his career. Some began to challenge him quietly while others sat back in anticipation. Then Bowes broke things wide open. He proudly announced that two "ring-leaders," Joe and one of the "losers," had "expressed a desire to go home and give phase four another try later." He broke out into a wide grin. But without hesitation two jocks stood up and cursed him vehemently. The class broke into a loud and prolonged cheer. I couldn't believe what I was seeing. Bowes stood at the front of the class seething with anger, and eventually stormed out of the room. He had lost control, and with it, all credibility as the Comco role model.

Bowes did not lecture to our class for the rest of weeks three and four. Five more students were sent home in week three for an unprecedented total of 10. There were no songs or skits for the rest of weeks three and four.

The tension was unbearable. We did not really know what our status in Houston, or even with Comco, was. Unit Managers were visibly uneasy lecturing to us. News of our class was flowing through the complex corridors. The jocks had the full support of the class and were in complete control.

On Friday of week five, after an evening of heavy drinking, a number of students including all the remaining jocks went on a destructive spree of company property. They damaged four company cars and destroyed the walls of a company townhouse. One of the jocks pulled up over 40 small evergreen trees around the company complex, rammed them through the walls of a company townhouse and placed the remainder in toilets throughout the complex. On Saturday, the police had identified those responsible and awaited Comco's request to file charges.

There was great apprehension in the class on Monday morning. I felt proud of the wound we had inflicted on Comco. At the same time, however, I could not help but feel guilty for our lawbreaking actions. To the surprise of all of us, we were given songs and skits for the first time in a week. We all sang with enthusiasm and the skits were appreciated. Then the biggest surprise of all: class was dismissed early and Tuesday's exam cancelled. No exam meant no studying! We had a night off! A couple of Unit Managers added that they would be buying rounds of drinks at a local bar that night. The whole class went down and enjoyed a night of good times on the company. It seemed to me that on this night the cliques began to disappear.

On Tuesday morning, the Director of National Education came into our class, introducing himself by his first name. He told us that Comco was a reasonable employer and announced that those responsible for the destruction of company property would not be reprimanded. Then he passed out his business cards, "in case any class member had anything to discuss in confidence."

We appreciated the company's attitude and

many bad feelings receded. Soon, morale improved and our performance improved dramatically. There were only three students who continued to do poorly. They were a cause of concern for us, so we got together to aid them. In spite of our efforts, by the last couple of days there was no way mathematically that the three could pass.

Final grades were to be distributed during a graduation party at a downtown restaurant. A pall hung over the party. We had become so close in the past few weeks. We were united by the ordeal we had been through. It didn't seem fair that the three couldn't graduate with us. Many planned to walk out on Bowes when he told the three students that they had failed.

Bowes arrived with 38 envelopes (there were 38 students remaining in the class). He announced that he had 38 graduation diplomas. A wave of emotion broke loose. We went crazy! We had all made it! We hugged and kissed each other as cheers were raised for the three marginal students. Then we cheered Comco and even Bowes. All was forgiven. We had sur- vived the worst of the training program. The next day we all returned to our home offices for preparation for the next term.

Three years after the training programme had ended, only two (myself included) of the 12 people from my region in that class had left the business. The rest continued on as happy, productive employees.

Discussion Questions

1. How effective is Comco's approach to training? Despite the debacle in this particular program, is the company succeeding in sorting out those employees who will feel committed to the organization?

2. To what extent is the training program an intimidation ritual?

3. David is obviously a somewhat embittered "outsider." How do you think one of the "winners" would feel about Comco's training program?

89

The Nomizu Sake Company†

The Nomizu Sake Company was founded in 1982 as a joint-venture between Nomizu International, a Japanese liquor importing firm based in southern California, and Woodland Farms Inc., an American rice-milling company with headquarters in northern California. The company was established in the San Francisco Bay Area, at an antiquated dairy factory which was renovated to suit the technological needs of sake production.

In its formative stage, the company brought over a team of Japanese sake makers from a small, agricultural village in northern Japan known for its sake making expertise. This team was led by a sake master, Mr. Toshiyuki Kawate, a good-natured, rotund, middle-aged man, characterized by his serene, Buddha-like disposition, steadfast traditional values, and sizable physical strength (he held a fifth-level black-belt standing in Judo). The Japanese team was originally housed in trailers on the factory premises and shared common kitchen and lavatory facilities. The younger sake makers took turns at being the group cook and shared housekeeping responsibilities. They worked long hours to set up the sake production area and develop a resilient yeast culture which would successfully serve as a catalyst for the rice fermentation process in the United States. A typical day for the Japanese team began with a thirty minute morning exercise routine which was led by Kawate, the sake master. Their day ended with a formal ceremonious work song which praised one another for their group effort and achievement for the day.

Nomizu Sake Company's management team was made up of Mr. Steven James, Sr., Chairman of the Board and President of Woodland Farms, Inc.; his son, Steven James, Jr., Executive Vice-President, and Mr. Kenichi Nagano, Vice-President of Distribution and President of Nomizu International. James, Jr. was the only one of the triumvirate with an office at the company site. Mr. Nagano was stationed at Nomizu International headquarters in Los Angeles and Steven James, Sr. at Woodland Farms, Inc. in Woodland. Steven James, Jr., a blonde-haired, blue-eyed, native San Franciscan, was typically American in his individualistic, entrepreneurial, straight-forward way of doing business. Outwardly cosmopolitan, he was in fact quite provincial in his attitudes toward the Japanese.

As the company grew, an American marketing, public relations and financial staff were brought in at company headquarters, as well as a Japanese/American salesforce. When full production commenced in the Fall of 1983, Mr. Kawate was promoted to Production Manager and additional production line workers were hired from the immediate vicinity of the factory to meet increased production demands. These workers came from a variety of backgrounds including students, expatriate house-

†SOURCE: This case was contributed by Mary Yoko Brannen, a Ph.D. student at the University of Massachusetts at Amherst; used by permission.

wives, student drop-outs, blue-collar workers, blacks, whites, Hispanics and Asian-Americans.

From the onset of the venture, management exhibited an awareness of certain problems that an international joining of this sort would produce. This awareness was limited, however, to the obvious communication difficulties that would arise from having monolingual Japanese nationals and Americans working under the same roof. Management made initial efforts to rectify this language problem by hiring Wendy Suzuki in 1982, at the company's inception, as the chief language instructor for the Japanese faction. A Japanese American born and raised in Japan, she gave private English lessons to the sake master six hours a week, after working hours, focusing on technical and basic survival skills. In addition, she conducted group English lessons for the junior sake makers.

It did not take much time to elapse before further problems of a more complex intercultural nature began to emerge in the company. As soon as full production began and production support was increased by hiring from the heterogeneous population of the San Francisco Bay Area, Kawate's monocultural methods of production management met with sizable resistance from the new workforce. A split in the workforce between the Japanese nationals and the multicultural Americans became pronounced. The newly hired Americans who had no cultural or artistic investment in sake making saw their job as a basic nine to five commitment of wage labor. They were characterized by their sense of individual identity, equal sense of status, informal style and direct assertiveness. In comparison, the Japanese nationals were characterized by a sense of group identity, respect for hierarchical status, formal style and indirect expression. Consequently, the American portion of the workforce, though initially intrigued by the novelty of Kawate's management techniques, soon grew tired of having to work past five o'clock p.m. to meet daily production quotas, as did their Japanese counterparts.

Consequently, Kawate called a meeting with James, Jr., to discuss the problems he was facing in the production area. James, Jr. called Wendy in to interpret for this session, and, after a brief discussion, he explained to Kawate that in America employees could not be expected to work overtime without some kind of monetary compensation. He went on to explain that since the Japanese workers were being paid on a salaried basis, overtime without compensation was not an unreasonable demand. If Kawate insisted that the other American workers, who were being paid on an hourly basis, should work overtime, then they would have to receive time and a half compensation. He further elaborated that because the Japanese workers would not have to receive extra compensation for overtime, and since they readily agreed to put in extra work, it was much more cost effective for the company to allow the Japanese to work overtime until production quotas were met and let the Americans go home as five o'clock as they wished.

As soon as the Japanese nationals saw that the seemingly aberrant behavior of their American co-workers was accepted by the management rather than reprimanded, they began to feel resentment and jealousy. Two of the younger Japanese workers followed the lead of their American co-workers and began punching out at five o'clock sharp. Group morale began to decline not only among the production workers as a whole, but also among the Japanese subunit as well.

By this time James, Jr., who had already increased Wendy's responsibilities to include becoming his private language tutor in an act of good faith toward the Japanese faction of the company, found it necessary to increase her responsibilities further. As more and more complex intercultural problems of the nature described above began to emerge and productivity and morale began to decline, she was called upon more frequently to interpret for James, Jr. and Kawate. These sessions which started out as short, thirty minute formalities, soon grew into frantic, five to six hour sessions of heated discussion, characterized by a high level of frustration on the part of everyone, where Wendy would continually try to find common cultural ground on which to center the issues at hand. James, Jr. was frustrated by what he called Kawate's "Japanese farmboy" mentality; Kawate was frustrated because he just could not understand why what he thought were "givens" in effective management practice were being questioned; and Wendy was frustrated because the sessions were too long and strenuous for effective simultaneous interpretation and because she could not stay impartial throughout the whole process; sometimes she took the American side, sometimes the Japanese, and many times she felt too embarrassed and compromised to translate the vulgarities and accusations that were expressed.

In 1984 a tasting room was opened to encourage the public to try sake, and a director of the tasting room was hired, Ms. Carolyn Yuen, a young Chinese woman from Taiwan who was a recent college graduate with a degree in Public Relations. Wendy was called upon at this time to provide advice and educational background for the tasting room staff so that they would be better prepared to answer the various questions that their customers might have regarding Japan and sake. In addition she put together a verbal accompaniment to a slide show to be shown at tastings on the sake making process.

Occasionally, to supplement her income and for job diversity, Wendy would help serve sake and speak with customers in the tasting room. On one such occasion, she witnessed a slide show and much to her surprise and embarrassment, she saw that the tasting room staff had added a slide of Mr. Kawate's portrait to which the verbal accompaniment went something like this: "Mr. Kawate, the sake master at Nomizu Sake Company, nobly left his hometown of Niigata, Japan to come to the United States on a mission to share his art of sake making. His mission was not without sacrifice because by leaving Japan, Mr. Kawate has blacklisted himself from the profession of sake masters in Japan, never again to be able to return and resume his position in Japan." Immediately upon hearing this Wendy spoke with the director of the tasting room, Carolyn Yuen, and asked her how this addition had come about. She said she did not know who originated it, but it was a gallant story and the customers were always interested in it. Wendy's response was that it was outrageous, unkind and insensitive to fabricate a story which was not only untrue, but also quite seriously an attack on Kawate's moral character. She added that perhaps this was all done in innocence, but that the cultural implications of Kawate's losing face among his colleagues in Japan were very serious and that this practice should be stopped immediately before Kawate would catch wind of it. Despite Wendy's admonition, the tasting room staff continued to use the same story.

Finally, in a culture session with Kawate he told Wendy that he was aware that his portrait was being used in the slide show and asked her to translate the accompanying storyline. He understood most of it but was baffled by the meaning of the word "blacklist." Knowing that she too could share in Kawate's loss of face by owning up to her role in the situation—in Japan the whole organization loses face when an employee makes an error—she apologized for not having been effective in putting an end to the story and then proceeded to translate it for him. Kawate's reaction was very grave, as she had anticipated it would be. He immediately took her by the arm and led her into James, Jr.'s office, entered without knocking, and had her repeat to James, Jr. what she had translated. He then demanded an explanation from James, Jr. James, Jr. assured Kawate that he had not known about this and that he would take care of it right away. He would have the tasting room staff discontinue the story and make Kawate a formal apology. After Kawate had left James, Jr. demanded an explanation from Wendy as to why she had not come to see him before this had gotten back to Kawate. He punctuated his anger with accusatory phrases such as "How could you have let something as inconsequential as this get so out of hand?" and "Where are your loyalties placed anyway?" The next day Wendy was told at a formal meeting of the tasting room staff that her services there were no longer needed. From that time on she was called upon less frequently to interpret and work as cultural liaison for James, Jr. Within a period of about three months she ceased to hear from the company.

Discussion Questions

1. How would you evaluate the way James Jr. handled this situation? Was his response more Western than Eastern? What could he have done to rectify the situation?

2. How would you evaluate Wendy Suzuki's behavior? Could she have been more effective?

3. How could the Nomizu Sake Company have done more to assimilate the Japanese contingent within the organization?

90

The Fortress Insurance Company

The Fortress Insurance Company, a major firm in the industry, had not entirely kept pace with the changing times. It offered only standard insurance services, and had taken little trouble to differentiate itself from its competitors or to cater to new public tastes and preferences.

This attitude had resulted in slower growth than had been foreseen, and Fortress's senior management had become distressed by the firm's poor record in attracting new clients. It had therefore reluctantly decided to venture into a new field of activity—the marketing of its services.

The reluctance of management to become involved with marketing was a natural outgrowth of the type of company Fortress was. As an insurance company, Fortress had always been an extremely conservative operation. Prudence, deliberation, and caution had been encouraged among employees, and those exhibiting these characteristics in large measure had often ended up in senior management positions.

The formation of the marketing department marked a departure from this scheme of things. On the advice of an outside consulting firm, and with some trepidation, Fortress selected Bill Storm, a brash young executive, as head of its new marketing department.

Storm, though bright, had not hitherto found his niche in the organization because of his aggressive and often unconventional approach to problems. Storm promptly set to work to develop this new department, and, by recruiting similar mavericks from within the company,

soon had a dynamic team gathered about him. The marketing department set to work to improve Fortress's market share. Marketing Fortress as the company that cares about people, they began to offer the public personalized financial planning assistance, do-it-yourself insurance portfolios, and other service-related insurance packages. Using television, radio, and print advertising as well as the services of a public relations agency, the marketing department drove its message home to all segments of the public. To the astonishment of senior management, within a year, Fortress, had begun to make substantial inroads into its competitors' market share.

As a result of its success, the marketing department gained considerable stature and autonomy within the organization. It was seen as the exception to Fortress' rule of caution in all things; the marketing department was allowed to be different because, apparently, its approach worked. The employees of the department saw themselves as an elite group, and took pride in being different from the majority of Fortress staff. Of course, these differences were fairly minor. For example, while most Fortress executives favored blue pinstripe suits and dark ties, marketeers dressed slightly more flamboyantly, preferring sports jackets, designer shirts, and bright ties. The monthly marketing banquet, a function instituted by Storm to draw department members together as a team in the early days, became something of an institution, and gossip about the wild goings-on at the banquet was endemic if not strictly factual. Departmental secretaries were invited to the marketing banquet, and this in itself was cause for talk, because in the other departments there was an unwritten law that executives never socialized with the secretarial staff.

These radical departures from Fortress's accepted practices were not smiled on by senior management, although they were tolerated. After all, the marketing department worked. Why it worked was, however, a mystery to the firms's top management. Indeed, some Fortress executives saw the department's deviations from Fortress's traditions and its relative autonomy as something of a threat. How did marketing fit into the organization as a whole? And if it got too eccentric, how could it be made to fit in, without, of course, endangering the market lead Fortress was now beginning to develop.

As the department gained recognition, it began to be perceived by ambitious young Fortress executives as a necessary rung on the ladder up. The result of this was that young climbers began to request positions in marketing, and the requests of those whom the company wished to advance were acceded to. As the basically conservative nature of Fortress had not changed, however, those whom the firm wished to promote were often of a cautious and conservative bent, very unlike the creative individualists who had originally staffed the department. Storm naturally had a veto on appointments to the department, but as he said in private, you can only refuse so many. Thus a split began to develop within the department between the original unorthodox staffers and the newcomers who conformed more closely to the traditional values of Fortress.

This split was noticed and welcomed by many senior management staff, who saw it as an opportunity to regain a degree of control over the department. They promoted Mr. George Tight to the position of departmental coordinator. This position was a powerful one, as it gave Tight, an employee of the "old school," control of the information flow within the department, as well as the right to control access to Storm himself.

Storm, aware of the problem, tried to bypass Tight as much as possible, and achieved some success in this measure. With a substantial part of the department "newcomers," and with Tight in a key position, however, the original marketing team was becoming increasingly frustrated. Many of their bright new ideas were being squashed by the newcomers, and Storm was no longer always accessible to give his support to innovative proposals.

The marketing department's creative drive gradually ground to a halt, and the results of this were not long in appearing. Fortress's market gains began to slow as old tried-and-true approaches were consistently favored over new initiatives. The short but spectacular surge of growth achieved by the firm leveled off. This in turn made the executive even more anxious to bring the department under control. It instituted a series of tough new reporting measures, which took much of the control of the department away from Storm. For example, bimonthly progress reports were now submitted to an executive committee outside the department, and the department's budget was adjusted on the basis of these reports. Since Tight was in charge of the preparation of these reports, he could effectively kill projects that were not to his liking or that of the "conservative faction." Control over hiring for the department was given to personnel, thus cutting Storm off from any new blood.

Storm, by this time frustrated and angry, accepted a position with another firm on the West Coast. He left, and Mr. Tight was promoted to his old position. Within a few months of this final change, top management at Fortress was able to congratulate itself on having gotten the marketing department under control.

Discussion Questions

1. Why did this organization block a successful venture?

2. Do you know of other organizations that have had similar experiences?

3. What advice would you give to Fortress's CEO on the lessons to be learned for this case?

4. How could Storm have been more effective in establishing the long-run success of the marketing department?

91

Rainbow Financial Services

Mark White saw the "Announcing" memo on his desk just as he returned from lunch. As the distinctive letterhead was used to communicate major organizational changes, Mark picked it up quickly wondering to himself what the big news was today. There had been so many changes at Rainbow recently that it was becoming almost routine to learn of a new acquisition or a new executive appointment every few weeks or so. But Mark was still taken aback by the new bulletin. It read,

Effective today, Art Brown, Vice President of Human Resources and Administration, is on sabbatical leave as he is undertaking a consulting assignment with Thompson and Peters. Because of the nature of this assignment, Art has relinquished his responsibilities in the Human Resources and Administration areas.

Art had been Mark's V.P. prior to his present job and it seemed hard to believe that he had been pushed out.

But stapled to the first memo was an even more stunning announcement from Rainbow's CEO, Robert Redding. Mark read on,

Because of the importance of Human Resources, I am delighted to announce that the board has appointed Ms. Doris Golden as Vice President of Human Resources, effective today. . . . Also, effective today, the reporting relationships of several departments within Human Resources and Administration will be transferred to other areas. The purpose of this change is to enable Human Resources to focus greater attention on an area Rainbow Financial Services is particularly committed to—the development of our personnel, their career plans and job satisfaction.

The memo went on to state that Brown's large division, which had consisted of a wide variety of functions such as printing, purchasing, translation, mail and shipping, human resources, premises, and customer services, was being broken up into pieces with one joining Data Systems, another joining Individual Marketing, and the third, consisting of Human Resources and Premises, becoming Golden's new division.

The new alignment did make more sense, Mark thought to himself—Brown's old divisions really had been too cumbersome. And the strengthening of Individual Marketing seemed consistent with Rainbow's stated aim of putting more emphasis on market research, product development, and other marketing activities. But what was harder to accept was the pace of change. This now means five new V.P.'s and one new president in the last three years, with three of the V.P. changes happening in the last month! Rapid change of any kind was still new for Rainbow, which for years had the reputation of being one of the more conservative members of the already ultraconservative life insurance industry.

Mark's mind wandered back over Rainbow's history as he knew it. Founded in 1897, Rainbow had grown slowly but steadily as a life insurance company by emphasizing traditional products and methods. A secure, paternalistic atmosphere had existed with the company's direction being set by the actuaries—the professional life insurance mathematicians. Mark recalled the standard joke about actuaries he heard soon after joining Rainbow 13 years ago

—an actuary was someone who really wanted to be an accountant but who lacked the personality for it! The place had a fetish for exactness and detail even when it was grossly inappropriate. He remembered senior employees telling him about the cafeteria in the old head office building. Staff would receive a menu showing the next day's meals and would send in individual orders. The cafeteria tables were small—seating only four—and staff were to eat at specific tables with the same table partners. Mark also remembered seeing the carefully worked out scheme of membership fee refunds for the company fitness center that one of the actuaries had done. Although the amounts were small, the calculations had been done to the dollar. But what really struck Mark was that the actuary who had so meticulously produced the schedule had been at the time the V.P. of Administration—in fact, Brown's predecessor. These images summed up Rainbow for Mark, at least until the last three or four years.

The changes had begun in the early 1980s. Rainbow had been acquired in the late 1970s by the Dynamic Investments Group, whose objective of putting together a financial services conglomerate soon became apparent. Slowly at first, then with an increasing pace, Dynamic had acquired interests in a bank, a trust company, and several property/casualty insurers in addition to life insurers. Through subsidiaries of member companies, the Group was also involved in investment management, property management, fitness and health services, and, most recently, the marketing of management training and development. Rainbow could no longer focus purely on life insurance. It now needed to expand its horizons to the whole financial services scene by coordinating with the other Dynamic Group members in ways that would allow all to benefit—cross-selling, networking, and integrating its strategy in personnel practices, purchasing, data processing, and so on with other Group members. As he turned back to his work, Mark suspected that Golden's ascendancy, Brown's demise, and the reorganization were somehow connected to these earlier changes.

The next day at lunch, Mark revealed his thoughts to Sandy Rouge, the young lawyer who had joined Rainbow a year earlier. "It's interesting," Sandy responded while sipping her soup,

"I didn't really know Brown except that I'd heard he was as tough as nails. And Golden I've hardly met—she arrived about the same time I did. But I agree with your comment about it being difficult to keep up with the changes. It's not only Dynamic that's creating the changes, it's the financial services industry generally."

Said Mark:

"Look at what's happening to the four traditional pillars of financial services (banking, trusts, insurance and investment dealers). For years the lines separating them were clear and hard—every pillar did its own thing and didn't interfere with the others. But that's not the way anymore. The lines are breaking down and everyone is invading what used to be another sector's turf. It seems hard to believe that it wasn't that long ago that banks weren't into residential mortgages at all. Now they are the leaders in it. You can buy insurance from a bank, get a GIC from an insurance company and purchase a mutual fund from all four. And look at how the banks are getting into discount securities trading—just the other day one of them said it was going to offer full services investment trading through a new subsidiary. The new rules on retirement saving plans are going to make the entire individual pension market intensely competitive. The insurance companies won't be able to take millions of dollars of annuity sales for granted anymore because not everyone will want an annuity.

"The whole thing is much more competitive and that means Rainbow is going to have to be a lot smarter in its marketing. I like the fact that Individual Marketing now has more clout—they'll need it if they're to be as innovative and adaptive as they'll need to be. No more sleeping on the job. The companies that will do well will be the ones who are quickest to grab new opportunities and exploit them like crazy. I may be wrong but I don't see a lot of significance in Brown being replaced by Golden. I mean its about time we had a woman on the Management Committee but I think the critical part of the change is that Individual Marketing is stronger. They have a big job to do."

* * *

After work that day, Mark was working out in the company fitness center. He had just started on one of the stationary bicycles when Louise Leblanc, his former colleague in the Human Resources department, walked in and started pedaling on the bike to his right. The conversation quickly turned to yesterday's announcement and Mark related to Louise his lunchtime chat with Sandy Rouge. "Well," responded Louise,

"I'm sure that the strengthening of Individual Marketing was one of their objectives, and I know you and Sandy are right when you talk about the changes in the financial services industry as a whole. But I think Art's departure and his replacement by Doris was inevitable given the direction Redding wants Rainbow to go. Just think of the six who have left or have had to leave over the past three years. In each case, the person either couldn't or didn't buy into Redding's strategy. Look at Jack Grey, who left the Investment Division just three weeks ago. Admittedly he was brilliant at the technical details but he never realized that at the V.P. level you can't survive if you can't manage people. And Grey couldn't, he tried to do it all himself. Ask any of the investment people—they were terribly frustrated under Grey. They're really excited about the new guy Joe Silver because they have heard he lets you do your job. I think it was a similar thing with Art.

"You know, when he arrived here in 1976 he brought in job evaluation, some management training, the new compensation system and later he instigated the current benefits program. It all seemed very innovative and progressive at the time—a very good start. But after that—nothing. Art brought those things in because he knew Rainbow wanted to join the twentieth century in terms of personnel administration but he had no personal interest in any of it. He never questioned whether the management training was effective, was having real results. It seemed to satisfy him if we had X number of programs per year or spent Y number of dollars per year. But don't, whatever you do, go over budget. Art would spend a lot of time analyzing his areas' budget loans and then watching to see if they were overspending. Don't get me wrong, budgeting and cost control are important. But Art considered it as the best way of checking up on people. You always had the feeling that he was suspicious of his staff, that unless he watched them like a hawk they would skip off work early and stuff

like that. I remember discussing the idea of incentive compensation with Art once. Well, it really wasn't much of a discussion. Art didn't really relish discussions. He scoffed at the idea, saying that the appropriate reward for doing a good job was being able to keep it. Art considered good management to be tough minded, decisive and quick to act. He prided himself on being intolerant of error or failure. Art certainly motivated his staff to get the job done but it was more out of fear of the consequences of not doing it than anything else. He certainly didn't inspire anyone to go the extra mile."

"OK," replied Mark, "most would agree Brown was more Theory X than Theory Y. But why do you say his replacement by Golden was inevitable?"

"For many of the reasons you and Sandy spoke of when you talked at lunch. The industry generally is changing quickly and Rainbow more quickly still because of our relations with the Dynamic Group. If you can believe what they say, life at Rainbow is going to be tougher but also more exciting. It'll be tougher because they'll expect more from everyone—thinking through things rather than just following directions. They're saying they want innovation, that the traditional methods won't be accepted unquestioningly anymore. They want everyone to be on their toes asking if this is the best thing to be doing, is this the best way to do it? According to Redding, the only way Rainbow will do well is if this approach becomes commonplace. Well, can you see Art Brown leading the way, as the Human Resources V.P. would have to, in that kind of environment? Art couldn't operate that way himself so how could the rest of the organization take him seriously about being innovative and adaptable? I'm sure you know that one of the major problems with the new performance appraisal system is not the system itself but the fact that Art never did any of his appraisals. No, I'm willing to bet that Redding wanted Brown out because he realized he was an obstacle to changing the way things are done around here."

"How much do you know about Golden?" Mark asked.

"Not a lot more than you," Louise answered.

"I know she has a background in psychology and organizational development but I haven't had many direct dealings with her. But from the times I've heard

her speak before employee groups here, she's polar opposite to Brown in a lot of ways. She seems more open, more willing to discuss things and to listen to what others have to say. She is tough in her own way but I think much more willing to accept a failure now and again so long as we learn from it and come out ahead in the end. I know it sounds terrible to say this but one of her biggest assets may be her inexperience in the life insurance field. And, especially important for a Human Resources person, I think she really likes people."

Several days later Mark had a chance to watch Golden firsthand at the quarterly meeting of supervisors and managers. Doris had been added to the agenda to talk about an upcoming initiative in customer service. As Golden started to speak, Mark listened intently, keeping the conversations of recent days in the back of his mind.

"As you probably know," Golden began,

"Robert Redding and the Management Committee have spent considerable effort over the past year redefining Rainbow's mission, goals and strategies. Of the four major goals identified—profit, being a leader in technology, similarly being a leader in developing our people, and attaining high standards of customer service—I have a special and direct interest in the last two. Before being appointed V.P. in August, two of my major responsibilities were management development and manpower planning. Some of you may very fairly ask what's to happen with these initiatives now that I have a bigger job. Well, I believe in these programs too much to allow them to disappear. I'm pleased to announce that Robert Redding has given me the OK to hire a new Director of Management Development to fill my old job and we expect to have him or her on board very soon. I know some of you recently participated in the management development seminars or management simulation exercises we have put on and the feedback from you—pro and con—was very useful. Under the new Director we plan to continue this type of thing and look for other ways to provide you with the tools for doing your jobs. I really feel that by sponsoring these programs Rainbow is showing that it considers you, its human resources, its most important assets, and is committed to your development.

"I'll finish off by mentioning one more initiative that I hope you'll find fascinating. In the next several weeks

you will see several job postings for a new department in our division reporting to the new Director of Management Development. This area will be responsible for the installation and maintenance of our customer service program. You have heard a lot of reference to customer service recently but now we want to really move on this—to make it come alive in this organization. I can't say exactly what the program will consist of—that will be the job of the new Director and Manger for the most part—but I can say we'll be considering quality circles, staff training programs and a whole system of planning, managing and monitoring for customer service. If customer service is to have any real meaning at Rainbow we have to manage it with the same amount of effort we put into our financial management. Any such program also has to be integrated with what we are planning in the way of incentive compensation and employee recognition. If the messages being received by employees are unclear, confusing or inconsistent we won't get the kind of behavior we want. It's not going to be easy. But if it's done properly it can have a profound effect on this organization. And I mean profound."

"Wow, she certainly means business," Mark thought to himself as he left the meeting. "Things are going to be different at Rainbow if she has her way."

In the next several weeks, much of the lunchtime discussion centered on the August 6 changes. Rumors circulated that Brown's departure resulted from an interpersonal conflict between him and Robert Redding. In some versions, the conflict was based on differences between the two on women's issues. Redding had made a real point of promoting women's issues by appointing several women to the Board of Directors, encouraging Rainbow to experiment with different marketing strategies aimed at the female life insurance consumer, and having Rainbow sponsor a home for battered women. Brown was much more traditional in his attitude toward women. In other versions, the conflict was based on other factors. But they were just rumors and Mike had no way of knowing if they had any foundation. Although the question of what really was happening remained an open one, Mike's enthusiasm for Golden's ideas grew and he was considering applying for one of the openings in her new department.

Discussion Questions

1. How would you characterize the changes taking place in Rainbow?

2. Do you think that the removal of Art Brown is politically motivated as a result of the conflicts with Redding, or an essential part of Redding's attempt to change Rainbow's direction?

92

The University as a Political System

One of the best ways to understand the dynamics shaping corporate politics is to take an organization that you know really well and document the interplay between the interests of key individuals and groups, and how these are expressed and advanced through various conflicts and power plays.

To illustrate, let's take the case of a university faculty or department.

Here's one way of representing the key stakeholders:

Within each of these groups, you may be interested in the political actions of key groups or individuals:

Who are they?

List them in the table below:

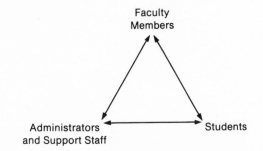

	Faculty Members	Administrators and Support Staff	Students
Key	_____	_____	_____
groups	_____	_____	_____
or	_____	_____	_____
individuals	_____	_____	_____

Now that have identified key groupings, identify the main areas (or issues) of conflict within and between these groupings.

List these in the space below:

Principal Areas/Issues of Conflict

Within groups:
  among faculty

  _____

  _____

  _____

  among students

  _____

  _____

  _____

  among administrators
  and support staff

  _____

  _____

  _____

Between groups:
  between faculty
  and students

  _____

  _____

  _____

  between faculty and
  administrative/support staff

  _____

  _____

  _____

  between students and
  administrative/support staff

  _____

  _____

  _____

Now, try to probe and explore the basis of these conflicts as thoroughly as you can: What are the rival aims, aspirations, and interests that underpin the conflicts that you observe?

For example, try identifying the task, career, and extramural interests of the various stakeholders and how they collide (see Chapter 6 of *Images of Organization* for guidance).

Type of Interest		
Task Interests	Career Interests	Extramural Interests
Faculty		
Students		
Administrators and support staff		

Finally, what sources of power do the various stakeholders use to pursue their interests? What other sources of power *could* they use? The table on the following page can be used to record your ideas.

The mass of detail generated through this exercise may prove overwhelming. But it should serve to illustrate how deeply ingrained the politics of university life can be.

You can forge the method into a tool for analyzing more specific situations in the following:

Think of a specific episode that seems to manifest a political conflict.

Now:

Diagnose in terms of the pattern of interests and power identified above.

Power Relations Between Stakeholder Groups

Power Sources Used by or Open to

Faculty
   (a) in their relations
      with students

   (b) in their relations with
      administrations and
      support staff

Students
   (a) in their relations
      with faculty

   (b) in their relations with
      administrators and
      support staff

Administrators and
support staff
   (a) in their relations
      with faculty

   (b) in their relations
      with students

You should be able to understand the basis of the political dynamics in operation much more clearly.

Familiarity with this mode of analysis can prove useful in reading the ongoing politics in any organization!

93

Global Inc.:
A Role-Play

This exercise focuses on a meeting of a special committee of the Global Corporation, a medium-sized manufacturer of electrical components.

The committee was established by Mr. Fred Zane, the CEO and President of Global, to make a recommendation to the CEO and Board of Directors on the issue of affirmative action in the company's hiring policies. An affirmative action program would involve a commitment to the promotion of women within the corporation generally.

The committee has been mandated

1. to decide—yes or no—should the company have as one element of its Five-Year Plan a commitment to the hiring and promotion of women? and
2. who should present the recommendation to the CEO and Board of Directors at the upcoming Policy Review Meeting? These are the two agenda items for the meeting.

The five members of the committee are

Ms. Jane Hudson—Director of Human Resources and Personnel Development
Ms. Louise Sadowski—Director of Public Relations and Corporate Communications
Mr. Joe McNamara—Vice President of Production
Mr. Bill Furillo—Vice President of Finance
Mr. Steve Elliott—Vice President of Marketing

The committee meeting will be played out in the classroom. Observe the role-play and try and make sense of events. How would you explain the dynamics of this committee meeting?

94

How Politicized
Is Your Organization?

Think of an organization, preferably the one for which you work.

Is it an arena where people join together to pursue an organizational goal, pursuing their own goals at the same time?

OR

Is the organization an arena where people tend to pursue their own goals, using the organization for their own ends?

It's a question of balance.

But detailed reflection on these questions will help you begin to identify exactly how political the organization is, in what areas, and in what ways.

95

Pluralist Management

The pluralist manager recognizes that conflict in organizations is pretty well inevitable, and usually requires careful management. He or she often adopts the role of *orchestrator* or *power broker* attempting to shape and manage the interplay of rival interests and the conflicts they produce.

Strategy A

When conflict is absent, this often involves generating an appropriate level of conflict to energize the organization, or when it is repressed, of bringing it to the surface.

Strategy B

When conflict is entrenched, bitter, and divided, ways have to be found to reframe and redirect divisions and disputes.

Discussion Topic

How can strategies A and B be implemented? Detail the precise methods that are available:

Strategy A: Examples of how repressed or latent conflicts can be brought to the surface and managed constructively:

_____

_____

_____

_____

Strategy B: Examples of how entrenched divides and conflicts can be reframed or redirected:

_____

_____

_____

_____

EXHIBIT 95.1

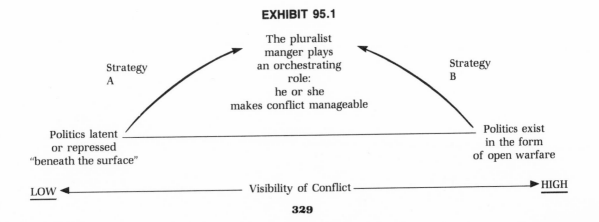

329

96

Meetings, Meetings, Meetings

You are 35 years old and the manager of special projects in a large construction and land development firm employing 1500 people, and specializing in the development of leisure parks and shopping centers. You are a professional engineer, and have been with the organization five years. You hope to stay at least another five, and to rise to the level of vice president of engineering services. Your present department employs 60 professional staff, and a further 30 support staff, and plays a central part in overseeing and managing the firm's major construction projects. It is a highly visible department, and regarded as a linchpin in the organizations's overall operations.

It is a Monday morning, and you are reviewing your calendar for the following month. You have three sets of clashing priorities.

1. There is a routine project review meeting, held on the second Monday of every month, that clashes with a special hospital appointment for your son. Your wife is out of town on the day in question, and you have been waiting for the appointment for two months.

2. The CEO of your company has called for a special briefing on a project that is in a critical stage of development. All departmental managers are expected to attend. Unfortunately, you have a high-profile visitor arriving from France as part of a special international delegation on shopping center development. This meeting has been arranged and carefully planned for six weeks.

3. A special daylong "retreat" of the corporate planning budget committee has been called to review financial plans that have a bearing on three of your projects. You are scheduled to give a luncheon address to the local chamber of commerce on the same day.

What are you going to do about each of the three clashes? What facts and considerations will have a bearing on your decisions?

97

The Sunnyvale Youth Center

The Sunnyvale Youth Center is a nonprofit institution devoted to assisting disadvantaged youth. Located downtown in a major city, it operates a drop-in center as well as offering counseling services, and special classes to children from ages 8 to 15. During the summer, it also organizes special day outings for various age groups.

The Center was started 12 years ago by a small group of volunteers. Over the years, it has grown to be a respected local institution, employing eight staff members as well as a number of volunteers. Its board has always included parents of children who have participated at one time or another in the program. Funding for the Center comes for the most part from the government, although donations from corporations and private citizens supplement its budget.

About a year before the situation described in this case, the president of the board, Mrs. Layla Grant, had persuaded her colleagues that the Center should be administered by a professional manager. After a good deal of discussion, the position of executive director had been created and advertised. A number of candidates were interviewed, and Marg Johnson, a social services professional with a special interest in systems, had been hired.

Six months after Johnson was hired, Mrs. Grant resigned from the board because of ill health. After a rather bitter wrangle between board factions, Mrs. Mila Hubbard had been elected president.

Mrs. Hubbard was a clerk in the office of a local supermarket. Both Hubbard's children participated in the Center's programs, and Mrs. Hubbard herself had been involved with the Center for some years, first as a volunteer and later as a board member. She had been opposed to the creation of the executive director's position, but had always got along well enough with Johnson after she had been hired.

* * *

It was almost the end of the day. The Recreation Committee had been in session for a full three hours, and there had been a lot of debate. Marg Johnson, executive director, looked at her watch. "Nearly five o'clock," she said. "I guess we'll have to postpone discussion of the other agenda items until next time." She began to stand, but Mike Thornton's voice arrested the action.

"Just a minute, if you don't mind, Marg. We haven't discussed the annual day trip to Glenbow Falls yet. Is it on or isn't it? I know it probably doesn't seem important to you, but it sure is to the kids."

The executive director sighed and sat down again. She had hoped that the meeting would not get around to this topic. Time had run out, but Thornton, the director of counselling services, was apparently determined to discuss it anyway. Thornton often insisted on discussing matters that were embarrassing to her and was, she had been told, saying things about her behind her back.

"Well Mike, I know the trip to the falls is something of an institution," she said, "but it looks as if we'll have difficulty running it this year. We just don't have the budget for it." Several people, including Ted Chillum, the young director of sports and recreation, nodded in agreement, but others looked unconvinced.

"Funny," said Thornton. "We have the money for a new microcomputer for the administrative office." He assumed that patient look that Johnson had come to detest. "Look Marg, I know you're a whiz with computers and that sort of thing, but you have to remember the human side of this operation too. And I can tell you, the kids will be really upset if the trip is canceled."

Johnson felt herself tensing up. Somehow Thornton always managed to cast her in the role of the bright but insensitive administrator, and it irritated her. Several of the staff were, she thought, looking rather accusingly at her. "We've gone through this business with the computer before," she said. "First of all, the money for it came from a one-time, take-it-or-leave-it special grant. The money had to be used for a computer or not at all. And secondly, as I've pointed out, I hope the computer will save us a lot of money in staff and administrative costs over the next few years. And the more money we save, the more we can spend on our clients." She smiled around at her staff. Some smiled back, but others did not meet her eye. With that, the meeting was adjourned.

* * *

As her staff filed out, Johnson wondered, not for the first time, how wise it had been to put Thornton in charge of the orientation of new recruits. At first, it had seemed a good idea to give the longtime staffer some additional responsibilities. But was it true, as rumor had it, that Thornton used orientation sessions to pass along his perception of her as an overtrained and callous person to new staff

members? Several recent incidents had made her think that it might be. For example, a recently hired recreation counselor had seemed surprised to be allowed to call her by her first name and had, when questioned, mumbled something about "thinking that she ran a tight ship." And the program director had come to her recently to beg her not to cancel the midsummer picnic, something she had never contemplated doing. Johnson frowned thoughtfully as she put her papers into her briefcase.

* * *

Johnson hoped that she had heard the last of the Glenbow Falls trip, but several weeks later, Ted Chillum knocked at her office door. "Have you seen this?" he asked, dropping a copy of the *Sunnyvale Spotlight*, the Center's newsletter, on her desk. On the third page was a cartoon of herself at the controls of a huge computer, which was printing out the message, "Glenbow Trip To Be Canceled." The cartoon made her look vaguely like a mad scientist.

Johnson stared at the cartoon for a moment, then picked up the phone.

"Calling Mike Thornton?" inquired Chillum.

"Darn right I am. He's the editor of this thing. Where does he get off, publishing a cartoon like this?"

"He says it was submitted by one of the kids. Marg, you can't get him for this, you'll just have to grin and bear it."

Johnson put the phone down. Chillum was right, she couldn't actually discipline Thornton for including the cartoon in the paper if it had come from one of the youngsters. "I suppose it's all in good fun," she said to Chillum with a smile.

But after he had left her office, she began to think about the episode. Thornton, she felt, was going too far. He was systematically trying to make her look bad. When she recalled the last staff meeting, it occurred to her that he might even be succeeding. Perhaps, she thought, the best thing would be to discuss the matter with Mrs. Hubbard. But would that be appropriate? As Johnson saw it, her job was to manage the place effectively without involving board members in matters of staff discipline. Aside from that, she recalled that Thornton had counselled both Mrs. Hubbard's children at one time or another, and had in fact been instrumental in landing the oldest a good summer job this year. Perhaps, it occurred to her, Hubbard's perception of the situation would be colored by this fact. Johnson decided to see how the situation developed for a short while before taking any action.

* * *

Several months later, Johnson gave her "summer wrap-up" report to the board. She was quite pleased with her work of the past few months. The Center's deficit had been eliminated through budget cuts and increased fundraising, and the organization's somewhat haphazard administrative procedures had been streamlined considerably. Yet despite her achievements, she sensed that some of the board members were not well disposed toward her. Perhaps, she thought, it was because many of them were new, having been elected since her sponsor, Mrs. Grant, had left. Most of the new members were friends of Mrs. Hubbard.

At the end of the presentation, there was polite applause, and then Mrs. Hubbard began to speak:

"Marg Johnson, I'm impressed. You've really done wonders in the administrative area. I'll tell you though, some of us are a little worried that the kids' welfare may be getting lost in the shuffle. We know you're a whiz with computers and all that, but we can't forget the human side of what we're doing. Now, I know that in our proposal the budget will be balanced for the first time in years, but on the other hand, for the first time in years the children will miss their trip to Glenbow Falls. And because I have two kids in the program myself I know how much that trip means to the youngsters. Now, maybe I've got the wrong slant—I'm only a mother with a high school education. But it seems to me that we have to make sure the kids are the first priority. So before we make any

decision on the proposed cutbacks I suggest that we put together a committee to look into which programs should be scrapped and which should be continued."

The motion was carried. Mrs. Hubbard was named head of the committee, to serve "with the advice and input of a senior staff member." Several days later, to her chagrin, Johnson found that Mike Thornton, not herself, had been selected as the "senior staff member" specified in the committee motion. Also on the committee were several of the new board members. Johnson considered challenging Thornton's appointment, but decided against it. For one thing, she felt it would appear petty to do so, and for another, she was very busy preparing budgets for next year, and so was not anxious to involve herself in endless committee wrangles.

The committee eventually recommended that many of the programs she had suggested eliminating be kept. Its recommendations were accepted. Johnson expected that the committee would now disband, but instead it was, at Hubbard's suggestion, instituted as a semipermanent "Financial Review Committee," to monitor the institution's spending. Its composition remained the same.

As a result of the committee's recommendations, the Center showed a deficit for the autumn. The board then instituted a number of austerity measures, including freezing Johnson's salary at its current level. Ted Chillum, the recreational director, was notified that his position would be eliminated and his job combined with Thornton's. In recognition of his increased responsibilities, the board voted Thornton a small increase in salary.

During this time, Johnson found that more and more of her decisions were being challenged by Mrs. Hubbard on the grounds that "the kids come first." Mrs. Hubbard was always very polite, but continually stressed that she, as a mother, could better judge what benefited the Center's clients than could Johnson. Thornton, whose work as a senior staff member carried considerable weight, inevitably sided with the president. The board usually voted to do things Hubbard's way.

Just before Christmas, Johnson's husband was offered a promotion and a transfer to head office. After some discussion, they decided to accept the offer, and so Marg Johnson resigned as executive director.

About a year later, she learned from a friend that Mrs. Hubbard had first been made acting director and then executive director of the Center.

Discussion Questions

1. How would you explain the course of events at Sunnyvale?

2. How could Marg Johnson have been more effective in her role as executive director?

3. What observations can you make about Mike Thornton's role?

98

Conflict at Riverside

Steve Williams and Rod Jessop find themselves in a new and interesting situation. They have recently become brothers-in-law. After years of viewing and dealing with each other from a distance—Steve is a senior manager and Rod a prominent trade unionist with a local engineering company—they now find themselves meeting socially on a regular basis. Given free choice, neither would seek the other's company. But because the Jessop family is a close-knit bunch that believes in doing things together, they have little choice. Anne, who is Steve's wife and Rod's sister, quietly insists that they try and get along "for the sake of the family." Both are good-natured fellows, and they resolve to do their best.

One Friday evening, they find themselves feeling very mellow. They have had a good meal, and just enough beer and wine to fall into excellent conversation. After a while, they find themselves alone, breaking an implicit taboo; they are talking about work. Both are in fine spirits, however, and are happy to continue. They are savvy operators and know that they will be able to steer clear of trouble. And who knows? They might just learn something useful from each other.

After some friendly jousting over the latest company gossip, Steve feels that the time may be right to find where Rod stands on contract negotiations at the company's Riverside plant. The plant had recently been selected for major redesign of production operations. Whereas the old design utilized fairly traditional systems of manufacture, new proposals had been de-

veloped to move toward a highly automated system involving a form of "group technology." Employees would work in teams responsible for major sections of the production process, rather than as individuals working on separate and narrowly defined jobs. Many traditional tasks would disappear, as computers and robots took over some of the routine functions, leaving the employees to perform the work requiring a higher degree of discretion and skill. The nature of the raw material being processed in the plant is such that this human element is still necessary. The management of the company had thus designed a plan to retrain employees for their new roles, and to guarantee that all would have a place in the new system. The project is being heralded by senior managers within the firm as a "cutting edge" development that will help the company to hold its competitive edge in the industry. The plan, however, has been greeted with considerable skepticism among many employees and their union representatives.

"You know," said Steve, "I'm having a really hard time in understanding what's happened at Riverside. By all accounts we have an ace production system that's absolutely essential if we are to keep abreast of new developments and remain competitive. The development department and the group handling the project seem to have worked out a scheme that will keep everyone happy. Better wages. No layoffs. A better quality product, and jobs that seem a darn sight cleaner and more interesting than those we have at present. It only makes sense that the contract should go through as soon as possible. It's the only way to secure the company's future. And we all win."

"Well, that's a matter of debate," replied Rod. "Sure, it looks like a great technology with a lot of advantages. But there's talk at the plant that this is the beginning of the end. Sure, it looks rosy up front, especially for you guys at head office. But many of the guys at Riverside and elsewhere have their doubts."

"What do you mean?" asked Steve. "How can there be doubts? Retraining, more money, and everyone has a job. No layoffs! What more can one ask for? Progress demands change, and this seems a change where everyone is being looked after. What do you mean this is the beginning of the end? It's the beginning of a new future for the company."

"For the company maybe," replied Rod. "But a lot of people on the shop floor think the writing is on the wall. Computers and robots are already replacing some of the jobs. The work force will decline by at least 20% over the next five years. I know that's being handled through retirements and general turnover, and there will be no layoffs now. But what about after the honeymoon? It stands to reason that the work force is going to decline as the system takes hold. Most of us may have no role in the company of the future. So why should we get excited? Sure, there's a sweetener. We are going to get a little more in the pocket in the short-run, and for many of us a change in work would be nice. But what about five years from now? How many jobs will be left then? And what about promotions? These changes are going to eliminate most of the supervisory jobs, so there will be no obvious path from the plant into management. We're going to find ourselves in a dead end as far as career is concerned. And a lot of the guys feel that Riverside is just the thin edge of the wedge. If the pilot scheme goes through here, then the other plants will follow. There's no guarantee that they will get the same privileges; there's nothing in the contract beyond Riverside. If the Riverside deal goes through, then everything may be lost. The new system of work breaks old job patterns, and

teamwork often ends up as a way of busting the unions. We may be giving up everything we've fought for."

"Ah, now we're getting down to it," said Steve. "The union is worried about how its going to work out for you guys who are holding all the power. When it comes down to the guts of the issue, its the old "us" and "them" mentality. You can't hold progress back. Riverside is the way of the future. If we don't go that way we're all going to be dead in our tracks."

"Right," said Rod. "We may end up dead in our tracks. But what's worrying many of the guys at present is that as far as the company is concerned *we're* going to be dead anyway, especially the guys in the other plants. There are absolutely no guarantees that they're going to get the same treatment as Riverside. If the company is allowed to go its own way, and make Riverside a success, there'll be jungle warfare. People in the other plants will know that the writing is on the wall for a fair number of jobs, and will probably scramble like hell to make sure that they come out OK. We've seen it happen so many times elsewhere. A company declares it's going to reduce its work force; certain people are in; certain people are out. Obviously those that are in are going to support the scheme; solidarity breaks down. It's the old principle of divide and rule! We're not stupid. The record of employee relations in our company is not great. We've had to fight tooth and nail for what we've got. And we're not going to give it away. It's not that the guys want to fight, or that the strong unionists want to hang onto their power. This company may be looking after you guys at head office. But it's certainly not looking after us. We weren't born yesterday. The Riverside deal does look good. But we may be crazy to accept it as it stands. It could mean the end of work for so many of our members elsewhere."

"Well," sighed Steve, "I guess we'll have to differ. I know that the people at head office are trying to take a fair and open view. I don't think that the Riverside plant is a danger to other plants. It's progress, man. We can't hang onto the same jobs forever. We've got to change with the times. I know there have been bad feelings in the company, especially since the big strike some years ago. But I think that's a thing of the past. The company learned from that. We have a new president, and by all accounts, among the best development engineering and organizational development departments in the industry. Many of the staff are locals, and I'm sure they have the interests of everyone at heart. I'm sure you're going to find you're off target on this one, Rod."

"Well," came the reply, "I guess we'll have to wait and see."

Discussion Questions

1. What is your view of the different "readings" offered by Rod and Steve?

2. How deep is the conflict between the interests of the workers at Riverside and those of the organization? Can it be resolved?

99

The Hand Grenade

Steve Johns was recently hired as a sales/marketing trainee for St. Lawrence Department Stores Inc. An enthusiastic diarist, he produced regular commentaries on his experience. The following extracts from his writings communicate his feelings as a newcomer to the organization.

Steve's Diary, January 30: I started working at St. Lawrence three months ago, eager and willing to climb the corporate ladder. Already, I've learned a lot. People are very willing to fill me in on the overall picture, and tell me stories—especially about others! The people and situations I have encountered are helping to show me the way at St. Lawrence. What follows documents my thoughts on the people I've encountered—at times I'm going to write as if they were speaking, telling us how I think they are seeing things.

Peter Williams, National Sales Manager: My name is Peter. I've been with the company for over fifteen years and have just been promoted to the position of National Sales Manager. Before my appointment I was the Regional Sales Manager. About a year ago I had a massive heart attack which damn near killed me. After being out of commission for eight months I received the doctor's approval to return to work and have done so, but with less commitment to my job. With my weak heart I've avoided rocking the boat with anyone, especially the marketing department. We've just hired a cocky young business grad who we

expect to bring through the management trainee program. Steve's a bright kid, and St. Lawrence is lucky to get him, but he's going to have to learn the ropes. I've taken him under my wing, so to speak. He has to learn to play the game and get ahead by doing the job right, without upsetting the applecart. Since I was the one who hired him I see him as my responsibility. Even though I have less power in my new role, I still have a lot of influence, and can do a lot that will be of positive value for this company.

Rick McCamus, Regional Sales Manager: I've been with this company for over ten years, four in sales in the East and six as the Western Region Sales Manager. I was brought in last year to replace Peter after his unfortunate heart attack. They have promoted him with seemingly more authority, but definitely less decision-making power. They can do that to Peter, but they aren't going to do that to me. I know that the Eastern Region represents more responsibility than my previous position, but, let's face it, it was a lateral transfer not a promotion. I am under careful scrutiny here, unlike out West where I was my own boss, but I'm still not going to take any crap from anyone. I do my job nine to five, and leave it at the office. My family life is precious to me and I don't need the added aggravation of having my family try to cope with a workaholic. I intend to be and will be the next Vice President of Sales. No one here is closer to that position than me. I just have to play my cards right and it should be mine within the year. Just how I am going to do that, you ask? Well, I'll tell you—right now I'm unsure of the ability of those working under me. I'm going to test each individual's ability to meet the task. I need to know who is part of the team and who isn't, I'll impress the higher-ups by improving this region. I have even more at stake when you consider that the big boys are constantly breathing down my back. I want to prove to every level of management in this head office that I'm an innovator, a team leader, and that I'm more than competent to take my rightful position as next V.P. of Sales. To help me with the big boys I'm going to take that new business grad, Steve Johns, and make him my assistant. I can use his analytical ability and creative juices to help me show these guys how I intend to shape things up.

Greg Hume, Account Manager: I've been with the company six years, four as a salesman, and the past two as an account manager. I worked for the competition before that for two years, but it didn't work out. I am responsible for six salesmen and try to make them feel as though they're my friends. I know they don't really like me, but I have to be the watchdog for the company's interests, especially now that I'm treading on thin ice. When I say thin ice, I mean that I made a mistake and was caught. About a year ago, I started taking money from my expense report (too complicated to explain!), at the expense of some of the salesmen's credibility. But why shouldn't I have—I mean they bring in these hotshot university grads and pay them more than I get after six years with the company, it's unfair! Skimming a bit off the top didn't bother me a bit, until I got caught. Well, lucky for me, though unfortunate for Peter, on the morning he was to talk to me about the skimming, he had his heart attack. I hate to get happiness from another's misfortune, but boy was I relieved. It took me off the hook for a while. During the time Peter was in the hospital no one approached me, so I assumed Lady Luck was on my side and I'd make it through. I guess I'm still scared though,

so I want to try and do a good job so they will never have a valid reason for firing me. Of course, Cathy, my wife, doesn't know about all this, and thinks another promotion is due. We just had our first child, and boy, expenses are mounting. I have to keep this job. I think those university kids are ambitious, though they don't know how to get by in this business like I do. I have to keep them from finding out my mistake. A few of them are cutthroat, and they'd get me fired without blinking an eye.

John Ramp, Sales/Marketing Trainee: I've been with the company for six months and already I can envision my way to the top. Sales training has been OK, but I really want to get into the marketing end of the business. Marketing controls money, and as we all know, money means power. I really want to make it for a number of reasons. But the main driving force is my fiancee's father. He's loaded. Although I've never been exposed to that life-style and never really expected it for myself, he expects it for his daughter. He wanted her to marry a doctor or a lawyer. I figure if I can hit the fast track in this organization he'll be impressed and things will smooth over so that we can get married with his blessing.

Steve's Diary, February 3: The courses I took at business school were good—but I'm wondering if they can be applied to real life? Today, I was told that my next major assignment will be with marketing, and I've also been asked to give a speech on my impressions of the company so far, to the next sales meeting. It looks like there is lots of room to move up the ladder at St. Lawrence. Peter told me a bit today about how to work with the people from marketing and sales and said just to tread carefully and watch, and I'd be on the way to the top. This is great because I really want to do well.

Steve's Diary, February 7: Spent today with marketing, and spent last Friday with the sales department. I think I'm ready to write my introductory speech for the sales meeting on Monday. They really stress competition in the sales department, and have hired a couple of other business grads in the past year in the same position as mine. I'm going to have to make myself look as good as possible because the one of us who gets promoted first is really on his way to the top. The marketing department is also very interesting. My "soon to be boss" at marketing warned me not to give a soft impression in sales, because as a future member of the marketing department he doesn't want them to think I'm vulnerable to their sales demands. I'm going to have to play my cards right and keep the other newcomers on their toes if I'm to move up through marketing.

It's funny—the sales people have been very unreceptive to my friendly advances. I suppose that they are scared that I may report something to their managers and that somehow this may cause problems with marketing. I know my own personal objective for marketing, and that is to look as good as possible and leave the impression with the people in sales that I'm competent. The covert rivalry I've observed between sales and marketing is interesting. I wonder if I can fit it into my speech on Monday?

Steve's Diary, February 8:   What an encounter with the harsh world of business! I worked on my speech last night, and thought I would perk it up a bit with inferences about the underlying conflicts between the salesmen and the marketing department. I went to see Peter with my speech today, just to get some approval. He had been very helpful in the past, so I trusted his opinion. I got to the jokes about sales and marketing. His jaw dropped. He said, "My God Steve—you have to understand, we don't want to offend anyone, especially marketing." Peter and I sat down and rewrote the speech. We made it appear as though there was a great deal of friendliness and cooperation between sales and marketing.

Steve's Diary, February 9:   The teamwork theme, much to my surprise, went over quite

well with the sales audience today. And the marketing manager, who was also present, commented on my quick grasp of the sales and customer relations' side of the business. Thinking it over, I realize that those whom I should be trying to impress in my speech are not the salespeople. It is the marketing department that I really want to shine with. Marketing has power over sales in terms of resource allocation—no wonder Peter didn't want to rock the boat. I guess that he was covering for himself as well, since it is well known that he has become a kind of mentor figure for me. Peter knew the consequences of my speech would be detrimental to his image as well as mine.

Steve's Diary, March 12:   What a long day. After working in sales all day long, Greg, the accounts manager, asked if I could work late tonight at his house—he needed some help preparing some graphs for the managers meeting tomorrow. Eager not to blow my image, I agreed. When I got to his house, he laid a pile of statistics on the dining room table and asked me to make some sense of them. Lucky for Greg, I had a few stats courses behind me, but it still took me a few hours of hard work. I was quite proud of the finished product. When I left Greg told me to put on my weekly report—4 hours administration, Greg's house. Obviously he wants the credit for himself. But did he truly believe that it would never come out that I had done the graphs? I suspect that Greg is over his head in his position. He obviously lacks the competence to do the work. But he's so consumed by the fact that I may find a way to get back at him. I'm having lunch with Rick tomorrow and I think I'll just feel him out on Greg's presentation.

Steve's Diary, March 13:   Well—some interesting things happened today. I had lunch with Rick. As I had expected, Greg took total credit for the work I had done. Rick even commented that he was impressed by Greg's analytic ability. Well I just couldn't take it, so I politely pushed it further and set the record straight. Rick didn't appear surprised. In fact, he brought me in on the "mistake" that Greg had made the year before. (He didn't know I already knew about it.) I understand Greg's desperation to keep his position, but he is going to get in deep trouble if he treats people like he's treated me. I found Rick very interesting today. At times I wondered if he was baiting me in the restaurant. I wonder what his motives are in this situation? Is he simply trying to recognize my abilities, and my underlying desire to move up in the company? Or is there some interest in it for him? Is he trying to set me up as a tattletale for other members of the organization? Rick is a goer though, and maybe isn't such a bad person to be aligned with.

Steve's Diary, March 19: I spent today preparing my presentation for the joint sales and marketing meeting tomorrow. I'm really nervous about it, especially since a few members of upper management plan on attending. I went out with John, who started in marketing six months ago, for a few beers after work, and he gave me the lowdown on exactly what happens during these presentations. Though not quite a lion's den, the top management will be receiving their first impression of me. John tried to reassure me that all will go smoothly, though I can't help but be apprehensive about the presentation.

Steve's Diary, March 20: The presentation went terribly, and I have John to thank for that. When I went into the presentation room John was quietly reassuring me. I was increasingly nervous as the room filled up, but I was confident I could show everyone that I was competent, and someone to watch for. Earlier, I had been told that the CEO would not be showing up. Though some people would have been disappointed at this, I was relieved that I had a chance to have more experience in front of an audience before facing the big guy. Well—thirty seconds before I started John handed me a note saying—"J.P. (the CEO) has just arrived." I searched frantically around the room, but could not see him. I panicked. Flustered, I started my presentation but did not regain my composure until a good two minutes into it. The damage had been done—everyone noted my confusion and lack of confidence. My image was blown. After the presentation I thought maybe I had missed J.P. slipping in and out. To make sure, I asked Peter (who had the best vantage point). He said that J.P. had not come.

John had given me a hand grenade with the pin out! Obviously, he plays the game pretty rough. Clearly, he sees me as a competitor—I'll have to watch out for him!

Discussion Questions

1. How typical is Steve's experience? Is he just looking for sinister motives and actions in every corner of the organization, or do people jockey for position in this way?

2. What conclusions would you draw from Steve's experience with regard to the process of building one's career?

3. What conclusions can you draw about the relations between sales and marketing? Does the case present a realistic view?

4. There seems to be a lot of impression management in this organization. Is this typical of situations when marketing and sales are dominant departments?

100

Jersey Packers

"It won't be easy," Marketing Manager John Ransom warned Cindy Wanstall, in the course of her final interview for a marketing trainee position with Jersey Packers, a large meat products firm.

"You'll start out as a cost control accountant, working in the plant. The job's routine, and the men in the plant won't treat you with kid gloves, just because you're a woman. And the training program takes perseverance—it'll be two years before you're a brand manager, don't forget. Furthermore, I won't be around to help you out—I've got my hands full supervising the brand managers, to say nothing of putting together next year's marketing plans."

"We've covered this ground before," Wanstall replied. "I want to be the first woman brand manager in the industry, and I'm prepared to work hard for that privilege."

"Well, just remember, I'm sticking my neck out hiring you," said Ransom. "No offense now, but some of my colleagues think our training program's just too tough for a woman. I hope you'll prove them wrong." He stuck out his hand. "Welcome to the Jersey marketing team," he said.

This conversation came back to haunt Wanstall in the months that followed.

Looming large in her decision to take the Jersey job was the fact that she wanted to be the first woman to break into this male-dominated firm. Seeing herself as a trailbreaker enabled her to put up with the prospect of several years of "rigorous" training. Furthermore, she was sure that if she worked hard and made some obvious contributions to the firm, her probationary period could be considerably shortened.

The first part of her training program was to take place in the plant itself, and Wanstall was a little apprehensive about her reception in this all-male environment. She had been assigned to work with a foreman who had a reputation for toughness, and for the first few days he and his fellow workers regaled her with dirty jokes, and made no effort to spare her from any of the dirty or unpleasant tasks found in a meat-packing house. Aware that she was being tested, Wanstall returned joke for joke and went about her assignments without complaint. In this way, she soon established a good working relationship with the plant employees. In fact, her foreman told her that she was "a lot easier to work with than some of those momma's boys over in the Administration Building." True to her original plan, she tried to show initiative and to do an especially good job. As a result, the foreman informally praised her work to her immediate supervisor, Rod Fuller, a brand manager. Wanstall's status in the plant was confirmed when she batted the winning home run in the interplant baseball tournament.

But while she was accepted by the plant people, she began to run into other and unexpected problems. It began to seem to her that a trainee was not "part of the marketing team" at all until he or she had completed the two-year probationary period. She tended to be treated with condescension by Fuller as well as by the other brand managers, and on numerous occasions was asked to do menial jobs—filing or typing—that seemed to her inappropriate for a management trainee to be doing. When she asked Fuller if male trainees were required to do the same sort of work, he merely smiled in a patronizing way and remarked that a male trainee would not ask that kind of question. On several occasions, she thought of discussing her problems with Ransom, but he had warned her he was rarely available, his time being filled with brand management meetings or executive conferences on mid- and long-range marketing strategy.

Involved mainly with low-level, clerical work, Wanstall found few opportunities to display her initiative or ability. The training program seemed to her not so much rigorous as downright boring. She began to feel that two years as "cost control accountant" with Jersey was a high price to pay for becoming the firm's first female marketeer and therefore began to look about for other employment.

Word of her job search came to the ears of Ransom, who as Marketing Manager kept an eye on the department's trainees. He called her in, and reproached her for her lack of determination. He had, he reminded her, gone out on a limb in hiring her in the first place. Was she going to prove his critics right in their charge that a woman "couldn't stick it out" at Jersey? Wanstall pointed out that the problems stemmed mainly from boredom but also that the marketing manager was not sympathetic.

"Look Cindy," he reminded her, "everyone else in marketing had to go through the mill. You've got to master the boring part of the job before you start on the interesting stuff. I hope you don't think you're entitled to special treatment just because you're a woman?"

Chagrined, Wanstall finally agreed to persevere with her training.

She did, however, begin to pester her supervisor for more challenging assignments. Fuller repeatedly disregarded these requests.

"Look Cindy," he said to her one day, "I don't like to say this to someone as pretty as you are, but you're getting to be a pain in the neck. If you want glamorous work, go apply to Mary Kay or something. Jersey's just a plain, old-fashioned company with old-fashioned rules, and one of those rules happens to be that you've got to walk before you can run. Right now you're learning to walk, so be a good girl and leave me alone."

Wanstall, incensed by what she considered his patronizing manner, became less and less diplomatic in her requests for interesting work, until, after about six months, she was barely being civil to her supervisor. Fuller, while ignoring her requests, never reproved her for her manner; he had been brought up to be polite to ladies, no matter what the circumstances.

After nine months of employment, Wanstall was called into Fuller's office to receive her first formal review. Her supervisor passed her the typed report and waited patiently while she read it. Wanstall was shocked and dismayed. The review charged that she was "emotional" and "impatient," and that she was "not a team player." Based on her recent performance, Wanstall privately realized that the review was in a small degree true, but not fair when her whole career with the firm was taken into account. She was also aware that to let the report stand would be tantamount to abandoning her career plans.

"I don't think some of these charges are justified," she said to Fuller, trying to keep the anger out of her voice.

"Oh? Which ones?"

"For example, the statement that I'm 'emotional.' I'm sure that my foreman in the plant would disagree with that, even in writing if I asked him."

Fuller look slightly worried at this, and Wanstall pressed her advantage.

"And how about this 'not a team player' business? No one in the whole plant would buy that description."

After a good deal of bargaining, Wanstall was able to have some of the more offensive adjectives removed and to have the tone of the review made more favorable.

Despite this partial victory over her supervisor, Wanstall saw that the writing was on the wall. At any point her career could be effectively blocked, either by Fuller or by Ransom. And supposing she did finally make the "marketing team," would there be any greater scope for creative work, or would the role involve, as her experience already suggested, retreading a well-worn path of routine? Wanstall applied for a job with a large packaged goods firm and was accepted.

Discussion Questions

1. What are the sources of Cindy Wanstall's problems in this company?

2. Is she being treated unfairly as a result of gender-related issues?

3. What could she have done to improve her situation?

4. Could she have achieved her aims in this company, or was she right to find another job?

101

The Department of Information Services

The Department of Information Services, a branch of the Regional Bureau of Administrative Affairs, came into existence in the mid-1960s. Its mandate was to provide the regional government with the automated information-processing capacity needed to fulfill its task of providing administrative services to other government agencies.

The department was divided into three sections. The Computer Systems Section looked after hardware and existing system software and did any required "troubleshooting." The Operations Section handled information input and routine tasks such as the copying and distribution of computer-generated reports. On this section's payroll were the clerks in the department's many branch offices, as well as the data processors and computer operators at the central office. Finally there was the Applications Section, which was charged with maintaining and periodically upgrading the department's software.

All of these sections were under the supervision of the senior administrative officer, who in turn reported to the department's executive director. Both of these officials were lifetime civil servants who had been with the bureau in other capacities before being appointed to the department.

For the first years of its operations, the department ran on what was officially called a "semi-manual system." During this time, its main function was to collect and disseminate information to government offices. A huge data base was built up to keep track of such diverse things as government property, government employment statistics, and budget information. To gain access to this wealth of information, branch offices filled in special forms that were then forwarded to the department's central office. There the requests were processed through the computer and the results mailed out by the clerks of the Operations Section.

This system, while it had advantages over the previous, manual system, did not entirely fulfill the government's expectations. There were often long delays before requested data were received, and other government departments were beginning to complain that they enjoyed few of the advantages that a computerized system should have brought them. Critics pointed out that a computer system should give users increased computing power, whereas all the Department of Information Services could supply was data.

In 1975, after an election that had been fought partially on the issue of "efficiency in government," the department was ordered to upgrade and improve its services, using the latest available information-processing technology.

William Brill, the department's executive director, responded to this request by asking Paul Jitney, head of Computer Systems, to report on ways to reorganize and improve the department. Jitney was the logical choice for this assignment as he was a career civil servant who had received considerable training in data processing through the government. After conducting a lengthy survey, Jitney submitted a solid but uninspiring, cautious report, which advised that regional offices be equipped with terminals allowing them to interact "on line" with the central mainframe. This option, while expensive, would speed up the transfer of information and eliminate much of the need for centralized data entry and retrieval. Jitney also recommended that a number of sophisticated financial planning and statistical software packages be acquired for the computer, so that branch offices could utilize the system's computing power as well as retrieve data.

The head of the Operations Section, Mike Cray, bitterly opposed these measures, not least, it was said, because they cut his section's staff by half. The head of Applications supported the report, which was soon adopted by the department. An unexpected by-product of this decision was the enhancement of the Applications Section, which played a crucial role in developing the new software necessary to upgrade the system.

The report received a great deal of discussion in the department and became a "high-visibility document," and moves were made to implement its recommendations in a gradual manner. Over the following five years, the department thus moved toward the new system, on the principle of making compromises whenever necessary and "minimizing pain." All the department's principal actors were happy with the result.

In 1982, the head of the Applications Section retired and his position was taken over by a newcomer to the civil service, Martha Dun. About the same time, the department was again beginning to come under fire for lack of efficiency. The microcomputer revolution had arrived, but the department was unprepared for it. Many "client" departments within the government had acquired microcomputers ("micros"), and were using them for many of the applications for which they had previously used the central computer.

Micros were becoming especially popular for spreadsheet and data base applications, for the software was more versatile and/or "user friendly" than the ponderous programs available on the department's mainframe. Although the central computer was acknowledged by most to be a superior machine, there was no doubt that micros were finding a ready market in the government.

Faced with a sharp decrease in log-on time (the measure by which the director habitually gauged his department's performance), the executive director circulated a memo calling a meeting of section heads. It was the first full-scale meeting that Dun had attended since joining the department, and she was not prepared for the way it was run.

The agenda was carefully laid out, and each section chief was allotted exactly 10 minutes to state his or her views on the problem of declining log-ons. Each presentation was followed by a five-minute question-and-answer period. Presentations were by order of seniority, and Dun therefore spoke last. This, she felt, was good, for it would give her a chance to assess the mood of the meeting and see what conclusions the others had come to. It was obvious to her that the department would have to incorporate the reality of microcomputers into its thinking, and she had several ideas on how this could be done.

The first person to speak was Computer Systems' Paul Jitney. "I haven't had much to do with micros so far," Jitney began. But I know enough about computers to know that micros aren't going to be able to compete with the services our mainframe can offer."

"That's true now," Dun interjected, "But what about three to five years down the road?"

The executive director looked at her reproachfully, "Please Ms. Dun," he said, "let's try to keep the meeting on track. You'll have your turn to speak." Surprised and hurt, Dun sat back and listened to the rest of Jitney's presentation in silence. The head of Computer Systems seemed to be saying in a roundabout way that the department should virtually ignore the micro revolution, a point of view she found ridiculous. What would the others say?

Next to speak was Mike Cray, from Operations. It soon became evident to Dun that he too did not know a great deal about micros. His proposal to study the technology with a view to integrating micro users into the system, however, seemed to make sense.

After Cray had fielded a few questions, the executive director consulted his watch and asked for Dun's presentation. Dun began with a brief discussion of the changes that could be expected in micro technology over the next few years. "And so we can expect to see great increases in memory capacity and processing power," she concluded. "So our task as I see it is how to integrate these machines into the department's operations." She paused to consult her notes.

"Very interesting," said the executive director. "Does anyone have any questions?"

"Oh, but I haven't quite finished," Dun protested. "I still want to discuss specific applications."

"I see," Brill looked pointedly at his watch. "Please go ahead then," he said reluctantly. "Can you keep it short?"

Aware that she had made a bad impression, Dun tried to condense her ideas into a three- or four-minute speech. From the executive director's manner, it was clear that a longer presentation would not be welcome.

At the end of her speech, the executive director looked around the table. "Any questions for Ms. Dun?" he asked. "No?" "All right then, I think what we need is a report on the impact of micros on the department. Mr. Jitney, you know the department's operations well, so I'd like to ask you to prepare the report if you'd be so kind."

"I'd be happy to," Jitney replied.

"Thank you. Any further comments?"

"No? Then the meeting is adjourned."

Dun was, to say the least, dissatisfied with the outcome of this meeting, but her dissatisfaction turned to outright disbelief when she saw the report produced by Jitney. It suggested that all government micros be "upgraded" so that they could "log on" to the department's mainframe. This proposal would, she thought, cost a lot of money, solve nothing, and merely delay the inevitable decline of the department.

Cray's remarks at the meeting had seemed sensible, and so after some thought, she sought him out and after some cautious probing confided her thoughts about Jitney's report.

As she had expected, Cray agreed that something had to be done if the department was to survive the coming micro revolution. Accordingly, the two department heads decided to prepare a joint report, to "supplement" Jitney's study.

After several weeks of intensive work, the report was completed. It called for the installation of micros in all the Bureau's branch offices. Operators were to be trained to use them, either as "stand-alone" devices or, as Jitney had suggested, as terminals to interact with the central mainframe. Both Dun and Cray were pleased with the report as it made an attempt to integrate micros into the overall departmental structure without downgrading the importance of the mainframe. It also gave both departments numerous development opportunities. The Applications Section in particular stood to gain a great deal of new work from the proposal by adapting and standardizing micro software packages.

Dun waited several weeks for a response, but none was forthcoming. Finally Dun's curiosity outweighed her caution and she approached the senior administrative officer, Cam Wells, to see what effect the document had had.

"None at all," Wells told her. "Mr. Brill didn't request the report, and so has no reason to review it at this time."

"But you've got to look at it," Dun insisted. "I'm telling you, if the department doesn't take micros into its planning process, it won't be around ten years from now."

"That seems unlikely," Wells replied politely. "I hope you won't mind Ms. Dun if I give you a piece of advice," he added in a friendly manner. "Both Mr. Brill and I have been here much longer than yourself, and we may well be here after you've left—I know how mobile you young computer people are these days. So let us worry about the long term and you worry about the day-to-day problems of your department. All right?"

Dun returned to her office and began calling friends in the industry to see if there were any suitable openings in private firms.

Discussion Questions

1. How would you explain what is happening in this case?

2. Do you think that Dun has behaved appropriately?

3. If you were Dun, would you have behaved any differently? If so, how?

102

Quality Co-Op

The Quality Co-Op was founded in the late 1960s by a group of young craftspeople describing themselves as "members of the counterculture." The co-op was located in an old building in a central but rundown area of the city. Although for legal purposes it was incorporated as a nonprofit corporation and required to have a board of directors, in practice it was run on the basis of decisions made at the informal, all-member meetings, which were usually held at least once every month.

Progressive values were shared by all the original co-op members, and it was an article of faith that the co-op was and should remain a part of the larger community in which it found itself. Thus members often did volunteer work in the surrounding neighborhood and even started several social programs to help local youth to learn craft skills.

As time went on, some of the original co-op members moved away or retired from the organization. There was no shortage of applicants to take their places, however. The reasonable rates and central location of the co-op made it an attractive place to locate a small business, and many tradespeople—carpenters, electricians, and plumbers—applied for and were granted co-op membership, along with the potters, leather workers, artists, sculptors, and glassblowers who were among the founding group.

Not all of these newcomers necessarily subscribed to the ideals of the co-op's founders. Indeed, at the weekly meetings, the membership began to split into two distinct groups. One of these led by Dorothy Blair, a potter, was composed of the remaining founder-members of the co-op. This group soon came to be known as the "Originals."

The other group was made up mainly of people who had joined the co-op after its first years. A number of them were trade unionists, and many were active in local politics. Some of this group felt that the co-op should be more politicized than it currently was, earning them the label of "Politicos."

Gradually, the two groups came into open conflict. A municipal election had been called, and the Politicos wished the co-op to throw its support officially behind one of the candidates. The originals felt that the co-op should remain aloof from politics, and be committed to the community rather than to any particular party.

As it happened, the annual board election was to be held several days prior to the municipal election. Unlike previous board elections, this one was hotly contested, with both the Originals and the Politicos running candidates for all positions. The main issue was that of which party, if any, the co-op should support in the upcoming municipal vote.

The co-op election campaign generated a good deal of bad feelings among co-op members. The Originals charged that the Politicos were trying to make the co-op into something it was never intended to be, while the Politicos accused them of clinging to old fashioned "hippie" ideals that were no longer valid.

The outcome of the election was a tie. Four members of each group were elected, a result that precluded any firm action on the municipal election issue, which was won, in any event, by the party supported by the Politicos. The main effect of the 1976 co-op election was to emphasize the split in the co-op's membership.

The elections in following years were fought with equal fierceness. The co-op's criteria for membership became an issue, with the Originals insisting that each case be treated on a "need" basis, while the Politicos urged that union membership be made a primary requirement. The balance of power swung back and forth, with the Originals sometimes gaining a majority, and the Politicos occasionally winning control of the board.

Eventually the split in the membership became more or less accepted, and representatives from both groups realized that they had to cooperate to some degree if anything was to be accomplished. This trend was encouraged by the fact that many co-op members were becoming tired of the continual bickering that had become the rule at the co-op meetings. Important initiatives to overcome differences were thus gradually launched on both sides.

A reconciliation between the two groups might have been brought about, but for a major urban development scheme that was unveiled early in 1985. The proposal, put forward by the municipal government, called for a massive cleanup and rezoning of the area in which the co-op was located. The area was to be used for subsidized housing, public buildings, and park land. After some informal negotiation, the city made the co-op an offer for the acquisition of its land and buildings, which included a large cash settlement as well as a new location in another part of town.

The Originals were strongly against accepting the offer. Its members argued that part of the co-op's purpose had been to boost the quality of life in the inner city. Many of the Originals lived in the area, and considered the existence of the co-op to be of major importance for the neighborhood as a whole. If the co-op relocated to the site suggested by the city it would, they felt, rapidly devolve into a sort of industrial condominium.

The Politicos, on the other hand, thought that the city's offer should be accepted. For a start, the offer had been made by the party most of them supported. Most of the Politicos believed that the urban renewal project would be good for the city as a whole, and would reflect well on the party. Another point was that, despite the restoration work done on the original building, it was old and rundown and maintenance costs were becoming a major issue. Relocation to a new building would be desirable from a financial point of view, and the proposed new location offered great market potential for many of the co-op's skills and products.

Once more, the board election became the focal point for tensions between the two groups. This time the election was fought with unprecedented bitterness, for it seemed the whole future of the co-op hinged on its outcome.

The election gave five seats to the Originals and three to the Politicos. The co-op accordingly refused the city's offer. By this time, however, the whole urban renewal scheme had become mired in legal and financial problems, and had been postponed indefinitely.

The election destroyed the budding accord between the two factions. The atmosphere at the co-op continues to be one of confrontation, and many members, tired of the whole thing, have moved to other locations. Those who remain would like to put an end to the division in the membership but cannot agree on how to do so.

Discussion Questions

1. To what extent do you think that the split in values, ideologies, aims, and objectives found in Quality Co-Op reflect a pattern in nonprofit organizations generally?

2. Co-ops are founded on democratic principles. To what extent do you think that the political hostilities described in the case ran counter to the co-op's ideals? Is there a paradox here? Can it be resolved?

3. How can the problems at Quality Co-Op be resolved in the long run?

103

Who Builds the Dillworth Extension?

Ultrex Developments Ltd. is a subsidiary of the Metro Group, a large development company that builds and manages commercial condominiums across North America. The parent company has the reputation of being a "bottom-line" firm in which no excuses are accepted for poor financial performance. Ultrex Developments has a central head office that handles finance, planning, and land acquisition. There are three operational divisions—West, Central, and East—each of which is responsible for the construction of new buildings as well as the maintenance of existing Ultrex buildings in its area.

Roy Snider, Vice President of Operations for the Western Division, was known in Ultrex as a man who got things done—at the best possible price. Snider had been with Ultrex since graduating as an engineer fifteen years ago, and had risen to his present position by building a reputation for always delivering the goods on time and on budget.

Under Snider were two line departments—development and maintenance—as well as a number of staff departments including personnel and purchasing. Line departments ran their own shows at the division level, while staff departments received direction from their head office counterparts.

The Maintenance Department was headed by Sid Farley, an old college friend of Snider's. It was responsible for the upkeep of the condominiums built by Ultrex. Farley had a permanent staff of two senior engineers, but he also had a team of anywhere from five to seven engineers on loan at any time from the Development Department. These engineers assisted with the inspection of Ultrex's numerous buildings and, more important, supervised the efforts of the independent contractors that were hired to do necessary repairs to the firm's holdings. All this work was, of necessity, "in the field," and so engineers assigned to maintenance were often involved in making major financial decisions in conjunction with management. Assignments to maintenance were looked on as a route to promotion.

The Development Department was responsible for the construction of new Ultrex properties. Headed by Myra Dell, an engineer, it employed about ten engineers. These engineers were responsible for reviewing tenders and for overseeing the firm's construction work. The actual construction work was performed by independent contractors. Once the contract was awarded, however, development engineers were responsible for making sure that specifications were met and that work was on schedule. With the multitude of large building projects under way at any time, this was a full-time job, especially because as many as half of the department's engineers were on loan at any given time to maintenance.

Evaluating tenders for new construction work was a two-part exercise. Incoming bids were first routed through the Development Department to see whether they met engineering specifications. Those that did were turned over to the Purchasing Department for further evaluation. Purchasing reviewed the tenders to be sure that prices quoted for material and labor were acceptable, and that the tendering contractors were reputable. Purchasing, on behalf of the Development Department, then concluded agreements with the contractors selected. Although nominally in charge of vetting maintenance contracts as well, by custom, Purchasing was only minimally involved with the activities of this department, as Farley preferred to deal directly with contractors. Head of the Purchasing Department was Harvey Basker, an ambitious young man with an M.B.A. degree from the local university. He saw Farley's ability to sidestep the Purchasing Department as an anomaly and a weakness in operating procedure, and had often wondered how to bring Maintenance "into line."

One day in the spring of 1984, Snider received a call from Ultrex's head office.

"Here's the situation," explained Bob Mills, Ultrex's chief of operations, after some polite small talk. "We have it on good authority that there are going to be some big changes in federal energy policy soon, with major implications for expansion of oil exploration. The energy companies are going to be looking for a lot of office space near where the action is and we think that the Dillworth area is where a lot of them will go."

"We have a building there already." Snider pointed out. "On a big lot too. But it's full up right now."

"Exactly," replied Mills. "So if we want to capture as many new clients as possible, we ought to expand. Can you push through a rush project to double office space in the Dillworth facility by the end of the year? If you can, we will catch our competitors with their pants down."

"I'd have to really look at it for a day or two," said Snider cautiously.

"Sure," said Mills. "Let me know what you think the day after tomorrow."

As he put down the phone, Snider realized the challenge he had been presented. If he managed to meet the deadline, he felt sure that he would clinch his claim for a promotion to head office. On the other hand, if he failed, it could well signal the end of the road as far as his career with Ultrex was concerned. He called in his department heads, told them of the development, then asked Myra Dell to report the following day on the feasibility of the project.

Next morning, to his surprise, he received a visit from Farley. "I was working late last night on the Dillworth project," said Farley. "Now just keep an open mind for a second while I suggest something new—how about letting the Maintenance Department do the job? We could do it faster than Development, and save money too. And it makes sense—after all, we're talking about upgrading an existing building, not building a whole new one."

"True," Snider admitted. "Go on, I'm listening."

"Well," said Farley, "Point one is that all the engineers are used to working with me. Actually, they know it's their show. So I have the same engineering expertise at my fingertips as Development. Point two—I'm more used to dealing with contractors than Development. I know how to beat them down, get the best out of them, make them trim their prices. I have to do it all the time in Maintenance. Don't get me wrong, Myra does a great job, but she doesn't know how to push the contractors like I do. For one thing, she's a lady, so she can't talk tough with them, if you know what I mean."

"There may be something in what you say," admitted Snider. "You'd better know though that I've just been talking to Myra, and she thinks she can beat the deadline and come in at cost as well."

"So my proposal is out?" asked Farley.

"Not necessarily. Put it to me in writing by the beginning of next week though. I have to have it on paper before I can do anything."

"I sure will," said Farley.

When his friend left, Snider phoned Bob Mills to tell him that he thought the project could be completed on time and that he would be pleased to get the go-ahead.

Meanwhile, word soon reached Dell that Maintenance was vying with her department for the supervision of the Dillworth job. Dell was well aware that if Farley succeeded there would be serious consequences for the department as well as for her career. At a minimum,

Farley could argue that Maintenance should have a larger permanent staff of engineers at the expense of development, and at worst, his success could pave the way for the amalgamation of the two departments. After some thought, she paid a visit on Harvey Basker in Purchasing to discuss the matter with him. Basker had long been waiting for an opportunity to "trim Farley's sails," as he put it, and so he agreed to a strategy of cutting into his time while simultaneously keeping him in the dark about the progress of the development counter-proposal.

Over the next few days, nothing seemed to go right for Farley. First of all, just as he began to prepare his written estimate on the Dillworth project for Snider, he learned that three of his engineers had been reassigned by Dell to a special development job, leaving him short staffed. When he complained to Dell, he was politely reminded that the head of Development could assign engineers to whatever project she thought suitable. Dell, however, promised that the engineers would return to Maintenance in several weeks, as soon as the special project was completed. Farley reassigned his remaining engineers to cope with the staffing shortage and recommended work on the Dillworth proposal. Then a flood of urgent queries from Purchasing arrived in the interoffice mail. These queries concerned recent department contracts and had to be dealt with to avoid disrupting work on several of Ultrex's key buildings. When he called Basker to complain about the sudden influx of work, he found that Basker had made a flying trip to head office to consult with senior purchasers there.

Farley spent several days trying to deal with the headaches caused by his shortage of engineers and the unusual load of paperwork. He managed to get rough estimates for work on the Dillworth project from several of his contractors but became increasingly nervous as the time to do a thorough job on the formal proposal requested by Snider slipped away. Moreover, the estimates proved to be somewhat higher than he had expected. But he was confident that they were lower than the estimates Development would receive. In try-ing to find out exactly what costs Development was projecting for the project, however, he ran into a brick wall. All the tenders had been routed through Purchasing, and Basker explained that it was impossible to give him figures for the project at this stage, as the contracts were being closely evaluated by his department according to a new and complex head office formula that took into account cost overruns and other factors.

Farley felt stymied. The deadline for submitting his proposal was only several days off, and staff shortages were still cutting into his available time. The proposal was a complicated one, and to do a "rush" job was to risk making serious errors. Furthermore, he was reluctant to submit a proposal without having some idea of what costs Development was projecting for the Dillworth job. What if his costs were higher than Dell's? It might, he reasoned, badly damage his credibility with Snider. It was even possible that the rival reports would be passed on to head office for further scrutiny. Faced with these alternatives, Farley decided not to submit a proposal after all. He explained to Snider that, although Maintenance could do the job at a lower cost, staff and time shortage had made the preparation of a proper estimate impossible. He promised, however, to submit a proposal for the next job of this nature. Dell was duly asked to supervise the building of the Dillworth extension.

Details of the affair soon leaked back to head office, and Dell's reputation rose rapidly. According to the company grapevine, she would be considered for a head office job after another year or so. An uneasy peace descended on the Western branch while Farley looked for another opportunity to expand his department, and Dell consolidated her position.

Discussion Questions

1. What forces are driving the interdepartmental competition within Ultrex Developments?

2. What strategies do Myra Dell and Harvey Basker use to undermine Sid Farley's initiative?

104

The Lakeside Literary Magazine

The *Lakeside Literary Magazine* (*LLM*) was started by five teachers at the local community college who felt that there should be a vehicle for disseminating creative literature (short fiction, poetry, and playlets) produced by the writers of their region. All of these teachers had dipped into their pockets to provide the magazine with a starting budget. One of them, Don Mucil, had also bullied the community college where he worked into supporting the magazine with a small grant.

After some discussion, the teachers decided to incorporate the magazine as a nonprofit organization, and to create a five-person board of directors to set policy. According to the magazine's charter, these directors would each year elect a new board, although there was no reason why any director could not continue to serve indefinitely if elected. The whole business of incorporation seemed to Mucil to be contrary to the spirit of the magazine, which he saw as a spontaneous expression of the community. Nevertheless, he was persuaded by his colleagues, especially Anne Ashley, who was the business head in the group, to go along with the formalities, for the sake of the magazine.

The first year, the magazine was well received. Sales, perhaps because of the regional content, were much higher than expected, and a local philanthropist donated a sum sufficient to cover the year's operating expenses and to provide the magazine with enough to begin its second year of publication. During this period, Mucil and cofounder Wilbur Josephson, a teacher of creative writing, served as *LLM*'s editors.

The second year, all five of the founders continued as directors, and Mucil was elected chairperson of the board. About halfway through the year, it became obvious that in order to process all the incoming manuscripts and to make required administrative decisions, an editor would have to be hired. This, of course, would be expensive. Fortunately, Mucil, who knew some people at the local Arts Council, was able to push a grant application through, and the board, after a rather hasty search, hired someone. It soon became evident, however, that the person was not as good as first thought, and was not really capable of doing the job. Mucil, exasperated, was all for firing him right away.

Ashley, however, pointed out that the magazine should be run in a businesslike way, and that to fire the new editor out of hand might result in *LLM*'s being sued for false dismissal. Mucil, under pressure from his fellow board members, was eventually restrained from firing the editor.

In the third year, two of the original founders declined to stand for reelection as board members, as the administration of the magazine was becoming too time-consuming. Mucil, Ashley, and Josephson continued as board members. After a good deal of debate among these three, Ann Ashley was delegated to follow up her suggestion that Helen McAdam be approached to see if she would like to sit on the *LLM* board.

McAdam was a well-known figure within the cultural community. She had served on the boards of various artistic organizations, and had a reputation for being a tough administrator, who expected her board to pull together. She was a member of a prosperous local family, and was able to devote herself to her works within the artistic community on a full-time basis. When approached by the *LLM* directors, she hinted that she would only consider serving on the board if she were made chairperson. After some consideration, the three founding members agreed to this. Mucil, the outgoing chairperson, was relieved to turn his responsibilities over, for, as he himself said, "I'm not really an administrator. I'm much more interested in the creative end of the magazine."

Another director still had to be found, and McAdam recommended Andrew Kollati for the position, arguing that he would be useful to the magazine because of his political connections. Originally a small building contractor, Kollati had built up his business and sold it. He had then gone into politics and had eventually become a member of the town council. Kollati did not have a great deal of formal education, and some people felt that this bothered him. Although a very busy man, he had, in the last few years, made an effort to associate himself with cultural organizations. Her suggestion was also accepted by the board.

From the start, Mucil had problems with McAdam, who insisted on following a tight agenda, and controlling the meetings of the board with rigorous rules of order. This approach seemed to Mucil to be at odds with the informal, let's kick some ideas around approach that had prevailed in the first two years of the magazine's existence. Also, Mucil, who prided himself on his ability to generate creative ideas for the magazine, was disappointed to see that the new board members preferred a more methodological, or as he characterized it, "plodding," approach to almost every issue.

Nor did he yet have a great deal of respect for Kollati, who was prone to make grammatical errors, and whose insight into literature was, in Mucil's opinion, nonexistent. Mucil wrangled almost constantly with Kollati over editorial policy, and at times only McAdam's insistence on the rules of order kept the meetings on track.

The real trouble began when *LLM*'s editor resigned his position and the board was faced with the necessity of replacing him. The position was advertised in local and national papers, and a dozen applications were received. Of these, four applicants appeared suitable. One was a local resident and a friend of McAdam's. Another had applied for the job when it was first advertised, but had been turned down. The third appeared to have precisely the qualifications needed for the job, but a quick check on her references revealed that she had not done well at her last several jobs. The last candidate had the qualifications sought, but seemed a bit young for the job.

Mucil insisted that they immediately hire McAdam's friend. They had to hire someone soon, he told the board, or the Art's Council would think that the magazine could get long without a full-time editor, and cancel its grant.

McAdam, on the other hand, wished to interview all the candidates, as that, she explained, would be the democratic way.

After much debate, McAdam asked all board members to call her the next day with their votes. Her friend was unanimously elected.

One evening, shortly after this episode, Mucil's phone rang. It was one of the magazine's founding directors.

"I'm afraid I've got some bad news for you," said Josephson. "You've been voted off the board."

"Voted off the board? I don't believe it!"

"Sorry Don," said his friend. "I'm afraid the vote went against you."

"But I didn't even know there was going to be a vote," Mucil protested, tugging distractedly at his bushy beard.

"It was a clear majority," said Josephson. "I voted for you, if that's any consolation. Someone'll be by to pick up the books in the next couple of days."

Mucil hung up, and looked distractedly around his cheerfully decorated apartment, its walls hung with original Eskimo prints. He could scarcely believe that he, Don Mucil, cofounder and charter board member of *LLM* had been voted off the board! Hadn't he worked long hours without pay for the magazine? Wasn't he the one with the creative ideas? Hadn't he been the one who had finally wrangled a grant from the Arts Council to cover the magazine's operating expenses? And this was his thanks!

As he reflected back, however, things became clear to him. Kollati had always considered him an intellectual and politically suspect, and no doubt McAdam had gone along with him. Ashley had never liked him much either, he suspected, and now she could do what she wanted with the magazine. Hurt and angry, Mucil vowed never to work with anyone outside the academic community again.

Discussion Questions

1. If the various members of the Board were asked for the rationale behind Mucil's dismissal, how do you think they would reply?

2. Is his dismissal rational?

3. Helen McAdam seems to place a lot of emphasis on the democratic process. How do you interpret her style of management?

105

A New Direction for the Upstage Theater

The board of the Upstage Theater Company had assembled to hear the Artistic Director's proposals for the following year's season. Mark Buck, the Artistic Director, had built a reputation on his staging of popular comic seasons, and most members of the board expected a similar proposal this year.

Buck entered the boardroom, and after a few general remarks, began to speak about his plans for the season. As he spoke, the board members began to look at each other with astonishment. Buck was proposing a radical departure for the theater, a season of serious works, starting with a Shakespearian tragedy and working up to a piece by Arthur Miller. At the end of this totally unexpected proposal, he looked round at his audience. "Any questions?" he asked rather blandly, while privately enjoying the obvious bewilderment on the part of the board. He loved surprising people!

Jean Carlisle, the chairman of the board, was the only one not surprised by the proposal, as Buck had approached her several weeks ago and dropped some hints about his idea. Buck, she had a shrewd suspicion, was out primarily to promote his own career. Known as a "comedy man" first and foremost, he was in danger of being typecast within the industry. Only by rounding out his production experience could he hope to progress.

Carlisle, however, could see a lot of possibilities in the proposal for a "serious" season, even though she knew it would be dismissed as foolhardy by a number of the established board members. Her involvement with the Upstage Theater was based upon a sincere commitment to the cultural development of the community. Lately she had been coming under some fire from her family and friends for not urging that more "culturally significant" work be performed by the theater. When she had first heard of Buck's proposal, she had decided to support it, and had accordingly begun to consider how best to get the board to support it as well.

Now she turned to Robert Ramsay, a board member who had been brought in for his connections with the business community. "Well, Robert, it's an interesting proposal we have in front of us," she said. "What do you think?"

Ramsay, she happened to know, had been considerably embarrassed in front of the board recently, as a result of his inability to raise money for the theater. She also knew that much of the resistance to corporate support of the theater had come from the fact that its plays were not considered serious enough. Thus Ramsay, she reasoned, would support the departure proposed by Buck.

This was indeed the case. "I think it's a marvelous idea. And I'm sure it's the kind of season the financial community would support," said Ramsay.

Several others on the board protested strongly against the proposed season. The most vociferous of these was Olaf Vickers, a local playwright of some repute. Vickers had had several of his comedy works performed by the Upstage Company over the years. The arguments presented by Buck, Carlisle, and Ramsay managed to quiet these objections, however, at least to the point where the board voted to examine the marketing and financial implications of the proposal and meet again in two weeks' time.

* * *

When the board met again, a month later, the battle lines were more clearly drawn. Olaf Vickers spoke first. "I move that we dismiss the proposal for a "tragedy" season, he said. "The theater has always had a reputation for comic works, and this reputation should not be thrown away lightly. I feel that our artistic director should go back and rethink his proposals."

Jean Carlisle, however, was ready with an answer. "I know how you feel," she said. "But I think we have to consider some other factors too. For years now our theater has been losing money, and how long the various arts councils will go on funding us is an open question. As I told you last year, some of the government people are very concerned that we develop more in the way of box office support and outside funding. Now as I see it, this proposal may give us a chance to do just that. I've asked Mark Buck to do an unofficial survey among the town's theater community, and I think you'll find the results interesting."

The artistic director now stood up. "We've been able to put together a random sample of theatergoers from the subscription lists of other theaters in town," he said. "I had a couple of people in the administrative office phone these people and do a straw poll survey of their preferences. The results indicate that a majority would patronize a new tragedy season. So I think we can expect some box office support for this proposal."

He sat down amid murmurs from the board members. Carlisle then asked Ramsey to address the meeting. "I've canvassed the business community," he said. "A number of corporations have indicated their interest is supporting a 'serious season' here. I think it's safe to say that we could count on fairly generous corporate support should we decide to go ahead."

A heated debate followed these announcements. While many of the previously uncommitted board members now leaned toward acceptance of the proposed season, a significant minority, lead by Olaf Vickers, opposed it. As the bylaws required a two-thirds majority to approve a policy change, the meeting adjourned without any decision being taken. It was decided to meet again the following week to resolve the crisis if possible.

* * *

During that week, Jean Carlisle paid a visit to Olaf Vickers. After some polite discussion of theater matters, she came to the point. "You know Olaf," she said sadly, "it's rather a pity you don't support the proposal for a 'serious' season."

"Why's that?" inquired the playwright suspiciously.

"Well," explained Carlisle, "it's just that I was talking to Buck the other day, and he wanted to commission you to write a work to wrap up the season. He says he's sure a serious piece by you would be just the thing to cap the year."

"I'm glad that he at least remembers part of the theater's original mandate," growled Vickers. "After all, the Upstage is supposed to be committed to the development of new local authors."

"And it's a commitment he takes very seriously," replied Carlisle. "And so do I, I can assure you. That's why if we were to go ahead with the season he suggests, I would move that your new play be commissioned immediately. I hope we can come to some agreement when we next meet," she added as she rose to go.

"Maybe," Vickers replied thoughtfully.

At the next meeting, Vickers announced that after some thought he had changed his mind and would now support the new season. Several weeks later, it was announced that, as local playwright, he had been asked to write a serious work to be performed as season finale.

Discussion Questions

1. To what extent, and in what ways, is this a case of organizational politics?

2. What are the principal factors shaping the decision-making process?

3. To what extent do you think that decisions are being made within board meetings or outside of them?

4. To what extent is the process involved here typical of meetings generally? In what ways?

106

Tipdale Engineering

David Tipdale, president of Tipdale Engineering, looked angrily around the boardroom table. "I'm telling you," he said, "there's no place in the company for an 'executive vice president.' Either I'm the boss or I'm not. And if I'm not, then this firm won't be the number one firm of wilderness construction projects for long either."

Richard Larkin, the new chairman of the board, made a gesture of frustration with one well-manicured hand. "Look David," he said patiently. "We've gone over this a hundred times. You're still the boss, even if we do decide to hire an executive vice president. No one here disputes that you're the force behind the firm. But you need some help. You can't run the whole company like you used to—it's grown too big for that." He turned to the other board members.

"Ladies and gentlemen, we've heard the arguments for and against hiring an executive vice president to assist Mr. Tipdale. I move that we now put the matter to a vote. All those in favor raise their hands. Carried, five to three."

* * *

The Tipdale Engineering Company was the creation of David Tipdale, professional engineer and maverick of the construction industry. Tipdale began his working career as an engineer with a large mining firm but soon found the corporate environment too restrictive and bureaucratic for his taste. His work with the firm frequently required him to solve nonroutine building problems at wilderness sites, but, to his disappointment, his often brilliant solutions to these problems usually were not implemented because they were "too unorthodox."

In 1961, Tipdale decided to go into business for himself. Working for the first year out of his home, he built up a solid base of clients who found that his innovative approach to the problems associated with wilderness construction often saved them a good deal of time and money. Five years after he had opened his doors, Tipdale found himself with a staff of 23, a large downtown office, and an excellent reputation in the industry. His experiments with foam domes as arctic housing units won him international publicity, and his successful use of local labor forces for on-site work made him something of a figure in several northern communities.

Creative, impatient, and somewhat disorganized, Tipdale relied strongly on his board, which at first was composed of personal friends, to keep track of the business side of his company's efforts. By hiring a reliable accountant as well as several experienced administrators, the board was able to ensure that Tipdale Engineering was run in a more or less businesslike way. Tipdale himself, after expressing some doubts about hiring administrators, came to like the arrangement as it left him more time to work on the engineering and architectural side of the business.

Over the next few years, Tipdale was often frustrated by the inability of construction companies to work to his exacting and often unorthodox standards, a fact he consistently complained about to his board. In 1974, it came to the attention of one of the board members that a construction firm was for sale. After some urgent meetings, Tipdale decided to buy the firm. As he disliked the idea of debt financing intensely, it was decided to sell stock in the firm to raise the necessary capital. Tipdale sold 60% of the shares, despite being urged by some of his friends to keep controlling interest. As he explained, "No one would dare put the squeeze on me! After all, without me, there isn't a company."

The construction firm was duly purchased, and the combination of design and construction facilities proved very successful. By 1980, Tipdale Industries was generating annual revenues of over $30 million.

All during this period, Tipdale insisted on being kept "in the picture" on all projects. He was also frequently abroad, consulting with other architectural firms, speaking at conferences, and keeping up with developments in the field. Thus, while he often made major contributions to the projects he was involved with, his insistence on being in on everything slowed projects, or even, on occasion, disrupted them entirely.

During this period, too, the composition of the board was slowly changing. Many of Tipdale's friends retired and some were replaced by nominees of the new shareholders. In 1981, Richard Larkin replaced the former chairman of the board. Larkin, the son of a wealthy family, had a variety of business interests, and was known in the business community as an aggressive and even ruthless operator. Larkin soon made it known that, in his opinion, Tipdale Engineering was operating well below capacity. The company could, he thought, easily achieve sales of $100 million with proper management and direction. His two main concerns were to increase the firm's efficiency by cutting turnover time on projects and to branch out from wilderness construction into suburban land development and commercial construction.

The second of these ideas was sharply opposed by Tipdale, who felt that the firm's whole reputation and its future lay in its special expertise. Such was his stature and his force of character that he was able to force Larkin to back away from the notion.

Larkin then turned his attention to improving the firm's efficiency, and here he found himself on firmer ground. It was clear that Tipdale was carrying a much heavier load than he could in reality handle, and that as a result the firm was not operating as efficiently as it could. After a good deal of lobbying, Larkin was able to persuade the board to hire an "executive vice president" to assist Tipdale with his work, as described in the opening portion of this case.

Hans Danson was appointed to this position. In addition to being a qualified engineer, he was a meticulous planner and administrator, traits that did not endear him to the freewheeling Tipdale. The two soon came into conflict over a project that had been stalled for a number of months. The engineering team on the project had been ordered not to proceed further without Tipdale's input, which had not been forthcoming. Danson, after looking into the matter, told the team to proceed. When the project leader protested, Danson insisted that work continue. Several days later, he received a call from the angry Tipdale.

"What do you think you're doing, telling the design team to go ahead with the Matawa River project?" Tipdale asked. "I had some special ideas for that, and I wanted to discuss them with the team leader before they went on to the next phase. Now it's too late."

"I'm sorry about that," Danson apologized. "But I've been putting together a comprehensive flow chart of the company's projects, and I noticed that the Matawa River project was way behind schedule. It's not the only one either. We've got to keep these projects flowing through somehow."

"I'll see that they flow through somehow," said Tipdale. "If there are administrative problems, you deal with them, but leave the actual design work to me, will you?"

"The slowdown in projects is an administrative problem," replied Danson.

The next few months were frustrating ones for Danson. Every time he tried to straighten out the administrative tangle that the firm was in, he found himself blocked by Tipdale. Most of the design staff, the heart of the company, were intensely loyal to the firm's founder, and so, although Danson possessed considerable personal skills, he found himself being treated as an interfering outsider. Tipdale refused to return his calls, and his memos remained unanswered. Whenever Danson made an appointment to meet with the firm's founder, Tipdale was always called out of town at the last minute on "important business."

Danson finally requested a private session with Larkin and informed him that, under the circumstances, he could do nothing. He therefore offered his resignation. Larkin refused to accept it, and instead called a special meeting of the board. He told board members that Tipdale was making it impossible for Danson to do his job properly. "Frankly, ladies and gentlemen, I feel we have no choice in this matter," he concluded. "If Mr. Tipdale wanted to run this business as a personal hobby, he should not have sold the majority of shares to the public. As board members, we have responsibilities to our shareholders, and one of those responsibilities is ensuring that the firm is well run. Either Mr. Tipdale must cooperate in our effort to manage this company better, or he must make use of his considerable talents in another milieu."

There was general agreement with Larkin's point of view, although several board members argued that without Tipdale the firm might lose much of its creative thrust. Larkin was given the task of communicating the board's views to Tipdale, and this he soon did.

Tipdale, although furious, was realistic enough to know that Larkin meant business,

and might indeed have enough board support to force his resignation. He, therefore, adopted a new "work to rule" strategy. He returned Danson's calls, but volunteered as little information as he could during the conversations. Files requested by the executive vice president were supplied, but they would often be incomplete. Key documents were often nowhere to be found. "Only goes to show how much we need to get organized," Tipdale would say ironically when Danson commented on the difficulty of getting things done under the circumstances.

Danson knew full well that he was the victim of a campaign of quiet noncooperation. The current situation was preferable to the one he had encountered when first employed, however. At least, he reasoned, he was able to get some work done. He therefore said nothing to the board, but forged ahead as best he could, and actually was able to streamline the firm's operations in several areas. Because he maintained a calm and nonthreatening demeanor, and because several of his innovations were clearly needed, many of the staff came to have a grudging admiration for him.

It is now two years since Danson was hired and the firm's efficiency has improved substantially, thanks to his reforms. Larkin, while still anxious to see the firm branch out into other fields, is not sufficiently sure of the board's support to push a showdown with Tipdale. An uneasy truce prevails.

Discussion Questions

1. Many companies founded by dynamic entrepreneurs experience problems as they hit different stages of development. To what extent is Tipdale Engineering facing this situation?

2. What other explanations can you provide?

3. What is your opinion of David Tipdale's relations with Hans Danson?

107

Problems in the Machine Shop

James Biltmore, a recent graduate of a highly respected business school, sighed as he sipped his wine and looked around the fancy restaurant a friend has brought him to for his 28th birthday.

"What's the matter?" inquired Jane. "Would you rather have had the Beaujolais after all?"

"No indeed," said Jim quickly. "It's just something at work that's on my mind."

"Tell me about it," his friend urged.

"Well, maybe I will. You're good at people problems. Me, I'm just an engineer by training, figures are more my thing, I sometimes think."

"You're doing very well," reported Jane. "You got a good job as soon as you got your M.B.A., and as you said last week, you're already in charge of a machine shop with 30 machinists reporting to you."

"Well, 36 to be exact," admitted Jim. "Actually, it's a problem with them."

"I thought you said they were all good people," interrupted Jane. "Most of them are old hands, aren't they?"

"They sure are," said Jim, playing with his fork. "About half of them, sixteen to be precise, are in their forties, six more are in their thirties, and the rest are about my age. Then there are seven more apprentices to round things out."

"So what's the problem?"

"Well," said Jim, "it may not sound like much to you. Last week we got a big order from one of our major customers. I scheduled the order, passed it along, and didn't hear anymore about it for a couple of days. I had to go down on the shop floor and check up. It seemed the order was moving along fine, but I wanted to be kept in the picture. So I told the guys who were supervising the work—two of the old-timers—to report to me on progress every day. Actually, I was a bit upset, so I made a big deal of it. I even put the order in writing. That was three days ago, and so far I haven't heard a thing."

"Nothing?"

"Nothing at all. Nothing in writing, nothing verbally. I think I'm being given the silent treatment."

"Hmmn, they're pretty cocky," said Jane thoughtfully. "Haven't they heard there's a lot of unemployment out there?"

"Not in their line of work," said Jim somewhat sadly. "Machinists are in big demand."

"Well, it seems to me that you'll have to put your foot down with them," said Jane. "After all, who's the boss there, you or them?"

"Sometimes I wonder," said Jim, sipping his wine. "Maybe we should have had the Beaujolais after all."

Discussion Question

What advice would you give to Jim?

108

Visibility, Autonomy, Relevance, and Relationships:
Four Factors Shaping Power and Influence

The power and influence one exercises in one's job are often influenced by how one approaches and develops that job. The following questionnaire, produced by Goodmeasure, of Cambridge, Massachusetts, provides a powerful means of coming to grips with key aspects of one's organizational role (in terms of visibility, autonomy, relevance, and relationships) and how one can enhance one's future power and influence.

ANALYSIS FOR ACTION†

This questionnaire serves two functions. First, it helps you analyze the *current* aspects of your job that contribute to your effectiveness and to your prospects for developing a reputation for effectiveness. Second, it urges you to think of *future* actions that can develop those specific parts of your job known to contribute to job efficacy and organizational power. There are two parts to most of the questions: part *a* asks about the way things now are; part *b* asks you to create action alternatives to improve the situation. Your responses to part *b* questions are an opportunity to *brainstorm* action possi-

bilities for yourself. Even if you do not see a way to follow through on an alternative at present, list it anyway. The task is to develop a range of alternatives for yourself, with a minimum amount of censorship or a priori restrictions. In a later step you will be able to select from among these alternatives the most feasible ones to pursue. But right now it is important to be as creative and expansive as possible. Leave no question unanswered, even if the alternative you suggest is seemingly small or insignificant. (If you do not know the answer to a part *a* question, use part *b* to list ways you could learn the answer.)

†SOURCE: © Copyright 1979 by Goodmeasure and Rosabeth Moss Kanter. Used by permission.

Visibility: The Extent to Which Your Work Is Known in the Organization

1. a) With whom in the organization have I shared my ambitions, my career goals?
   b) Who else could help me if they had more such information about me?
2. a) How is what I do in my job communicated to the larger organization (both informally and formally—e.g., meetings, conversations, reports)?
   b) How can I improve on this communication? What other forms are available to me?
3. a) Who are the influential people *within* my department who know about my work?
   b) What additional information about me could be useful to share with them?
4. a) Which of my job activities bring me into contact with people beyond my department or organization?
   b) How can these activities be expanded?
5. a) Who are the influential people *outside* of my department who know about my work?
   b) How could they learn more about me?
6. a) How often do I participate in committees, task forces, or other work groups that include people from across the organization?
   b) What other activities of this type can I become involved with?
7. a) What groups and professional associations outside of my employing organization do I belong to?
   b) How could increased participation in such groups benefit me?

Autonomy: The Amount of Discretion in Your Job

1. a) At present, what types of decisions do I make acting on my own authority (e.g., budget expenditures, hiring, staffing, etc.)?
   b) In what other areas could I expand my discretionary authority? How could I get such authority?
2. a) What parts of my job allow me the opportunity to act on my own initiative, to demonstrate my creativity?
   b) How could I make these a more central part of my job activities?
3. a) Are there any new projects or activities in the organization or within my job that would give me the opportunity to create and develop something?
   b) How could I get involved with these projects or activities?

Relevance: The Value of Your Job to Pressing Organizational Issues

1. What are two to four crucial issues that my institution faces within the next three years?
2. a) Which aspects of my job play a role in addressing these issues?
   b) How can I further develop my job to become more involved in these issues?
3. a) What skills do I have that are the most value to the organization?
   b) How can I use these, or trade on them, to improve my job situation?
4. a) What other skills could I develop or improve on to make me more of an asset to the organization?
   b) How can I go about this?

Relationships: Supports and Alliances on the Job

1. a) How often am I in contact with my peers?
   b) How could I benefit more from these interactions?
2. a) How often am I in contact with women in roles similar to mine?
   b) How could I benefit more from these interactions?

3 . a) Among my subordinates, who are the most promising?
   b) What things could I do to help these people develop and advance in their careers?

4 . a) At present, what responsibilities do I share with my subordinates?
   b) What other of my responsibilities could be shared with them?

5 . a) Which senior person(s) could best help me do my job more effectively?
   b) What can I do to develop this relationship(s)?
   c) How can I be of help to this person in his/her job?

6 . a) Who is the most senior person with influence who has shown an interest in my career?
   b) In what ways can I make my skills and ambitions better known to this person?
   c) How can I be of help to this person in his/her job?

7 . a) What contacts, both in and outside of the organization, do I have that are of most value to the organization?
   b) How can I use these, trade on them, to improve my job situation?

8. What contacts could I develop that would make me more of an asset to the organization?

Action Planning

From the many alternatives you have suggested to yourself, select three to five that, given your particular job situation, would do the most to increase your job effectiveness and/or career prospects. Let these be your goals. Write down each goal in the space provided. Then, for each goal, list one or two specific actions you can *immediately* do to begin achieving that goal.

GOAL: _____

1st ACTION(S): _____

_____

_____

GOAL: _____

1st ACTION(S): _____

_____

_____

GOAL: _____

1st ACTION(S): _____

_____

_____

GOAL: _____

1st ACTION(S): _____

_____

_____

109

Profit and Organizations:
A Story of Exploitation?†

A formal debate often serves as a good tool for exploring the different sides of an issue.

The following four statements have been designed to provide the basis for an inter-group debate on the exploitative aspects of modern organizations. Your instructor will provide details of how the debate is to be organized.

Debating Issues

1. There is a basic and irrevocable split between the interests of those who own and manage business organizations in the capitalist system and those who are the rank and file workers. Therefore, there will always be exploitation of workers to some degree.

2. The pressures on those who own and manage profit-making organizations to maximize profits are so great that there will always be a tendency to downplay occupational health and safety (unless forced to do otherwise).

3. The pressures on those who own and manage profit-making organizations to maximize profits are so great that there will always be a tendency to downplay environmental pollution control and conservation as well as consumer health and safety.

4. The centralized profit maximizing objective of large multi-national corporations inevitably leads them to exploit host countries in the third world by creating dependence, failing to develop human resources, creating internal divisions and keeping them as "hewers of wood and drawers of water."

---

†SOURCE: An exercise contributed by Vic Murray, York University, Toronto, Canada; used by permission.

110

Final Offer

Final Offer is a Canadian Broadcasting Corporation video presenting an inside and incredibly frank view of hard-fought negotiations between the Canadian arm of the United Auto Workers and General Motors. The video features tensions between union and management, and within the union itself. It is particularly important as a historical document illustrating the background to the split between the Canadian and American union leaders, and the establishment of the Canadian Auto Workers, as a union in its own right, under the leadership of Bob White.

Watch the video, and think about the following questions:

1. What does the video tell us about power relations on the factory floor, especially between workers and supervisors?

2. To what extent do you think that GM management and the American leaders of the UAW struck a partnership to defeat Bob White and the Canadian branch of the union?

3. How would you characterize the pattern of politics illustrated in this case: as unitary, pluralist, or radical?

4. What does this case tell us about the power relations between unions and management more generally?

About the Author

Gareth Morgan is widely recognized as one of the most innovative thinkers in the field of management today. A lively and inspiring speaker, he has delivered hundreds of talks, seminars, and addresses throughout Europe and North America. In 1987, he was elected life fellow of the International Academy of Management, in recognition of "an outstanding international contribution to the science and art of management."

He has written five other books and numerous articles, including *Images of Organization* (1986), widely acclaimed as one of the most important contributions to management over the last decade, and *Riding the Waves of Change* (1988).

He holds degrees from the London School of Economics and Political Science, the University of Texas at Austin, and the University of Lancaster, and has served on the editorial boards of the *Academy of Management Review, Administration and Society, Journal of Management,* and *Organization Studies.* He is currently Professor of Administrative Studies at York University, Toronto.